The Political Theory
of Salvage

SUNY series in New Political Science
_____

Bradley J. Macdonald, editor

The Political Theory
of Salvage

JASON KOSNOSKI

SUNY
PRESS

Cover image from Wikimedia.

Published by State University of New York Press, Albany

© 2022 State University of New York

For information, contact State University of New York Press, Albany, NY
www.sunypress.edu

Library of Congress Cataloging-in-Publication Data

Names: Kosnoski, Jason, author.
Title: The political theory of salvage / Jason Kosnoski.
Description: Albany : State University of New York Press, [2022] | Series:
    SUNY series in New Political Science | Includes bibliographical references
    and index.
Identifiers: ISBN 9781438491196 (hardcover : alk. paper) | ISBN 9781438491219
    (ebook) | ISBN 9781438491202 (pbk. : alk. paper)
Further information is available at the Library of Congress.

10 9 8 7 6 5 4 3 2 1

Contents

Illustrations

Acknowledgments

As is hopefully apparent, the core concept of this book was inspired by many people I know in Flint, Michigan. I was especially inspired by the people I met during the Occupy Flint encampment, and the Peace Mob Gardens project which combined salvaging abandoned houses, urban gardening, sponsoring plays and other arts activities, with community building in Flint. I would especially like to thank my former student Brian Morrisey for both his leadership in both these efforts, and his introduction to so many of the participants of Occupy Flint.

I would also like to thank many people who read early chapters of the work: Daniel Birchok, Clara Fisher, Rich Gillman-Opalsky, Kojiro Miyahara, Justin Joque, and Rob Mickey. I would especially like to thank Clara and Connor Morris for organizing the "John Dewey and Critical Philosophies for Critical Times" conference at University College Dublin where I presented some of the concepts in that appear in the book for the first time.

It has been a pleasure to work with SUNY Press Editor Michael Rinella, as well as the editor of the SUNY Series in New Political Science, Bradley J. Macdonald, who have been extremely supportive and helpful. The University of Michigan—Flint Office of research also generously provided funds to help with publication.

Finally, I would like to thank my family for their support during the seemingly interminable amount of time that it has taken to finish this book. My children, Gabe and Leah, and the seeming "messes" they have made, have been constant sources of inspiration for thinking about the creative resistance that comes from using what others see as useless. My wife Dana has been a constant source of support and happiness—and without her I would never have been able to complete this work.

Introduction

In the winter of 2012, I sat on a rickety chair, huddled around a wood-burning stove ripped from an abandoned house, in a structure built with twisted boards, garbage bags, and other pieces of what many would consider trash, talking about Italian Marxist Antonio Gramsci. I was in the Occupy Flint encampment, and its inhabitants had dealt with the harsh Michigan winter by building a dense ecology of structures comprised of only what they could salvage to protect themselves from the cold. These shelters were much more elaborate and sturdy than the flimsy tents and lean-tos found in most Occupy encampments in U.S. cities—they had to be, due to the climate. The community the activists had constructed instead appeared as if it could have been found in the community-built, informal[1] neighborhoods of Caracas or shanties of Lagos due to the sturdy structures made of salvaged material. These scraps of what others would call waste were used to construct tools and buildings that served almost every need that could be found in a permanent neighborhood.

The permanence of the Flint encampment stemmed from the fact that it was located on an abandoned vacant lot, and thus it lasted much longer than other occupations—no police came to destroy it as they had in New York, Oakland, and so many other cities. So when the winter came, the campers faced the problem of the weather with greater freedom than other occupiers. Yet they still faced constraints caused by their poverty. On one side of the encampment, an occupier had pulled up a decrepit old yellow school bus that served as a wall to keep out the wind and any unannounced visitors. Activists who stayed overnight could sleep in tattered hammocks slung over its tattered seats. There was a media structure where occupiers composed their communications on laptops and phones they could recharge by connecting to portable electric generators. In the encampment's kitchen, activists heated dented

1

pots on a wood-burning stove and served tea in chipped cups as they talked about both high theory and the mundane tasks required to keep the encampment going. It was like a small medieval hilltop village, but instead of terracotta bricks built by guilds of artisans and twisting streets that had slowly, organically developed over the years, it was hastily constructed with no greater plan (see figures I.1 and I.2), using salvaged rubbish collected by the students, the unemployed, the fast food workers, the veterans who comprised its ensemble of "citizens."

Why were they there, especially after so many occupiers had gone home? Why did they sleep, eat, and work outside in the harsh Michigan winter surrounded by what most would consider trash? Whereas participants in Occupy Wall Street were brought together by general opposition to the increasingly wide gap in incomes and wealth between the "1%" and the rest of the nation's population, the activists in Occupy Flint, while certainly decrying economic inequality, had a more local goal— to restore democracy in Flint. The State of Michigan had declared a "financial emergency" in Flint in the fall of 2011 and had appointed an emergency manager who would take over the functions of both mayor and city council in December. The activists were acutely aware of how this event was tied to what they saw as the conscious destruction of Flint by powerful political and financial elites. The lack of democracy caused by the Emergency Manager Law was to them an inevitable outcome of the general lack of democracy they saw in American political and economic life. They had hoped that their encampment would act as both an example of, and eventually an exemplary replacement for, the democracy

Figure I.1. Occupy Flint. Author Photo.

Figure I.2. Occupy Flint. Author Photo.

that Flint had lost to the logic of neoliberal austerity and the political forces in the state representing this economic program. In order to spark democratic culture, they held both small, internal general assemblies where more involved occupiers collectively decided the best way to undertake the tasks needed to maintain the camp, and larger, community-wide general assemblies that addressed how the citizens of Flint might re-start the tasks of governance of which they had been robbed by the state. As one activist put it, "We thought the general assemblies would *be* the city government after the state took it away."[2] But the encampment was not only meant to replace established political institutions; it also acted as a laboratory where a diverse group of residents talked about, constructed, and reflected upon new ways of production, collaboration, and enjoyment that might assist them in fixing the numerous cracks within their broken landscape. They would refurbish the houses the city could not fix and the banks would not fund. They would provide energy through windmills because the residents could not afford their electricity bills. And they would decide these things together using the democratic voice of which the governor and emergency manager had robbed them. And because the suburbs, state, corporations, and national government provided nothing, they would have to use only what they could find—like the camp itself, theirs would be a government built on salvage.[3]

The Occupiers of Flint were exemplary of a larger community of the disadvantaged being forced to use what others throw away to rebuild their lives due to the destruction wrought by neoliberalism. Reacting to this trend, scholars are beginning to articulate accounts of the greater social and political significance of salvage. For example, Anna Lowenhaupt Tsing, in *The Mushroom at the End of the World: On the Possibility of Life in Capitalist Ruins*, uses the foragers of the matsutake mushroom in the Pacific Northwest to describe an increasingly occurring way of life she calls "salvage accumulation" or "the creation of capitalist value from non-capitalist value regimes" (Tsing 2015, 128). She describes how these mushrooms, which grow especially well in forests damaged by intense industrial logging, are foraged by the "displaced and disenfranchised" (Tsing 2015, 5) who form transient, nomadic communities that converge around sites where mushrooms can be found. According to Tsing, foragers, at least the successful ones, develop a particular sense of where to find the buried mushrooms, reading the landscape to find hidden topological clues such as patterns of roots and trajectories of mounds that subtly suggest the presence of their hidden quarry. Furthermore, when actually searching for mushrooms their efforts exhibit a "rhythm both impassioned and still" (Tsing 2015, 242) that, while seeming chaotic to outside observers, actually is led by their careful senses of hidden clues within the landscape. And while these mushroom foragers might not see it as such, Tsing's ethnography suggests that salvage is not simply a concrete set of practices for survival, but also a general orientation toward shattered environments that might lead to new practices of work, freedom, and community.

Accounts such as Tsing's that remain focused on salvage in and of itself do not explore the many recent manifestations of salvage in explicitly activist contexts. From the squats of Berlin to the *favelas* of Brazil, the salvaging of discarded materials has become an important part of contemporary protests against capitalism. Furthermore, just as occurred in Flint, occupations of public space in Cairo, Tel Aviv, Athens and New York were marked by salvaged structures that housed activists for the duration of their protests. While many have focused on nonhierarchical decision making as the political essence of such encampments,[4] very few have noted how the practice of salvage itself has accentuated the radical political potentials of such activism. In a sense, the survival of these salvage protests constitutes a political act in itself due to authorities' aggressive efforts to evict them from spaces deemed off-limits. But my claim goes deeper, that the act of salvage—the abilities, attitudes, and perceptions that accompany this activity, when undertaken in certain contexts—both intensifies the radical potential of these forms of resistance and nudges that activism into realms of critique on which it might not have otherwise focused. To explore these connections I want to introduce the term *political salvage* to describe the increasingly occurring nexus between these two activities in contemporary radical activism.

But how does salvage particularly influence the anticapitalist politics of all of these diverse forms of protest and activism? In *Mushrooms*, Tsing herself bristles at the suggestion that salvage represents a revolutionary or emancipatory activity, an attitude shared by many who see salvage as a mere coping skill in the face of a physical and social environment increasingly damaged by neoliberalism. She states that what she calls the "latent commons" and other possibly emancipatory social forms that can form due to the activity of the foragers

> cannot redeem us. Some radical thinkers hope that progress will lead us to a redemptive and utopian commons. In contrast, the latent commons is here and now, amid the trouble and humans are never fully in control. Given this negative character, it makes no sense to crystallize first principles or seek natural laws that generate best cases, instead I practice arts of noticing. I comb through the mess of existing worlds-in-the-making, looking for treasures—each distinctive and unlikely to be found again at least in that form. (Tsing 2015, 255)

Tsing here offers an ambiguous account of the practice of salvage. While certain examples might constitute "treasures" that offer the possibility for progress, she warns that theorists and activists should not try to look to such manifestations as blueprints for future action. Salvage and the latent commons that often coalesces around its practice should only be thought of as negative examples that offer up few if any guides for the future. Efforts to construct a political theory of "first principles" or "laws" betray the unique, contingent, and unstable nature of the social forms, values, and practice displayed by the salvagers.

But what if the characteristics of salvage that Tsing identifies as anti-utopian—the lack of complete human control, the arts of noticing and not acting, and the contingency of the communities it forms—constitute the exact characteristics upon which anticapitalist movements might rely? What if the "chaos" of salvage activity, its rhythmic as opposed to linear paths of construction and destruction, can be used to undermine the ideological separations upon which the alienation and reification produced through capitalist experience relies? I argue that as opposed to the pessimism of Tsing and others, her description of the actual practice of salvage points toward a normative kernel lying within its practice that stands in stark opposition to the contours of capitalist experience. This kernel is grounded in the lack that prompts the act of salvage itself. During the activity of salvage, its practitioners often find themselves led to acknowledge, respect, and open themselves to the new and unseen. One must focus one's attention intently not only on what an object is, but what it could possibly be. The salvage environment calls upon a person, and if they heed this confusing call rife with possibilities it can lead them to seek useful materials in the most reviled places and ponder the unexpected possible uses of seemingly broken and repellent items. Therefore, this activity draws attention to the unique qualities of an object as opposed to its quantity or exchange value. Furthermore, to salvage is to think in terms of assemblage and combinations. During salvage one often asks, How can this new object be connected with this other thing with which it would normally not be associated? Instead of buying something new, one must scavenge what is around them, and use that to repair what is broken. I use the observations above to argue that within this activity lies an anticapitalist potential, that, while not constituting a classical Utopia that prefigures the best, or even a better society, does contain the outline of practices that can be useful in both resisting our commodified lifeworld and imagining new futures beyond that of our contemporary, increasingly ruined capitalist landscape.

Salvage does not solely embody a set of skills and practices but also suggests a particular form of political community. The contemporary practitioners of salvage, whether in Flint or Zuccotti Park, the barrios of Tijuana, or the squats of Amsterdam, use land and materials in new ways—taking possession of them as a group, not ceding to public government control yet not dividing them up into individual parcels, resulting in ownership neither public nor private, but common property. Also, such groups act autonomously, commonly, and collectively, reaching solutions to their shared problems while salvaging the necessities of their own existence. Finally, they form communities comprised of shifting and novel relationships with both the human and nonhuman elements of their environments, so that the commons they build is generative and constantly becoming something new. While such relationships seem like weak reeds upon which to build a politics that could effectively counter the juggernaut forces of capital, they might play an important role in generating new habits and subjectivities, which activists might use in their confrontations with power.

This identification of the radical potential latent within communities of political salvage constitutes the main claim upon which I build my next argument—that salvage communities can be cultivated and the radical potential of their practices deepened through particular design innovations, spatial strategies, rituals, and habits. Salvage constitutes a concrete activity focused on the concrete materiality of items to be used in concrete spaces. As such, thinking about how particular informal communities, squats and occupied public spaces have activated, maintained, and strengthened these activities allows me to identify the characteristics of salvage communities that might be accentuated to further cultivate the anticapitalist characteristics present but underdeveloped in the examples I highlight. It is important to emphasize that by identifying practices that might intensify the political consequences produced through participation in such communities and then thinking about them as what I term "radical workshops," I am not suggesting that salvage results in one particular strategy or that radical workshops must assume a particular institutional configuration. Furthermore, I am not claiming that each of these qualities I identify will necessarily lead to the generation of the others. My conceptualization is meant to act as a weak organizational form and a general political strategy. While such a strategy accentuates the political possibilities inherent within in salvage, the act of salvage in and of itself does not lead to anticapitalist attitudes and practices. Furthermore, the examples that I offer and the theoretical literature I use to analyze these examples are meant to highlight the conditions that might strengthen the radical power of combining salvage with certain types of radical political action. This means that there is no one example to use nor predetermined combination of innovations that will ensure success. Even if there were, and every possibility that I highlight were somehow implemented, episodes of political salvage would most likely continue to be fragile and perhaps fleeting. Instead, I aspire to articulate this political theory of salvage to highlight the conditions which activate and sustain the manifestations of political salvage that increasingly rise up within the ruins left by neoliberal capitalism.

Before continuing, it is important to identify some things my conceptualization of a political theory of salvage is not. As one looks around the contemporary capitalist landscape, one often see spaces, buildings, and items that are "salvaged" by "artisans." Artisanal vinegars, factories renovated into high priced lofts, rusted bicycles transformed into pieces of mobile art, are examples of the new hipness of salvaged items, especially among city dwellers.[5] This work does not embody the type of salvage I explore—using an old thing in a new way does not, in itself, possess political implications. The salvage I examine, as suggested by Stavros Stavrides, constitutes a "craft of the poor" (Stavrides 2016, 126).[6] When turning an old factory into a mall or high-end condominiums, the shell might be retained, but the materials, and more importantly the idea and the planning process are commodities, things that are bought new. But when the poor salvage, it is not a choice. They must use primarily what surrounds them and work with the people around them. They are often led to intently pay attention to the qualities of the items and spaces that constitute their landscape in order to discern the possibilities within them. They must try to sense the vibrant potentiality latent within the items that they have because they do not have the means to obtain others. They must use these items in new ways and must use them before they are sure their interventions and repairs will work. Thus, they will fail frequently and must start over and reassess more frequently. Furthermore, not only can they not pick the environment from which they salvage items, they cannot pick the uses for which they will be employed. Challenges to living cannot be avoided and are more frequent due to the precariousness of poverty. Finally, I want to emphasize that when poverty is understood in this sense, activists are poor. This precariousness of poverty mirrors the precariousness of the political activities that employ salvage, as the vagaries of life under the stress of state harassment, internal disagreement, and shifting political winds force activists engaging in salvaging public spaces and encampments to deal with unforeseen, messy, and unavoidable circumstances. Restoring an old bicycle meant to be ridden on weekends through the park is a choice that one need not make, whereas restoring a bicycle to power an encampment generator is an act performed in the context of necessity. It is this unavoidable salvage, salvage that must happen to fulfill an essential, unavoidable, or immediate task that imposes burdens on its practitioners, yet it is in these impositions that one can find its unique attributes and anticapitalist promise; promise that does not necessarily lead to political action, but constitutes a situation that increases its likelihood.

I also do not offer an all-encompassing account of contemporary salvage activities and their relationship to political movements. There are many examples of the involvement of political activism and salvage that I do not discuss.[7] This is because this book, despite the fact that it draws on material from many fields of inquiry, remains a primarily theoretical endeavor. I undertake the investigation from the perspective of political theory largely as a means of clarification and intensification. The work is itself a type of salvage,[8] in that I attempt to roam around the messy landscape of contemporary social theory and political activism, gather works that seemingly could never fit together, and jury rig them into a tool that might aid in imagining the construction of a revolutionary subject. Thus, while this work will draw heavily on the work of others, it does not aspire to be a comprehensive examination of salvage. It only hopes to clarify what I deem to be the concepts, values, and practices that might constitute a political theory of salvage using theory and example. Once again, not every act of salvage by the poor will result in political salvage, and thus I will focus on examples that I see as pointing toward the conditions that have increased the occurrence of such as the fusion of salvage and politics, and, furthermore, that constitute the conditions that have maintained this linkage. Although manifestations of "political salvage" as I call it have been increasing in number, such activity has not been acknowledged as a specific mode of activism with its own specific repertoire of actions, consequences, and attitudes.

I want to introduce one final qualification to this study. In trying to articulate a political theory of salvage, I examine many empirical examples of activists engaging in political salvage. In my examination, I highlight the political promise of these activities using conceptual analyses. This is not meant to discount the difficulties, errors, and perils faced by these movements. Salvage constitutes a precarious activity in many different ways. One might not find what one is looking for, and an item might not behave in a way that one might have thought. Furthermore, contestant politics in itself entails risks, with the best laid plans falling prey to either fortune or overwhelming odds. I state these seeming truisms to emphasize that the movements and activists I discuss in this work are not flawless—they have made mistakes, have failed and fallen prey to internal, petty discord like any other political endeavor.

Despite these failures I will not be assessing these movements on the basis of their "practical" success—I will be engaging in a theoretical exegesis, using these examples of the potentialities I see within these movements in hopes of suggesting strategies for extending the nascent political implications I identify. Furthermore, when talking about the potentials of these movements and activists, I do not wish to diminish the desperate circumstances that most often prompt political salvage. It is the poor who undertake political salvage, and although I see promise that transcends particular effort, this is not to romanticize these efforts or the situation that prompts them. I look at the poverty that prompts salvage not as some form of redemption, but a circumstance that prompts attitudes and practices that can be recreated in any situation after they are identified and analyzed.

While acknowledging such limitations, I do claim that a theoretical examination such as this can help to clarify and define political salvage, orienting political inquiry to examine it as a distinct form of contemporary protest. Furthermore, in articulating a political theory of salvage based upon the core concepts inherent in its practice, one might begin to think about how to deepen and intensify its practice, and apply these concepts to new situations where it is not presently undertaken. As Sheldon Wolin (2016) points out, political theory does not simply examine and clarify concepts, but offers a vision of political practice, helping to redefine the world it examines. The "vision" produced through a political theory of salvage, with its origin in material situations of extreme contingency and breakdown, cannot be expressed in any concrete representation of a better world. Instead, as we shall see, it is better expressed in jury-rigged experiments that must be constantly modified. Isabel Stenger argues that this mode of experimentation without vision, or perhaps, experimentation that will hopefully lead to vision, should be the goal of a political theory that truly grows from and listens to the contingency that I place at the center of salvage. As she puts it:

> [T]he challenge for political theorists may then be to learn how to situate themselves in relation to such empowering experimentation, the role and importance of which can easily be dismissed or assimilated into the background noise, unable to seriously disturb power relationships, or equally

to be misrepresented as a model embodying a new idea of democracy. What theorists have to do is to learn how to relate to something that involves true experimentation on its own ground. (Stengers and Bennett 2010, 22)

Thus, through articulating a political theory of salvage, I write as both a scholar of salvage and as one engaged in salvage, attempting to dig myself and my community out of the muck that surrounds me in a way where I do not simply survive, but build something new and, perhaps, better.

Chapter Outlines

I will begin my argument in chapter 1 by presenting examples of what I call "political salvage" or the growing imbrication of anticapitalist political activism with scavenging and the construction and repair of spaces using salvaged material. I organize the chapter around common themes I find within these examples. From a simply descriptive and qualitative perspective, Tsing's observations on "salvage accumulation" constitute my starting point in portraying the "arts of living on a damaged planet" necessary to exist in a world of climate change, neoliberal austerity, and political authoritarianism. Other ethnographies describe the daily struggles of those who salvage refuse for a living. In the midst of this struggle, these examples demonstrate how individuals develop salvage skills and forms of community that not only allow them to subsist, but also to develop new concepts of freedom and modes of consciousness. I then explore the growing recognition that salvage has become an important mode of contemporary activism and a common value upon which many build their communities. Whether it be the informal community dwellers salvaging to build their neighborhoods, the "crafts of the poor" that Athenians are forced to employ in their fight to survive austerity, or the jury-rigged gas masks and tree-borne shelters cobbled together by activists in the midst of their struggle I outline three categories of political salvage, occupations, squats and barrios. I conclude by arguing that the defining concept of this "political salvage" lies in its "plasticity" or the fact that salvage can lead its practitioners to creatively reinterpret the uses of the materials and environments in which they are forced to exist.

In chapter 2, I explore the significance of the fact that salvagers particularly rely upon their sense of the affective qualities they experience

when interacting with their broken environment when both scavenging and repairing, and how affect lies at the core of salvage's political
potential. Not only have theorists attempted to flesh out a theory of
affect in order to describe how people experience the potentialities
of their interactions with damaged environments, but also some have
begun to explore the affects produced through existence within contemporary capitalism and how this sense of the everyday might play a role
in perpetuating its legitimacy, undertaking what they call a "political
economy of the senses." Theorists have not limited their use of affect
to describing the many ways that capitalism constitutes a particular
affective landscape that encourages identities and perceptions shaped by
reification and alienation. They have begun to argue that any attempt to
overcome such affective infrastructure gains power through the cultivation
of particular affects—affects that begin to resemble those described by
salvage theorists. Specifically, I argue that nascent affects of "love" and
"depression" are often produced through salvage, and by identifying and
accentuating such affects its practice can gain political power. I conclude
the chapter by arguing that the work of William Connolly, and especially
his grounding of democracy in a "A World of Becoming," constitutes
the best contemporary political analog to the love/depression dynamic
I describe and consequently to the critical potentiality of salvage as I
understand it. In his understanding, democratic citizens form relationships
with others based not on compromise or shared identity, but instead
grounded in creative transformations they experience through following
the subtle resonances that result from opening themselves up to the
hidden multiplicity of their pluralistic surroundings. The affect-enabled
plasticity of salvage labor mirrors the plasticity of this democratic, anticapitalist becoming, and thus I claim that salvage, when practiced in a
way that intensifies such affect, can be seen as a generator of the ethos
of radical democracy articulated by Connolly.

In chapter 3, I examine the abilities, skills, and habits that might
intensify the political potentials of salvage. As I said before, some have
interpreted salvage as a "craft of the poor." Using this insight as a spring-
board, I analyze salvage through accounts of artisan practices presented
in the work of Richard Sennett and Gilles Deleuze. They highlight
how craft workers rely upon habits that accentuate the propensity to
follow contingent affects and thus increase one's likelihood of adopting
"plastic" flexible habits. I then employ both Deleuze, John Dewey, and
others to claim that being able to fully take advantage of the affective

sense produced through one's interaction with one's environment to engage in creative, subversive becoming should be undertaken with the rhythmic form exhibited by craftwork. In this way, craftworkers exhibit "disciplined" becoming that better enables practitioners to sustain their plastic labor and could thus increase its political consequences. I also claim that craftwork is best practiced communally and in spaces that encourage the development of rhythmic, affective, craft habits. To explore such spaces, I demonstrate how John Dewey's model of the progressive schoolroom is designed to assist students in adopting a pro- ductive aesthetic form to their thinking, and Deleuze's schema of the Baroque House is meant to highlight the proper rhythmic alternation necessary for the nomadic "minor" sciences. Thus, I contend that such spaces, which I call "radical workshops" encourage what I call "rhythms of resistance" that might encourage a critical praxis of salvage. If these craftlike characteristics of salvage were acknowledged and accentuated, then its practice might more powerfully break down reified perspectives and allow for the construction of alternatives to the ruined landscapes of contemporary capitalism.

After articulating the various political potentialities lying within salvage—reliance on affect, embodying a rhythmic form, and occurring in urban spaces—in chapter 4 I discuss how the practice of salvage becomes political. I argue that the work of Henri Lefebvre helps us to imagine a "macro choreography" where the entire city becomes the "stage" that encourages salvage-based insurrection. I demonstrate that the dynamic of capitalist development within cities, that of creating abstract centralities primed for capitalist accumulation and segregated peripheries where discarded materials, workers, and spaces themselves create dialec- tical tensions within the cities, has often led apolitical salvage cites to engage in political contestation. For example, when salvage cites that are ignored because of their locations on peripheries come to be the tar- gets of capitalist appropriation, the members of such groups often resist. But, using Lefebvre's methodology of "rhythmanalysis" I show how the plastic, affects felt by salvagers in their local salvage spaces might also be produced by the contradictory geography of the capitalist city itself. Thus, Lefebvre can help to understand how the potentialities within in the micro practice of salvage that I identify are often actuated by the macro dynamics of the capitalist city, and therefore how larger political forces can transform salvage as a survival strategy into salvage as an act of resistance.

In chapter 5, I explore the spatial qualities that accentuate and diminish the possibility for political salvage in particular spaces. The main concept I use to enter this discussion is that of anticapitalist "choreography" as discussed by Derek P. McCormack and Brian Massumi. I use these works to discuss how spaces, such as the "radical workshops" I examine in chapter 3, might be arranged to deepen individuals' sense of the resonances that surround them and to use these affects to deepen their likelihood to undergo radical becoming or to engage in what he calls "experiments with experience." I then go on to discuss a number of actual protest "spaces," such as Occupy encampments, urban squats, political art installations, and informal communities, that display aspects of productive choreography, and then suggest how this choreography might be improved to encourage salvage. Such choreography centers on establishing rhythms of interactions between people, things, and spaces that create an affective background conducive to the dereifying, relationship-creating, and sensing of different resonances that can encourage what I call the affective "rhythms of resistance." With choreographic attributes of such "radical workshops" articulated, perhaps future occupations and examples of salvage politics might be endowed with a weak structure that would address the charge of the "tyranny of structurelessness" levied by so many toward Occupy Wall Street and the other self-organized political actions involving salvage it has inspired.

In chapter 6, I begin to discuss how all of the conditions that I have suggested sustain and enhance political salvage might be expressed within a political movement with discrete political goals. Such a vision centers around the concept of the "commons." In numerous case studies and ethnographies of political action within poor communities, theorists have described the product of such autonomous productive activity as the "commons," meaning a space neither publicly administered by governments nor privately held by individuals. Michael Hardt and Antonio Negri in their *Commonwealth* have been especially enthusiastic concerning not simply informatively supporting this concept as a goal of politics, but also showing how the contradictions produced through biopolitical production has increasingly led to acts of resistance that produce common spaces, communities, and businesses. Through linking Hardt and Negri's understanding of the commons to salvage, I can further clarify what I see to be its concrete political implications. The commons plays a fundamental role in Hardt and Negri's articulation of the political subject they refer to as the "multitude." They describe the multitude as a loose network of self-organizing groups resisting biopolitical extraction of value from the commons. Although they briefly name salvage as a promising site for the constitution of the multitude, they do not develop this insight. I claim that through choreographing spaces that encourage the craft of salvage and its rhythms of resistance, salvage can act as a powerful practice encouraging the formation of the multitude. This insight leads me to a larger political claim—that salvage can act as a loose political structure based in shared practices that that lie somewhere between a crowd and a party. Hardt and Negri rely too heavily on their assumption that the multitude constitutes a self-organizing political subject that rises due to the contradictions of what they deem to be the contradictions of the new form of biopolitical capitalist production. My understanding of salvage as a craft that best occurs in choreographed spaces suggests that through self-imposed regulation and practice, the multitude can be cultivated—not by organizers working for a hierarchical party, but instead by adopting preexisting rituals and training procedures in choreographed spaces. Thus, the craft of political salvage, as I imagine it occupies a median space between socialist and anarchist practice, displaying both structure and spontaneity. Therefore, the political theory of salvage can contribute to the diminishing the acrimony that currently divides the Left.

Conclusion

As with the other Occupy actions, the salvaged village of Occupy Flint was eventually dismantled, in this case with a whimper and not a police-induced bang. Flint's state-requisitioned local autonomy was not replaced by political horizontalism and numerous general assemblies, but instead returned through the same executive fiat through which it was taken away. By that time, the damage had been done—its water had been poisoned by the policies of neoliberal austerity. Was Occupy Flint a failure, as so many had deemed Occupy Wall Street? I argue that it was not. Just as the resonances of the Occupation of Zuccotti Park could be felt in the aid efforts of Occupy Sandy, where New Yorkers formed autonomous communities of mutual aid to help with hurricane relief, the influences of Occupy Flint could be heard in the community upris-ing to combat the Flint water crisis.[9] Remember, the import of salvage does not lie in the act, but in new habits, attitudes, and relationships that it fosters. If, as John Dewey stated, democracy is a way of life, then perhaps salvage is the way of enacting democratic, anticapitalist life in a broken world. Some episodes of political salvage persist and some die. Yet salvage as a political strategy transcends its own individual manifestations. As capitalism creates increasing numbers of ruined landscapes and more and more poor people who inhabit such landscapes, salvage will continue to constitute a necessity to survive. And with this increase in salvage comes the opportunity to implement the observations that I make concerning the qualities that increase the possibility and sustain the practice of political salvage. Furthermore, in many ways, efforts to resist such phenomena have been in decline: reactionary governments have been on the rise in both the industrialized and industrializing world, oftentimes using the ruins of capitalism to justify their authoritarian and exclusionary practices. Despite this, salvage will continue to be linked with politics as more movements attempt to reclaim, refurbish and reinhabit their environments. If salvage is acknowledged as an integral, and, more importantly, a positive and constructive part of not simply coping with ruin, but of overcoming it in a hopeful and possibly revolutionary way, then perhaps the ruin of the world might be thought of as representing the opportunity to make a new one.

Chapter 1

Salvage and Politics

Introduction

In 2016, the radical political and cultural journal *Salvage* began its inaugural issue with an essay by its editors entitled "Amid this Stony Rubbish." The authors enjoin their readers to transcend the utopian stupor they believe most political radicals inhabit and mercilessly acknowledge the reality that the Left has been reduced to a state of rubbish. The authors' pessimism is not confined to radical moments but extends to democracy itself as neoliberalism continues its march to colonize public institutions with the logic of capitalism. They claim that what has worked in the past to resist such forces will not work in the future, and revolutionaries must "search history's dump to reclaim the best of what the left has discarded" (Salvage Editors, Anon. 2015, 4). But in the midst of this search, the essay implores, those defending economic egalitarianism, political democracy, and ecological justice must not become overly optimistic. The authors seem to be saying that the "dump" of the contemporary world yields only weak material with which to build an alternative to the neoliberal order. They lament the difficulty of discerning exactly what might bring success and what might fail in a broken world where old solutions produce seemingly random, futile outcomes. While the Left cannot expect history's dump to produce anything hopeful in the traditional sense of the word, the authors do claim that the Left must adopt an attitude indicative of

> the German *Sehnsucht*. In this expression of utter yearning, for something familiar yet undiscovered, is a sublation of delight

and sorrow that C. S. Lewis described as "the inconsolable longing in the heart for we know not what," and "unsatisfied desire which is itself more desirable than any other satisfaction." "Joy," in fact, was an idiosyncratic translation, a joy he insisted be "sharply distinguished both from happiness and from pleasure," and "might almost equally well be called a particular kind of . . . grief. But then that is what we want." (Salvage Editors Anon. 2015, 14)

This call to grief-filled joy (or joyful grief) raises a number of interesting questions. Is such grief-joy a motivation or something that one must endure? If this attitude can spur action and indignation, what actions might it lead activists to take? What type of fuel or material does one need to feed one's joyful grief, or, in other words, what type of evidence compels us to experience more intense feelings accompanying this experience? Finally, how does one sustain this attitude toward the broken world? All of these questions become more acute and pressing in light of the authors' claim that any hope of "fixing" the broken world in the near future remains an impossibility. They argue that "'we have to stop imagining,' in Judith Butler's recent words, 'that repair is possible. That full repair is possible.' But still we struggle to jury-rig tools, to rise" (2015, 15). Notice here the equivocation in the use of the word *repair*—the uneasy juxtaposition of repair and full repair. This uncertainty in the possibility of fixing a broken society reveals a profound ambivalence concerning the strategy and ambition of radical politics. But, whichever attitudes, tools, and strategies those who wish to stem the rising tide of neoliberalism are forced to adopt in this world of trash, the essay argues, the process of salvage will be ongoing. Salvaging radical politics constitutes a process that has no foreseeable end, no set of tools whose effectiveness will persist throughout the process, and no ground rules for what material might constitute the best building blocks for any improvements. Even though they invoke salvage as a new paradigm for the Left, they articulate salvage in a pessimistic mode that offers little solace and few easy solutions.

In this chapter, I will introduce an alternative understanding of salvage based not in theory but in actual practice. This understanding is rooted in the claim that the practice of salvage possesses heretofore unacknowledged emancipatory possibilities. But it is important to first examine how the concept of salvage has begun, if haltingly, to appear in radical political discourse. Like the sentiments expressed above, these discussions have largely taken the form of pessimism, using salvage as a metaphor for the lack of widespread radical possibilities within the contemporary political situation and the necessity to step back and reassess. I will chronicle some of this Left-pessimistic interpretation of salvage while introducing the main theme of the work—that those who study the actual practice of salvage identify radical potentialities within the practice, and salvage often plays an important role in contemporary political struggle. Thus, while not a panacea, salvage can be seen not only as a strategy indicative of retreat and defeat, but also a constructive and radical practice in and of itself.

To continue with my portrayal of contemporary Left interpretations of salvage, other theorists have used the metaphor of salvage as a basis for rethinking political strategy with negative, or, to be fair, skeptical tones. For example Left cultural critic Evan Calder Williams articulates what he sees as a "salvage punk" aesthetic developing in reaction to the increasing ruin and pessimism created through contemporary neoliberalism. He notices this particularly reflected in pop culture such as the *Mad Max* franchise and other films that feature a postapocalyptic word filled with the ruins of industrial capitalism. But whereas such "reactionary" visions of the breakdown of contemporary society result in images of a Hobbesian war against all that merely confirms the most aggressive, hierarchical, and conservative stereotypes concerning human nature, he sees a more progressive interpretation of this cultural imaginary. He imagines this Left salvage punk a "post-apocalyptic vision of a broken and dead world . . . shot through with the hard work of salvaging, repurposing, *detourning* and scrapping" (Williams 2011, 17).[1] The actual intellectual and material labor that goes into such salvage involves both "to clear away the waste—the wreckage at once *material* (the produced crap and scraps of our production processes) and *theoretical* (past gestures, manifesto fragments and strategies for repurposing)—to make a space for what can be made from it," and "making and remaking, not the smoothing of compromised synthesis, but welding, stitching, rewiring" (31). Calder Williams claims it is the embracing of the "punkiness" of this vision that saves it from banal or reactionary emphasis upon merely valuing the old. It hopes to retain the "innate venom of things" [2] that undercuts what he sees as the "inherent flatness and equivalency of postmodern cultural production" (40). In the final evaluation, he argues that salvage punk as contestation must take the form of "the work of construction," not simply gutting to see what can be sold back to the industrial suppliers[3] but a production of "valueless times" to see what "values might emerge outside of the loops of circulation and accumulation" (41). Thus, for Calder Williams, salvage punk constitutes a social-cultural practice not where ideas come to be reused and perhaps refurbished in an already existent system, but instead where discarded items are used to build disruptive machines and spaces that both create and maintain cracks in the larger economic and cultural order.

Yet when it comes to describing the method for constructing salvage-punk machines, Calder Williams's descriptions manifest themselves only in the negative. While he does invoke modes of cultural and physical production such as montage and the Situationist *detournement* when attempting to further articulate how might one engage in salvage, he primarily casts these actions in terms of what is taken away, not what is built. When actually practicing acts of progressive salvage punk, he emphasizes that one must "sort, sever, untangle, and grasp objects of insistent value from the wasteland," and that salvage punk entails "a hacking apart of those past moments saving something and tossing away more, particularly those traditions in which we've invested too much to see them for the lumbering hindrance they have become" (Williams 2011, 40–41). He sums up the activity of salvage punk through characterizing it "fundamentally a negative operation, even at its moment of construction. . . . The goal is never the restoration of a positive entity, but rather an assemblage of negatives: cast out by the system, or in the longer task of montage, cut out to be put together otherwise" (68). He implies that because of the nearly insurmountable logic of commodification, the fact that anything can be repurposed as something to be resold, the only tool a true salvage punk can construct is a hammer, which is used to smash. Salvage punks sift through the trash heap only to find implements that can further break the system that created the trash heap in the first place. The attempt to construct, however temporary or open to modification, ideas, methods, or strategies for contestation will simply be reassimilated into our contemporary capitalist reality. What Calder Williams offers through his vision of salvage punk constitutes an embrace of this activity only in what he sees as its depressing authenticity. To him, living in the scrap heap of our contemporary condition requires that we realize how badly off we really are. The salvage punk hopes to wake us up to the true dire nature of our situation and nothing else—for to imagine that salvage might bring about actual improvement or political change is to undermine the radical potential of the trash heap of society itself.[4]

As I suggested in the introduction, Anna Tsing presents a somewhat pessimistic understanding of the relationship of salvage to radical politics. For her, salvage constitutes a strategy for living within the cracks of the contemporary capitalism that plays a small role in a larger, contemporary economic formation increasingly constituting a phase of global supply chains. She defines this role as "salvage accumulation," which she describes as "taking advantage of value produced without capitalist control" and a "process through which lead firms amass capital without controlling the conditions under which commodities are produced" (Tsing 2015, 63). She goes on to state that "sites of salvage are simultaneously inside and outside capitalism; I call them pericapitalist" (ibid.). This hybrid under-standing of the relationship of salvage to capitalism remains true to what she sees as the empirical dependence of capitalism upon noncapitalist forms of accumulation, especially in the age of our current neoliberal disasters. She juxtaposes her understanding of salvage and other non-capitalist forms of accumulation against the views of theorists such as J. K. Gibson-Graham and Michael Hardt and Antonio Negri. She states:

> Gibson-Graham advises us, quite correctly I think, that what they call "non-capitalist" forms can be found everywhere in the midst of a capitalist world—rather than just in archaic backwaters. But they see such forms as alternatives to capi-talism. Instead I would look for the non-capitalist elements on which capitalism depends. (Tsing 2015, 66)

For her, the fact that salvage currently exists within capitalism most likely leads her to eschew fully examining the tensions that might exist between these two forms of value extraction. Her position seems to be that salvage exists within the capitalist world and to fully represent this activity one must emphasize its connections to capitalism and how its practitioners do this merely out of desperation and not as a manifestation of politics or resistance. Such salvage pessimism can be summed up by Tsing's assertion that I quoted in the introduction, that the relationships and communities built by the foragers of matsutake mushrooms take the form of a "latent commons" that "cannot save us." Salvage, to her, remains too episodic, chaotic, and intertwined with capitalist production ever to constitute a form of political resistance.

Despite such minimalist and pessimistic interpretations, a number of authors have adopted a more productive and contestatory interpretation of the political potentialities of salvage. For example, in Katherine Millar's study of the community of salvagers who have established themselves in the landfills of Rio de Janeiro, she criticizes "scarcity as a persistent paradigm for understanding lives lived in precarious conditions" (Millar 2018, 6). She goes on to argue that during the act of salvage, "reclaiming these particular objects and many more is also an act of remaking the world" and that "waste lies at the heart of both relations of inequality and transformative social projects" (33).[5] She grounds her assessment of salvage in the work of E.P. Thompson, whose work on the "riots of the belly" undertaken by the poor to better their conditions she sees as helping to "disrupt such conventional narratives of deprivation" (12). Subsequently, she claims that such an inquiry might suggest how the tools and procedures used by salvagers point the way to a more explicit understanding politics and activism. A similar attitude is evinced in Mike Davis's recent essay "Learning from Tijuana." Here, he discusses what he sees as the implications of the city's residents' "bootstrap urbanism" where they salvage and repair their built environment:

> [I]n the Do It Yourself City, bricolage supplants master plan-ning, and urban design becomes a kind of *art brut*, generated by populist building practices. If only by default, the masses become the city's true auteurs, and architecture is not so much transcended as retranslated through its dynamic vernacular context. (Davis 1996, 35)[6]

Whereas Davis points to salvage in a metaphorical sense and Millar's work centers upon the concrete practices of a discrete community, both of these statements point toward a more affirmative interpretation of the radical promise of salvage. Kristin Ross emphasizes a similar radical political potential in salvage, when she emphasizes not simply the importance of the barricades for the defensive needs of the Communards during the Paris Commune, but also the larger significance of their construction. She observes that during the construction of the barricades, "monumental ideals of formal perfection, duration, or immortality, quality of material and integrity of design are replaced by a special kind of bricolage—the wrenching of everyday objects out of their habitual context to be used in a radically different way" (Ross 2008, 36).[7] These are diverse exam-ples but they are united by the supposition that salvage does not simply constitute a tactic of survival, but can also represents an expression of autonomy outside the official structures of state and society.

Although the previous examples come from actual practice, a tradition exists using the concept of salvage to engage in transvaluation of oppressive culture and reconstruction from catastrophe. For example, take Benjamin's invocation that "the debris of industrial culture teaches us not the necessity of submitting to historical catastrophe but the fragility of the social order that tells us this catastrophe is necessary" (Buck-Morss 1989, 170), and ruin "refers also to the loosened building blocks (both semantic and material) out of which a new order can be constructed" (212). Furthermore, Michael Thompson also offers revaluation of what society discards in his *Rubbish Theory: The Creation and Destruction of Value*, when it states, "[W]hen that which we have excluded from our scene of things nevertheless intrudes and forces its attention on us, our sense of order, hence our ability to control our external world, [are] seriously threatened" (Thompson 2017, 232). He recommends a "metabolic" approach to rubbish—the acknowledgment that excluding rubbish stems from social conventions, and acknowledging such artifices can lead to an embracing a fluid exchange between what is seen as trash and what is understood as valued. He goes on to claim that the way to change such an impression would be for the city to accept the trash it excludes, leading to "all manner of physical and social re-construction of the dividing line between purity and impurity" (249).[8] Thus, the acceptance of trash comes to be seen, ironically, as the way that an environment comes to be seen as less trashy. And although Thompson does not interpret the process of "picking" through detritus to salvage hidden utopian nuggets, his work does further indicate the growing prominence of the interest and transvaluation of rubbish into a resource as opposed to a burden.

This brief introduction to some recent work that alludes to the political promise of salvage opens the door to a much wider understanding of how this theme has been emerging in social science and popular culture. In claiming that salvage embodies a novel category emerging within political action that possesses radical potential, I must define it. In order to do that, I must undertake a brief survey of some of what I see to be the themes that have emerged in the work of those who have engaged in empirical work on salvage. I will identify social and political theorists who discuss salvage, even when their discussions do not constitute the primary focus of their work. I will link these disconnected discussions into common themes of affect, plasticity, space, and community to construct a preliminary theory of salvage that identifies both the primary experiential characteristics of this activity as well as the physical and social environments in which salvage tends to occur. Yet in addition to conducting a survey I will also be building that case that, as opposed to the pessimists I identify, salvage might, in fact, play an important role in "redeeming us." Millar's assertion that deprivation need not be the only aspect of salvage, but also can inspire new understandings of what she calls, invoking E. P. Thompson, the "arts of living" that might point a way forward to new political tactics and social understandings.

Occupations, Squats, Informal Communities: Political Salvage

As anyone who has ever tried to find a public bathroom while walking around lower Manhattan knows, taking care of the most basic necessities without knowledge, funds, or cultural capital in this unforgiving urban landscape can be a challenge. That the participants of Occupy Wall Street not only managed to provide basic necessities such as food and bathroom facilities for themselves and visitors, but also articulated a critique of capitalism that captivated the country for three months while the city government repeatedly tried to evict them, seems nearly miraculous. One of the strategies the Occupiers pursued in order to maintain themselves, their encampment, and their political message was to salvage discarded material and repurpose it for their own ends. Anthropologist Michael Taussig notes the prevalence of salvage when recalling his time at the camp. He talks of how he and his compatriots "looked in heaps of garbage for plastic bags to cover us if we try to get some sleep" (Mitchell, Harcourt, and Taussig 2013, 19). He goes on to observe how activists used such recycled material not simply for the necessities of living, but also for their political expressions. On the east side of the park, facing Broadway, Occupiers set up a row of signs made from recycled material, most frequently boxes originating from donated pizzas called in from around the country. Taussig talks about these signs as if they were idols emitting incantations from the salvagers, stating:

> [I]t is the handmadeness of the signs, their artisanal crudity, art before the age of mechanical and digital reproduction that facilitates this hop, skip and jump. . . . Put another way the sign has a talismanic function, an incantory drive and is of divine inspiration, the gods in this case being of mirthful

disposition, feeling quite at home in the park. (Mitchell, Harcourt, and Taussig 2013, 27–28)

One need not share his interpretation of the "talismanic" properties of the Occupiers' salvaged placards to note the importance and power of the recycled signs. He stresses that their messy, salvaged, and rudimentary form did not detract from, and instead increased, the impact of their message. This pattern of salvaging materials for both the reproduction of the camp and the creation of its political message was repeated in instance after instance—from the bicycles repurposed as pedal-powered electric generators, to furniture, structures, banners, and even gas masks constructed from trash, salvage was one of the major tactics used by activists in their occupation and maintenance of Zuccotti Park as a protest camp.

This phenomenon of political salvage has not been confined only to Occupy Wall Street. In their study, *Protest Camps*, Anna Feigenbaum, Fabian Frenzel, and Patrick McCurdy claim that a "hands on and DIY practice is central to how protest campers approach politics and it is also the best way of researching protest camps" (Feigenbaum, Frenzel, and McCurdy 2013, 27). They recount instance after instance where discarded materials are employed for both maintenance of camps and political activities. The activists engage in such acts of salvage, the authors claim, because if one does not have funds to purchase something, or is prohibited from getting what one needs, then one must make do with what others have discarded. This salvage practice has been noted by others in their explorations of contemporary protest. Catherine Flood and Gavin Grindon's exhibition *Disobedient Objects* explores example after example of activists salvaging prosaic objects and reemploying them for subversive ends. For instance, they discuss the multiple ways activists have repurposed wooden pallets:

These mass produced wooden frames designed for disciplining labor and circulation commodities become around the world a shared infrastructural basis of the first 1970s tree sit-ins in New Zealand; furniture and barricade elements in 1970s Kabouter squats in the Netherlands, or those of Okups in Spain, and more recently the base of 123 Occupy designs to support the protest unit of Occupy Wall Street Tents. (Flood and Grindon 2014, 14)[9]

This salvage dynamic can be further observed in other encampments, whether on Rothschild Boulevard in Tel Aviv, Tahir Square in Cairo, or Syntagma Square in Athens.[10] These examples, both *Disobedient Objects* and *Protest Camps* demonstrate that the process of salvaging for the maintenance of the camp remains inexorably tied to the politics of the camp. As Feigenbaum, Frenzel and McCurdy argue, "[P]rotest camps are places where republican politics and social reproduction often coincide and mutually depend on each other" (Feigenbaum, Frenzel, and McCurdy 2013, 25). The fact that activities that sustain the occupations themselves often take the form of salvage has not been emphasized and points toward unexpected opportunities for political analysis—although at this point the ways that the "productive" politics expressed by the activists and the "reproductive" salvage activities that maintain the spaces from which this political activity originates remain opaque.

Salvage has also been regarded as an important aspect of less overtly political activities undertaken by subaltern groups. For example, squatting, while not inherently resulting in direct activism such as protest marches, attempts to change policy and organizing, and often leads to overt political activity as municipal authorities attempt to evict activists from the buildings they have taken. But additionally, squatting is in itself is a political act that challenges capitalist conceptions of property. In the process of refurbishing derelict buildings because no other housing is available, many squatters use recycled material in these efforts, and not simply through necessity. As Alexander Vasudevan relates in *The Autonomous City: A History of Urban Squatting*, squatters often deem salvage as a principled part of their efforts. He describes how "Lower East Side squatters rejected government funding and relied on recycled materials . . . and their own building skill and experiences which were passed on from house to house" (Vasudevan 2017, 221). Thus, we can see that salvage was not simply a tool squatters used to maintain their homes, but a shared ethos that defined the self-identity of the LES squatting movement. Although each squat was governed autonomously by its own members, a consciously cultivated common culture of salvage united these seemingly disconnected endeavors. Through his discussion of the Bauhof Handicraft Collective in West Berlin, Vasudevan demonstrates that this salvage ethos was not confined to North America. He recounts that

> [t]he Bauhof took on a key coordinating role within a wider activist milieu in Kreuzberg that encompassed a growing number of handicraft collectives that had emerged during the

1970s as a part of an expanding network of radical self-help activities. The Bauhof supplied squats with inexpensive building materials that were either recycled or purchased cheaply in bulk. . . . Ultimately the Bauhof became a site where squatters and architectural professionals often met to debate, discuss and experiment with new and innovative approaches to participatory design and adaptive reuse. (Vasudevan 2017, 137)

Thus, the act of salvage in this Berlin squatter movement not only constituted a unifying practice supported by institutions and spaces that transcended individual sites, but also it a represented political and creative principle that animated a new community dedicated to democracy and the participatory restructuring of the urban landscape. Once again, in this example, although it is not explicitly acknowledged, the salvage activity of "handicraft" and supplying squats with "inexpensive" salvaged material not only constituted an important part of maintenance of the squats, but also was the basis for the formation of their community and its subversive practices.

Besides refurbishing individual buildings, squatting can result in small acts of subversive, autonomous effort to try to salvage community resources and spaces. In North American cities such as Detroit, residents of underserved neighborhoods build their own city services such as utilities, street lights, and internet.[11] Others have examined the "bottom up" salvage design of the environment in Tijuana. It is important to remember that these authors interpret bottom up in two senses—both literally, in that additions to houses often take the form of new levels that are built on top of one another, and figuratively, in that the people who built the structures themselves make decisions concerning their architecture, often collectively. Lesley Stern discusses one of these common projects. She describes how in Tijuana a theater is constructed from salvage:

The seating and the stage are made from tires. When [local activist and engineer Oscar Romo] began, with the community, clearing the site, it was filled with trash and tires. So instead of engaging in more schlepping, they used the tires just as people have habitually done, to build walls, particularly retaining walls. A politician, in a random and rare act of civic cooperation, came in to clean up the area and yanked all the natives out, believing them to be weeds. Gradual replanting is happening. (Tsing et al. 2017, g24)

This story highlights the linkage of salvage to particular places and to the building of particular types of community. So many used auto parts from San Diego end up dumped in Tijuana that many have noted the preponderance of junkyards in the city with their mountains of tires. Thus, the community used the constituents of its damaged environment to fulfill both social and environmental needs.[12] And note how the offered political intervention, while neither aggressive nor meant to negate the community's salvage project, was still destructive in its own small way. Here, the state attempted to impose its understanding of order, while the community expressed its own, collaborative vision and thus learned how not to "see like a state."[13] And as residents push back against such maladroit efforts at reform and improvement they express a sense of autonomy for their community. This case and others suggest how states intervene, not simply through innocent attempts at "improving" the autonomous salvage activities of communities but also in more aggressive attempts to clear what salvagers have built expressed in, for instance, slum clearance and gentrification in reaction to the self-organized salvage activities of communities, and how such intervention can stoke mistrust and resistance to officialdom.[14]

The final manifestation I will discuss, seems to lie solely within the realm of aesthetics, or of art as aesthetics. This area possesses seemingly the most tenuous relationship to politics, but in fact salvage art projects often occur within squats, informal communities, and occupation, blurring the line between performance and resistance. In the book *Strike ART*, Yates McKee invokes many cases of such political salvage art, particularly the work of Thomas Hirschorn's Gramsci Monument, to assert what he believes to be the political import of such salvage art projects. The monument is one of a series that Hirschorn has undertaken to embody the thought of modern philosophers. The Gramsci Monument was constructed in a public housing complex in the Bronx, New York, with Hirschorn providing a rough outline for a construction crew made up of neighborhood residents. The actual monument took the form of a built landscape constructed with materials donated and found within the neighborhood itself, with various spaces dedicated to food, discussion, a workshop, and other activities, as opposed to passive exhibits. The monument acted as a mini-educational community, decorated with quotes by Gramsci, sponsoring academic talks, plays, and dances, and a general gathering space for discussion, construction, and recreation. McKee states:

[I]ndeed along with other degraded materials like packing tape, tinfoil . . . cardboard features prominently in the ramshackle participatory monuments of radical philosophers created by Thomas Hirschhorn during the 2000s which were nominated by leading art critic Hal Foster to exemplify a zeitgeist of precarity. Hirschorn's transient shanty-style construction often featuring loosely designated areas of activity such as computer stations, kitchens, playgrounds and libraries were in fact likened by philosopher Simon Critchely to the provisional architectures and spontaneous zoning of the Zuccotti Park settlement. (McKee 2017, 106)

Much in this quote hearkens back to the examples that have been previously discussed in this chapter. Mckee's invocation of the "shanty style" of the monuments, including the observations that the monument contains various areas dedicated to their own reproduction just like the Occupy encampments, that these areas were constructed out of salvage materials themselves, and that the monuments were participatory in their construction and maintenance, suggests that a community of salvage formed around the piece of art itself. In essence, the Gramsci Monument and other manifestations of political art represent the construction of a "barrio" within the modernism of state housing. There are numerous examples of similar contemporary "salvaged" art exhibiting similar methods of cooperative construction meant to critique the throwaway culture of capitalism and highlight this culture's ominous consequences.[15]

This brief survey of political salvage—occupations, squats, informal neighborhoods, and the art produced by salvagers in these spaces—is meant simply to introduce the growing significance of salvage as a political concept through what I see to be some provocative, concrete manifestations. Remember, many people use old things in new ways, many comb old garage sales in hopes of finding treasure in trash, but this is not what I mean by salvage. What all of the previous examples have in common, first, is the necessity of salvage. Even artistic endeavors such as Hirschorn's philosophers installations, not only are built and maintained by the poor from materials they are forced to use because they are surrounded by them, but also represent the unavoidable precarity of poverty in contemporary societies. All of these examples involve salvage both as a strategy of reproduction—the establishment and the maintenance of their spaces of salvage—and as an important part of the creation of an anticapitalist political action. Furthermore, all of these examples of salvage-established communities (remembering all the time that these groups diverge in important ways from communitarian understandings of association) neither originated in nor maintained themselves in isolation—even the autonomous squats of European cities banded together to share knowledge and create a culture of salvage. I will elaborate more on these specific themes as the argument proceeds, examining how contemporary inquirers hone in on particular characteristics of the actual work of salvage, the qualities and relationships indicative of salvage communities, and other subthemes. At this point, I only want to highlight the unique places and endeavors that characterize the new work on political salvage, in order to justify my focus upon this activity and its political import.

The Affect of Salvage

As I previously demonstrated, during Occupy Wall Street, observers were struck by the frequent usage of recycled material both for construction of the infrastructure necessary for the maintenance of the camp and for more explicitly political activities. Predictably, the authorities used this "trashy" aesthetic as an excuse to cast aspersions on the participants' cleanliness, and by extension, their morality. Furthermore, the city used the supposed filthiness of the camp as an excuse to exert actual pressure to remove it, citing the "public" health dangers it represented.[16] The discourse on the smell, look, and general feeling of uneasiness felt by the critics of Occupy is revealing not simply for what it reveals about their efforts to discredit the occupation. More importantly, it suggests how the experience of Occupy, its sights, sounds, and the sense one felt when actually in the encampment, played an important role in its reception. Recall that I noted how Michael Taussig emphasizes the ineffable, "talismanic" qualities of the Occupy experience and that this was intimately intertwined with its salvaged nature in his observations of the signs inscribed with political messages made from the boxes containing thousands of donated pizzas that fed the Occupiers. Although Taussig locates the "graven" quality of the sign in the interaction of the way the sign holder and sign corporeally interacted and fused into a "centaur"-like hybrid, his description also suggests that the salvaged "crudity" of the signs contributed to an ineffable sense that augmented their substantive messages. The signs, of course, acted as symbols using language to engage thoughts, but due to their salvaged qualities, they also possessed something more, in excess of their symbolic meaning. Experiencing the signs led Taussig to suggest a quality with its own "drive" and "inspiration," a sensed affect that interacts in strange and surprising ways with the known substance of the signs. This inarticulate fascination concerning the affects expressed by the construction of and interaction with salvaged material, both in its construction and reception, can be found in many recent works and represents an important aspect of the increasing interest in salvage and its political implications.

An emphasis of the importance of the affects created by activists' relationship with salvaged material can also be seen in the exhibition *Disobedient Objects*. In this exhibit the curators chronicle the many ways that activists salvage discarded objects to construct gas masks, barriers, tree slings and other implements necessary to protest. Such objects are produced within particular contexts, socially, materially, and geographically and each one possesses, in a sense, its own story and agency. This link between the object and its unique circumstances of construction leads the curators to search for "an archaeology of resistance" that "invites us to listen to these objects, discover their stories" (Flood and Grindon 2014, 42).[17] Indeed, one of the most evocative contentions of the curators is that such disobedient objects possess power themselves—power to influence, to call out new feelings and ideas, and to play a part in their own development. They claim that the use of salvaged material in recent anti-neoliberal globalization actions "speaks to us of what objects can compel the body to do, call for touch, for care, for action drawing us into their world" (Flood and Grindon 2014, 35) leading them to observe that "we see this notion of transformative affect expressed in many protesters' descriptions of actions and events" (Feigenbaum, Frenzel, and McCurdy 2013, 20).[18] Notice here the emphasis upon what the objects evoke in the body—touch, action, feelings of care and interest. The objects produce in people with whom they interact effects that they cannot, at least immediately, put into words or know as facts. They possess "talismanic" qualities, as Taussig might state, in the sense that they manifest themselves as ineffable, vibrant, "spirits" that seem to possess autonomy in themselves. Thus, the particular affect produced through the reception of the salvaged object plays a significant role in how observers receive and interpret the meaning of these actions.

Tsing herself emphasizes that searching the damaged forests of the northwestern United States for matsutake mushrooms demands that the pickers pay acute attention to the affects produced through their work within the broken environment in which they salvage and thus open themselves to their vague, affective sense of the landscape. She repeatedly documents how foraging engaged the affective sense rather than knowledge on the part of the foragers. To describe this activity she invokes composer John Cage's assertion that hunting mushrooms required "a particular type of attention; attention to the here and now, of encounter in all of its contingencies and surprises" (Tsing 2015, 46). She goes on to state that in her own fieldwork "her senses were changed" during her scavenging (48) and that to find a good mushroom she "needs all her senses" (241). To find a mushroom, one cannot look for the mushroom itself; rather, one must search for indications of where it might potentially reside. She observes that

> foragers have their own ways of knowing the matsutake forest: they look for the lines of mushroom lives. . . . I am search- ing for the signs of the mushroom's growth, its activity line. Mushrooms move the ground slightly as they grow, and one must look for that movement. People call it a bump, that implies a well-defined hillock, very rare. Instead I think of *sensing a heave* [jk] an effect like the inhalation of breath in the chest. (Tsing 2015, 241–42)

This sense of qualities such as the presence of a particular object in a ruined environment, how the world possesses not only simple, discrete objects, and the dynamic and potential relationships between objects can be seen in other descriptions of salvage. Similarly, Millar notes in *Reclaiming the Discarded* that salvaging for cardboard and other "waste" material within the landfills of Rio de Janeiro often leads practitioners to follow vague paths that, especially at first, cannot be clearly discerned and only sensed.[19] Both searching for plastic and discerning what types of plastic might be recyclable, she claims, depends on the salvager's sense of the possible location and the possible qualities of the plastic (whether or not it is recyclable), and demands that the salvagers make estimations based on vague feelings and senses. Whether working in a chaotic ruined forest or a landfill made up of the discarded ruins of society, salvagers must rely upon guesses, senses, and affects in order to find the potential, hidden treasures obscured by the disorder that surrounds them.

Another example of the close tie between affect and salvage can be found in the efforts of community members in Tijuana to construct and repair their neighborhoods. The physical environments of many barrios in the city are constantly shifting and transforming due to the fact that waste is constantly dumped into them by the affluent, the fragile structures they build frequently fall, and the land itself upon which the neighborhoods are built crumble and wash away due to both weather and uncoordinated construction and excavation. Because of such physical precarity of their environment, residents must be sure to build up a sense of the unpredictable patterns of spatial change within this shifting landscape. "The movement of things," writes Leslie Stern concerning the salvaged landscape of Tijuana, "things like tires," constitute an important part of the activities of those who wish to salvage the landscape—not only in terms of "finding" resources that can be used, but also in terms of how the landscape itself might be reconstructed and repaired in ways that are both resilient and beneficial to the community. The Tijuana activist Oscar Romo is undertaking an effort to chart how the environment of a particular neighborhood "moves" and flows due to the constant influx of trash and its effect upon the environment. The participants in the "sensing project are more interested in sensing the movement of things than of people" (Tsing et al. 2017, G23) and in the end they espouse a view of the neighborhood that emphasizes the "boundaries that are permeable" (G28). The potential "movements" of the neighborhood and the canyon in which it is located reveal themselves through a general sense of how the landscape might develop and change along those borders. What the citizen-scientists who engage in this salvage project mean by using the word *sense* indicates a perception not precise enough to produce definitive projections. For them, the landscape itself gives a sense of how it might undergo change, which residents must use and follow if they hope to successfully salvage within it.[20] Such senses, while unpredictable, do allow them to evolve a fairly trustworthy awareness concerning the developmental trends within their physical environment, and good guesses concerning the consequences of their modifications of this environment. Because the landscape is damaged it "moves" and develops in complex, unforeseeable ways, and thus their salvage repairs and interventions must be made through multiple iterations of trial, error, and observation.

Just as the damaged forests and trash-filled barrios can produce affective qualities that their inhabitants sense while undertaking their salvage labor, participants in constructing and maintaining the bricolage, recycled habitat of the Gramsci Monument report that the space of the monument itself seemed to repeatedly "speak" through vague, affective senses. They describe how the monument was "like a magnet, pulling people" (Hirschhorn 2015, 255) toward it from both the housing project in whose common area it was built and the surrounding neighborhood. Another participant recounts:

> Because the physical environment of the Gramsci monument was so novel it exaggerated peoples' body language—it became very clear what different people were thinking, feeling, fearing and loving about the project. I think any real experience of this work was also tethered to an experience of one's physicality. Physically, psychologically and emotionally I experienced a profound surrendering of myself and my notion of time to this project. (Hirschhorn 2015, 230)

The language within this passage remains particularly evocative in terms of efforts to describe how an individual's somatic interaction with the various constituents of a landscape produces affects. The exaggerated body language, the physicality of the communication, and most importantly the "surrendering" of oneself all point toward how the monument led participants to sense the contours of their relationship to others and their environment. In addition, the passage suggests that the connections between those within the salvaged environment of the monument were the result not of cognitive choice, but of affected tone, pace, momentum, and potential. Not surprisingly, most of these descriptions remain vague—not only were these accounts given by participants, but they were not asked to focus on their understanding of the affects they experienced throughout their time on the monument.

As recounted by Tsing during her efforts to find the matsutake, the ineffability of affect renders it difficult to convey, but the presence of strong senses as a notable and unique aspect of participants' experience of moving through the landscape of this monument links it to the previous accounts I presented of an emerging linkage between salvage and its powerful reliance upon affect, and the contention ecosystem of affects produced by the spatial and temporal flow of actors in relation to a particular environment might constitute a unique attribute in salvage spaces. Exploring the "talismanic" qualities of the signs held by Occupy Wall Street activists and the "sense" of movements displayed by the geography of the Tijuana barrios led to questions concerning the political implications of such ecosystems of affect. While it is true that confusing, tension-filled affects can be experienced through a multitude of activities, these theorists point toward the fact that salvage both produces these affects and engages our perceptions of them in unique and powerful ways. Exploring the relationship of salvage and such affects leads to questions such as, What exactly constitutes the revolutionary potential of such a "sense?" How does it work itself into actual practices, and how do these practices translate into revolutionary action? It is to these questions that I now turn.

More than Just a Bottle: Plasticity and Salvage Labor

To most, plastic is just plastic. But different types of plastic have particular feels—smooth, hard, flexible to various extents—and individual pieces always feel that way due to their internal composition. This feel refers to more than its texture—you can get a feel for what you can do to a particular piece of plastic. You bend it, scrape it, tap it, and then, after a while, you get a sense of what it can do, or better yet, what you can do with it. Similar to other objects, one can get a sense of how it moves, and even how it might move, bend, and break in other situations. But in a sense, everything is plastic to various extents, although this does not seem to be true at first glance. Some things are more flexible than others and thus more amenable to change—some objects seem inflexible, natural, characterized by an essence. Furthermore, some ideas, institutions, and even people are more flexible than others. When searching for things with "plastic" qualities that can be used in a number of particular salvage efforts and then attempting to use such items in unknown precarious situations, one must undertake many forms of testing, experimenting and building, and thus one's labor in and of itself can be said to become plastic. Consequently, salvage often leads those who undertake it to take on the characteristics of the material they seek itself—their activities and even their conceptions of themselves and their abilities become flexible and plastic.

I now want to begin to explore how some contend that the "plastic" or, in other words, changeable character of salvage labor can be seen as a profoundly political act. Think of the sentiments expressed in the following quote by a protester talking about cutting a fence:

Cutting the wire and taking down the fence is damage to property. Is that violence? Where do you draw the line? A carpenter takes a piece of wood and cuts and planes and shapes it into something else: a house, a bed or a child's toy. The wood is cut but we don't call that violence. We do this all the time: cutting wheat to make bread, melting metal to reshape it, burning wood on our camp fire. We are transforming things for our purposes. That's what creativity is about. . . . With our own HANDS we pull down the fence, making a huge door in the base. (Feigenbaum, Frenzel, and McCurdy 2013, 135)

What activists describe here is the practice of physical plasticity as a radical political act. The combined sense of both the discrete material of the wire and its relationship to a particular social context gives activists a "sense" of its potential plasticity. This activist regards not only the fence as plastic, but also what the fence represents—a border between the legal and illegal, the official and the forbidden. And as the fence is transformed, the sense changes, the potentiality unfolds as the shape of the cut, the goals of the action, the strategy of its attainment all develop in ways unforeseen by the activists and seemingly unattainable using the materials at hand. It is important to remember that not all construction involves acts and attitudes characterized by transformative plasticity. Following instructions and using premade modular parts involves no contingency or possibility. This is why the combination of radical political action and the plastic use of materials exhibits their similar creative and subversive possibilities. For the most part, within our capitalist economy characterized by the division of labor, plasticity within the process of production, is not only discouraged, but is deemed subversive.[21] Consequently, undertaking activities such as the one described above where activism combines the plastic use of materials represents particularly radical possibilities.

Unsurprisingly, pronounced plasticity, both literally and figuratively, is also a quality of the dump. A huge amount of plastic finds its way into urban landfills, and as Millar states in *Reclaiming the Discarded*, to the salvagers who work within the dumps of Rio de Janeiro, this material is not simply highly valued for the price it can garner, but plasticity becomes a value in itself. She asks, "What would it mean to envision not only the materials *catadores* [salvagers] collected but their work itself as plastic?" (Millar 2018, 127). What she means by this is not simply that salvage reveals that materials can be used in different ways, but that the work itself is plastic—such labor comprises a collage of different skills, goals, and co-workers. Although many try to characterize the work of laborers, not only salvagers in dumps but also street vendors, handicraft repair practitioners, and others, as "informal," Millar insists that this term only conveys a negative impression of what the work is not—located within a state-recognized firm or institution, stable in terms of its hours, dependent upon some type of specialization. She instead insists that the work of these salvagers possesses a form and content in and of itself. She encapsulates the distinctive quality of such work in terms of its plasticity. During her time in the landfill she observed:

> Plastics and plasticity were all around me . . . as I learned to squeeze bottles or bend flip-flops to determine their form; as I listened to *catadores* explain how certain materials can leave imprints on the skin; as I watched jumbled piles of containers being transformed into monochromatic regular blocks; as I discovered that these blocks would take on yet other forms such as that of rope, produced for other markets in other parts of the world; and as I traced the ever--changing relations between the city, waste, *catadores*, scrap dealers, etc. (Millar 2018, 132–33)

What I draw from this passage is that plasticity can be seen as a type of work with its own habits, practices, characteristics, much of it having to do with attuning oneself to the specific plastic qualities of materials. It is true that plastic labor, as suggested by Millar, does not entail rigid procedures that can be contained in a training manual. How could it when it is so dependent upon the practitioner's sense of potentiality within the material and situation? But this does not mean that plastic labor does not entail certain styles and congruities across different instances of its practice. I will now review some recent literature that centers around this concept of the "plasticity" of labor, especially in the context of salvage.

The practices undertaken by *catadores* who salvage plastic and subsequently transform it into other things suggest not only a new form of labor, but one with radical potentiality. Whereas plastic in and of itself it valued in production for its malleable properties (it can be shaped using a mold of any shape and size), the salvager does not work with plastic in this preproduction form. In the dump, plastic is already molded into not simply a shape, but a commodity used for a specific purpose such as a bottle from which to drink, packaging meant to protect a specific object. Yet, because the plastic found by *catadores* does already possess the form of a specific commodity, but is still both assessed by the *catadores* and used by others for the qualities that allow it to be used ways other than for which it was designed, this form of labor constitutes not only a transformation of the original material form, but also the transformation of its commodity form. It is not simply that a piece of wood comes to be transformed into a table, but a bottle of Coke or Pepsi comes to be used as insulation, the face shield for a mask, or a simply another receptacle for liquid, sand, or toys. Thus, it is not only the supposed material limits of the material that is being challenged, but also the artificial limits that already bear and display, literally, the shape of consumer capitalism and its ecologically destructive culture of disposability. The plasticity suggested by the *catadores'* salvage activity, and the plasticity indicative of salvage in general, might constitute the practical basis of an anticapitalist social critique based in the everyday life activity.[22]

In precarious conditions, labor often assumes plastic forms, but for Donna Haraway, the origins of plastic labor go much deeper and can be traced to biological processes undertaken by organisms attempting to exist in stressed environments. She states that she is committed to "art, science, activism as sympoetic practices for living on a damaged planet" (Tsing et al. 2017, M31). The type of labor she sees as the product of such a stressed environment remains rooted in "stories of mutation, adaptation and natural selection" that are forced on organisms who must undergo changes due to shocks outside of their regular experience. These mutations and adaptions force organisms into new, precarious, and sometimes uneasy relationships. To explore this she outlines

> a theory of ecological relationality that takes seriously organ-isms' practices, the inventions and their experiments crafting interspecies life and worlds. This is an ecology inspired by a feminist ethic of response-ability, in which questions of species differences are always conjugated with attentions to affect, entanglement and rupture; an affective ecology in which creativity and curiosity characterize the experiential forms of life of all kinds of practitioners, not only humans. (Tsing et al. 2017, M32)

When a species faces threats, it must change itself and what surrounds it. Thus, in this interpretation "plastic" can mean not only flexible, but sticky and likely to bond with other things. Haraway argues that one of the changes organisms often make, and the labor they undergo to make these changes, is that of forging new tendencies of responsiveness toward their surroundings. As Haraway notes, linking her to my previous discussion, the potentials of these relations can be felt through the affects produced by these changes. The ability to be open to the affects produced through experimental actions and responses constitutes this work, which Haraway refers to as indicative of the period of what she calls the "Chthulucene" (invoking H. P. Lovecraft's mutant, octopus, demigod) where insecurity and destruction force strange hybrids of organisms and environments. She claims that in this new era of "partial healing and modest rehabilitation" the main imperative remains "to join forces to reconstitute refuges, to make possible partial and robust biological cultural-political technological recuperation and recomposition which must include mourning and irreversible losses" (Tsing et al. 2017, M33). In sum, to adopt the ethos of the Chthulucene requires work, the work of changing, bending, and making plastic. This work does not entail simply transforming material things, although it does involve molding and crafting new environments from distressed landscapes. It also leads to the work of forging new symbiotic relationships, as with wasps and orchids and their mutual dependence, each taking from and giving to the other. These new hybrids follow no predetermined path, and flow from vague senses and affects that necessitate their being constantly modified. The work of the Chthulucene is a work of repair and attempts to cobble together parts that might or might not "work" together to comprise a machine that might or might not function in a way that fixes the problem at hand. Thus, Haraway suggests a precarious type of labor uniquely suited to repairing precarious environments, which constitutes, in her mind, the best hope for overcoming precarious times.

Another example, in which a recent theorist has conceptualized a plastic form of labor that sheds light on salvage labor, can be seen in Jack Halberstam's *Queer Art of Failure*, where he claims that the estrangement from "normal" heterosexual society causes queer folk to have to invent and extemporize frequently, due either to the ambiguity or the hostility of their environment. Learning how to fail, how to recover while knowing that one will most likely fail again, represents a fundamental queer skill, and salvage labor is nothing if not an activity that will frequently lead to failure. This art of failure has been invoked by others in the specific context of salvage. The curators of *Disobedient Objects* claim that the activists who jury-rig their protest implements from the trash around them are also engaging in this sort of queer art. They claim that the activists engaging in the Queer Art of Failure "work by any medium necessary, often under conditions of duress and scarcity they tend to foreground promiscuous resourcefulness, ingenuity and timely intervention" (Flood and Grindon 2014, 12). They go on to state that "their acts of composing things otherwise, in defiance of all that is wrong around them, are beautiful failures that throw deontelogical definitions of success into question" (Flood and Grindon 2014, 13). Cthulu-like mutations of quotidian objects are bound to fail—how could they not when faced with the fragility of their raw materials and the herculean tasks in which they employ them? They must also fail in that their usage is temporary—they are designed for use within a particular context and a particular time, both of which will necessarily change in the situations of precarity that constitute damaged landscapes. Thus, the plastic is also fragile—their forms, because they are broken, are amenable to restructure and repair.

If the plastic labor of salvage necessitated by the Chthulucene results in strange couplings, deformations, and mutations of the familiar that frequently fail, the actual processes of this labor must also take on new forms—bricolage, collage, and improvisation. Thus, it is a labor composed of many distinct activities, an observation that is reflected in literature concerning protest and salvage. The book *Protest Camps* describes how the participants building and maintaining these radical spaces engage in plastic labor under conditions of instability and stress. The communities that form within these encampments not only lack significant resources, but must quickly adapt to pressures from the state. They are comprised of individuals of differing backgrounds and experience, and thus the activists must form quick, and sometimes messy, relationships working with others in order to address pressing problems. These forced, experimental conjugates lead to a labor of contagion, where individuals trade skills and perspectives with others and projects take the form of a bricolage of different activities. Due to these conjugates, "the time and space that protest camps can offer for exchanging skills and knowledge, makes them fertile ground for tactical innovations" (Feigenbaum, Frenzel, and McCurdy 2013, 139). They go on to describe how these encampments not only constitute environments ripe for developing shared skills and bricolage labor, but how because of their compactness, looseness, and constant need to adapt, they force even more dramatic fusions of seemingly disparate labors and activities. A similar intermixture of labors, this time between specialized and traditional, high and low, can be seen, according to Tsing, within the groups that form to collectively salvage items within damaged landscapes. In their efforts at managing the landscape damaged by incessant forest cutting, officials are forced to work with pickers who already use the forest for salvage accumulation. During this process, to "rebuild themselves, citizens' groups mix science and peasant knowledge. Scientists often take leadership roles in . . . revitalization but they aim to incorporate vernacular knowledge; here the urban professionals and scientists consult elderly farmers for their advice [about the contours of the landscape]" (Tsing 2015, 236). *Rubbish Theory* also recommends such plastic, bricolage labor to deal with discarded and waste material, calling for an "interplay between government science, engineering science, market science and community science" (Thompson 2017, 244). Peasant knowledge mixed with the scientific method leads to efforts that can address the specific needs of specific spaces. And these needs and solutions come to be thought of as emergent and becoming, as opposed to manifesting themselves as predetermined by fixed and accepted metrics. The quantified generalizations of the specialists are intermingled with the affective, qualitative generalities of the local "peasant" knowledge to create communities of inquiry that focus on the plasticity of environments, and not their unitary potential for economic exploitation.

The intense and frequent fluctuations, and adaptations that occur during the work to maintain these encampments, according to the authors of *Protest Camps*, can lead to a situation where "the split between work and leisure which is a feature of capitalistic society is broken down and work becomes enjoyable and satisfying" (Feigenbaum, Frenzel, and McCurdy 2013, 213). Thus, the authors claim that the hybrid nature of work transcends the category of work itself as individuals come to combine their labor and their desires, singing, laughing, and even philosophizing as they engage in seemingly quotidian tasks. Furthermore, activists from a wide variety of backgrounds choose together how they will engage in their tasks, mixing work and pleasure in ways that they determine themselves and thus further breaking down the rigid hierarchies between necessity and play, labor and leisure, so prevalent within capitalism. As one activist describes their experience:

> After the General Assembly that night there was both a talent show on one side of the plaza ("This is what a talent show looks like!") and an Anti-Patriarchy Working Group meeting (which became the Safer Spaces Working Group) on the other. In some ways the juxtaposition of both these events happening at once is emblematic of one of the splits at the park: talent shows across the square from anti-patriarchy meetings, an announcement that someone has lost their phone. Maybe this is how movements need to maintain themselves, through a recognition that political change is also fundamentally about everyday life and that everyday life needs to encompass all of this: there needs to be a space for a talent show across from an anti-patriarchy meeting. There needs to be a food table and medics, a library, and everyone needs to stop for a second and look around for someone's phone. (Blumenkranz et al. 2011, 36)

Notice here that the close proximity of the activities within the confined space of the encampment intensified the plasticity of the labors within their day. Also, although the above passage does not emphasize this fact, the library, the food table, and other infrastructures within the park were constructed from salvaged material. Thus, while activists undertook juxtaposed specific activities such as engaging in antipatriarchal discussion and food distribution, they also interspersed styles of activity such as discourse, play, and salvage. The plastic nature of this labor manifests itself as a hybrid of pleasure and labor, high and low art, crafts and technology. The work of building cathedrals that act like carnivals, or carnivals that inspire like cathedrals, necessitates the most varied, collage-like and plastic of labor, and Ross's linking this type of labor to the building of the barricades and other salvaged structures during the Paris Commune ties it to the plasticity that characterizes the labor undertaken by the *catadores* of the Rio landfills.

After introducing examples of how plastic labor results in strange couplings of both its products and its processes, the question arises whether one can identify any common qualities. In her account of the plasticity of labor she saw in the Rio landfills, Millar suggests one provocative characteristic of such work. She states that because plastic labor remains so dependent upon the vague affects produced by the landscape and material, it places a high value not only on giving form to the object upon which an individual is working, but on receiving form. She states, "[A]s both the capacity to receive form and to give form, plasticity disrupts the dualist framework of the formal and informational in representation of the economy, allowing us to see how system and structure are molded in practice and that what appears unregulated or disregulated produces its own order" (Millar 2018, 132). A procedure characterized by alternation between these two distinct endeavors and their requisite attitudes and skills seems vague and limited, but it is not the substance of this description that contains the seeds of an account of the practice of plastic labor, but its form. It is the interplay between giving and receiving that constitutes the primary characteristic of such labor. The different understandings of the task of salvage, testing, tempering, and tampering might seem to be a rhetorical flourish, but they also reveal an openness to different strategies in the face of the uncertainty that characterizes plastic labor. Thus, because of the plural, plastic nature of labor called upon by salvage, alternation between these different modes seems to be an important quality of the form of such labor. No matter whether conceptualized as an art of failure, a Chthulucene method for producing strange couplings, or a multifaceted endeavor to maintain a protest camp, it seems that plastic labor constitutes a process involving multiple iterations of both making and observing, constructing and repairing. And if salvage labor constitutes an example of such plastic labor, then this rhythmic quality seems like a characteristic that might be further explored. Of course, many types of fabrication and human activity involve creativity, the employment of different techniques, and the necessity of modifying one's production plans due to unexpected qualities of one's materials. To be sure, I am not claiming that salvage represents the only type of labor that exhibits these plastic characteristics. What I hope to emphasize is that these descriptions of the plasticity of salvage labor can used to articulate one of the many conditions that constitute an environment conducive to the manifestation of political salvage.

Spaces of Salvage

Salvage, when undertaken by the poor, cannot simply center around particular projects. The needs are great for those existing in damaged landscapes—simply repairing a leak in one's roof will not put food on the table, educate one's children, or produce clean drinking water. Thus, they must salvage entire landscapes and construct spaces that will help them undertake these tasks. Contemporary accounts stress that salvagers occupy squares, take over factories, build community centers, and refurbish houses. As mentioned above, many have noticed that in salvage communities, although they possess the internal differentiation and liquid qualities of assemblages, participants often experience the shared characteristics of autonomy and unity through affect. This is not the only shared characteristic of these communities noticed by recent observers. The spaces salvagers build themselves also often possess similar physical geographies and designs, and such spatial arrangements can play an important role in establishing and sustaining them. The common qualities of political salvage spaces highlighted by these authors are intimately related to their substance and goals—salvage designs accentuate the perception of affect, the plasticity of labor, and the diversity and liquidity of their assemblages. Although it might seem unnecessarily difficult to do under a situation of extreme hardship, many salvagers devote time and energy to consciously rearranging the layout of their occupied or refurbished spaces. Sitrin relates that "in some workplaces, the physical structure or organization of production has been changed so as to facilitate conversation. In recuperated workplaces such as Grissinopolis [in Buenos Aires] workers have moved their machinery to face one another so that they can be in assemblies and discussions whenever they desire, thus limiting the amount of time needed to break for conversations about production and running of the plant" (Sitrin 2012, 141). Sitrin recounts how other salvagers discussed the value of their spaces specifically in the context of how they produce and protect affects:

> Call it whatever you want to call it, but it needs to create a particular affective space. It's as if we live in flux moving at a certain speed, like little balls bouncing all about and then suddenly, the assembly is our intention to establish a bay, to momentarily pause time and space and to say let us think about how to avoid being dragged and bounded about and simultaneously attempt to build something new ourselves. (Sitrin 2012, 174)

The assembly here is not valued by participants solely as a decision-making body, but instead as a space or "bay" for establishing affective environments that stand in stark contrast to the "flux" that constitutes the background sense characterizing daily life within contemporary neo-liberal capitalism. The squats described in *Autonomous City* often also place a premium on the design particularities of their salvaged spaces. Vasudevan recounts how, in one reclaimed space, "walls were removed in order to increase the size of social spaces, including kitchens, while stairwells were created to produce a new geography of movement through the buildings, now connected and held together by a network of doors, passageways, courtyards and vestibules" (Vasudevan 2017, 138). Here, the emphasis is not upon one particular space dedicated to assembly, as recounted in the previous examples, but the relationship between discrete spaces within a larger structure, and how this geography leads individuals to move through these spaces, their usages, and the individuals devoting themselves to these particular tasks at particular times. Such a focus on design, how particular spaces arrange bodies and their movements, as will become apparent, constitutes the last emerging theme within my survey of the contemporary literature on salvage.

One of the most common themes within recent discussion of the political qualities of salvage spaces highlights the significance of the internal diversity of these spaces in that they often contain areas dedicated to different usages. In *Reclaiming the Discarded*, Millar recounts that, after the landfill where she had previously worked was shut down, many of the factories that had once received this recycled material also faced closure. Some of these abandoned factories were occupied by the salvagers who were no longer able to make their living collecting materials from the landfill. During their recuperation and transformation to new methods of production, they became more than simply factories, but communities in themselves. Millar recounts that one of its worker/residents

> told us that there were 40 families living in the factory. Newcomers were building houses in the yard, often with old material they found on the factory grounds. Everyone divided the electricity bill and shared a well for water. . . . I was amazed by all the ways this abandoned factory had been transformed. The dump had closed in Jardim. . . . But the work of reclaiming the discarded clearly had not. (Millar 2018, 187)[23]

In a similar vein, Raul Zibechi, in his *Territories in Resistance: A Cartography of Latin American Social Movements*, explains how builders of informal communities, when constructing spaces, often design them with internal differentiation and plasticity in mind. Zibechi argues that such internal variation forms a microgeography where, even though activities take place in separate areas, the compactness of the entire space and the numerous connections between the individual areas encourages residents to intermix their activities through frequent movement. He claims that within these spaces there exists an "integration of time wherein there is a dissolution of the divide between working time, leisure time, and domestic time" (Zibechi 2012, 28) and that such efforts stem from an attempt to "reunite time fragmented and parceled up by the system" (36). Thus, Zibechi ultimately portrays the internal diversity of activities and design within these spaces as leading to even deeper and more affective melding of activities, where participants' experiences flow from one task to the next, placing each previously separate activity into new perspectives and relationships. The space encourages the breakdown of the capitalist division of labor, and the plastic forms of work that develop result in the residents experiencing new affects. These spaces both encourage and are reflective of the plastic labor that produces them. Thus, the spaces in themselves become plastic—mirroring the plastic salvage labor that constructs and maintains the space in the first place.

I will return in later chapters to such spaces and how they emerge through and support the practice of salvage, but at this point I only want to emphasize that the internal complexity of the salvaged neighborhood and reclaimed factory undermines efforts to control its population—it remains a direct rebuke to capitalist and modernist forms of urban planning. It remains a rebuke in many ways, but firstly their salvaged, scattered, bricolage labyrinthine spaces that are constantly built and rebuilt call on inhabitants to use their bodies, conduct their daily activities, and interact with others in new and unforeseen configurations. Such variations of movement and activity, while challenging previously held knowledge and habits, help to activate the inhabitants' attention toward affect. Both building and residing in such spaces rely upon one's vague sense of how a scavenged piece of material might persist and behave in a new function or arrangement. One must make guesses based on sense to answer questions such as "Will it fit?" "Will it last?" "how should I hold this?" and, "Where can I find more of this?" Furthermore, the chaotic arrangement of spaces encourages juxtapositions of activities normally separated and distinct within the capitalist division of labor. Manufacturing, child rearing, political discussion, and festival become intermixed as new Chthulu-like combinations of activities lead those in salvage spaces to salvage not material, but their own lives and identities, employing supposedly discarded actions, interpretations, and techniques from their past to deal with these strange new combinations of activities. These new arrangements come to exist due to the necessities of both life and politics. Existing in the broken landscapes and jury-rigged spaces that come from this struggle can call out new, precarious, oftentimes failing responses. The solutions that salvagers concoct to meet their pressing needs are formulated in spaces that they have salvaged themselves. The physical bricolage that surrounds them prompts bricolage solutions and constantly mutating bricolage habits. Even confronted with oppression, their resistance takes on such plastic, bricolage qualities. Fragile, site specific, and wildly nonconforming to conventional understandings of organization and ideology. But for the examples of political salvage that I have invoked in this description, the spaces they construct in their pursuit of both their prosaic and their political aims stand in stark contrast to the rationalized spaces of capitalism, and therefore contain the potential to act as locations where alternatives to this system are both generated and nurtured.

Some might claim that much contemporary radical activism, especially actions such as occupations of public space, squats, and other activities characterized by horizontal decisionmaking and autonomy from hegemonic political and economic institutions, should be characterized as an example of "prefigurative politics" or actions embodying the practices and values of an ideal society. But Feigenbaum and her co-authors stress that these actions should be seen as "laboratories of insurrectionary imagination, spaces in which experimental collaboration and richly creative actions are dreamed up and deployed" (Feigenbaum, Frenzel, and McCurdy 2013, 116). As opposed to the advancement of specific interests or even a particular vision of the future, they see the practice of collective creativity, no matter where it might lead, as the core political activity of such encampments. They also argue that participants' sense of the affects produced through the encounters in these camps act as one of the primary drivers of such collective, experimental becoming. If experimentation constitutes the main political goal of such insurrectionary actions, I contend that salvage might play an important role in cultivating such an "insurrectionary imagination." Under the right conditions, the "plastic" labor" indicative of salvage practice can contribute to the undermining of the division of labor and reified consciousness constitutive of capitalist consciousness, and therefore clear the way to radical rethinking of society.

Salvage Communities

Salvage communities are made of leftovers—leftover materials and, often, leftover people. People might be left over in a literal sense, an impoverished population not able to find the means of subsistence in a particular capitalist landscape, but *leftover* can also describe those who feel alienated from the prevalent norms in their community. Participants in salvage communities acknowledge their surroundings as broken and in disrepair, and thus undertake the plastic labor of salvage, together. And make no mistake, often, in the contemporary accounts of salvage that I have been recounting in this chapter, one finds individuals working together while salvaging—as Rebecca Solnit recounts in her *Paradise Made in Hell*, precarious situations often bring together people aware of their vulnerability, as opposed to prompting a Hobbesian war of all against all in competition to gain forced resources. But contemporary studies suggest that communities that some see as formed exclusively to survive disasters in fact embody a much more complex constellation of goals. For example, the squatters who salvage abandoned buildings relate that they undertake this task for a variety of reasons beyond the necessity of housing. Recounting the motivations for the foundations of one squat, *The Autonomous Cities: A History of Urban Squatting* reports:

> The occupation represented far more than an act of rehabilitation and renovation. It was also widely understood as an ongoing process through which a meaningful social infrastructure was assembled, sustained, and extended. As was the case with any squat, the *Regenbogenfabrik* places particular emphasis on horizontal decision making and collective self-management and applied these practices to both the day to day life of the squat and to projects that supported a larger community (cycle repair shop, carpentry workshop, day care, cinema, hostel and community info shop). (Vasudevan 2017, 78)

Instead of individuals banding together to advocate for a particular slate of policies (although they sometimes do, usually in the case of squats centered around housing policy), they engage in emergent processes of political creativity and becoming that *Autonomous Cities* describes as "world making," a process of "making" that includes the activity of salvage. Furthermore, this "world making" interpretation of the goals of salvage communities constituted a shared goal across autonomous groupings: "Islands of flats grew together to form an alternative social structure—they affirmed a self-determined lifestyle and developed a common culture" (141). Their salvaged spaces, in this recounting, act like labs or workshops, bringing people together to collaborate on projects, as opposed to clubhouses or barracks that house unified groups. While necessity might bring these groups together, they soon develop much more complex and varied goals that often lead to the transformation of the self-perceptions of their participants.

The bricolage character of the salvage construction process is reflected in the nature of the groups who undertake it, and this is why they are often described as assembled—groups that have fallen together as opposed to assembling as the result of conscious construction. One can see this when Tsing uses the term *assemblage* with its connotations of co-presence and not coherence, to describe salvage landscapes. Because, as she states, "Matsutake also illuminate the cracks in the global political economy. . . . Many matsutake foragers are displaced and disenfranchised cultural minorities" (Tsing 2015, 8). The communities that form around this activity are comprised of inhabitants from many different backgrounds and identities. The precarity created by these cracks creates a situation wherein groups of salvagers are "unable to rely on stable structures of community" and are thus "thrown into shifting assemblages, which remake us as well as others. We can't rely on the status quo; everything is in flux, including our ability to survive" (Tsing et al. 2017, 5). But assemblages, while chaotic, are not inscrutable—they always take on the form (albeit a temporary form) of patterns of unintentional coordination, and it is our job as salvagers to "notice such patterns" (ibid., 23). I have discussed that many claim that noticing such patterns in landscapes, whether it be the result of mushrooms, plastic, or other supposedly trash-like materials, is an effort to sense affects they produce by their movement through the landscape—but social environments possess such patterns also. Tsing emphasizes that groups do form around mushroom picking—often housed in encampments made of recycled materials—comprised of individuals from varied backgrounds, united only by their alienation, both materially and culturally, from the capitalist economy. Assemblages fall into more or less organized and coherent states, but the potential for the formation of the community always remains a possibility, despite the level of seeming chaos and discord of a particular moment. Yet for her the assembled qualities of these groups results in their ambiguous promise as bases for more radical political formations.

When these groups do attempt to coordinate their actions, Tsing notes the unavoidable necessity of acts of translation that build upon the nascent congruities present within the assemblage at a particular point in time. These acts of translation, she asserts, depend upon participants sensing nascent commonalities and collective actions shared among the group, and then translating such senses into a more articulate plan they can debate and discuss. Tsing recounts how the formation of the salvage community of the matsutake pickers is comprised of "fugitive moments of entanglement in the midst of institutional alienation," which is why she refers to this possibility as a "latent commons" of possibility that cannot be assumed to necessarily flow from the activity of salvage nor take the form of a group with a predetermined identity. She argues that "any gathering contains many inchoate political futures and that political work consists of helping some of those come into being" (Tsing 2015, 254). Thus, assemblages, whose characteristics become accentuated in situations of salvage, while containing potential alliances and common-alities, exhibit extreme fragilities and fluctuations. For her, the process of forming and maintaining such commons using translation represents a vague and fraught potentiality but not one that that leads to radical political action or the formations of communities of resistance.[24]

Despite the assembled nature of salvage communities, it is important to note that one pattern of potential "salvage politics" latent within such attempts is that whatever the common goals and relationships within a particular assemblage, the process of developing these potentials is undertaken by the participants themselves. The scattered, vulnerable nature of salvage landscapes does not present inevitable solutions for their repair, and the assemblages of alienated denizens are thrown together by precarity and necessity, not conscious groupings around sim-ilar identity. These are forgotten places and people, and therefore their salvage efforts must be undertaken by themselves and only themselves. Sitrin observes that "spaces on the periphery such as shanty towns and slums in post-industrial areas . . . are rapidly becoming sites not only of struggle but of organization in ways that involve autogestion" (Sitrin 2012, 175). Autogestion, or autonomous self-rule, often comes to be the organizing principle of these salvage efforts as individuals undertake efforts to collectively recuperate their physical and social environment. Sitrin goes on to argue that an important aspect of the autonomous character of such salvage efforts is the generation of feelings of autonomy within the participants themselves. She relates this interpretation of the value produced through salvaging, or recuperating an abandoned factory in Argentina by Ernesto Lalo Paret:

> The process has all of the problems that you could imagine but it has made the factories viable which for the previous owners were not viable. Also, what is viability in a society full of shit? An economist might tell me about what something is worth in cash flow, but it is the person who is recovering their self-esteem, recovering their self-worth and confidence in themselves that puts the factory back to work. How much does it cost that this guy be an example to his kid? And what is it worth to recuperate a factory for the community, for a family and for society? (Sitrin 2012, 177)

Here, the value salvaged by the factory is expressed in terms of the self-confidence and sense of agency required by autonomous action—while the physical factory is recovered, so are the participants who have been battered by austerity in the same way as the economy. In interview after interview, Sitrin goes on to recount how those collectively occupying and salvaging factories and public spaces in Latin America see themselves as establishing "a relationship that helps us to recuperate ourselves as active people, bringing back our creative ability, helping to bring new meaning to life" (Sitrin 2012, 163). Their salvage communities are self-directed and self-affirming—autonomously building participants' sense of autonomy. And it is the messy, broken, and ruined nature of the materials and landscapes with which they must work that allows for the cultivation of such autonomous actors and communities.

I want to discuss one further trend that prompts the formation of communities engaging in political salvage—that of climate change. The disruptions caused by increasingly catastrophic weather disasters, while affecting all, affect the poor with particular vehemence. As poor neighborhoods are made unlivable by both individual catastrophic events such as hurricanes and long-term environmental trends such as increasing heat, soil erosion, and lack of water, their residents find new ways to survive. They migrate and build new informal neighborhoods, they squat in abandoned buildings, all the while using what they can find to construct their new living arrangements. And, as with other instances of salvage by the poor, the actions taken by these climate refugees often prompt backlash from authorities, prompting the poor to undertake defensive actions to preserve their hard-gained if precarious existences. But the political possibilities contained within the actions of such climate refugees do not remain limited to attempts to preserve temporary housing against authorities intent on enforcing zoning, property, and other laws meant to preserve the status quo of urban design. Ashley Dawson observes that efforts to rebuild after climate disasters can lead the way to the significant rethinking of social and political norms and the cultivation of radical political possibilities. She calls this phenomenon "disaster communism," or the phenomenon of the forced mutuality that is often produced by attempting to live through catastrophes transforming itself into Left solidarities and forms of political critique. She states, "Disasters can often further strengthen capitalism and profit for the rich, but they can also offer a glimpse of what radical political theorist Jodi Dean calls the communist horizon, the sense that the oppressive conditions of the present can be overcome and new forms of solidarity discovered." (Dawson 2017, 236). She discusses many instances, but most relevant to my argument is her interpretation of Occupy Sandy, the mutual aid efforts that developed from Occupy Wall Street to help distressed communities in New York City.[25] Although she does not specifically mention how salvage might play a role in disaster communism, she does invoke the "self-built" communities in South American cities such as Caracas, communities that I demonstrate often use salvage in their "self-building" as examples of how the poor often construct both physical infrastructure and radical social forms in reaction to natural disasters. Thus, the increasing "disasters" prompted by climate change, while causing undeniable despair, might increase the possibility of radical social transformation engendered by salvage.

In light of the frequency of self-organization and recovering self-worth reported in the previous accounts, it is important to note that Tsing's pessimism concerning the political potential of salvage communities is not unfounded. Although she does occasionally interpret "picking mushrooms as the practice of freedom" (Tsing 2015, 94), the freedom she observes as inherent in the practice and the communities that form around it are fleeting and contentious. Salvage communities contain the potential for new understandings of community and democracy, but she is correct to point out that this potential remains highly contingent and fragile. If a political theory of salvage can be cobbled together from these actual, yet highly variable groups of people mutually scavenging, repairing, and occasionally resisting, then Tsing's criticism of the salvage commons must be taken seriously. The question of whether or not the qualities that make the salvage commons unique—its members' reliance on vague sense to ground their efforts to solve problems and deal with contingency, its lack of a division of labor and production of plastic habits and identities, and its location within bricolage salvage spaces—all seem to militate against any effort to organize, regularize, or theorize procedures or guidelines that might contribute to the resilience or propagation of such communities. Can one hope to pull any political potentialities from such spontaneous inventions as the latent commons that might transform the salvage communities and the encounters from which they spring into a political formation that can not only defend the squats, barrios, and occupations that spring like mushrooms from the ruined landscapes left by capitalism, but transform capitalism itself? If capitalism is a global phenomenon, can the "latent commons" also somehow coalesce into a transnational movement? Furthermore, do social circumstances and political-economic trends exist that might increase the likelihood of groups that originate in a latent commons developing into communities that undertake contestant politics? If autogestion comprises one of the potentialities of the latent salvage commons, how can the attitudes, skills, and procedures that sustain such horizontal decision making be cultivated by participants? Only through providing viable answers to questions such as these will a political theory rooted in salvage practice be able to actually contribute to contemporary radical politics.

Conclusion: Salvaging Anticapitalism

This has been a necessarily limited survey of works that I see as particularly provocative contemporary examples of writing on the political implications of salvage. Furthermore, I have only partially examined many of the works cited in this section, and I will return to some of these examples later, tying them to theories and concepts that will provide further elucidation. Finally, I have highlighted many terms and concepts discussed by these authors, such as plasticity, affect, space, and assembly, without fully analyzing their meaning or how they might constitute a political theory of salvage. This chapter was meant to explore a number of authors whose work suggests a connection between the efforts of the poor to use salvaged materials to sustain the reproduction of their communities and the production of political affects upon themselves and others that stems from these activities. At the beginning of the chapter, I discussed some of those I call "salvage pessimists" such as Anna Tsing, who believe that salvage activity can only result in temporary adjustments to the ravages of disasters, such as climate change and neoliberal austerity. It might be unfair to characterize them as such, but my examination of salvage does lead me to go forth with the project about which Tsing expresses ambivalence—to look for the nascent "vision" of anticapitalism contained within its contemporary practice. Needless to say, Tsing's work is impressive on many levels, and good portions of the following argument will consist of my expanding upon many themes that she introduces. But I do have one particular disagreement with Tsing and the other pessimists—or perhaps it might be better to say a difference in emphasis. Instead of the difficulties, I focus on the potentials—although the difficulties involved in such a project certainly exist. In the previous survey, one aspect of salvage labor that becomes apparent is how such activity constitutes a reaction to instability. Salvage landscapes display heightened assemblage characteristics—shifting internal constituents, porous, membranous borders, heightened and unfolding possibilities that create intense affects for those who exist in them. The "creative" destruction caused by neoliberalism creates landscapes and communities that need to be salvaged. Yet, as has also, hopefully, been apparent in the previous discussion, the nature of salvage, and its practice, can intensify the possibilities for affective, plastic transformation within these same landscapes and communities. Because the materials—spaces, buildings, and identities—become so broken and twisted by the unstable winds of neoliberalism, so do the possibilities that the products will also form strange hybrids, mutations, and relationships.

Of course, simply because salvage is a product of plastic labor, plastic community, and plastic spaces does not mean that its practice in itself will lead to the downfall of capitalism. Through this difference in emphasis I hope to identify the radical kernels within salvage that might be cultivated, deepened, and specified to form a radical political project. Such a project is not merely a projection of my own political beliefs— salvage, undeniably, as it is practiced among poor communities in waste spaces and is, hopefully, apparent from the previous chapter, remains an important part of many contemporary radical projects. And if one looks back at the argument in this chapter and the broad conceptual categories I have outlined, the transformative and even subversive tendencies within the practice of salvage cannot be easily ignored. For example, take the observation that salvage accumulation depends to a high degree upon the perception of the affects produced by the interaction between the salvager, the thing to be salvaged, and the salvage landscape. These affects, at least among the writers I have highlighted, constitutea vague sense of the vibrant developing relationships between things. This sense reveals not the substance of the relationship, or, in other words, its particular cause, or the substance of a similarity, but, instead, its tenor, where it might be going, or its potentiality. Because sense suggests possibilities, it possesses the possibility of leading to transformative reinterpretation of one's surroundings—the structures of ideologies, the built landscape, and our political institutions might not change but the pattern of one's body's movement within these environments modifies and the affects produced by these travels result in unique perceptions of sense and quality. Focusing on affect and its necessary interrelationship with cognition and, subsequently, action suggests an attitude of transformation, of what might be and not what is. And salvage, by possessing the potential to lead its practitioners to pay more attention to affect, leads them to focus on what might be, both in terms of scavenging and repairing. Unlike the salvage pessimists, I regard the affects that are called forth in the process of salvage as harbingers of its transformative potential and as an indication that salvage will very likely not remain within the social and physical confines, such as a particular neighborhood or capitalism itself, in which it is presently located. Thus, salvage, while now coexisting within the cracks of capitalism, contains a bubbling energy that occasionally pushes it out into new social realms where it can challenge current understandings of production, social space, and community.

When recalling the other themes I have culled from recent literature on political salvage, similar implications can be reasonably drawn—that salvage as I have defined it constitutes a subversive activity that undermines social categories and, when practiced in the context of contemporary capitalism, might possess radical implications that could be strengthened. The theme of plasticity suggests that such landscapes and such labor leach in unexpected ways beyond the boundaries set for them by present norms and institutions. Communities conceptualized as assemblages, as opposed to those united by unitary understandings of interests and identities, are united by the ways in which multiple relationships might enable new possibilities for creative development and new forms of problem solving. And the spaces that these communities build, using salvage materials and methods, deepen the perception of affect, enable plastic labor, and help maintain fragile assemblages. Although salvage, as it now stands, can often be found in relation to capitalist forms of labor, community, and space, because of what I have argued as its inherent tendency to undermine categories and challenge individual understanding of oneself and others, it allows a shift in focus from what it is, namely, a coping strategy to deal with the ruins created by capitalism, to what it might be, a transformative political practice.

Chapter 2

Sense, Becoming, and Political Salvage

Introduction

The qualities of salvage politics I discussed in the last chapter highlight precarity and scarcity. One does not *choose* to salvage in the sense that I use the term. Simply using discarded material during a construction project or deciding to repair an item, as opposed to replacing it, is not the type of salvage I am discussing. For the poor, salvage is never a choice, it is a necessity stemming from the precarity of their situation and the materials they must use to address their quest to fulfill their needs. They must build even though they do not know how a material might respond to a new situation, how a particular change in their environment might spark new and possibly harmful changes, how individuals dealing with the same precarity might react to their interventions. Precarity can be avoided by those with resources, and it can be overcome through better tools and more labor. Those with resources might refurbish but they do not salvage.

Having said this, what techniques are used by the poor to survive in such circumstances, and how might these skills and practices possess political import? How is fixing a wall using found material experimentally different when undertaken by a wealthy or a poor person? Assertions such as these misunderstand the actual experience of precarity and its relationship to salvage. The unpredictability of the broken landscapes that constitute the raw material used by salvagers cannot simply be dispelled with more precise techniques of measurement or better tools—the precarity of these landscapes is real. The perplexing inscrutability of damaged landscapes cannot be precisely discerned because they defy such attempts at quantification. The indeterminacy of things, and thus people's reactions to things, are real phenomena. And this indeterminacy is profoundly heightened by broken landscapes. The constituent elements of these landscapes move and combine into unstable environments and thus are highly pregnant with possibilities both dangerous and advantageous. But how does one discern something as indefinite as possibility? It cannot be measured or quantified. Furthermore, because such landscapes constantly change, they cannot be contained within the confines of a particular space of experimentation, as happens in a laboratory. Thus, the question presents itself of how one might use the real, vital, precarious contingency of one's ruined landscape to both scavenge and repair, the distinct activities of salvage.

One can begin to answer such questions through the work of Jane Bennett. In her *Vibrant Matter: A Political Ecology of Things* she emphasizes the reality of such material indeterminacy through a discussion of a pile of trash she encounters on a Baltimore street. She recounts how while observing a storm drain during a walk, she began to compile a list of what she saw: a glove, a dead rat, matted clump of oak pollen, a bottle cap, and a stick of wood. Here, she presents five things with distinct qualities: all are inanimate and they are able to be expressed in a neat list. But then, after another moment of reflection her focus changes and she muses:

> As I encountered these items they shimmied back and forth between debris and things—between on the one hand stuff to ignore, except insofar as it betokened human activity (the workman's efforts, the litterer's toss, the rat-poisoner's success), and on the other hand, stuff that commanded attention in its own right as existents in excess of their association with human meanings, habits or projects. In the second moment, stuff exhibited its thing-power: it issued a call even if I did not quite understand what it was saying. At the very least, it provoked affects in me: I was repelled by the dead (or was it merely sleeping?) rat and dismayed by the litter, but I also felt something else: a nameless awareness of the impossible

singularity of *that* rat, *that* configuration of pollen, *that* otherwise utterly banal, mass produced plastic water-bottle cap. (Bennett 2010, 4)

The "thing power" of the refuse that she has sensed lies in its singularity—the uniqueness of each item in its relation to its own history and its own unique relationship to the things with which it finds itself in association. No one could have predicted the exact contours of the pollen as it found its way to the Baltimore drain, and no one could have predicted that a bottle cap and that pollen not only would have ended up together, but also the affects that this vibrant congeries would produce through its interaction with Bennett. She goes on to state, "When the materiality of the globe, the rat, the pollen, the bottle cap, and the stick started to shimmer and spark, it was in part because of the contingent tableau that they formed with each other" (Bennett 2010, 5). The shimmer, or the obscure, affective sense she experienced, came not from simply how the trash pile came to lie in that arrangement, but what that arrangement might become and how the trash "called" her to notice certain aspects of its contingent potentiality. The trash is unstable, it will move in the short run, develop (or devolve) in the long run, and the exact path this transformation will take is both unpredictable and immanent—a different grouping of things in the exact same situation would express different qualities. Others highlight how her arguments demonstrate that disasters exhibit many of these same vibrant, emergent qualities as this trash heap, acting as "ruptures that allow her to highlight the active role of non human materials in public life" (Danisch 2020, 200).[1] Such ruptures confuse previous understandings, disrupt habits, and scramble meanings in a way that brings one's vague affective sense of one's relationship with one's material surroundings to the foreground of consciousness. For Bennett, the disordered nature of trash heaps and disaster constitute a vital assemblage with agency. This material agency, because it confounds expectations and overwhelms those with whom it interacts, produces novel, jarring, and perhaps exciting affects. Effects such as these that come from confrontation with the jumbled, confounding, and, initially, even repellent pile of trash, while not necessarily prompting the adoption of "plastic" habits that constitute the radical political potentiality of salvage, do open the door to such transformation.

This experience of opening oneself to the vital movements and potentialities of a ruined landscape, which for Bennett is, in this instance, something with which they chose to engage, constitutes a frequent activity for the poor who are forced to salvage. They encounter not simply trashy puddles on the way to work, but ruined buildings, rivers, and neighborhoods in which they must live and which they must use to survive. The contingencies inherent in such environments pose questions to those who must negotiate them, such as what might fall, what will keep out the wind, where one might find food. The basis upon which to make such assessments changes every day. The feeling that something might change in a way that could create difficulty constitutes an imposition difficult to ignore, especially when a decision seems unavoidable and pressing. Thus, for the poor the "vibrancy" of the environment is not simply something that evokes affects that include indeterminacy and a sense of wonder. The poor are often called to observe and even interrogate their ruined environments to cull opportunities for collecting resources that might play a role in meeting their needs. Sensing the multiple, resonant currents of disordered vibrancy that surround them, suggests how a situation might develop, how a particular item might be stretched, cut, or combined, the impact an intervention might have upon an unstable, vibrant environment. Sense thus constitutes a matter of life and death for the poor, and to be able to best discern the vague clues offered by these affects in the process of their salvage constitutes a vital skill.

In this chapter, I attempt to articulate new forms of political agency that might result from focusing on the affects one experiences through salvaging in broken environments. I do this by exploring how sensing the affective contingencies produced by the vibrancy of environments plays an important role in the generation of novel interpretations and actions. Furthermore, I investigate how affect plays a fundamental role in the radical political potential of the plasticity with which I characterize salvage. To make this argument, I discuss authors who, for the most part, do not use the term *salvage* but do invoke many of the concepts I identify as important to contemporary theorists of salvage. Next, I will discuss how one of the most important consequences of the contemporary "affective turn" has been for theorists to begin exploring how this concept might be relevant to political analysis. A prime example of this can be found in Lauren Berlant's *Cruel Optimism*. She claims that affects she describes as cruel optimism form an overarching "infrastructure" that functions in many ways like a disempowering ideology. I will continue by describing how a number of theorists suggest that, due to the pacifying consequences of this affective background to life in contemporary capitalism, affective strategies are needed to overcome them.

I conclude by arguing that certain affects that often accompany the act of salvage, which many describe in terms of love and depression, if first identified and then accentuated can deepen the critical potential of this activity and result in the embrace of plasticity. I then claim that much of this literature concerning the potentiality of critical, radical, or democratic affects can be summarized as a politics of becoming, and is most provocatively explored in the work of William Connolly. He asserts that if capitalism produces affects of staccato inwardness and impasse, critical thought and democratic agency produce affects of letting go, expansiveness, and development. And it is becoming, the willingness to be open to the indeterminacy of where these resonances might lead in terms of both action and conceptualization, that ties it to the plasticity at the core of salvage. For just as salvage labor is indelibly tied to the concept of plasticity, both in its operation and its results, becoming is an inherently plastic process, which leads not only to unforeseen outcomes but also to unforeseen changes in the participants involved in this process. Thus, I conclude that political salvage, when it occurs, can possibly reflect a particularly potent manifestation of becoming, and thus can contribute to propagation of the "ethos of pluralization" envisioned by Connolly.

Sensing Contingency, Sensing Salvage

The contingency sensed by those who dwell in salvage landscapes is real. Such a sense derives from the actual vagueness inherent in a situation comprised of many interrelating elements that might develop in many, equally likely ways. Such contingency is not chaos—it can give clues as to the manner in which relationships within environments might change, reconfigure, and affect each other. Contingency is an aspect of situations, not things. An isolated thing in itself, for the most part, stays the same—it is designed, or it has evolved, to have some sort of internal stability which makes it identifiable as a particular thing. But nothing exists by itself. Everything stands in relationship to something else, whether in actuality or potentiality. We might focus on particular things, but we always experience things within a web of relationality characteristic of a situation.[2] Laboratory experiments are designed to diminish these situational characteristics, isolating a limited number of influences upon a particular process or thing. Unlike these controlled environments, situations, with their inherent contingency, are not simply complex, but their boundaries shift, with webs of influence expanding and contracting as different influences gain prominence and fall away. The changes within situations might be characterized as fast or slow, accelerating or decelerating. Situations can complexify or simplify. Their boundaries might grow and widen or, conversely, shrink and become circumscribed. A situation might exhibit many of these qualities at the same time and thus hang together with only chaotic relationality, or exhibit a constant quality of smoothness. It might be in equilibrium, exhibiting very little change, or be falling out of this state and embodying increasing states of chaos. Thus, the vitality that situations exhibit, or in other words, the agency Bennett claims matter displays, manifests itself in terms of a general quality—indicative not necessarily of what it is going to do, for that would involve a prediction impossible to make, but of what it might become.

As mentioned, the fact that human beings are always part of situations leads Bennett to suggest that she does not simply observe, but in fact becomes a part of the "situation" of the trash heap on the Baltimore street. She observes the individual parts of the waste, the dead rat, the glove, while she senses the vitality of each of its parts in relation to what is there now, what came into relation before, and thus what it might become. Another name for the sensation of the vitality indicative of the qualities of a situation is *affect*. Kathleen Stewart claims that "affects are the varied, surging capacities to affect and to be affected that give everyday life the quality of a continual motion of relations, sense contingencies and emergences" (Stewart 2007, 2).[3] Alternatively, she explains them as the way meanings "pick up density and texture as they move through bodies, dreams, dramas and social workings of all kinds" (Stewart 2007, 3). This affective texture, as Lauren Berlant argues, is an outgrowth of the change within our environments and our locations within them, which she claims "is an impact lived on the body before anything is understood and as such is simultaneously meaningful and ineloquent, engendering an atmosphere" (Berlant 2011b, 39).[4] In sum, affect constitutes the property by which we sense the quality of the relationship that temporarily forms between our bodies and our environment. Situations can be jumbled, smooth, at rest, or agitated. These arrangements also change, with trajectories of increasing or decreasing organization in multiple domains of that situation. These affective qualities reveal something real about situations—a disjointed situation and the affect it produces is a situation not stable and thus rife with potentials. Contingency, of course, leads to uncertainty—this is why so many avoid it. But that uncertainty can be mitigated through attention to the resulting affects experienced by those in such situations. Affect can indicate general trends, points of promise, and paths to be avoided. Paying attention to the real phenomenon indicated by these seeming internal and arbitrary feelings can mitigate some of the uneasiness that comes from existing in contingent situations. Of course, this requires effort and time in an attempt to cull the vague clues suggested by the affects one senses. But through their emphasis upon the empirical origins of affect, these theorists make an argument for the potentiality of such efforts.

It is important to remember that one's situational environment is not comprised only of one's body and the material world. Bodies sustain minds and minds are constituted by language and meaning, all of which play a role in the constellation of facets that comprise a situation. Some theorists focus almost exclusively on the interaction of meaning and environment and the affects these relationships produce. For example, Todd May, while interpreting Deleuze's account of the sense and affect, states that "sense is what happens at the point at which language and the world meet. It is the happening, the event that arises when a particular proposition comes in contact with the world" (May 2005, 100).[5] While May seems to focus exclusively on the mind and its reception of the larger environment in this quote, it needs to be stressed that "the world" includes the body, and thus his statement should be taken as acknowledging thought's inextricable linkage with the multiplicity of the material world. All thoughts, and the bodies to which they are tied,[6] are further linked to their physical plural surroundings, and this relationship constantly produces a string of "happenings" that produce affects.[7]

Oftentimes one aspect of this complex relationship between body, mind, and place comes to the foreground of experience. Everydayness, often, is comprised of routines, habits, and unquestioned norms that do not require conscious thought or choice. But when something new occurs, it is accompanied by a jarring affect as the pattern of previous relationships that has constituted the script of our actions undergoes disruption. This sense of novelty can be perceived even before the actual source of the novelty is known—in fact, it often is. We sense that something is wrong, something is new, something has shifted, often before we know exactly what has changed. Brian Massumi notes how two bodies interacting can result in "predictable causation," but three or more bodies interfere with each other in unique ways that cause "resonance" that spreads across one's environment in unpredictable ways. Stewart claims that such resonances cause us to be "tuned into" changes, to shift our attention to them. These senses can later be tested, thought about, and evaluated. She also describes this mobilization of attention to newness that is characteristic of affect as when "matter can shimmer with undermined potential and the weight of a received meaning" (Stewart 2007, 28). The shimmer she describes here represents heightened attention to novel affects. According to anthropologist Deborah Bird Rose, "[T]he shimmer, the brilliance . . . is a kind of motion. Brilliance actually grabs you. Brilliance allows you, or brings you into the experience of being a part of a vibrant and vibrating world" (Tsing et al. 2017, G53). And when this shimmer occurs, it imposes itself upon us and "lingers for a little while as an irritation, confusion, judgment. thrill or musing. . . . Its visceral force keys a search to make sense of it, to incorporate it into an order of meaning" (Stewart 2007, 39). This is the "call" produced by the shimmer of the trash pile described by Bennett—the sensed immediacy when the affect of a contingent world imposes on us in unknown ways. When newness is something that is noticed through sense it disrupts the usual banality of the everyday and calls upon us to establish a new relationship with the world. This is the sensed "vibrancy" as described by Bennett. Salvage environments are replete with such shimmer. The novel affects they produce grab attention and shock individuals out of their habitual reactions. Individuals experience this as pulsating because of their pronounced change and contingency, and the novelty and strange ambiguity can often become an object of desire, stoking interest in the object and "calling" our attention to it.

The ineffability of affect, its perception on the margins of consciousness, and the general character of the web of relationships renders it difficult to describe with words. People, especially those who are overwhelmed by the affects that accompany a rapidly changing situation, grasp at words to convey the experience of change, and often express such feelings in terms of being overcome, one's body taking over one's consciousness and being led by an unknown force. Although such experiences of the ecstatic that prompt such affective reactions have frequently been associated with religion and spirituality, political activists also describe such overwhelming affects accompanying their actions. Francesca Polletta, in her *It Was Like a Fever: Storytelling and Protest in American Politics*, grapples with what she deems as the confusing ambiguity of the stories many activists tell concerning their experience of protest. For example, during the civil rights movement, many activists described their protests as spontaneous, despite the fact that they were both planned and coordinated with larger groups. What Polletta finds is that the spontaneity described by those participating in sit-ins and protests referred to the vague but powerful sense of being led or inspired to act by something outside of themselves. She asks of the participants in the civil rights movement, "Why do activists cast themselves not as strategic actors but as swept up by forces over which they had no control?" (Polletta 2006, 33).[8] Over and over again, she finds activists narrating their experience of protest as "bursting, breaking, exploding, sweeping, surging, ripping through the city like an epidemic of students, fired by the spark of the sit-ins and a chain reaction" (Polletta 2006, 40). For her, constructing coherent narratives from almost indescribable experiences is an attempt to make sense of the "unfamiliar," but as opposed to focusing on activists' attempts to render their overwhelming desires and emotions into communicable narratives, I would rather focus on the sensed, affective quality of the experiences they are describing. The words they use in Polletta's account—sweeping, surging, bursting—all suggest trajectory and potential, all indicate the general direction and tempo of a group of related and dynamic actions, institutions, ideas, and individuals.[9] These activists are trying, however haltingly, to describe their sense of the affects inherent within the situation in which they found themselves—the dynamic feeling of changing and being changed by the events around them, that in many cases motivated them to action.

The affects that these activists feel reveal something real about their relationship to their environment, a phenomenon possessing important political implications. To explain: bodies encounters other bodies; some of these bodies are human, some are not. A body, in the discourse of affect, is something that can be affected, changed, diminished, and, most importantly, augmented. Encounters palpitate situations and they initiate changes that resonate in unpredictable ways. Such encounters, as Deleuze describes, using Spinoza, can combine to form a more powerful whole, or sometimes can decompose each other. He states that we experience joy when a body encounters ours and enters into composition with us, and sadness when, on the contrary, a body or an idea threatens our own coherence. When bodies (and bodies can be humans, things, or ideas) enter into such composition, our own body becomes more powerful—in the sense of being more likely to be affected in ways that add to that complexity. Power is an affect, a surging, a smoothness that allows bodies to traverse many situations and to enter into combinations—the more combinations the more capacities and actions. Most importantly, power can be felt. As our bodies are more able to be affected, we sense the flowing relationality, the increase in the range of our physical, cognitive, and affective movements, and thus become connected with a wider situational environment. For the activists described by Polletta, the power, agency, and autonomy they sensed indicated real increases in their potentiality for political action. As actions resulted in expected outcomes, previously unrelated elements of their environment began to make "sense" in their consciousness as they experienced smoother, more integrated affects that seemed to "surge" and "sweep" them up into greater acts of political involvement and understanding.

Even after presenting powerful narrative accounts of the affects that accompany activists' experience of political work and transformation, one might still ask whether such accounts remain insignificant to larger political and social analysis and describe only subjective reactions to local encounters. Protevi helps to link the previous discussion of affect and situations explicitly to their political consequences. He emphasizes that

> although cognitive sense-making constitutes and reproduces bodies' politics by the patterns of its action, this action is itself patterned by virtue of the sociopolitical and historical embedded of bodies politic. In other words the differential relations of our autonomous reactions and their approving or disapproving reception by other form patterns of acculturation by which we are gendered and radicalized as well as attuned to gender, race and other politically relevant categories. (Protevi 2009, 35)

Thus, the spatial boundaries of situations are not limited to what one's body can immediately touch, feel and hear. Human existence involves unavoidable imbrication within many fields of relationality defined by one's immediate environment, one's local community, the language one uses, and the social and political contexts of these more circumscribed ecologies. Protevi integrates the differing scales into a theory of political affect by arguing that the constitutions of "bodies politic" occur on a number of different levels or "orders." He describes how "first-order bodies politic are at the personal scale, whereas second-order bodies politic can be either the group or the civic scale" (Protevi 2009, 37). These different scales co-constitute each other, producing simultaneous affective resonances depending on the particular relationships occurring through interactions of bodies with bodies, and bodies with the systems that privileged particular meanings, identities, and somatic habits. He goes on to observe that the "orders" of the body politic cannot be limited to two scales, and he therefore posits the existence of multiple larger scales, claiming that "the body politic of a nation is composed of multiple levels of subordinate collective (second-order and above) bodies politic. There are also multiple overlaps of bodies politic as first-order bodies politic can belong to many different second-order (and higher) bodies politic, which creates resonance and dissonance at various levels (Protevi 2009, 42). Because political, social, and economic systems structure our daily movements, language, and understandings of ourselves, we can sense the affects produced throughout daily interactions with these systems. Protevi's account highlights this important point and provides theoretic and political context for the qualitative accounts of the affective thresholds experienced by activists described by Polletta.

A full account of what the implications of embracing the potentialities of affect might mean for political action—and specifically the political actions that constitute a theory of salvage activism—will be discussed later. At this point, it is important to note that affect and precarity are intimately interrelated, and that relying on vague affects can be a powerful strategy to transform confused situations into those infused with power and political potential, in that affect can focus attention on new realms of inquiry and possible action. When we do not know what to do, when our cognitive interpretations fail us, these theorists point us toward relying on our senses. These senses are not simply internal or emotional states, but indicators of the relational and thus spatial and temporal characteristics of the environment. These affects, the constant combining and recombining in which our bodies engage with other bodies, tell us something not simply about what is happening, but what might happen. Relying on our sense of affects does not always result in increasing the power either to be affected or to affect situations in a way that brings them to greater equilibrium. Situations change, and change in novel unique ways that might overwhelm and confuse our repertoire of habitual actions and interpretation, and we might not be able to recover immediately from such profound ruptures. Furthermore, situations reveal not just the specifics of their changes but how they are changing—the speed, direction, tendencies, and more importantly, the potential developments—and although our bodies can sense these changes, they are felt vaguely and can often be misread. What the sense of precarity offers is an opportunity, not an eventuality. But this opportunity can help us to understand how precarity cannot simply be overcome, but be transformed into a resource for personal and social transformation that can be embraced.

As demonstrated earlier those who study salvage emphasize, this opportunity for transformation can jump to the forefront of experience when one finds oneself immersed in landscapes of heightened precarity, a precarity that forces individuals to search the ruined ecologies that surround them for any potentials that might help them meet their needs, even potentials as vague and discordant as one's sense of affect. Damaged landscapes of salvage and disaster present an ecology of scattered and unknown practices,[10] where affects manifest themselves in wildly discordant and jarring matrices of relationality. But these patterns, because of their wild contingency, also offer many possibilities for modulation and recalibration. They can wake up individuals to the possibilities for change around them and call for changes to the ecology of practices that builds around them. They often disarm previous understandings and bring one's sense of affect to the foreground of consciousness. Such interest stems from the necessity of interpreting and planning action based on the affects stemming from interaction with the immateriality of their damaged ecology—previously held understandings simply don't result in expected results in such chaos. Under the right conditions, they inspire plasticity by encouraging individuals to lessen this chaos, at least initially, not through conscious action but by modulation through affect, a process that leads to unforeseen paths and novel relationships. Affect is the core of developing both material consciousness and plasticity, and the damaged landscapes where salvage often occurs provide a fertile background in which to develop such characteristics.

Capitalist Affect

A person experiences affective sense of their situation through its vague qualities, but this observation deemphasizes the fact that the qualities of the actual ecologies of affect that most face in their daily lives can exhibit consistent tendencies, forms, and patterns. Damaged landscapes do not constitute the only ecology that individuals, even the poor, might encounter in contemporary capitalism. If one is poor, one faces an increased likelihood of encountering such a landscape, but other types of landscapes abound in capitalism. Catastrophes constitute states of exception to everyday life within capitalism—and "functioning" environments, where people work regular jobs, buy regular clothes, and live in regular neighborhoods, constitute stark contrasts to the affective ecologies that inspire salvage. A number of scholars have begun to use the concept of affect to describe the everyday experience of life in capitalism and, more importantly, how the specific affects created by capitalism might serve to legitimate its existence and hide its consequences. Thus, examining the affective landscape of everyday life in capitalism not only provides a contrast to environments I previously discussed that encourage plasticity, but also highlights the obstacles that any political theory of salvage based in affect must overcome.

Bennett is one such theorist, as can be seen when she argues, "American materialism, which requires buying ever-increasing amounts of products purchased in ever shorter cycles, is antimateriality. The sheer volume of commodities and the hyper-consumptive necessity of junking them to make room for new ones conceals the vitality of matter" (Bennett 2010, 5). By claiming that the rampant consumption produced by capitalism results in a prevailing sense of antimateriality, Bennett suggests that exposure to certain social systems can diminish the ability to sense the vibrancy of one's environment. Attention to both the vitality of one's surroundings and how one's body is affected by the vitality demand not only acknowledging, but taking the time to sit with sense. As situations change, so do their affect, and therefore one must let sense happen to oneself over a period of time in order to truly receive a helpful impression of what it conveys. Yet, as Bennett notes, contemporary neoliberal capitalism thrives on quick replacement. Instead of devoting the time to sense the contours of one's surroundings, capitalism encourages establishing radically new ecologies with different constituents through the purchase of commodities. This abandonment of sensing the developmental properties of an ecology can occur not only in terms of the simple materiality suggested by Bennett—not simply new stuff, but new jobs, new communities, new friends—all of these replacements and "new choices" chop off one's sense of the affect of one's environment. Thus, it is the "antimateriality" that Bennett, perhaps ironically, claims to be the consequence of capitalism. Although consumer culture clearly results in individuals accumulating more things, they do not pay attention to the things they have and thus lose the full sense of their vital materiality. The "thingness" of things drops out and they become mere extensions of our own interpretive frameworks.

Others have given more detailed accounts of how the affects produced by commodified ecologies impact those who exist within them. The quality of our relationship with commodities—the choppy, episodic relationship we have with the things we buy and frequently replace limit our tendency, and even ability to sense and thus understand them as parts of dynamic situations with their own agency. We undergo a greater number of qualitatively similar experiences in a capitalist society that elevates commodity production and consumption to the paradigm of all interaction. Jonathan Crary observes that increased working hours, technology that forces workers to undertake tasks at home, and incessant onslaughts of entertainment media have led to a twenty-four hours a day cycle of work and play. Instead of cycles of work, rest, and sleep, waking life comes to be experienced as an incessant "transient flux"[11] where labor and commodity consumption mix, and even replace rest and sleep. The constant experience of life with such spatial and temporal qualities impacts individuals in many ways beyond simple exhaustion—more importantly for this argument, Cray claims that "there is an ongoing diminution of mental and perceptual capabilities rather than their expansion or modulation. Current arrangements are comparable to the "glare of high-intensity illumination or white-out conditions in which there is a paucity of tonal differentiation, out of which one can make perceptual distinctions and orient oneself to shared temporalities" (Crary 2014, 34). Notice here Crary's references to types of perception outside the five senses—his emphasis upon the inability to perceive (or sense) "tonal differentiation" or orient oneself to "shared temporaries." A lack of sleep and living within an environment comprised of a flux of staccato and disconnected, commodified moments does not rob us of our vision, but instead dulls us to quality. Individuals sense their extended exposure to such spatial and temporal qualities as a background sense of bland affects, even though the changes we experience occur at an increasingly blinding rate. Crary states, "To be bland is a becoming smooth, and distinct from the idea of a mold that the word conformity often implies. Deviations are flattened or effaced, leading to that which is neither irritating nor invigorating" (Crary 2014, 56). Stewart invokes similar bland affects as characterizing the social ecology of capitalism, describing such environments as enacting "the dream of pure circulation itself . . . being in tune without being involved . . . nothing will happen to us and nothing we do will have real consequences . . . like a flotation device" (Stewart 2007, 50–51) and "dull with anxiety" (58). Once again, notice the terms that connote modes of affect: "breezy" as a smooth and superficial movement; "not being involved" in the sense of not being affected by others, a similar situation as that of not experiencing "consequences"; and, finally, floating along with no sense of agency or power on currents with trajectories beyond one's control. This quality of experience, while only vaguely sensed, not only expresses something real about life in capitalist society, but also profoundly impacts one's ability to perceive the relationships that comprise the larger social environment.

When Stewart discusses the "dull anxiety" she sees as the general affect produced through daily life in capitalist society, it is important to note that her use of the term *dull* does not imply inactivity—a statement one might make about a town or a movie where nothing happens. By dull, she means "dulling" or "dulled" of particular perceptions, most notably devoid of how affect can reveal the resonances between different aspects of our situations and the overall potentials and tendencies within particular situations. Lauren Berlant describes the affects produced by daily life in capitalist society as characterized, perhaps ironically, by such complex dullness and varied uniformity. They argue that the unique quality of these environments originates in their constitution as strings of "impasse." They explain this term by stating:

> [U]sually an impasse designates a time of dithering from which someone or some situation cannot move forward. . . . The impasse is a stretch of time in which one moves around with a sense that the world is at once intensely present and enigmatic such that the activity of living demands both a wondering, absorptive awareness and a hyper-vigilance that collects material that might help to clarify things, maintain one's sea legs and coordinate the standard melodramatic crises with those processes that have not yet found their genre of event. (Berlant 2011b, 4)

To them, life in capitalism consists of situational patterns experienced as both moving and standing still, where we attempt to understand the processes in the larger world that create our lived distresses, but where these quests only end in frustration. We attempt to look but cannot find why bad things happen to us, why we lost our job, why our nephew became addicted to methamphetamines, or why our water makes us sick as opposed to quenching our thirst. We collect facts, but cannot put them together into a coherent picture of the forces and actors that impact our lives and why the world seems to be hostile to our interventions. We produce too many solutions that are too quickly attempted and discarded—we buy a new self-help book and then throw it away when we see another—and thus we adopt the commodity form as the form of all our solutions. Although we attempt to assign "genres" to the various events in our lives, or, in other words, an explanation with a particular narrative containing protagonists, antagonists, a dramatic arc, the larger meaning of our experience remains enigmatic. They state that impasse should be represented as "a vision of the everyday organized by capitalism . . . that is disorganized by it, and other forces besides" (Berlant 2011b, 8). Thus, impasse becomes the general and driving affect that surrounds us, a prevailing, amorphous irritant that cannot be cured, and, perhaps ironically, a powerfully motivating force of action.

Despite the disorganization of atmospheres of impasse, individuals must live, must make decisions concerning the mundane and the profound. The primary strategy that takes form in reaction to impasse is that of cruel optimism, a repertoire of "skills for adjusting to the newly proliferating pressure to scramble for modes of living on" (Berlant 2011b, 8). Because the affective potentialities that might be sensed within the daily life are difficult to discern, due to the crosscurrents and riptides of capitalist affect, the attempts we make to take control of our lives do not produce desired consequences and do not address the root source of our problems. But the act of trying, of attempting to make attachments, whether they be relationships with persons, places, ideas, or modes of life, provides everyday solace, structure, and a genre of response in an opaque world. Hence, the "cruelness" of the hope provided by such actions. They state that "what's cruel about these attachments . . . whatever the content of the attachment is, the continuity of its form provides something of the continuity of the subject's sense of what it means to keep on living on and to look forward to being in the world" (Berlant 2011b, 24).[12] Cruel optimism inspires the hope that there will always be another job if we lose the one we have, another friend we can make after our current one leaves, another neighborhood to which we can relocate. Such interventions constitute "a relief and not a reprieve or a repair" (Berlant 2011b, 117), and eventually accumulate and form an "affective infrastructure of the ordinary" that hides and overwhelms affects that might be produced by a different positioning of oneself, a different orientation of oneself in relation to the situation one finds oneself in. Furthermore, these affects provide "bland" and "breezy" sensations that while not solving one's problems, constitute a different and competing nexus of desires that at least lessen the psychic impact of deprivation— undermining the anxiety produced by the disconnection and contingency of these events by placing them within a larger affective background. Although one might suffer loss, the affect surrounding that loss is one of optimistic smoothness, a sense that the loss remains one small bump in the road that can be overcome with effort and "stick-to-itiveness." Individual obstacles and responses are stitched together into a cruel quilt that obscures the actual causes of the problems we face.[13]

Berlant's observation that cruel optimism can compensate for the experience while not addressing the causes of the reification that structures life in capitalism opens the door to a pathway of analysis of affect that links it to specifically Marxist concepts. An example of an incomplete but promising attempt to form such a link between affect and such categories can be found in Anita Chari's *A Political Economy of the Senses: Neoliberalism, Reification and Critique*. In this text, she argues that the reification Lukács and others claim to be the consequence of a life saturated by commodities produces heretofore unacknowledged aesthetic modes that strengthen the potency, and thus the damage, wrought by this process. To explain this contention, she claims that reification takes three specific forms: formalism, fragmentation, and dissociation. Whereas she describes all of these subcategories of reification in terms of their ability to mold cognition through particular modes of aesthetic presentation, I would argue that each of the modes of reification she identifies is also experienced through particular affects. Formalism, which substantively encourages individuals to regard and interpret all things in terms of commodities, for Chari also results in individual experience as "schematic," wherein things are thought of as "necessary." Affects that are formal, necessary, and schematic are affects of similarity and repetition, as portrayed by Berlant. Cruel optimism drapes all experience in a veil of similarity, where any obstacle is amenable to improvement and any disturbance has been anticipated. The formalistic affect is one of continuity; thus, the sense of this manifestation of reification undermines any excesses, disturbances, dissatisfaction, and even difference produced through vibrant situations. For Chari, disassociation reflects a "detached, unengaged point of view from which to judge internal events rather than events in the world. . . . Lukacs refers to this detached stance with the world *Teilnahmslosgkiet*, or lack of participatory involvement" (Chari 2015, 118). Because of this disassociation, the capitalistic individual "is not fully feeling or experiencing the sensations of affects of her actions" (113). Such detachment, or, as Stewart would put it, "light and breezy" affects, are a further consequence of the formalism of affect that overwhelms the difference that reification obscures. It is an anesthetic that works against the "shimmer" and vibrancy indicative of the damaged environments where salvage is likely to occur.

Finally, and perhaps most damaging to the practice of radical politics, Chari states that reification fragments our consciousness, diminishing our ability to construct "cognitive maps" of society that might render clear the systemic origins of our personal problems. Martijn Konings, in his *The Emotional life of Capitalism: What Progressives Have Missed*, describes the consequence of such fragmentation by stating:

> The sheer complexity of modern life means that we often do not know what performances are at the root of our trouble and what changes we should be making. As a result paradoxically it is often an intensified commitment to existing routines and iconic meanings that promises relief from our problems. (Konings 2015, 35)

Fragmentation not only manifests itself cognitively and emotionally, as Konings suggests, but also in a particular affective background to our thinking about society. When discussing the construction of totality, Chari introduces Fredric Jameson's likening of the construction of such holistic pictures of social reality to the "creation of totality in the work of art [in] Schiller's atheistic principle of the play impulse" (Chari 2015, 125). Such a playful construction of totality would take the form of a narrative, which derives aesthetic, and therefore motivational, power "from a kind of political plot construction whereby a new relationship to action is established which invests the world with connections that break out of the immediacy of the disengaged, contemplative mode of cognition characteristic of capitalist culture" (126). Reified narratives are constituted by cruel, paranoid, choppy relations that, while constant, are not consistently unified. They exhibit the form of a life replete with constant purchases of new items that represent new lifestyles, never cohering into any larger project or understanding.

While it is necessary to grasp the importance of particular modes of narrative structure when interpreting the consequences of reification, Chari's description of the aesthetic only through the substantive concepts of narrative such as plot and substantive connection needlessly limits the power and novelty of her analysis. When interpreting the aesthetic not only in terms of a narrative, but instead as a sensed affect, fragmentation might mean not simply the inability to cognitively discern the connections of one's own life to larger social forces, but also the inability to feel the affects society has on us and the affect our actions might produce in other environments. Furthermore, perhaps the aesthetic construction of totality might be dependent upon cultivating the ability and propensity to sense shimmering resonances that might "break out of the immediacy" of the affective background of cruel optimism that undergirds a daily life of reification. A fully affective interpretation of reification would not only connect Chari's work to the discourse of affect, but would more fully portray the complexity of lived experience in capitalism and the complex interrelationships between sense and cognition. Furthermore, by presenting this aesthetic interpretation of reification, I am attempting to highlight a consequence of life in capitalist society that could be productively counteracted through exposure to a contrasting ecology of practice, such as salvage.

Another affective interpretation of Marxist ideological categories can be found in Frederic Lordon's *Willing Slaves of Capital: Spinoza and Marx on Desire*, yet this example more fully embraces an understanding grounded in the individual's experience of affects. He does this by discussing how alienation sculpts our general patterns of desire. He claims that "a distinct feature of domination is thus to rivet the dominated to minor objects of desire, in any case those needed so by the dominators who keep the other objects for themselves. With joy rather than fear—this is no doubt how the dominators govern most effectively; but they delimit the joys strictly, rigorously, selecting the object of desire that will be offered" (Lordon 2014, 107). The object of desire, Lordon stresses is not any particular commodity or benefit, and not even a specific set of desires, but instead a particular form of joy that creates a particular affect. He explains that "consumerist joy is indeed a joyful affect but it is an extrinsic one. The neoliberal epithumogensis [deliberate engineering of affects] undertakes to produce intrinsic, joyful affects, that is affects that are intransitive rather than deeded to objects outside the activity of wage labor itself." Thus, capitalism "fixes the power of individuals to an extraordinarily limited number of objects" (52). He states, "[I]f the concept of alienation is worth rescuing, it would be for the sake of giving it the meaning of the 'stubborn affect' (Spinoza's *Ethics* IV. 6) and the occupation of the mind—the condition of the mind filled with too few things but completely so, thus impeded from expanding comfortably" (145). Konings also contends that the limited field of desire produced by capitalist alienation specifically revolves around money and consumption, observing that "moderns . . . do not experience money as involving a dismal uniformity but as offering unconditional universal access to difference" (Konings 2015, 61). For Konings and the other theorists of Marxist affect that I have been discussing, alienation is a type of fixation, "closure and contraction" that results in passivity and the circumscribing of the ecology of affects to which one's body is exposed. In a sour, commodity-filled existence the sense of affect sculpts desire as much as the content. It is the concentration of affects that are too powerful and that overwhelm other affects. Thus, their "intransitive" nature—these are effects that do not resonate but instead absorb other passions, foreclosing the realization of any possibilities outside the real or the "acceptable" as defined by capitalist ideology. These affects constitute a rigid background, in stark contradiction to the plasticity encouraged through salvage, and thus constitute a powerful obstacle to any political program based in salvage practices. The "stubborn" affects of "consumerist joy" described by Lordon flow from the same reified affects described by Chari. If affect indicates flow and connection, and the affects experienced in unsettled environments signal that those connections contain multiple and developing potentialities that resonate outward, capitalism produces environments that obscure such affect.[14]

In sum, all of the affective manifestations of life in capitalism I have discussed, cruel optimism, reification, and alienation, share the consequence of diminishing the "power" or the ability to be affected by other bodies within one's ecology of practice, and thus decreasing the likelihood that individuals will undergo encounters that will lead to the novel, surprising changes conducive to their development. Instead, their desire becomes attached to affects that isolate them and therefore lead to disempowerment. Many of these phenomena are characterized by affects comprised of difference that leads to sameness. For example, when experiencing cruel optimism, individuals find themselves undertaking different interventions in their lives to deal with the insecurity caused by the neoliberal capitalism that led to the same impasse. But this substantive impasse comes to be accompanied by the affect of forward motion, seeming novelty, and pure activity that accompanies action. We feel good and powerful because we are doing something, not because the actual action addresses our problem. The act of anticipation negates the specific nature of the phenomenon, which for the most part cannot be predicted in times of intense precarity and insecurity, and thus a smooth, even soothing affect accompanies even the most incongruous and contingent events. Cruel optimism can be clearly related as experienced affective constituents of Chari's account of reification. Both result in the dissociation that discourages individuals from "fully feeling or experiencing the sensations or affects of their actions." Consequently, such disassociation leads to a formalism where different experiences come to possess similar affects, resulting in a general anesthetic quality to life where even if a potential connection between oneself and one's environment can be discerned, it is bathed in affects that make it difficult for individuals to recognize it as such.

These observations point toward the existence of what Berlant refers to as the affective "infrastructure" of a society. As opposed to the economic and political institutions that require certain behaviors, embody particular ideas, and empower discrete groups and populations, they observe that "what constitutes infrastructure in contrast are the patterns, habits, norms and scenes of assemblage and use. Collective affect gets attached to the sense of its inventiveness and promise of dynamic reciprocity" (Berlant 2016, 403). Although Berlant here posits the existence of a "collective affect" that possesses fixed patterns similar to an institution, they emphasize that such *sensus communis* does not remains fixed and that infrastructure "holds statements up in a tensile structure that is always making things different as they course through the material world" (404). Furthermore, this social realm cannot be characterized simply as culture, civil society, or the political activities of what Gramsci might call the "War of Position," but it instead it refers to how all of these daily activities create a general yet internally fluid "how" of "what" people do. It constitutes the collective atmosphere of a society and the spatial and temporal character of the patterns of its "dynamic reciprocity." Because such an infrastructure composed of innumerable encounters, individualized habits, and unique situations could never possess the stability of an institutional structure, it constitutes a realm of both instability and potentiality. It possesses a general tenor that can be sensed, but is only that, an affective infrastructure that surrounds individual actions that serves to augment social and economic systems of injustice.

Manifestations of capitalist affective infrastructure contribute to the formation of alienated desires—and while there is much activity within this circumscribed ecology, all of the aims and actions of individuals further reinforce this boundary and rob them of the possibilities of experiencing expanding encounters that might increase their power to be affected. If affect helps to constitute desire, and especially constitutes the force that breaks out of ideology and helps to create new desires, individuals experiencing affective alienation grounded in commodity consumption are forcefully separated not only from their labor, but also, as Marx would term it, their species being. By species being, I mean their ability to take a conscious role in constructing the world around them with others. Sensing the intricacies of every relationship that constitutes the complex web of bodies and encounters that constitutes the world is impossible, of course. To overcome affective alienation would entail the ability to get a sense of the world as an affective horizon, the propensity to be open to, and even to desire, the resonances created by the vibrancy of other bodies, and finally the ability to use the senses to construct provisional linkages between concepts and make predictions on the consequences of actions based on the potentialities discerned from sense. Thus, becoming attached to capitalist patterns of affect and the institutions that create them leads to desiring actions more varied in their superficial differences yet more uniform in their constricting, limited, and blinkered qualities. But if one possesses the ability and desire to allow other resonances to "shimmer" and break free from the affective patterns that help to unconsciously legitimize capitalism, then one might gain the power that comes from allowing oneself to be affected and the novelty and creativity that might result from interacting with a much wider ecology of practice. Of course, to simply claim that possessing the ability and desire to embrace the "shimmer" of contingent qualities begs the question of under what circumstances one is likely to gain such abilities and desires. Yet at this point it is enough to highlight how theorists of affect emphasize the potentials within shimmering affects and how they possess political implications.

All of these theorists of capitalist affective infrastructure argue that our sense of the capitalist landscape constitutes a stark contrast to the affective characteristics of salvage ecologies and labor I discussed in the previous chapter. These forms of affective "false consciousness" that lie within a society's infrastructure bolster traditional understandings of capitalist ideology through revealing how daily life is not simply rife with substantive propaganda and distraction, but also a background landscape of affect that modulates experience in such a way that it breaks apart connections between self and society that would be the basis for any systemic understanding of their personal crises. The uniformity charac-teristic of affective reification described above undermines the plasticity indicative of the multiple senses of possibility one experiences through interacting with salvage landscapes. What renders such manifestations of ideology so powerful is that even "true" information and "accurate" descriptions of society lose their significance due to being bathed in deadening affects. Thus, the "consciousness" described here does not consist of "false" portrayals of society fed to individuals by government or media, but instead, constricted, bland affects that forestall the possi-bility of making connections and pursuing the possibilities of where these facts might lead. They create an anesthetic environment diametrically opposite to that of salvage.

Love Is Depressing, or Anticapitalist Affects

If capitalist affect fragments and circumscribes, it stands to reason that anticapitalist affects, if they are to encourage plasticity and becoming, should push outward, join, and be amenable to profound difference. Remember, salvage activists claim that engaging with waste material "speaks to us of what objects can compel the body to do, call for touch, for care, for action drawing us into their world" (Flood and Grindon 2014, 35). A number of recent theorists have begun to hypothesize that objects, people, and the environments they constitute can draw the body outward by prompting affects of "love," especially loving affects manifesting themselves in political and social contexts.[15] And while the use of the word *compel* in this case implies a much too powerful result, examining the affective inclinations, tendencies, and inducements of the "loving" and other affects involved, even in limited forms, in the activity of salvage constitutes a promising entry point into identifying the affective infrastructure that might counteract cruel optimism and reification I discussed earlier.

For example, Martha Nussbaum in her *Political Emotions: Why Love Matters for Justice* describes love not as a romantic or sexual bond, but instead in more relational and, I would argue, affective terms. More specifically, she casts love largely as a spatial and temporal phenomenon, as in the numerous instances in which she uses the term *overflowing* to describe both the experience and the consequences of love. What she means by using the word *overflowing* as a description of the "consequences" of love is that love overcomes the self, and leads individuals into new pathways for actions and perspective. She claims that love results in "a suspension of conscious demands for control . . . it is an outwards moving curiosity" (Nussbaum 2015, 176). When one experiences losing oneself, and one's limits become porous, one is drawn into new and surprising realms of oneself and what surrounds them, surprising oneself with desires that they did not realize they possessed. Regarding love as an emotion deems it as an inner mental state, while interpreting it as affect shifts focus to situations and how they might exhibit "loving" affects. While this might seem strange, certain environments, whether social or material, can be loving in the sense described above. They might be welcoming and overflowing, drawing participants out of their limited perspectives and overflowing their previous borders in dynamic development. Of course, individuals are always part of situations, and thus the "love" possibly exhibited by them will be sensed as gushing, expanding affects. But the main utility of interpreting love in these affective terms is that it can be used to describe not simply relationships with other people but also environments, objects, and even futures. If love is an affect, anything that affects an individual can be the object of an inspiration for love. Consequently, love, in this perspective, is personal and impersonal—one does not simply fall or feel in love, one can be in loving situations that inspire these affects.

Another articulation of such a nonromantic, politically oriented, and affective understanding of love can be found in Michael Hardt and Antonio Negri's work, especially in *Commonwealth*. For them, love is not an identitarian emotion whereby individuals share mutual affection for a common set of ideals, but instead is constituted by affects very similar to those described by Nussbaum. For them, love is a force pushing outward, curiously seeking the new and the strange while opening up individuals to new experiences. To explain their view, they ask readers to "think of Walt Whitman's poetry, in which the love of the stranger continually reappears, an encounter characterized by wonder, growth and discovery . . . love of the strange, love of the farthest, love of alterity can function as an antidote against the position of identitarian love which hinders and distorts love's productivity by forcing it constantly to repeat the same" (Hardt and Negri 2009, 183). This understanding of love results in "rupture with the existent and creation of the new" and also the formation of new "singularities," or unique arrangements of individuals and environments in common relationship. In this account, love, once again, is not simply a bond between two individuals or groups of individuals, but between humans and their vibrant human and non-human environments, reciprocally affecting each other.[16]

A description of affective, expansive, and political love can also be seen in the accounts of salvage landscapes such as the Gramsci Monument I discussed in the last chapter. Lex Brown, a poet who developed and oversaw the Children's Curriculum for the monument, claims:

> Love was an explicit and crucial part of the *Gramsci Monument*. It's the word for the kind of energy that people could feel when they were standing in it and on it. The way the kids reacted to the monument, the work and participation that the residents put into it, the dedication of the people working there. . . . Love in a social context is often dismissed as sentimental, superficial or naive, but in reality it is tough, powerful and complex. Real love is not pity, charity or an opportunity. During the monument, I learned that love is showing up, again and again, and doing your work because you believe in it. It is listening to other people with the knowledge that you don't know everything—even about yourself. (Hirschhorn 2015, 232)

Notice that this account of love as "energy," "work," and a tendency to listen and thus grow and develop casts its experience not in terms of internal emotion, but instead as a relationship not only of dedication, but more importantly for this conversation, openness to the other. Brown emphasizes that the love she experienced was grounded in an acknowledgment of how the hidden, surprising aspects of oneself are engaged though encounter. Furthermore, the "energy" she claims people felt suggests that the relationships of love sensed by participants in the monument were felt more than known. Affective love-energy is sensed as the mutual, creative becoming of a group of people moving together in a supportive space. While the participants within this monument were not engaged in the same activity as they moved through and co-created within this salvaged landscape, they were united by the shared sense of collective love that bonded them in their differentiation, creativity, and mutual aid.

If love is expansive and playful, according to these theorists, it will spread, forming the basis of a nonidentitarian community. When Hardt and Negri discuss the Spinozian origins of their interpretation of desire (*cupiditas*) that evolves into love (*amor*) they see love as resulting from a "striving for freedom and the common [that] resides at the most basic level of life . . . love consolidates the common institutions that form society" (Hardt and Negri 2009, 193). I will discuss this notion of the common more fully later in the argument, but at this point notice that their understanding of freedom is tied in with the common and love. When one maximizes the ability to be affected by others, one gains more options, perspectives, passions, and techniques for living and is liberated from the circumscribed ecology of practice constitutive of alienation and reification. To allow oneself to be affected more is to be freer. In this view, actions come about through relations, and to have more open and varied relations is to possess a larger repertoire of action and, furthermore, to desire and feel "joy" when exercising this wider repertoire. As Todd May argues concerning the affective joy and freedom that results from love, "[T]he poetically important thing about joy is therefore its function as a principle of mutuality. Active bodies will seek to maximize the mutual sympathy of their combinations: but this does not entail that they should strive to meet bodies they perceive as wholly similar resulting in a politics of community based on identity and sameness" (May 2005, 23). Thus, the joys of love are mutual and diverse, shared but always expanding and challenging previously established relationships. According to this understanding, love develops or it dies, it is continually passed on or it stops. It results in a community where the love is at once less than romantic love, in that it does not require permanent devotion and sacrifice to partner and family but can result in boundless possibilities for growth and expansion. Finally, love, because of its expansive, conjunctive consequences, embodies affects diametrically opposite to the separation and alienation characteristics of the capitalist landscape described by Chari and the other theorists of capitalist affect.

Although these theorists make a strong argument that affective love can counteract the reification that results from everyday existence in capitalism, not all embrace love as the core of their strategy of affect-based resistance. If, as Berlant claims, optimism, albeit a cruel variant, constitutes the form of affective infrastructure supporting contemporary neoliberalism, it stands to reason that, she claims, depression might play a role in liberating us such from false hopes. In fact, Berlant argues that depression constitutes a powerful strategy for demystifying the haze created by cruel optimism. They state that "in a Deleuzian sense it is a minor work of political depression that . . . makes a world from political affect in which practices of politics might be invented that do not yet exist" (Berlant 2011b, 229). Whereas cruel optimism is characterized by affects produced through a staccato pattern of meaningless actions that lead to perpetual impasse, depression is slow. When we are depressed we lack energy, we dwell upon our problems, and we think not about some possible (if unlikely or harmful and subtly repressive) future solution, but our past losses. If all of our repertoires of reaction are molded by the affective patterns of cruel optimism, and if all of our actions lead to affectively satisfying yet substantively disempowering results, the solution might be not to act. Berlant advocates the adoption of genres of action that lead to a process of

> breaking the patterns of cruel optimism of normative liberal civil society models in [their] turning away from those models. I say turning away rather than refusal because these works are not in a melodramatic modality. They are adverse to the in-in-your face modes of on-the-street protest. They manifest a politically depressed position but without seeking repair in an idiom recognizable in the dominant terms. (Berlant 2011b, 249)

To not act, to hide and "wallow" in one's depression, constitutes a profoundly political act, even more than protesting, according to Berlant, because quick resort to action can easily conform to the patterns of cruel optimism. They go on to explain the benefits of inaction by stating that "a deflationary aesthetic stretches out the space between cause and effect, stimulus and response." This stretching "splits off the loop from feedback, throwing the spectator into a space that does not yet exist . . . a space of potential political agency circulates in the atmosphere" (Berlant 2011b, 250).[17] If a person unconsciously and compulsively repeats actions that lead to a state of impasse, they claim, their depressive stretching of the interval between stimulus and response constitutes a potent tactic for breaking this pattern of behavior and, as is implied by the quote, setting the stage for new and liberating agency.

Berlant is not the only theorist to offer an account of the political benefits of depression. Using the work of Melanie Klein, Sedgwick gives a seemingly similar account to Berlant's when she lauds the benefits of depression to counteract the anxiety created through capitalist affects such as cruel optimism. She argues:

> The depressive position is an anxiety-mitigating achievement that the infant or adult only sometimes and often only briefly succeeds in inhabiting: this is the position from which it is possible to turn to use one's own resources to assemble or repair the murderous part-objects into something like a whole—though I would emphasize not necessarily like any pre-existing whole. Once assembled to one's own specifications, the more satisfying object is available both to be identified with and to offer one nourishment and comfort in turn. Among Klein's names to the reparative process is love. (Sedgwick 2003, 128)

Berlant criticizes this approach as conflating love and depression. For them, the inward affects of depression do not form a direct pathway to repair. They comment that portraying depression as a direct pathway to love establishes the risk of merely recapitulating cruel optimism. They state that

> such an arc and a rhythm [between depression and loving repair] can also amount to attempts to sustain optimism for irreparable objects. The compulsion to repeat a toxic optimism can suture someone or a world, to a cramped and unimaginative space of committed replication, just in case it will be different. Political realism can be tyrannical; it can become a foundation for change. Political fantasy can be ridiculous and self-defeating; it can ground and sustain as aspirational thinking beyond pragmatics that insists on a new materialism. (Berlant 2011, 259)

What Berlant here suggests as the first step toward breaking the cycle of cruel optimism and, by extension, the compulsive affective passions that underlie capitalist affect, is to acknowledge that the world is broken, to get depressed about the ruins that surround us, and to actually take them for what they are. Depression, in the context of salvage, allows us to truly observe the trash heap of what our world has become. Even though Sedgwick's understanding of depressive repair suggests that her repair respects the damaged state of previous situations in that it results in only "something like a whole" that bears the scars of its origins in ruins, Berlant still suspects that her interpretation would result in actions that do not fully respect and recognize the depth of damage that surrounds us in our present social situation. For Berlant, depression does not constitute a position where one can "turn to one's resources" and begin thinking of concrete repairs—such a move would betray the necessity to sit with one's depression for a sufficient length of time so that it can truly overcome the cruel optimism that pushes toward action, any action, that might provide compensation for the struggles of life in capitalism.

The invocation of repair in Sedwick's account of depression points toward the discussion of Halberstam's *Queer Art of Failure* by the curators of *Disobedient Objects*, the exhibition chronicling the use of salvaged items by activists. They observe how the fragile, jury-rigged gas masks, shelters, and other tools constructed by activists often break or do not perform in the manner imagined by activists. Although activists often feel acute pressure to quickly move on from such failures and try again to salvage what they need in light of the demands of their situation, Berlant and Sedgwick suggest that they should embrace the depression they sense due to their failure. Depression halts actions and gives the room to observe and rethink. It embraces the failures that inevitably come through salvage. And thus, thinking of depression and failure as an important and productive part of salvage helps to define the conditions under which this activity possesses the most potential for prompting an embrace of the plasticity that constitutes its normative core.

Even if one interprets the result of depression in a way similar to Berlant by eschewing a direct relationship between it and repair, this does not mean that a relationship might not be imagined that aids in imagining anticapitalist affective infrastructure. When Berlant raises the possibility of a "rhythm" arising from depression and repair that results in a toxic optimism, this does not mean that they eschew repair—they suspect it only within an "idiom recognizable in the dominant terms." It seems that what they want to avoid is easy repair, or a mode of repair that does not follow a significant period of reflection that results in questioning not only methods, but one's values and even identity. They insist that depression must change us, and depression in itself does not produce affects of love and repair. It seems to them that another intervening agent must provide a link between depression and love, lest love negate and replace the depressive state leading toward actions that do not truly reflect the "deflationary aesthetic" that they value. Thus, a "rhythm" between love and depression might be imagined even when interpreting depression as Berlant does, but it constitutes a rhythm much more complex, alinear, and difficult than that suggested by Sedgwick. As Berlant suggests, "Stretching out the space between cause and effect, stimulus and response" does not mean that no response will ever be produced through a depressive state, it merely posits the question of how and why, and in fact whether, if at all, one leaves the space of depression. Furthermore, the fact that Berlant does not discuss the transition "out" from depression suggests that they see depression as a possibly continuous state, as something that informs all of our actions. But this understanding perhaps underestimates the dangers of depression, in that depression can lead to not acting at all, or even self-harm. But, of course, positing depression and love as all-encompassing affective states does not speak to the possible complexity of experience. Love and depression might exist simultaneously—with some relationships in a situation resulting in expansive affects and some prompting deflation, which combines into a complex polyrhythm of senses that highlight various possibilities and relationships simultaneously. Thus, while Berlant remains wary of a hasty exit from depression, this does not mean that their work does not allow for a relationship between it and love to address cruel optimism.

No matter that the relation between the love and depression constitutes the most powerful antidote to capitalist affect, a discussion I will undertake in the next chapter, at this point it is productive to point out that this dynamic mirrors many of the affective properties of salvage I discussed in chapter 1. Depression focuses our attention on what is truly around us without imposing particular activity or interpretation upon this environment, just as material consciousness leads those who possess it to be able to sense the affective possibilities inherent in their relationship with an object. Meanwhile, love, when interpreted as an affect, prompts individuals to open themselves to the unpredictable vitality leading us into unpredictable transformations of our selves and our surroundings in a way that closely resembles the plasticity encouraged by salvage. Linking salvage to this love-depression rhythmic dynamic suggests a tantalizing political implication for salvage. Berlant and the other theorists I have cited in my affective reading of love and depression undertake their efforts to hypothesize how affect might contribute to a radical political program. If the love-depression cycle can counteract the affective environment produced by capitalism, and salvage can lead to the experience of this cycle, then salvage possesses inherent underacknowledged anticapitalist potentials. Thus, a situation where undertaking salvage activity prompts the presence of both affects constitutes the "best case scenario" for salvage undermining the capitalist affective infrastructure of everyday life. Reification breaks down as we undertake repeated cycles of depression and love and thus become more likely to acknowledge the plasticity of our selves and society. Of course, such a perspective on society and its relations to the self could be cultivated and organized to play a more prominent role in Left politics. But, as a precursor to such a politics, the rationalized, regularized "thingness" of capitalist society must be undermined and transformed into an acknowledgment that things possess an inner, plastic vitality that can be increasingly sensed and embraced through the love-depression cycle, or the act of salvage.

Affect and Politics, or Becoming Anticapitalist Salvagers

Although the previous discussion of love and depression was meant to provide insight concerning the political potentialities of the affects accompanying salvage practice, the exact way in which one might perform or live an anticapitalist politics of love or depression most likely seems quite opaque at this point in the argument. So now I want to begin surveying a number of theorists who advocate political strategies of mobilizing and prompting affect. These theorists, instead of speaking in terms of finding the "correct" or most "universal" interest that might unify resistance or a particular rhetoric that might break individuals free from capitalist ideology, speak of organizing encounters that might prompt affects that could both form the unifying basis for critical movements and prompt contestatory action. They imagine a "counterhegemonic infrastructure" that counteracts the control, cruel optimism, and reification that trap individuals in cycles of impotence and create huge difficulties for them to make connections between the crises in their daily lives and the larger social forces that cause them. The theorist whose work best represents this joining of affect and politics is William Connolly, whose work on what he deems the "politics of becoming" I will argue embodies many of the themes present consonant with the work I have previously discussed in this chapter.

To begin an investigation of the political implications of the loving and depressive affects that constitute the political potentialities of salvage, I want to discuss Berlant's provisional translation of their depressive stance into a more concrete politics. As might be expected with their focus on affect, they identify the quotidian and everyday as their focus. This focus on how seemingly apolitical, banal affects actually structure our political consciousness leads them to identify their politics with anarchism, because those who espouse this politics do not attempt to change, or even establish new institutions, but instead try to imagine a new position of autonomy and collectivity that springs purely from daily practice and encounters. They claim that the beginning of a political translation of affective depression is an "anarchist/DIY (do-it-yourself) aesthetic of the ordinary that, at least points to a politics and aesthetics that is genuinely dramatized and embedded in the new ordinariness, which is organized by a postspectacular articulation of banality, catastrophe, and structural crisis" (Berlant 2011b, 232).[18] Consequently, despite the enormity of the ruin of our contemporary landscape, to be a political depressive means focusing on what we ourselves can perceive directly and how we might cope, and indeed grope through efforts to contend with how the world seems to be ruined in the everyday. They identify in particular with anarchist David Graeber who they claim

> advances a kind of philosophical pragmatism that involves becoming a political subject whose solidarities and commitments are neither to ends or to imagining the pragmatics of a consensual community, but to embodied processes of making solidarity itself. . . . In this view one's individual or collective attachments to the political would ideally be an attachment to the process of maintaining attachment. In psychoanalytic terms, the anarchist political depressive would enact repair by performing a commitment to repairing politics without needed clarity or consensus on either of the two traditionally legitimating motives for political action: an ends-oriented consensually held good-life fantasy or confirmation of the transformative effectiveness of actions. One "does politics" to

> be in the political with others, in a becoming-democratic that
> involves sentience, focus and a comic sense of the pleasure of
> coming together once again. (Berlant 2011b, 260)

Notice how such a politics involves "sentience" and "focus" as qualities needed to be able to perceive the vague sensations produced by affects in one's environment, affects upon which individuals must rely when they do not possess the "needed clarity" toward an end that accompanies most traditional political activity. When living in a ruined landscape, Berlant observes, there is no assurance of the "transformative effectiveness" of our action, yet repair must occur anyway, repair of what we find around us, without any possibility of simply abandoning our damaged landscape and starting anew. The only resource, they claim, that we know we possess is the possibility of constructing shaky relationships of solidarity through the pragmatics of community and encounter—a DIY politics in an age when one cannot rely upon any previously constituted institution, or even a set of values or practices that previously provided a trustworthy set of tools, with which not simply to undertake political action, but to live everyday lives. As I suggested before, while I see the construction of such solidarity of "attachment to the process of maintaining attachment" and repair that does not need "clarity or consensus" as an expression of affective love, at this point, what remains important to emphasize is that Berlant sees their politics as resulting in an anarchist politics of the everyday where individuals focus on building a foundation of solidarity upon which larger acts of contestation rest.

While they do not specifically mention salvage as one of the manifestations of this DIY/anarchist politics, the similarities are striking. When Berlant claims that such a politics constitutes an "aesthetics" of "banality, catastrophe, and structural crisis," they invoke the "aesthetics" and thus the affects of the experience of salvage. Whereas a dramatic reaction to catastrophe might involve dramatic, public, and contestatory action, the banal reaction to such events involves simply doing what one has to do to survive on a day to day basis. While structural crisis is recognized through this position, the DIY/anarchist attempts to pragmatically repair their attachments with no "good life" fantasy to guide them. Such is also true of the salvager, who pragmatically looks at what surrounds them to guide their repairs. Their attention to their catastrophic environment constitutes their guide for banal repairs of their attachments to their human and nonhuman surroundings. And while DIY/anarchist depression does not fully encompass the political promise of salvage, it can play an important explanatory role.

I want to punctuate the discussion by arguing that William Connolly's "politics of becoming" possesses strong linkages to the political consequences of the love-depression cycle I discussed earlier in this chapter and that of political salvage I discussed in the last chapter. In sum, I want to argue that salvage constitutes a particularly strong ecology of becoming. Like the theorists of the affects of capitalism I presented earlier, Connolly bemoans the "acceleration of several domains of life" (Connolly 2008, 62–63) where the "complexity, volatility and messiness of the capitalist assemblage" leaves individuals vulnerable to what he deems the "evangelical capitalist resonance machine" (12). In this affective infrastructure, similarities between seemingly disparate cultural and political elements, such as "Christian family eroticism," George Gilder self-help, and Rush Limbaugh resentment "morph[s] into energized complexities of mutual imbrication and interinvolvement, where heretofore unconnected or loosely associated elements fold, end, blend and emulsify and resolve incompletely into each other, forging a qualitative assemblage resistant to classical explanation" (39–40). What acts as the basis for this assemblage is not a set of substantive similarities, but affective resonances—movements and propulsive forces, similar to the accounts of consumerist alienation that provide freedom within a circumscribed field and thus produce joy, yet this joy is both limited and tied to aggressive resentments of those outside its boundaries of acceptability. Connolly describes the affects characterizing this resonance machine for its adherence as "the one and only site in the mundane world that legitimately copies the creativity of God: it is the prime site on earth of risk, uncertainty and creative action. These guys are Deleuzians of the Right. God, creation and capitalism; capitalism, creation and God" (31). Thus, "joyful" affects not only join these elements into an interpretive web, highlighting aspects of these traditions and the world that reinforces its existence, but they provide the structure of desire that attracts, and even compels, individuals to maintain and even further the ideas and institutions that constitute this resonance machine's "worldly" manifestations. The contingencies that are exacerbated by neoliberal capitalism are both captured to develop a bounded creativity and resented as something that is created by otherness.

Connolly stresses that affective power created through this resonance machine remains so resilient because it works in the recesses of consciousness and subtly ties desires to ideas and actions. Arguments alone cannot break the power of such a machine by themselves; such a counterhegemonic project requires both argument and the experience of new affects. He argues that only a "series of positive existential orientations, relational tactics, local strategies, academic reforms, microeconomic experiments, large social movements, media strategies, shifts in economic and political ethos, state polices, and cross-state citizen actions are needed to reduce" (144) the power of this resonance machine. The tactics he names that are most closely related to an affective politics of the ordinary center around an effort to build what he calls "gratitude for this world" produced "through engagements with ourselves, church assemblies, films, media events, professional meetings, dinner conversations," which will "induce, fuse, care for the future" (ibid.) into not only our political actions but everyday life. Gratitude for the world produces care for the future. This is because, in Connolly's rendering, the shifting, vibrant potentials of the material and social world, if embraced, confound the limitations of the evangelical-capitalist resonance machine. Through attention to multiple affects, truly sensing their presence and becoming open to the creative energies, solutions, and relationships present within every situation, a new structure of desire based in "care" and not "resentment" can compete with the powerful passions accompanying capitalist affects.

This focus on "local strategies" and "relational tactics" leads Connolly to claim that a politics of becoming must encourage participants to be "capable of becoming responsive to unexpected shifts and turns in the flow of time" (Connolly 2005, 117) that can be sensed through attention to one's relations to one's surroundings, or one's sense of affect. He goes on to claim that such sensitivity creates a sense of wonder and even mysticism, although such mysticism remains a radically empiricist mysticism grounded in the vibrancy of the world and not the supposed vibrancy of the spirit. This attitude of the mystic

> proceed[s] primarily by attraction and example applied to new circumstances, not by commands attached to eternal laws. True mystics simply open their souls to the oncoming wave. That which they have allowed to flow into them in a stream of flowing down and seeking through them to reach their fellow men; the necessity to spread around them what they have received affects them like an onslaught of love which each of them stamps with his own personality. A love

> which is in each of them an entirely new emotion, capable
> transposing life into another tone. (Connolly 2005, 117–18)

Although Connolly, somewhat misleadingly in my estimation, refers to
the "love" for the world expressive of the attitude of the mystic in terms
of emotion, the substance of his description exhibits strong similarities
to my account of the political significance of affect. His love does not
manifest itself in terms of specific desires, but instead manifests itself as
"transposing life into a different tone." In order to fully embody a mystical attitude, he claims, individuals must not adhere to eternal laws, but
instead "open their souls to the oncoming wave" and allow the potentials
of their encounters to "flow into them in a stream." Just as Polletta suggests activists in the civil rights movement described a sense that they
were "swept up by forces over which they had no control," Connolly's
language of flow, stream, and wave all indicate the importance of allowing oneself to be guided by affect in his understanding of democratic
politics. All of these characterizations describing an attitude of "caring"
about the world and approaching it with gratitude, which clearly refers
to opening oneself up to a new affective ecology that might counteract
the resonance machine supporting contemporary neoliberal capitalism.

Connolly characterizes the mystical "opening" that transposes life
into a different tone as becoming open to what he calls "a world of
becoming." The structure of desire stemming from such an ecology of
practice finds its basis in the same "creativity" upon which the "evangelical
capitalist resonance machine" grounds its attraction, but this creativity
is not circumscribed, based in limited horizons and rigid practices. The
true pluralism, dynamism, and vibrancy of the world's characteristic
becoming leads individuals to take on the vibrant, shifting potentials
of experience. Connolly emphasizes that openness to the world leads
to "those protean moments when we are hit by surprising events and
movements that throw aspects of our previous projections into disarray.
These are precisely the moments, first, when the experience of time as
becoming becomes most poignant, and second, when the public virtue of
critical responsiveness becomes most crucial to pluralist politics" (Connolly 2005, 128). Here, Connolly translates this attitude of the mystic
to what he deems a "pluralist politics" experienced by allowing oneself
to be fully affected by the novel encounters indicative of our world of
becoming. Pluralist politics, although certainly accompanied by affects
that seem at first glance mystical, should be characterized more fully by

experimentation upon the world and oneself. Connolly states that in daily activities, or what I referred to as an affective infrastructure characterized by pluralist politics, "experimental and experiential perspectives circulate back and forth with each sometimes triggering a surprising change in the other." A rhythm of activity (the experimental) and the passive (the experiential) characterizes the general form of practices that are constitutive of such a tactics of plural politics. He goes on to state that "we must become involved in experimental micropolitics on a variety of fronts" (37) that "cultivate subliminal experiences of vitality further even as we work to diminish the risks that accompany acting recklessly on its fruits" (137). He calls for such experimentation to constitute not simply an individual ethos, but a community based in mutual becoming, or in other words, a plural ecology of practice. Thus, embracing a world of becoming leads to a plural politics based on practices that lead to affects of joyful movement and love based in the new, and not simply repeated iterations of the same circumscribed creativity and resentments of the evangelical-Christian resonance machine.

This articulation of a politics of plural becoming depends upon a gratitude toward the world that opens its practitioners to the flowing, contingent, and emergent affective resonances that are produced through the immanent vitality of the world and all of the bodies, both human and nonhuman, that constitute it. As is, hopefully, clear, such a politics embodies many of the themes revolving around the recent spate of work concerning the politics of affect. Certainly, one of the main similarities is the focus on how sensing the promise of the vital affects inherent within one's situation has the potential to break us out of the rigid confines of the everyday life of capitalist perception, whether it be characterized as cruel optimism, reification, or alienation. Connolly describes such a politics taking the form of the "experimental and experiential," a characterization reminiscent of the "laboratory of insurrentionary imagination" I invoked earlier, requiring attitudes of both activity and reception, or in other words, love and depression. He calls for engaging in "micropractices of the everyday" that mobilize affects that have the power to replace passionate resentment with passionate becoming—a plural, democratic, and common ethos that appreciates the uniqueness of others and how encounters with such uniqueness might lead to unexpectedly welcome paths of personal and collective development.

What remains most provocative in relation to my argument concerning this politics of plural becoming is the possibility of linking it to the political potentials inherent within salvage. Remember, a broken environment in which one salvages is an environment of heightened, vibrant contingency—one must salvage a landscape (remembering that landscape is simply another word for environment of situation) when the action within it does not result in expected outcomes. A broken landscape is not simply depleted of resources, but instead is broken in terms of the way we encounter it. The relationships inherent within a broken ecology are unknown to us because they are characterized by more contingency than we are used to—the constituents of the situation relate and develop with irregular rhythms and unknown trajectories. And even if we come into contact with a broken ecology, so much of everyday life in capitalism is bathed in affects of cruel optimism, alienation, reification, and control that undermine our perception of the potentialities lying within them. Yet it is because of this contingency that broken landscapes can call on those who exist within them to develop techniques to reconcile themselves to the ruin around them that can overcome capitalist affects, and thus offer them the opportunity to become something else in the midst of that ruin. Thus, salvage can encourage "gratitude," as Connolly might term it, for a broken world—the thankful, unexpected finds of salvaging that come from the necessary acute sensitivities to the potentialities inherent in the broken landscapes left by global capitalism. To be a successful salvager, one must truly have gratitude for the world, a gratitude that entails closely attending to the surrounding environment as it is, for it constitutes the only materials from which one can rely upon one's sustenance.

This understanding of gratitude, which I am interpreting as a sensitivity to and appreciation for the affects that surround us, can be linked with other affective interpretations of the concepts Connolly uses to explain becoming. For example, when Connolly invokes "those protean moments when we are hit by surprising events and movements that throw aspects of our previous projections into disarray" as the situations that prompt generosity, it is clear that this statement mirrors the descriptions of the shimmer and vibrancy produced through the affects that accompany experiences of precarity. Furthermore, Connolly explicitly recommends that those interested in fostering an ethic of plural becoming "cultivate subliminal experiences of vitality" using language, especially that of vitality, that many of the theorists of affect invoke. Finally, when Connolly recommends cultivating the "public virtue of critical responsiveness," while this certainly means this virtue involves responding to others, in light of the similarity of both his language and conceptual framework to the theorists of affect, this responsiveness can also fruitfully be interpreted as a responsiveness to the "vital" affects produced from situations of "disarray." Although Connolly does not specifically use the term *affect*, he does frequently emphasize the importance of resonance, and thus he can be grouped with these theorists, and thus be used to tease out some of the implicit consequences and implications of their "politics of everyday life."

Even though I argue that Connolly's plural politics of becoming constitutes the most fully developed political translation of the recent concern with affect and politics, and despite the fact that the politics of becoming can be interpreted as particularly congruent with salvage, this does not mean that questions do not remain concerning the actual practice of such a politics. Connolly calls upon those who would engage in a politics of becoming to undertake micropractices that might cultivate a sensitivity to the vitality and potentials within the world that might lead to gratitude, as opposed to resentment of that vitality. But although Connolly presents long lists of the areas of life where such an ethos of pluralization should be cultivated, he does not describe the experience of actual activities that might constitute such ecologies of practice. Therefore, many questions remain for a full articulation of a political theory of salvage. For example, how might the dynamic between love and depression, activity and passivity, necessary for such becoming translate into particular styles of practice? Furthermore, I have identified many affinities between the politics of becoming and the plasticity with which I earlier characterized practices of salvage.

But questions remain concerning how becoming and salvage might lead to politics such as in the examples I presented in chapter 1, such as occupation, squats, and informal communities. Are all salvaged landscapes equally promising for the practices of a politics of becoming? Furthermore, I have identified how theorists such as Nussbaum, Hardt and Negri, Berlant, and Sedgwick suggest that undergoing a process characterized by affects that alternate between those of "love" and "depression" might counteract the affective infrastructures of capitalism. But how might such a rhythm be sustained and encouraged, and cultivated and propagated. If these affects constitute the sensed core of the "becoming" described by Connolly, how can they be translated into a political program that can be communicated to others, that can be used as a tool for organizers and activists? If a salvage/becoming politics of the everyday involves the experience of alternating affects, perhaps prompted by spaces that encourage these affects, what everyday practices and environments might lead people to both endure, and even want the experience of such affects? And how might this rhythm play a role in salvage? Also, one might ask for a more detailed account of the particular spaces that encourage becoming and the attributes of these spaces. Finally, after equating salvage with the politics of becoming, one might ask, What specific political goals and even policies might accompany such a politics? How might one design ruined spaces that encourage the types of encounters leading to such attitudes? It is to questions such as this that I now turn.

Chapter 3

The Craft of Salvage

Introduction

I began by claiming that political salvage constitutes a craft of the poor and thus remains quite distinct from the contemporary trend of refurbishment so often portrayed in reality television and seen in gentrifying neighborhoods. Political salvage as a craft of the poor represents not salvage as an aesthetic choice but instead as a survival tactic employed by those forced to exist in ruined landscapes. As I previously noted, I take the term *craft of the poor* from Stavros Stavrides, who introduces the term in his study of poor urban dwellers who form communities in marginalized neighborhoods. He contextualize his discussion of these crafts within the larger discourse of what the calls the "tactics of the powerless" employed by those who are displaced by lack of steady work, shelter, and other sustenance. He describes that

> [t]hese crafts of the poor have deeply influenced the practices of communities of movement. People have carried into their movement this collective wisdom and this ability to improvise by making use of what is available. This inventiveness is transmitted by . . . tacit knowledge which implicitly molds models of action and patterns of practice (building crafts focused on *"bricolage,"* recycling etc.). (Stavrides 2016, 126)

While Stavrides's identification of "recycling" and building crafts focused on "bricolage" clearly invokes salvage, he does not expand upon how such crafts might constitute "tactics" that might contribute to either resistance or any greater politics. Furthermore, by referring to salvage activities as crafts, he begs the question of how such activities, which are usually understood as mere improvised activities undertaken without thought or foresight, might be equated to the activity of craftworkers who cultivate their craft through long periods of practice and apprenticeship. Stavrides's brief equation of salvage activity with craft is further complicated by his claim that the practices of "communities of movement" influence such crafts. Craftworkers, ensconced in their workshops and following long-honed traditions, seem to embody the antithesis of communities that must move and adapt. Thus, naming salvage as a "craft" raises many provocative yet difficult questions and seems to obscure as much as it clarifies.

I want to argue that interpreting salvage as a craft can not only help to understand how individuals and communities undertake this task, but, more importantly, sheds light on how the political potentials of salvage might be transformed into actualities. As I have argued, vulnerable and disempowered populations increasingly find themselves surrounded by the debris-strewn landscapes produced by neoliberal capitalism, so that they are increasingly enveloped by the contingent effects resulting from their interactions with such ruined landscapes. Yet the question remains of how salvagers capitalize on such affective potentialities (love, depression, becoming) as they experience during their political and nonpolitical struggles. Simply stating that one should adopt a particular attitude or pay more attention to the ineffable affects they experience in their daily lives offers little help—especially due to the fact that so many institutions, cultural norms, and expressions of power seek to bolster the reification, alienation, and commodification that I claim salvage might overcome. In other words, if salvage increasingly constitutes a component of radical political practice, the question presents itself: What particular practices constitute salvage? The acknowledgment that salvage can be defined as an activity of scavenging discarded materials and using them to either build or repair useful items does not highlight the actions that might hone the skills necessary to undertake this practice, particularly as I have interpreted it. Such a deep, phenomenological articulation of the practice of salvage would have to focus on the affective skills of perception, felt deep within the body, that capitalizes upon the sensed potentialities emphasized by so many of the salvage theorists I discussed. It would have to describe a form of production where practitioners are both led by the materials they use while actively attempting to impose form, direction, and intention upon their creations. Finally, this description would have to explore the role of the relationships that form during salvage and thus articulate, if not rules, norms of common behavior that would encourage collaboration while not imposing group conformity.

It is through interpreting salvage as a craft that I answer such questions concerning the practice of political salvage. In particular, Richard Sennett, in his *The Craftsman* and *Together*, presents an understanding of craftwork comprised of habits and practices quite similar to the politics of becoming that I claim are the normative core of salvage. Deleuze also presents an account of nomad artisans engaging in salvage that can also help conceptualize what a more political understanding might resemble. These accounts portray an activity combining the utilitarianism of *techne* and the creativity of *poesis* resulting in a hybrid, which James Scott refers to as *metis*—a "peasant" form of construction based in informal rituals, where goals and aspirations constantly change due to the demands and limitations of the environment. Furthermore, as discussed in its original ancient Greek context, *metis* possesses even richer implications for my interpretation of political salvage in that it was often invoked to describe the cunning displayed by tricksters and the guile displayed by the weak to defeat the strong. Thus, craftwork-*metis* becomes not simply a way to cope in the face of uncertainty, but a weapon that may be wielded by the disempowered. This understanding of craftwork undertaken by the poor as an example of *metis*, I will show, demonstrates how salvage can be further understood as a subversive activity well suited to augment efforts dedicated to resisting capitalism.

Today, craftwork is often thought of as production by artisans: highly trained, specialized producers of expensive items. The analyses that I use to construct my understanding focus instead on the often marginal position occupied by craftworkers. Deleuze and others emphasize the itinerant and nomadic nature of artisan existence. Sennett emphasizes that an essential component of craftworker training entailed not production of precious luxury goods but repair of everyday household tools. Furthermore, the practice of craftwork is not limited to a particular time or product, but instead should be understood as an attitude toward work and one's material. Sennett provocatively claims that the creation of modern open-sourced software (often undertaken by contingent, mobile workers) exhibits many similarities with ancient crafts such as the construction of pottery. The similarities lend credence to an understanding of craftwork not as solely the purview of those tied to exclusive guilds that zealously protect their secretive and lucrative skills. For example, he emphasizes how the genesis of Linux, the free, open sourced operating system, embodied a "public craft" that relied upon the concept of a "bazaar" model where anyone might participate. He emphasizes that, in distinction to understanding craftwork as a set of traditions rigidly controlled by artisan masters and passed down from generation to generation, Linux workers, in the mode of craftworkers, constantly updated their skills in reaction to the problems they faced. He claims that "the experimental rhythm of problem solving and problem finding makes the ancient potter and the modern programmer members of the same tribe" (Sennett 2008, 26). Thus, if one takes Sennett's view, one begins to see that thinking of types of contemporary production not commonly perceived as crafts can embody the same procedures, attitudes, and relationships as this supposedly ancient and antiquated practice. Furthermore, presenting open sourced coding as a type of craft introduces provocative linkages between craftwork, *metis*, and anticapitalist resistance. As opposed to the rigid and often exploitative conditions experienced by code-producing workers in giant tech firms, open sourced crafts embody freedom, creativity, and common ownership. Thus, even coders practice the "crafts of the poor" that can be seen in the actions of those undertaking political salvage.

I begin my argument by presenting Sennett's contention that whether one produces pottery or code the primary characteristic of craftwork lies in its particular affective attentiveness to the materials at hand. I then discuss the importance of the workshop to craftwork. I emphasize that both salvagers and craftworkers depend upon affect to guide their activities, and how particular rhythms inform their process of scavenging, repair, and creation. Next, I stress that both political salvagers and craftworkers tend to form communities characterized by autonomy, open inquiry, and reciprocity. In conclusion, I assert that salvage is a type of craftwork, and that the accounts of political salvage can be deepened through analyzing them under the guise of the thick phenomenological framework presented by the theorists of craftwork I present in this chapter. Specifically, through acknowledging that craftwork can be improved by adopting particular rituals, habits, and designing spaces that encourage a rhythm between affective perception and conscious construction, which leads to experimentation and critical becoming, I argue that envisioning a "craft" of salvage can add important details to envisioning an anticapitalist politics of becoming. Such a vision helps to clarify the possibility of constructing a model of the "rhythms of resistance" that might inform an analysis of the further radical potential of political salvage.

The Body and Craftwork

To be forced to salvage is to be forced to form one's livelihood from rubble and ruins—ruins that are chaotic, vibrant, confusing, and potentially desirable. Such debris possesses both promise and danger to the salvager, presenting questions such as, Will this piece behave as I think it will when it is under stress? And, What can I do with this thing, can I use it to plug this hole, support this wall, or break this rock? The question of how to open oneself to the effect that vibrant materials have upon us, and how salvagers' continuing interaction with rubble can be evaluated through the background texture that is produced by one's continuing interaction within it is the same question that faces craftworkers. Richard Sennett embarks upon a deep phenomenological analysis of the actual practice of crafts, grounded in the need of the craftsperson to develop what he refers to as "material consciousness." Craftspeople undertake a variety of activities—sometimes making and sometimes observing. Unlike those who work under the regime of the division of labor, "the craftsman, engaged in a continual dialog with material, does not suffer this divide" (Sennett 2008, 125). This dialog consists of the craftworker intertwining their conscious design for the item under construction with the constraints and vibrant potentialities inherent within the material at hand. Deleuze, in A Thousand Plateaus, adds a further layer to this description by claiming that "an artisan who planes follows the wood, the fibers of the wood," and that an artisan must undertake a "surrendering to the wood, then following where it leads by connecting operations, to a materiality, instead of imposing a form upon matter: what one addresses is less a matter submitted to laws than an immateriality possessing a nomos" (Deleuze and Guattari 1987, 409). Material consciousness constitutes the ability to "surrender" to the internal "nomos" or, in other words, guidelines, within matter and follow them where they may go. Invocations such as "surrendering" to the material invoke the expansive, affective descriptions of love that I introduced in the last chapter. But this consciousness is not simply passive, with Sennett stressing that material consciousness comes about through the act of interacting with materials, stating that "we become particularly interested in the things we can change" (Sennett 2008, 120). Material consciousness constitutes a surrendering to potentialities, created through transformative work, that change both the material and the person undertaking the work. It focuses attention on one's immediate environment in a way that counteracts the affective infrastructures produced by capitalism. And it can constitute the first step in embracing the contingency of salvage environments that can generate the liquid practices upon which the ethos of plural becoming is built.

Because material consciousness constitutes an activity in which craftworkers prod, pull, poke at things to stoke their perceptions of where the vibrant materiality within objects might lead, Sennett stresses that such consciousness can be cultivated. But the craftworker does not adopt such consciousness through purely cognitive processes, and instead it must be cultivated through the body. He claims that "all skills begin with bodily practices" (Sennett 2008, 10). The necessity of such a somatic grounding of skill comes from the fact that the potentialities within materials are sensed, at least initially, through the body. Sennett emphasizes that "the relational, the incomplete are physical experiences" (Sennett 2008, 44). He is very clear that sensing the relational trajectories produced by cultivating material consciousness manifests within craftworkers' bodies as much as their minds. He states, "Craftwork establishes a realm of skill beyond human verbal capacities to explain" (95). It is important to emphasize here that the skills exhibited by craftworkers are more "felt" than "known." They are located in the body through muscle memory, and are guided by affective senses produced through physical interaction with materials. Craftspeople touch, turn, knock, and bend the things they hope to use and transform to get a sense of how those things will react in different situations—how they will bend, slide, and fit into other things. The body, in effect, leaps in first, giving a provisional assessment based on the affects produced by the interactions, and although, of course, the qualities of materials can be cognitively assessed later, crafts are practiced as much with the body as with the mind.

The fact that one must "get hold" of a thing, whether a machine or simply a piece of raw material, to ascertain and sense the tendencies of its behavior in various relationships with other things, as opposed to simply reading instructions or descriptions, suggests that the skills and methods of the artisan need to be cultivated through practice. Such practice cannot follow a predetermined methodology—it consists of adapting one's own particular body to a set of unique materials, and subsequently modifying the undertakings themselves. This is why craftworkers not only acquire knowledge of their craft, but also the habits that allow them to actually practice their craft. Such subconscious interactions between bodies and their environment happen constantly (the reason we need not think about how to walk) as bodies adopt repertoires of responses that are built up over time—in other words, habits. Yet habits need not be mechanical repetitions of the same activity. Some habits are expansive, for example, one's body might react to a particular sensation by waiting to receive more sensations, as opposed to acting upon a sense. Of course, one learns a habit through repetition, but, Sennett asserts, "[R]epetition can go stale. . . . Refreshment occurs by ingraining a habit, then examining and enlarging it consciously, then ingraining it again as unconscious behavior" (Sennett 2012, 90). Craftworkers must cultivate expansive habits, because each time they construct an object they work with different materials and thus must undergo new rounds of adaptation and becoming, and not simply implement the application of a preexisting principle. The habits they must employ are those of attention, persistence, and the ability to translate vague affects into actions. These habits themselves are modified through the practice itself, and thus craftwork takes on the form of an affective dialog between craftworker and material.

More importantly for this argument, habit is the faculty, at least initially, that reacts to affect. We can never "know" an affect as we know quantitative attributes. We can never read affect as clearly as we can read an instruction manual. Often times we react to affect without even knowing it. In normal, expected experience bodily habits both perceive and react to these qualities without our even consciously knowing it. Think of how we drive a car and react to the road and other cars on the margins of our consciousness. By emphasizing the relationship of habit to affect what I want to do is to highlight that our reactions to affect are shaped by personal characteristics. Affect, while representing real relationships and their potentialities in the environment, comes to be molded by our habits. The same affect can evoke different reactions, depending on the person experiencing it, or no reaction at all if we do not possess the habits that are attuned to affect. Furthermore, by stating that habits constitute the human faculty that initially reacts to affect, I highlight the fact that the way in which an individual reacts and perceives sensation can change. Desirable habits can be cultivated, and undesirable habits can be undermined. Of course, one cannot simply choose to drop a bad habit—such a change requires practice. And by examining habit within the context of its status within craftwork we begin to think about a systematized way of sculpting habit and thus consciously modifying our reaction to affect. Finally, with such systemization we can see the beginning of a political theory, because, with an articulated, if flexible, procedure such as the method by which craftworkers cultivate the habits necessary to their activity, one can begin to see how the political ethic I claim as the normative core of salvage—that of plural becoming, might also be propagated.

Sennett emphasizes that the craftworker's qualitative sense of the dialog between themselves and their materials never results in clear and precise information concerning the best way to construct an item. In fact, he asserts that if the dialog is being undertaken to its greatest potentiality, it will lead to greater amounts of confusion. He states that "to do good work means to be curious about, to investigate, and to learn from ambiguity" (Sennett 2008, 48) and forces the craftworker to "dwell in temporary mess. Wrong moves, false starts, dead ends" (161). It is within frustration that curiosity is born. Craftspeople cultivate a response to difficulty and failure that leads them use such experience as a resource. Sennett claims craftworkers must surrender themselves to these confusing and frustrating senses and "work with resistance" (Sennett 2012, 209). Being able to sense the contours of this frustration and chaos constitutes one of the most important habits craftworkers must cultivate, according to Sennett. He states that "intuition begins with the sense that what isn't yet could be. How do we sense this? In technical craftsmanship the sense of possibility is grounded in feeling frustrated by a tool's limits or provoked by its untested possibilities" (Sennett 2008, 209–10). Thus, being aroused by working with a material, whether with one's hands or with a tool, and sensing the frustrating yet engaging affect constitutes the soil from which craftworker's curiosity grows. And such frustration can be seen as one of the "arts of failure" invoked by the curators of *Disobedient Objects* to describe the salvage practices of activists constructing their gas masks and other protest implements during their acts of resistance.

It is important to emphasize that, at least within Sennett's account, learning craftwork relies as much upon repairing malfunctioning items as creating new items. He claims that "making and repairing form a single whole" (Sennett 2008, 199) and that "dynamic repair" constitutes an activity that will change an object's form, and because of the ambiguity produced through repair one can never tell when a seeming simple repair will metamorphose into a dynamic repair. As with his expansive understanding of craftwork that encompasses the material and the nonmaterial, Sennett emphasizes that repair constitutes an attitude applicable to many realms, not simply to physical objects. He invokes Freud's work on mourning to claim that "mourning is a type of repair work." Such repair work on oneself "issues a call to return to the world, outside the worker's own emotional history . . . work promises re-engagement" (Sennett 2012, 255). This invocation of Freud ties mourning to the craft of repair. It emphasizes the indeterminate length of the procedure, in that no one can tell the exact time when mourning will cease, and perhaps it will never, just as the tinkering and repairing of an item might continue indefinitely. Both mourning and craftwork entail sitting with one's frustration and confusion, not rejecting it but truly turning toward what can be rebuilt in the "ruin" of one's life. Thus, through interpreting craftwork through the lens of repair and creation, Sennett deemphasizes the elements of perfection, attention to detail, and exclusivity that so many see as inherent within both contemporary and current artisan experience, and thus creates space for the type of "depressive" affects I discussed in the last chapter to contribute to the process of craft. To engage in craftwork in this understanding entails not only giving oneself to one's materials but also being committed to the frustrations, false starts, and failures that a true embrace of messy and broken immateriality might bring. Viewed in this light, artisanship does not produce perfection, but instead constitutes an acknowledgment of, and even admiration for, imperfection.

The flexibility and spontaneity that springs from craftwork's reliance upon the individual's ability to sense and then follow the affective clues produced through her interaction with their environment possesses one final social implication to many who have written on the nexus of artisans, craft, and social formation. Theorists of craft have also noted the unsettled, nomadic nature of craftworker's lives, with Deleuze stating that, due to the emergent potentials resulting from the affect of the artisan interacting with vibrant materials

> artisans are obliged to follow in another way as well, in other words to go find the wood where it lies and to find the wood with the right kind of fibers. Otherwise they must have it brought to them; it is only because merchants take care of one segment of the journey in reverse that the artisans can

> avoid making the trip themselves. But artisans are complete only if they are also prospectors; and the organization that separates prospectors, merchants, and artisans already mutilates artisans in order to make workers of them. We will therefore define the artisan as one who is determined in such a way as to follow a flow of matter, *a machinic phylum*. The artisan is the itinerant, the ambulant. To follow the flow of matter is to itinerate, to ambulate. (Deleuze and Guattari 1987, 409)

The itinerance of metal workers, Deleuze claims, constitutes a particularly defining aspect of the metallurgic crafts. Furthermore, his claim that to be a metalworker entails "following the flow of matter" links the necessity of affect-based craft to a mobile and nomadic lifestyle. He claims that both the nature of minerals and ores as particularly amenable to transformation through smelting and molding, and the widespread geographic location of these materials, impel particularly strong itinerant characteristics upon their work. He states "artisans-metallurgists are itinerant because they follow the matter flow of the subsoil" (Deleuze and Guattari 1987, 412). This necessity to follow the pockets of minerals they use to craft their wares leads them to change the nature of their very dwellings. He goes on to argue that "smiths are ambulant, itinerant. Particularity important in this respect is the way in which smiths live. . . . [S]miths may have a tent, they may have a house, they inhabit them in a manner of an 'ore bed,' like metal itself in the manner of a cave or a hole a hut half or all underground" (413). Thus, their homes follow their search for materials. They settle and then they move and thus transform their own understandings of themselves and their craft as they encounter new techniques and craftworkers. Sennett notes a similar phenomenon, especially in terms of the metalurgic crafts when he cites the Islamic philosopher and sociologist Ibn Khaldun. He reports that the goldsmiths seemed to him like Berbers, made strong by travel and mobility. Sedentary guilds, by contrast appeared to him inert and "corrupt." The good master, in his words, "presided over a traveling house" (Sennett 2008, 59). Thus, despite the stereotype of an artisan's existence as highly structured and rather privileged as compared to "poor" unskilled workers, in fact, many artisans lived precarious lives—following their materials and their markets wherever they might lead.

Deleuze's linkage of artisans and nomads manifests itself in another form, particularly relevant to my discussion of salvage. Remember, the nomadic/artisan movement that undermines rigid political borders comes about due to the necessity of "following the matter flow of the subsoil" which necessitates that artisans act as "prospectors." This searching closely resembles the activity of the foragers of matsutake mushrooms described by Tsing and the scavengers Millar describes searching for plastic in the Rio landfills. Just as nomadic metallurgists must scour the land to find hidden clues that indicate the presence of precious metals, mushroom foragers must "look for the lines of mushroom lives" hidden under the topsoil. Whether a craftworker needs, wood, metals, trash, being able to forage for the proper raw material forces them to move across a landscape. The difference between artisan nomads as described by Deleuze and salvage craftworkers is simply that the latter must move across landscapes that are more intensely damaged and contingent than others. Even salvagers such as those described by Millar at the landfill in Rio de Janeiro, who foraged in a single place, eventually were displaced, forcing them into new, unknown environments.

The larger implication is that artisans and salvagers are confronted with strong incentives to move due to the very nature of their activity—and thus their existence challenges geographical boundaries and static formations of community and political membership. Deleuze notes that "we know of the problems States have always had with journeymen's associations, or *compagnonnages*, the nomadic or itinerant bodies of the type formed by masons, carpenters, smiths" (Deleuze and Guattari 1987, 368). He goes on to claim that "if the State always finds it necessary to repress the nomad and minor sciences, if it opposes vague essences and the operative geometry of the trait, it does not because the content of the sciences is inexact or imperfect, or because of their magic or initiatory character, but because they imply a division of labor opposed to the norms of the State" (ibid.). The reason that these minor sciences oppose the norms of the state lies particularly in their potential for subversive becoming. Deleuze defines the destructive power of such endeavors precisely within their tendency toward movement and emergent becoming, claiming, "There are itinerant, ambulant sciences that consist in following a flow in a pectoral field across which singularities are scatted like so many accidents (problems). For example why is primitive metallurgy necessarily an ambulant science that confers upon smiths a quasi-nomadic status? This is only true to the extent that ambulant procedures and process are necessarily tied to a striated spacealways formalized by royal science—which deprives them of their model, submits them to its own model"

(Deleuze and Guattari, 1987, 372–73).[1] The minor, nomadic sciences, to Deleuze, constitute reactions to the poverty and exclusion of their practitioners, as they are forced to cobble together their own sustenance without the aid of others. Yet it is this very poverty that gives them their critical potentiality. He states, "The alleged poverty is in fact a restriction of constants and the overload an extension of variations functioning to deploy a continuum sweeping up all the components. The poverty is not a lack but a void or ellipsis allowing one to sidestep a constant instead of tackling it head on, or to approach it from above or below instead of positioning oneself within it" (104). Such an understanding of poverty as a position denormativizes the concept and suggests the existence of both inhibitions and opportunities for those who occupy it. The "minor sciences," while not a panacea for poverty, do provide new pathways for both living in such circumstances and, perhaps, transcending them. Most importantly for my argument, though, is the supposition that the poor develop their own methods, habits, and even epistemologies. This insight points to elective affinities between the concepts of "craft of the poor" and "minor sciences" and how both may be used to understand salvage.

Lest it be thought that nomadism constitutes an activity confined to the past that has been eliminated due to the rise of the state and its geographic controls, Ashley Dawson suggests that nomadism can be seen as not simply an increasingly prevalent phenomenon in contemporary society, but also a harbinger of radical political change. Whereas most see the solution to the problem of climate refugee status as protecting lands vulnerable to inundation by rising seas, or providing permanent homes to the displaced, Dawson sees both of these solutions as unrealistic. She sees the amount of resources needed to protect land from rising seas as so great that they will be expended only on those with political influ-ence, and finding new "safe" homes for the displaced, especially in areas vulnerable to rising sea levels, constitutes only a temporary solution at best due to the unpredictability of where climate disasters might occur. She instead recommends that the most effective and just perspective to take in light of the unavoidability of destruction caused by climate change would be to adopt the perspective of "liquid urbanism." By this term we mean that the city, and human habitations in general, should not be thought of as a fortress to be defended from the onslaught of rising waters and other extreme weather events, but instead as possessing flexible, plastic borders and structures as much as possible, to facilitate frequent movements of population and infrastructure. She states that liquid urbanism is a "conception of a city that is integrated with the delta . . . here fluid dynamics structures the city . . . and hydrological issues serve as starting points and frameworks for future urban planning and design decisions" (Dawson 2017, 277). Such a fluid urban planning strategy would facilitate the just and egalitarian relocation and modification of communities when they are hit with climate catastrophe. Fundamental to such implementation of a strategy of liquid urbanism would be the modification of the entire geography of the city in reaction to necessary climate recalibration: both the poor whose neighborhoods are directly affected and the rich and business communities whose locations are better protected from rising waters would be subject to rethinking. Thus, nomadism, in the sense of both communities moving, but also being modified to possess the "smoothness" that facilitates such nomadism, would become part of urban design strategy. And as I have demonstrated previously, nomadism, at least as conceptualized by Deleuze, with its links to metallurgy and other crafts indicative of *metis*, encourages the plasticity I have characterized as fundamental to plural becoming. Perhaps more fundamental to my argument, though, than this theoretical linkage is the actual salvage practice undertaken by contemporary "nomads" displaced by either climatic or economic devastation. As poor communities move, build, and defend what they have built, they often are forced to rebuild with materials that others deem useless. And, as even previously affluent communities become increasingly impoverished when they suffer climate catastrophes and are forced into nomadism, they increasingly rely upon salvage to maintain themselves and their communities.

Thinking of salvage as a nomadic, minor craft in a Deleuzian mode further highlights its critical and political potential. Embracing the characteristics of salvage highlighted by Deleuze through these concepts also should lead to further inquiry into the specific attributes of how such minor sciences can be further strengthened. For while Deleuze might bristle at the possibility of "formalizing" such minor sciences, it is clear that attempting to apply Sennett's understanding of the flexibility of craft and its habits would not undermine Deleuze's conception. Minor sciences can be both flexible and regularized, spontaneous and cultivated. While Sennett's understanding cannot be legitimately translated as a model for a traditional organization such as a political party, it does lend guidelines for regularization and transmission to what in Deleuze's account seems to be a somewhat haphazard operation. Self-organization does not necessarily mean random, and the rituals and principles contained in Sennett's account of craft point toward methods for strengthening and perpetuating the minor sciences—especially salvage when it is conceptualized using Deleuze's thought.

To truly shift perception of artisanship as an activity undertaken by exclusive brotherhoods creating precious works of luxury goods in a way that creates distance between the heterodox yet mostly unpolitical understanding presented by Sennett, I want to compare the understanding of craftwork I have presented thus far to the account of peasant *metis* given by James Scott in his *Seeing Like a State*. I also want to introduce this concept because it creates a stronger linkage between the concepts of craftwork and salvage. To begin, in contrast to creative *poesis* and purely reproductive *techne*, Scott claims that most peasants undertake production best characterized by common sense experience or knack. He claims that activities that entail "adapting to capricious physical environments, the acquired knowledge of how to fly a kite, fish, shear a sheep, drive a car, ride a bicycle" (Scott 1999, 313) require a sense of one's vibrant, "capricious" environment upon one's activities. Such a "feel" for affect constitutes one of the primary skills of what the ancient Greeks described as *metis*, and it is only learned through repeated bodily activity. He goes on to explicitly tie *metis* through craftwork by stating, "No wonder that most crafts and trades requiring a touch of feel for implements and materials have traditionally been taught by long apprenticeships to master craftsmen" (314).[2] It is an apprenticeship in discerning the shimmer of the vibrant contingent matter that surrounds the peasant, in developing the *metis* of sensing contingent affects.

Lest one be led to believe that such peasant skills or "knacks" constitute skills appropriate only to traditional societies, and thus inappropriate to contemporary, complex, and changing environments Scott contends that "the context of *metis* is characteristic of situations which are transient, shifting, disconcerting and ambiguous, situations which do not lend themselves to precise measurement, exact calculation or rigorous logic" (Scott 1999, 320). Thus, *metis* constitutes an activity relevant to the contemporary, liquid world of neoliberal capitalism—especially the poor, who are most likely to live in in the environments most subject to destruction. Scott explicitly casts *metis* as a craft of the poor, stating, "[P]overty or marginal economic status . . . is itself, I would argue, a powerful impetus to careful observation and experimentation," and, "The innovation of metis will typically represent a recombination (*bricolage*, to use Lévi-Strauss's term) of existing elements" (324). Remember, bricolage constitutes a pattern I have previously identified as characteristic of salvage environments constructed by the poor. Scott's presentation of *metis* as a type of craft, explicitly a craft of the poor, constitutes a forced attention to the affects that changing, volatile environments have upon their action and links it to both Sennett's and Deleuze's accounts. Furthermore, that such attention manifests itself as a knack or a sense of these affects, ties *metis* to the centrality of affect to craftwork, as in the previous accounts. In Scott's understanding of *metis* it becomes clear that craftwork constitutes a form of activity with particular potential to use the confusing and frustrating affects produced through life surrounded by salvaged environments and not to simply despair in their rubble.

Metis has also been seen as a skill employed by all successful politicians. Such effective political actors engage in "octopus"-like deception and resourcefulness. In this interpretation, "The politician taking on the appearance of the octopus . . . involves not only possessing the logos of the octopus but also proving himself capable of adapting to the most baffling of situations, of assuming as many faces as there are social categories and types of men in the city, of inventing the thousand ploys which will make his actions effective in this most varied of circumstances (Detienne and Vernant 1991, 39–40). *Metis*-based trickery surprises not only the opponent, but also the perpetrator of the trick itself in that the performance of good *metis* requires guesses and estimations that might lead to surprising outcomes. That the mutant god Chthulu invoked by Sedgwick also possesses an octopus head constitutes a fascinating link between the two concepts. Thus, *metis* can be seen as a "weapon of the weak"[3] particularly suitable to a life surrounded by refuse where one must use cunning and seemingly otherworldly observation. It demonstrates that the affect so important in the activity of skilled artisans is the same as that used by those refurbishing squats, constructing gas masks, and repairing the buildings, streets, and infrastructure of informal communities.[4]

Those employing *metis* undergo self-transformation reminiscent of Connolly's understanding of becoming, and must constantly contend with "fluid changing realities." And because the reality to which *metis* is best suited is that of contingency, the wielder of such skill must also become "more supple and more polymorphic" than the unknown situation or opponent (Detienne and Vernant 1991, 27) and display this important skill. To discern the shifting future one must be able to develop a shifting sense. Homer calls *metis* "not one, not unified but multiple and diverse . . . when taught by Athena and Hephaestus, the deities of *metis*, the artist also possesses an art of many facets." When this art is practiced it must be particularly attuned to *poikilos*, the "sheen of a material or the glittering of a weapon. This many-colored sheen, or complex of appearances, produces an effect of iridescent, shimmering and interplay of reflection which the Greeks perceived as the ceaseless vibrations of light" (Detienne and Vernant 1991, 18). This reference to the "shimmer" that is displayed by shifting contingency hearkens to the "shimmer" invoked by Bennett and others when discussing the vibrant materiality she began to perceive through close observation of the Baltimore trash heap. The Greeks frequently linked *metis* to a particular type of perception able to notice what is moving, shifting, contingent, and becoming. Although they could not cast this ability specifically in terms of affect, it is far from inappropriate to equate the ability of the person deftly employing *metis* to discern the "shimmer" of a situation with the shimmering, resonant affects cited by Bennett and the other theorists of the new materialism. In both sorts of *metis*, the skill and the situation are shifting and thus display this shimmer. "Why does *metis* appear thus and multiple, canny, colored shifting, because it's field of application is the world of moment, of multiplicity and ambiguity . . . in order to seize upon the fleeting *kairos* [right time to act] *metis* had to make itself even swifter than the latter" (Detienne and Vernant 1991, 20). Just as affect suggests the path of development within an otherwise confusing and shifting situation, those employing *metis* "must be able to look and foresee a greater or lesser section of the future" (27). Thus, peasant craftworkers, in their cunning, display what must seem like trickery, to pull victory from the jaws of what seems to be sure defeat. They use their sense of what to others seems invisible to predict a likely future. They transform themselves to conform to their transforming situation, and thus remain powerful despite that fact that they are weak.

With my invocation of *metis* as an evocative description of the relationship of affect to craft I have attempted to both highlight an important yet underappreciated aspect of this activity and transform common understandings of those who undertake it. Sennett's description of the activity of craftwork, while undermining the stereotype of the artisan as an elite laborer tied to a static tradition, does not explicitly refer to the act of salvage nor cast artisan labor as a "craft of the poor." This understanding of *metis*, as expressed through both Scott's work and the concrete ancient Greek cultural context of its origin, provides such a linkage. The peasant, the trickster, the octopus who dwells in the shadows, these are figures easily imagined as dwelling within a trash heap, using what to others seems only to be a broken stick as a lethal weapon.

But *metis* does not only possess a similarity to salvage in that it constitutes a "craft of the poor." At a deeper level, *metis* embodies the same core activity with which I identified salvage, the plasticity necessary to live within environments of contingency. The peasant's undertaking of a process of "touch and feel" that produces the knack of *metis* is simply another way of describing how a craftworker cultivates "material consciousness." Both of these activities encapsulate the skills possessed by salvagers, who must "touch and feel" the broken landscape around them to cultivate a "material consciousness" that suggests possibilities for scavenging and repair. More importantly, introducing the concept of *metis* demonstrates that the skills involved in salvage are just that, skills that might possibly be cultivated and improved through practice. To say that the act of salvage is a manifestation of *metis* allows one to identify some the core abilities possessed, even unconsciously, by those who practice it, and furthermore to imagine how one might intensify the potency of such "knacks" and the results of such improvements. Although, traditionally, those who undertake *metis* do not learn from an instruction book, and thus the practice seems resistant to systematization, identifying this "minor science's" primary characteristics and abilities can help to envision how one might improve its practice. Interpreting salvage as a craft that employs *metis* not only leads to further analytic clarity, but also suggests how salvage might be employed as part of new understandings of political action. Gaining the habits of *metis* is also a process of gaining the habits of becoming. By possessing such habits, the plasticity indicative of salvage practice can be intensified, as the affects one experiences moving through ruined landscapes become more easily noticed and followed. Possessing such habits constitutes a powerful enabling circumstance that one might value and adopt the political ethos of becoming when salvaging ruined landscapes.

The Rhythms of Resistance

The dialog between active creation and affective reception indicative of craftwork constitutes the general form of building the material consciousness that arouses the creative becoming experienced by craftworkers. But casting craftwork as possessing two distinct modes of activity that produce two distinct modes of affect does not actually reveal how the worker combines these two modes. I want to now describe how craftworkers engage in not simply rhythmic production but also rhythmic becoming. They not only go back and forth between observation and receptivity of the sensed affect and also a rhythm of development within themselves. This observation lies at the core of Sennett's account, and leads him to claim that "there is a rhythm which governs the development of human skills" (Sennett 2012, 200) comprised of ingraining habits, questioning habits, and then re-ingraining them within the body. This focus on the importance of rhythm to the development of habits and potentialities within the human body can also be seen in performance studies and human geography. Just as a scavenger experiments with the possibilities of her body moving within her broken, ruined physical and social environment, a craftworker experiments with her body in the particular gripping of a tool, how to bend, press or stretch a particular piece of metal without breaking it, and how to stretch her own body when trying to insert a particular piece of material into a particular hole. As these different rhythms, some slow, some fast, some chaotic, some regular, begin to reveal the possibilities within a particular piece of material, new bodily habits emerge to address how to use a tool or perform a particular action with a particular thing. Craftworkers sense how different rhythms produce different effects upon their materials and themselves, experimenting in a way not guided by an image of what they intend to make, but trying different rhythms and sensing how they affect the developmental trajectories of their materials and their own bodies. They undergo alternating patterns of activities productive of expansive love and depressive withdrawal. And thus understanding how craft is enacted through rhythmic patterns of activity that produce rhythmic experienced affects constitutes an important step in understanding salvage as a craft of the poor.

Deleuze's works synthesizes these more empirical observations concerning rhythm and craft into a theory of the importance of rhythm to becoming. To begin, Deleuze makes it clear that rhythm does not entail mere repetition of the same. He differentiates between the two through his identification of milieu as the organizing form of experience. Human experience can usually be characterized by distinct groups or styles of actions that can be identified as distinct milieus. Deleuze emphasizes that rhythm occurs only between changing milieus, not through simple repetition. He argues that "there is rhythm whenever there is a transcoded passage from one milieu to another, a communication of milieus coordination between heterogeneous space-times" (Deleuze and Guattari 1987, 313) Such passages between milieus represent the basic form that all development (material or psychic) takes, with Deleuze claiming, "When a body combines some of its own distinctive points with those of wave it espouses the principle of repetition which is no longer that of the same but involves the other, involves difference. . . . [T]o learn is indeed to constitute the space of an encounter with signs in which the distinct points renew themselves in each other" (Deleuze 1995, 23). The "wave" Deleuze refers to here is the milieu, or general pattern of the actions, not the singular movement or phenomenon. He goes on to state that "to change milieus, taking them as you find them such, is a rhythm. . . . A milieu does not in fact exist by virtue of a periodic repletion, but one whose only effect is to produced difference by which the milieu passes into another milieu. It is the difference that is rhythmic; not the repetition that produces it" (Deleuze and Guattari 1987, 314). In passages such as this one can see that Deleuze asserts that rhythm is a combination of the seemingly dichotomous difference and repetition: when patterns representing different milieus repeat, they form larger chorus-like territories that slowly develop and transform themselves. Thus, ironically, creativity comes from patterns of the same.

Rhythm constitutes such an important part of artisan craft because the juxtapositions it establishes between different bodily movements, modes of perception, materials, actions, and relationships produce affects that the craftworker relies upon to guide her construction. "Surrendering" oneself to one's material, especially when attempting to work with the unknown qualities of novel, disorganized, or volatile material, acts as a powerful strategy when one's previous knowledge fails to produce expected outcomes. When discussing the efficacy of rhythm to becoming in the work of Deleuze, Brian Massumi discusses the important of "non-sensuous similarity" in the transformation and development of bodies. He claims that enacting repeated alternations between movements and environments "brings differences together, cutting across world lines and identities conserved along them. This transversal linkage between world lines combines non local linkages" (Massumi 2013, 108). These transversal, or oblique, strange, and potentially transformative linkages form what he calls "activation contours" that form even stranger, less expected, and potentially transformative linkages. Massumi goes on to posit that the "whole concept of the activation contour is that the same contour can be found across modes in the rhythm of seeing, of touching, of hearing. Rhythm is admodal, it is the abstract shape of the event as it happens across whatever modes it happens with" (Massumi 2013, 125). John Protevi makes a similar point concerning the transformative power of rhythm due to its ability to tie together nonsimilar actions and codes in a process of spatial and temporal similarity. He states, "[R]hythm is critical, it ties together critical movements. Critical here means a threshold in a differential relation, a singularity in the link . . . of change of a living system in its ecological niche" (Protevi 2010). Then, when linkages of logic, meaning, and substance break down, rhythm can act as the form that creates ties between differences that reveal the novel linkages that not only connect what seemed to be disparate and unlinkable but the transversal potentialities that undermine traditional ways of doing and knowing.

It is important to note that moments of nonsensuous similarity produce tendencies that lead to the perception of multiple possibilities. Yet it is by undertaking this difficult process that creativity occurs. Sennett describes how intuitive leaps occur by establishing "adjacency" between two objects, which causes surprising reactions within oneself. He describes that "although you were preparing for it you didn't know in advance precisely what you would make of the close comparison . . . you begin dredging up tacit knowledge into consciousness to do the comparing—and you are surprised" (Sennett 2008, 210). Similarly, Manning and Massumi talk of how engaging in rhythmic becoming produces a similar experience of enthusiasm with its accompanying unique affective sense. They state, "[E]ven moments of confusion or discord are attunements, in that they intensely re cue the participant to what is happening" (Manning and Massumi 2014, 118). This "re cuing," or reorientation, leads to paths of exploration not available before, and thus thrusts the body's exploratory movements forward in ways that revivify and thrust forward rhythmic development even after frustration and incoherence have seemly stymied progress. This pushing forward, or loving affect, derives from the desire for harmony and fusion, no matter the exact form of this fusion. Its rhythmic affects are experienced not as regular rhythms, but as "polyphony" where crosscutting patterns must be closely attended to in hopes of discerning the individual threads that constitute the confused jumble of immediate experience. Consequently, the rhythmic affects established by the habitual rhythmic procedures sustain the process of temporarily fusing disparate elements of one's experience to each other so that one can sense the new affects these juxtapositions create, even when frustration and confusion create difficulties in sustaining this process.

One way that such rhythmic habits can be cultivated is through undertaking rituals that support this process. Sennett argues that rituals, are not only adaptive and plastic, but are the foundation of a craft-worker's becoming. Remember, craftwork, especially when understood as *metis*, often comes about through dealing with unknown materials and indeterminate situations. In order to commence the process of rhythmic alternation between sensing affect, acting upon the hunches of these senses, observing the affect that one's intervention produces within the material and within oneself and one's plan for construction, artisans adopt rituals of action. They begin with rhythmic rituals that structure their initial interventions, because, when the actual path of construction is not clear, due to the hidden potentialities of one's material, the process of ritual provides a formal starting point for one's actions, which, while previously known, opens up the craftworker to the unique qualities of the process of producing that unique item. Sennett states that those who study ritual "emphasize this adaptive process; rather than static, ritual is continually evolving form within" (Sennett 2012, 88). Furthermore, he argues that the core of craft ritual is not its substance or its ties to arcane practices but instead its form. He describes that "rituals depend of repetition for their intensity. We usually equate repetition with routine, going over something again and again seeming to dull our senses . . . repetition can take another course. Playing a passage again and again can make us con-centrate ever more on its specifics, and the value of the sounds words or bodily movements become deeply ingrained" (Sennett 2012, 90). While such a focus on the specifics of a movement (and how that movement produces an affect when interacting with a substance) might seem to turn the person who performs the ritual inward in an attempt to replicate the smallest bodily movements, Sennett states that such attention can play a role in transforming actions and enlivening them. He describes how "repetitions have to follow a certain course in order to stay fresh. Refreshment occurs by ingraining a habit, then examining and enlarging it consciously, then ingraining it again as unconscious behavior" (ibid). And such ritual transformation does not remain at the level of inarticulate sense leading to somatic reactions. He observes that "rituals . . . transform objects, bodily moments or bland words into symbols," and goes on to describe how rituals contain both symbols of representation that recreate meanings and evocations that inspire new meanings, and that

> rituals draw on both kinds of symbols, but sort them out through the rhythm of practice. Directions are first given us, which we ingrain as habit; these directions dissolve into evocations we try to use more consciously; the pursuit is not endless; we recover our sense of direction in an enriched habit, re-ingrained as tacit behavior. In rituals, objects and bodily gestures, no less than language pass through the transforming process becoming dense in meaning. (Sennett 2012, 91)

Bodily ritual, according to this account, constitutes the initiation of a process of becoming involving object, symbols, and the body itself. The process of rhythmically intertwining these different aspects of experience creates new combinations and relationships between them, resulting in "enriched" habits and "reimagined" objects. Rituals help to sustain and even restart the difficult, failure-strewn process of craft, and can thus be seen as a possible aid to the difficult, failure-strewn process of salvage. Furthermore, although rituals might constitute a consistent starting point for craftworkers, their propensity to scaffold and support rhythmic becoming means that they result in surprising juxtapositions of materials and activities as aspects of the larger process of construction. Thus, rituals can lead to surprising outcomes, and encourage both plasticity and the ethos of becoming.

What remains most provocative concerning these multiple dissertations on the importance of rhythm to both craftwork, and specifically its properties of becoming, is that such references create an even stronger conceptual bond between this discussion and salvage. When Tsing claimed that searching for mushrooms in damaged environments "has a rhythm both impassioned and still" (Tsing 2015, 4), perhaps unknowingly she was invoking a wide literature involving both craft and becoming. Her description of a rhythm "impassioned and still" possesses provocative similarities to the rhythm of love and depression I discussed earlier. In her description of the rhythm of mushroom pickers she goes on to state that the passion that mushroom pickers feel is frequently accompanied by periods of passive observation. She claims that "no one can find a mushroom by hurrying through the forest: 'slow down,' I was constantly advised. . . . Calm but fevered impassioned but still: the picker rhythm condenses this tension in poised alertness"(242). Notice that the juxtaposition of activities accompanied by these two qualities ends in alertness—a greater propensity to notice the subtle and unique qualities of the environment. Without the combination of each distinct phase, searching would either halt in depressive stillness or spin off in unproductive, uncontrollable love, like passionate diversions. She refers to the multiple, differential rhythms experienced by salvagers as "polyphonic rhythms" and explains that "polyphony is music in which autonomous melodies intertwine" (23). She goes on to state, "When I first learned of polyphony it was a revelation in listening, I was forced to pick out separate simultaneous melodies and listen to the moments of harmony and the dissonance they created together" (24). Such an account of the "polyphonic rhythms" that involve both "impassioned but still" rhythms and their attendant affects possesses many similarities to the above account. Most importantly to my argument, both Tsing and the other theorists of rhythm have demonstrate the ties between creativity and rhythm, especially when such creativity springs from contingent, unpredictable situations.

Furthermore, when Tsing claims that "thinking through salvage rhythms changes our vision. Industrial work no longer charts the future . . . livelihoods are various, cobbled together and often temporary" (Tsing et al. 2017, 133) she stresses how salvage craft often involves activities separated by the capitalist division of labor, and thus subtly suggests critical political potentialities latent within the rhythms of salvage. Yet this discussion differs from hers in that it suggests that salvage rhythms are not simply reflective of a particular phase of capitalist production and experience, but can in fact undermine the depoliticizing consequences of such experience, an assertion I will continue to develop in this chapter. Salvage rhythms, when conceptualized in terms of craftwork and *metis*, result in both plastic identity and understandings of one's material and social surroundings, as opposed to exposing the reification lying at the core of capitalist ideology. When seen in this light, salvage rhythms can be described as "rhythms of resistance" that do not simply reflect the ruins of capitalism but form a practice that might assist us in overcoming it. Plural becoming and the plasticity of habits that sustain this political ethos set the stage for creating mutations that undermine the reified separations of capitalism. Seemingly "natural" social phenomena lose their "thingness" through the process of rhythmically sensing the possibilities produced by fusing disparate materials, ideas, and identities in the process of salvage. Both finding useful items in seemingly useless places and forcing them to play roles that one might have previously thought they could never have played requires persistence, yet results in destabilization of previously unquestioned assumptions. Undertaking repeated rituals of rhythmic inwardness and outwardness as sensed through affects of depression and love might allow salvagers to "practice" their craft, and further intensify its consequences of plasticity and the ethos of becoming. Thus, the rhythmic form of craft also can be seen as the rhythmic form of critical inquiry that undermines reification and alienation.

Craft and Radical Salvage Workshops

Although I have only tangentially addressed the relationships that craft-work has historically engendered, they constitute a fundamental aspect of the practice of craft. The communities that form around craftwork have often practiced in particular spaces, or workshops, that also aid craftworkers in their undertakings.[5] As Sennett demonstrates, many medieval workshops operated more like laboratories where craftworkers collaborated and experimented. He states, "This was an age in which scientific experiment lodged itself in workshops, making some of them places of research, research with no practical end immediately in view" (Sennett 2012, 112). He notes that socialist Robert Owen attempted to revive this understanding of the laboratory/workshop, as opposed to the oppressive factory that he considered a more "primitive" form of production. Sennett makes the claim that a "modern variant of the workshop is the scientific laboratory, which Owen explicitly foresaw" (ibid). For both Sennett and Owen, the workshop encouraged experimentation, in contrast to the regimentation and strict discipline of the capitalist workplace. For Sennett, the workshop represents a hidden space of innovation that was one of the factors driving the scientific launching of the Renaissance. For Owen, it represented a form that would hopefully overtake capitalism, grounding production in unalienated labor free of exploitation. Both Sennett's and Owen's work demonstrates how a particular space and the communities that form in this space played an important role in supporting craftworkers in their activity.

One of the primary qualities of the workshop that encouraged experimentation were the collaborative practices grounded in the non-cognitive sense of affect it facilitated. Sennett describes how the free flow of ideas and skills in the workshop created a sense of informality among the participants. Helping, trying new things out, supporting one another when they experienced failure were all part of this casual form of interaction. Such almost constant reciprocal interplay often took place through subtle looks, expressions, and movements. He claims that within the workshop, "bodily gestures take the place of words in establishing authority, trust and collaboration. . . . Gestures of movement, facial expression and sound endow the social triangle with sensate life" (Sennett 2012, 205–206). He goes on to state:

> [E]ven speech can be infused with an easy visceral feeling, as in open conversations, more relaxed more pleasurable more sensate in their flow than comprehensive argument. Yet the sensation of informality is also deceiving if we imagine "informal" to be the same as "shapeless." The settlement-house workers knew this was not to be true when they gave a shape to informal language classes and dramatic performances; we know also in our bodies that informality is shaped, when we gesture appropriately to our circumstances and gesture well. (Sennett 2012, 208)

It is important to highlight that Sennett defines informality as "flow" grounded in sensed affect between craftspeople, for instance, the sense of how a hammer hitting a piece of metal is transformed into a gesture, which is immediately sensed by another craftsperson who communicates back with a gesture of approval or disapproval. As people in the shop become accustomed to each other they can support, criticize, or collaborate using only their faces and bodies. As one person experiences productive interventions as she and her material become something new and exciting, others in the shop can encourage this process through simultaneous gestures of excitement. And because gestures rely on proximity, the manner in which the craftspeople move about the shop—their pace, direction, and speed—influence how these gestures are both combined and received. Relationships form and dissolve on the basis of gestures, and thus this form of communication, received in terms of both their individual impact and their placement within the flow of the overall affect of craftpersons' experience over a period of time, fundamentally shapes the labor process. Thus, the informality produced by affective gestures can lead in surprising directions and facilitate creativity due to their vagueness and possibility. Gestures play the same role as the affective feedback produced through the craftworker's interaction with their material, supplying clues to the quality of the relational development between two people. Furthermore, gestures of informality open people to sensing their affective potentialities with their surroundings, creating a greater possibility that individuals will perceive the affects produced by their interactions.

Although gestures originate in the spontaneous affects created by the relationships between craftworkers in the workshop, Sennett observes that the conscious employment of rituals both encourages and sustains this flowing informality. Such rituals can bolster the habits of craft not only when working with physical material, but also when "working with" (both constructing and repairing) relationships with others. One person who he claims was an expert in using community rituals was the American Socialist Normal Thomas. Sennett describes that, while Thomas was not a traditionally skilled orator and his speeches often involved well-worn themes of economic exploitation, "his usual listeners would recite these themes by heart." The reason, Sennett claims, that those who interacted with him felt such a strong and enthusiastic bond was because Thomas was so skilled in deploying rituals of informality such as handshakes, facial expressions, and other movements. Such rituals conform closely to Sennett's understanding of the workshop, which he characterizes as exhibiting "dialogical communication and informal association" (Sennett 2012, 113). Sennett relates that Thomas

> always placed his own seat in the middle of a group, a circle if possible, rather than holding meeting where the chairman sits elevated at the front in a room. At the end of a speech he never called for raised hands, but sought out, by an intu-ition he could never explain, those people too shy to speak up. After meetings, he usually spoke to people while gripping them by the forearm, and he didn't let go while he talked. (Sennett 2012, 271)

The spatial and somatic rituals he describes, such as the ability to sense through their facial expressions what others are experiencing, constitute the rituals of informality. Establishing rituals that initiate informality, especially among people who do not know each other, can stoke affective receptivity. Rituals rhythmically help to bond individuals to each other. It is not just that rituals activate the somatic properties of becoming I have been stressing throughout the entire argument—decentering the cognitive and tying thoughts to actions, emphasizing sense through the body in relationship to the mind; these sociable rituals mirror the processes undertaken by craftspeople in their creative becoming. Sennett makes this connection when he states that "sociable experts address other people in their unfolding prospects just as the artisan explores material change; one's skill of repair is exercised as a mentor; one's guiding standards are transparent, this is comprehensible to non experts" (Sennett 2008, 251). Thus, rituals of informality such as those practiced by Thomas not only create informal bonds between people, but also create an informal, flowing milieu for interacting with the world, rooted in both ritual and the material practice of the workshop. Informality allows for openness to the vibrant affects that lead to becoming, and social rituals embodying this attitude, according to Sennett, complement the craft rituals practiced by artisans during the act of physically working on their materials.

I want to emphasize one further provocative benefit of workshops being interpreted through the lens of their laboratory-like characteristics. Remember, Sennett describes the workshops as not encouraging specialization but instead acting as spaces of "interdisciplinary thinking." One of the reasons such interdisciplinary thinking was encouraged by workshops was the lack of a specific division of labor. Craftworkers engaged in many skills and many productive processes when building their wares. Their workshops contained many different tools and had to stockpile many different types of materials. Although Sennett does not specifically claim that the close spatial proximity of these different activities and individuals contributes to the laboratory-like creative, collective, rhythmic, affect-based becoming he describes in these spaces, other theorists have discussed how the arrangement of spaces can contribute to this process. Workshops, and more concretely the spatial characteristics of workshops, matter because they prompt individual movements between activities and those undertaking them in different parts of the shop and encourage the mixture of relationships between individuals as they go about their movements within the shop. Some philosophers have imagined how movement through particular spaces might aid in this process. They hypothesize that existing within spaces that display certain architectures can heighten the perception of affect and rhythmic movement that they see as crucial to collective creativity, becoming, and the undermining of capitalist reification. And although they do not specifically cast their spaces of becoming as "workshops," they do see these spaces as encouraging becoming, and thus one can use their understandings to develop one's own grasp of my interpretation of the potential of the workshop to explain communities of salvage.

For example, John Dewey presents a schematic that portrays what he sees as the layout of an effective schoolroom, emphasizing a spatial arrangement conducive to the interdisciplinary experimentation with which Sennett characterizes the workshop. Furthermore, this schematic emphasizes that the experimental becoming that both students and their objects of study undergo is produced through the students' rhythmic movement between the different areas of the school. The figure portrays two levels, with the first level showing particular rooms dedicated to discrete areas of activity/study that surround a library (see figures 3.1 and 3.2).

One of these rooms is explicitly identified as a workshop, but each of these activity-dedicated spaces allows for the development and experimentation, due to their close proximity and connection with the workshop. The diagram also depicts the connection of the school to areas of society such as businesses, schools, gardens, and the "country" surround-

Chart III

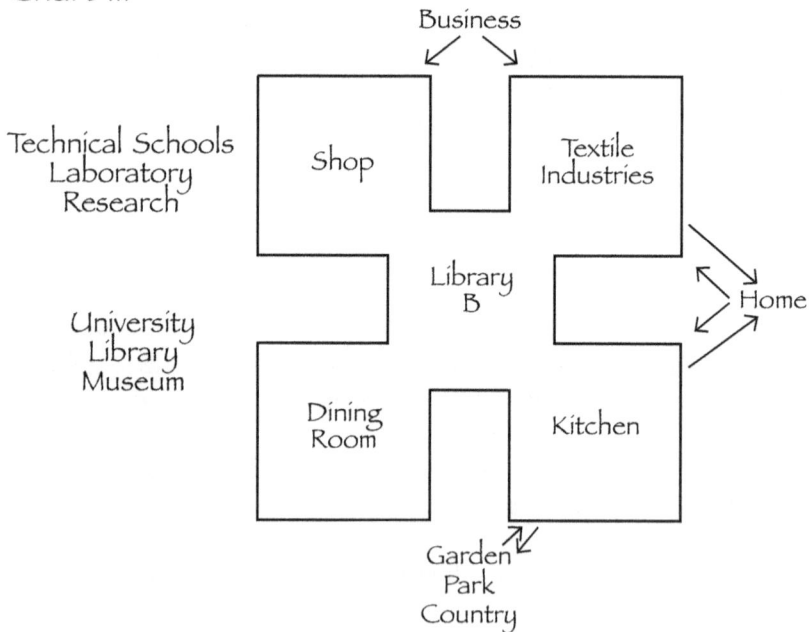

Figure 3.1. Conceptual Plan for Dewey School: Dewey, *School and Society*, 1983. Fair use.

Chart IV

Laboratories
Research

Physical
and Chemical
Laboratories

Biological
Laboratory

Museum

University
Library
Museum

Art

Music

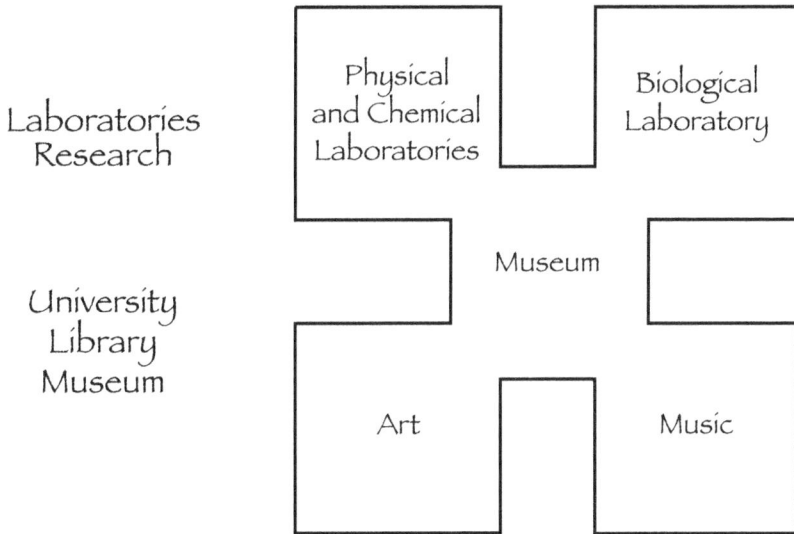

Figure 3.2. Conceptual Plan for Dewey School: Dewey, *School and Society*, 1983. Fair use.

ing the school. The second floor also contains four interconnected rooms, except on this floor the rooms represent areas of traditional scholarly and artistic endeavor, all of which surround a museum. Dewey imagines that groups of pupils will enter rooms relevant to problems they face in their lives. For example, a problem that a student encounters at home might lead to an investigation within the kitchen. As they begin to physically experiment with these model environments, he sees students traveling to the library to formalize their knowledge. Furthermore, Dewey suggests that exploration in one room will most likely lead to inquiry in other, connected rooms, as students begin to perceive the relationships between the seemingly disparate aspects of their daily existence. He explains that before the students know the nature of these connections, they sense them, with the students' experience of similar affects in different rooms leading them to develop more formal links between seemingly disparate endeavors. During this process, the design of the school, with individual yet interconnected rooms, facilitates this process by encouraging both movement between rooms and restful attention within rooms. Dewey stresses that, all the while, students are led to move and sense new combinations of relational qualities in conjunction with attempting to gain substantive knowledge. After a sustained effort to appreciate the resonances of the different aspects of their daily lives, as represented by the rooms on the first floor of the school, students then proceed to the second floor, where they continue to add layers of significance to their investigations of their daily problems through study and experimentation with more esoteric, and traditionally academic methods of inquiry. Thus. the rhythmic and not simply repetitive nature of the movement: students move between different rooms on one floor, forming small milieus of activities, each with its own pace and structure, and then switch to the upper floor, where they repeat this process. This development produces an affective sense of increasing pace, intensity, and moment that helps to propel thought forward, assisting the students' progress through their investigations.[6]

When these investigations consummate, Dewey contends that the students will collectively represent their journeys through the various rooms of the school within its museum. The map they create is then displayed in the museum to emphasize not discrete solutions to particular problems but instead to illustrate "that experience has its geographical aspect, its artistic and literary, its scientific and its historical sides" (Dewey 1983, 54). In other words, the museum displays the map of the students' cognitive, spatial, and temporal environment and their collective journey of becoming through it. He goes on to state that "through the map, every new traveler may get for his own journey new benefits of the results of other explorers' explorations" (Dewey 2008a, 284). These maps, Dewey claims do not represent predetermined solutions to problems, but instead lead to the "increase of ability to place our own doings in their time and space connections," and, thus, "our doings gain in significant content" (Dewey 2008b, 216). The use of the term *significant* here is not haphazard—it emphasizes that maps not only increase knowledge, but also perception of quality and affective connection to these larger surroundings. And his desire that students produce a map indicates his concern with the social and political potentialities resulting from this process. More importantly than any map are the habits that the construction of a map helps to cultivate. The classroom thus acts as a type of physical ritual that aids in the sustaining of the rhythms of resistance nascent within the practice of salvage.

Deleuze also offers a diagram that can be used to imagine a space productive of a rhythmic movement of bodies, which encourages affects that can facilitate anticapitalist, critical becoming. Although he does not present a workshop space, his previous focus on craft and rhythm merits the inclusion of this ideal structure in this discussion. To begin, in a similar fashion to Dewey, Deleuze argues that the nomad best undertakes her journeys with others, in what he refers to as a "pack." The wolf in a pack symbolizes for Deleuze an internally flexible and shifting yet coherent group that senses its belonging with others in the group. He describes the wolf as "the instantaneous apprehension of a multiplicity in a given region . . . not a representative, a substitute, but an I feel. I feel myself becoming a wolf, one wolf among others, on the edge of a pack" (Deleuze and Guattari 1987, 32). Among the further characteristics of a pack are, "small or restricted number, dispersion, nondecomposable variable distances, qualitative metamorphoses . . . impossibility of a fixed totalization or hierarchization . . . lines of deterritorialization" (33). Thus, the wolf pack, because it is a qualitatively conjoined entity, or, as he states, an "I feel," encourages its members to sense the possibilities of the folds within their experience, and thus encourages rhythmic production of difference, both within the pack and in the territory in which the pack travels.

While Deleuze suggests that engaging in nomadic inquiry within a pack heightens the qualitative aspects of deterritorialization, he also suggests that movement through geographies exhibiting particular spatial characteristics will further intensify resonances productive of becoming. His Baroque House, similarly to Dewey's laboratory schoolhouse, contains two floors and also serves as an ideal/typical schema that rhythmically structures collective becoming. Deleuze hypothesizes:

> Baroque architecture can be defined by severing of the facade from the inside, of the interior from the exterior and the autonomy of the interior from the independence of the exterior but in the conditions that each of the terms thrusts the other forward. . . . What makes the new harmony possible is first the distinction between two levels or floors which resolves tension or allots the division. The lower level is assigned to the facade, which is elongated by being punctured and bent back according to the folds determined by a heavy matter forming an infinite room for reception of receptivity. The

upper level is closed as a pure inside without an outside, a weightless, closed interiority, its walls hung with spontaneous folds . . . it's [sic] walls are hung with spontaneous folds that are now only those of a soul or a mind. (Deleuze 1992, 29)

The above quote stresses that while the lower floor possesses multiple openings and constitutes a realm of receptivity to the world, the upper floor, while closed off from experience, "thrusts" this reality into a multiplicity of differences and potentialities within self or the "soul." Deleuze envisions that those entering the house rhythmically alternate between the floors because the upper floor remains "folded" over the lower floor (see figure 3.3).

This architecture leads him to describe the Baroque House as a "musical" machine that acts an affective background facilitating the rhythmic folding and unfolding, with the lower floor revealing and producing folds in experiences produced though receptivity to resonant qualities and the upper floor containing the folds and multiplicities within the self. It is only through the affects produced through rhythmic reiteration between the different modes of activity on the different floors that the true potentiality of each can be capitalized upon, or, as Deleuze puts it, "it is in melody that harmony is achieved" (Deleuze

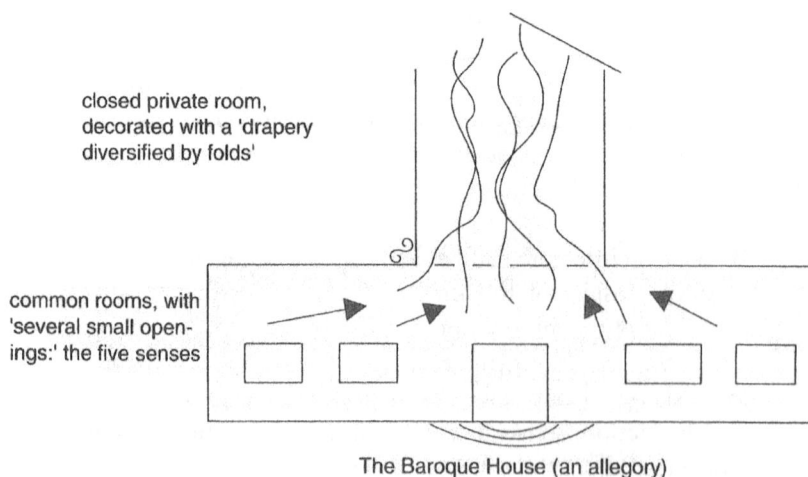

closed private room, decorated with a 'drapery diversified by folds'

common rooms, with 'several small openings:' the five senses

The Baroque House (an allegory)

Figure 3.3. Conceptual Plan for Deleuze, *The Fold: Leibniz, and the Baroque*, 1993.

1992, 135). As with a Baroque concerto, the smaller progressions of stac-cato notes rhythmically wind their way forward into a harmonic whole, yet a Deleuzian concerto always possesses an unforeseen outcome due to the deterritorializing potentialities released through such unfolding.

Similar to Dewey's school, Deleuze's nomadic becoming structured with the rhythmic characteristics of the Baroque House produces a map that represents a provisional portrayal of not only the territory of the nomad, but the deterritorializations undertaken by the nomad to transform and occupy their environment. Todd May describes these Deleuzian maps as developing "transversal connections—since they cut across traditional political identities—they are invisible to liberal political theory" (May 2011, 131). He stresses that these maps reveal hidden pathways through which individuals might become other than what they are by virtue of their interactions with their environment. Furthermore, Deleuzian maps reveal opportune points of intervention where individuals might mold their environment in new and unexpected ways. The map, of course, is not the primary goal, but instead a tool of becoming and a spatial framework for encouraging transversal connections. Furthermore, the map represents the development of new, plastic, habits of becoming in that the more flexible, integrative, and responsive the habits the wider the scope and complexity of the map. The layout of the Dewey School and the Baroque house encourage both such juxtapositions and the mutations in which they result. Their internal diversity and connected, distinct spaces, lead inhabitants to sense a multitude of affects created through various transversal connections. Furthermore, they encourage the rhythm of testing, sensing, and then tensing again using the potentialities indicated through affect. They constitute "idiorythmic"[7] spaces that allow for the experience of affects discouraged by everyday life in capitalist landscapes. Because they contain spaces dedicated to diverse activities concentrated within a discrete area, they stand in stark contrast to the separated, reified daily life of capitalism. And the webs of connectivity that individuals form through their activity come to be formed by both knowledge and effect due to the concentrated proximity of the inner spaces. And because these spaces act as spatial rituals encouraging such plastic habits, they might help to further intensify the possibility that such spaces can act as the "laboratories of insurrectionary imagination" that the activists who establish salvaged protest camps describe them-selves as constructing.

The Craft of Salvage and Radical Workshops

Perhaps counterintuitively, at the end of this exploration of some of the underacknowledged properties of craft and artisanship I want to reiterate that salvage itself can be seen as a craft. As opposed to a haphazard, improvised practice, we recall, salvagers approach their activity through the lens of sense—they feel the potentials within their environment to suggest where to forage materials and what those materials might be used for in either construction or repair. Both artisans and salvagers begin their work by interacting with their materials—they tinker, prod, and observe and then allow the potentials to unfold. They do not try to impose their predetermined plans upon their materials, they engage in a dialog with those materials, which results in surprising outcomes. Artisans focusing on repair often, through their dialog with their materials led by vague senses of prospective transformations, inadvertently mutate the original objects into forms much different that the objects with which they began. The idea that salvage constitutes a craft can be most potently seen when it is interpreted as a manifestation of *metis*. James Scott, while not naming *metis* as a practice that its practitioners would specifically name as such, or even acknowledge as a distinct style of action, persuasively argues that peasants and the poor—those who live in highly precarious situations they cannot avoid—undertake similar modes of reacting to that contingency, which employ similar abilities, attitudes, and relationships. Thus, *metis*, the knack for sensing the possibilities in contingency, can be said to constitute a flexible yet consistent process involving constantly invoking routines and rituals across differing situations. This encourages the conclusion, if one acknowledges that artisans are less rigid and salvagers more regimented than most believe, that salvage can be thought of as a craft. And with the linkage of craftwork to *metis* an understanding of craft can be constructed that focuses on its linkages to the wily strategies that the poor must use to survive in their daily lives and thus acknowledges the craft of salvage as a "weapon of the weak."

I have tried to show that artisan communities and spaces play a fundamental role in the cultivation of the affective aspects of craftwork that build upon the potentialities for salvage to act as a generator of plural, anticapitalist becoming, and, more specifically, that workshops intensify salvage's reliance on sense, rhythm, amateurism, becoming, and by inference radicalism. I have discussed that the workshop was a place of creativity, more similar to a laboratory than a household, and that the workshop was characterized by rituals of informality that encouraged experimentation, risk taking, and learning. Just as communities of salvage are fluid and diverse, these artisan workshops are not united by similar identities but instead by rituals that encourage relationships of sharing, openness. This sharing and openness can manifest themselves in design elements that both embody and strengthen the experimentation and becoming that is indicative of the workshop. Both Dewey's classroom and Deleuze's Baroque House encourage rhythmic becoming and the unfolding of potentialities, because their structures both separate and connect. They establish different areas for different subject matters (the schoolroom) and styles of inquiry and attention to one's surroundings (the Baroque House) yet ensure that their structures allow for easy alternation between these different areas. These spaces represent both structure and openness, and both diversity and relationship. These spaces, ironically, both structure and undermine the structure of artisan community and relationships. They lead to the critical rhythmic becoming that one sees in squats, artistic spaces such as the Gramsci Monument, and the various Occupy Wall Street encampments. These spaces, which arose spontaneously, and were built through rhythmic *metis*, reflect this process in that they contain additions that were excreted through the slow processes of unacknowledged dialog between groups of salvage crafters and their materials in dialog itself with conscious dialog between the participants. The value of juxtaposing these real salvage/political spaces against these ideal/conceptual models is that the comparison emphasizes the specific design features of the salvage environments that might not be apparent even to the builders of the spaces productive of the critical becoming they experience. With this knowledge concerning the importance of spatially induced differential rhythm to the construction of salvage workshops, these characteristics might be more consciously and critically applied during their construction.

I want to stress one final political implication for thinking of salvage as a craft that groups collectively undertake in "radical workshops." One continually vexing problem for Left movements concerns the level of organization and hierarchy necessary to maintain political effectiveness and longevity. It might seem that the occupations, squats, and informal communities that I have asserted constitute the primary manifestations of political salvage occur spontaneously and without any coordination. At this point, I have not articulated any possible linkage between either the individual examples that I discuss or the larger categories of political salvage activity. Yet thinking of salvage as a craft establishes a possible linkage between these seemingly disparate instances of political salvage. As it stands now, many protest camps, such as Occupy, while comprising seemingly isolated, local, and self-generated events, act not only as sites of resistance to specific injustices but also as sites of education and transmission of the traditions and skills activists have gained through their participation in past protests. For example, in one protest camp activists recount that "many of these . . . tactics involved learning process, including reading training guides as well as attending training workshops and skill sharing sessions at the camp" (Feigenbaum, Frenzel, and McCurdy 2013). While the "training guides" used by the activists were handwritten, photocopied, and stapled-together hand-me-downs, and the workshops sometimes occurred in trees they were trying to save from clear-cutting, the educational activities undertaken in protest camps demonstrate a continuity of practices between these events that constitute the nascent linkages that might constitute a more coherent political formation. One can also see such skill sharing in squats that not only establish tool libraries but also workshops on repair.[8] My conceptualization of salvage as an anticapitalist craft of the poor adds a further layer to the possible continuities between such seemingly isolated activists. Shared practices such as those cited, while not constituting formal rules of conduct, might add a further layer to these unifying yet flexible tactical repertoires that establish unifying relationships across space and time between autonomous activist spaces. Furthermore the craft of salvage's ethos of anticapitalist becoming can become further intensified when constituting a part of this shared activist tradition.

In sum, I contend that the all of the aspects of craft outlined by the theoretical accounts I have discussed—itinerant, cunning, sensitive, rhythmic, workshop-collaboration—can be seen to various extents in the accounts of political salvage I presented in the first chapter. Furthermore, they specify and thus present the possibility of amplifying both the accounts of effective-critical becoming I present in the second chapter and thus the possibility of acting as the basis for practices particularly potent in counteracting the disempowering affects I recounted of capitalist daily life. Thus, this presentation of the labor undertaken by salvage craftworkers in radical workshops constitutes the beginning step of actualizing the political theory of salvage into practices and social formations. The next step I will take is to think not about the how of this political theory but about the where.

Chapter 4

Salvage and the City

Introduction

In the last chapter I explored micro practices that sustain political salvage. To further develop a political theory of salvage, I will now explore the macro conditions that might increase the likelihood of individuals engaging in this form of resistance I will focus on the larger social and economic context in order to examine where salvage most frequently occurs and the many dimensions along which its occurrence can vary. I also identify characteristics within this landscape with the intention of deepening their potential to sustain radical political transformation. To summarize, I claim that the dynamics of geographic change within capitalist cities have often encouraged the development of individual acts of salvage into communities of political salvage, and recognizing this fact might help activists to further deepen the radical implications of this seemingly mundane activity

As the populations of many previously affluent cities in industrialized nations shrink[1] while cities in the developing world grow due to the increased presence of informal communities, the "ruined" and "filthy" city has become a focus of interest in terms of its potentialities for rethinking the concept of salvage. While urban debris might seem worthless, some see in the ruins of the cities a resource, in terms of both the physicality of the resultant debris and its meaning. Referencing Benjamin, Beaumont claims that "one of the city's archives is its detritus" (Beaumont and Dart 2010, 1), and that the reason to collect this detritus is "to expose the hidden histories of familiar monuments" and to "familiarize the city" (9). As cities become increasingly characterized by economic dislocation and environmental harm, they also produce more and more ruin. Capitalist cities, due to the frequent geographic "creative destruction," caused by capitalist redevelopment contain abandoned, marginal, and ruined spaces that become "loose" and thus prime sites for use in surprising new ways. Urban looseness comes about when "[l]acking officially assigned uses, leftover spaces and abandoned spaces lie outside the 'rush and flow' as well as the control of regulations and surveillance that come with the established uses of planned urban public space" (Franck and Stevens 2012, 8). Thus spaces that were designed for a specific purpose now come be used in a variety of different ways, hence their "loose" character. These abandoned spaces, of course, possess their own histories and physical geographies and thus are not places of complete freedom and creation. In effect, many claim, they act as spatial catalysts that might "loosen" the habits and thought of those ensnared within capitalism's infrastructure of daily life.

Such urban looseness also increases the possibilities for political salvage. Urban centers in capitalism are concentrations of materials, people, and social systems devoted to the smooth flow of commodities. They are also spaces of division among zones devoted to different predominant uses, such as residential, industrial, leisure, and waste—whether, in the last instance, these waste spaces result from conscious placement of dumps and landfills or constitute unplanned concentrations of abandoned buildings, decaying streets, and piles of garbage. The anticapitalist occupations of 2011 in New York, Madrid, Athens, and Tel-Aviv all developed in public areas where small numbers of dedicated activists built encampments that drew a wide array of city dwellers to the sudden eruption in their midst. Squatting is often an urban phenomenon.[2] As once-abandoned buildings in abandoned neighborhoods increase in value and thus become the objects of municipal and commercial forces of gentrification, squatters fight to retain the spaces they have refurbished. Finally, slums form in direct relation to the growth of more affluent areas of the city. Despite the fact that poor residents get squeezed out of urban centers, affluent areas still rely upon the service labor that they provide. Thus, slum dwellers seek to build residences in proximity to their jobs in more affluent areas, building in the urban "cracks" by using only what they can find, while the people who employ their labor try to push them away. Struggle ensues as each segment of the population attempts to occupy the urban landscape, yet, as with occupations and squats, each segment, in a strange way, depends on the other, developing dialectically due to the forces of capitalist urbanization. This struggle over space frequently leads to the transformation of mere salvage into political salvage, as salvagers struggle to keep their spaces while they are forced by necessity into spaces where they are not welcome by capitalist elites.

In order to explain the dynamics of the geographies of political salvage, I will rely heavily upon the work of Henri Lefebvre. Lefebvre notes that capitalist cities are realms of segregation, in that, while distinct districts within disparate cities exhibit uniformity (for instance, the financial district in any major global city displays spatial characteristics and architectural styles similar to the financial districts in other cities), cities themselves come to be starkly divided, especially between rich and poor, capitalist and worker. Bankers circulate freely within their own particular districts within cities, and between the financial districts of different cities, while never traveling to other districts. Poor districts are constantly penetrated by capital through the purchase of buildings and businesses characteristic of gentrification, while the movement of the poor into the districts of capital is severely restricted. Using a technique of social criticism he calls "rhythmanalysis," Lefebvre tries to demonstrate that the geography sculpting everyday life in such spaces causes the inhabitants' bodies to move in such a way that it creates patterns of experience that habituate urban dwellers to an abstract, quantified consciousness supportive of capitalist ideology. Thus, he shows how the capitalist city both contributes to an affective infrastructure that bolsters capitalism and, dialectically, contains affective inducements that might lead to resistance. By employing his analysis, I am able to expand the discussion of the ways the affective, rhythmic capitalist "infrastructure" sculpts the desires and identities of contemporary citizens and offers a bridge between the micro and macro political qualities that lie inherent within the practice.

Despite the subtle power of such affective infrastructures to depoliticize and rob citizens of their propensity to sense the affective textures of their daily lives, Lefebvre asserts, city dwellers undertake frequent efforts to undermine the abstract spaces of contemporary urbanity both through small, everyday acts of improvisation and more conscious efforts of resistance. Human bodies, in their everyday experience within these capitalist urban structures, find ways around the restrictive limits placed on their movements in capitalist space. Tired people sit on steps meant to usher bankers in and out of their highrises, and street vendors set up shop in immaculately tended public plazas. Police try to curb these practices and people resist, or move on and act in the same way when they believe the authorities are not there. Opportunities for such creative reimagining of abstract space are greater in peripheral areas where capitalist control is less intense. There, ostensibly dilapidated buildings are transformed into vibrant community centers, and trash-strewn lots are planted with vegetables. Abandoned factories are redesigned and recommissioned to build items chosen by workers and their communities. To inhabit a space is to transform it and make it one's own through large and small modifications.

Lefebvre even mentions, albeit briefly, that salvage communities represent a potent manifestation of inhabitation. Thus, his understanding of inhabitation can help to explain what salvagers do when they salvage not simply an item, but an entire space, an activity that helps to explain the occurrence and dynamics of political salvage. Thinking of salvage as an instance of Lefebvrian inhabitation also places this activity within the context of a larger and vibrant social theory. I expand upon this observation to explore how political salvage undermines the propagation of abstract space and segregation, which Lefebvre identifies as the manifestations of the capitalist restructuring of urban space. But I go on to make a larger claim—that Lefebvre relies too heavily upon the contradictions within capitalist urban space to act as the catalyst for urban resistance. He seems to believe that self-organized groups will undertake the reinhabitation of abstract centralities and thereby push the boundaries of segregation purely as a result of the spatial dynamics he identifies. I will argue that political salvage, in the way that I have envisioned it, as a craft that best occurs in radical workshops that intensify the affects leading to becoming, might constitute a consciously employed tool of inhabitation that can play a role in the organization of political activity to reinhabit the capitalist city. Political salvage thus can constitute a tactic of inhabitation that does not simply spontaneously occur, but can act as a rallying cry and unifying practice for those fighting for their "right to the city."

Rhythms of the City

Lefebvre grounds his understanding of space as a product of body, mind, and environment in his understanding of rhythm. He argues this most explicitly in his book *Rhythmanalysis: Space, Time and Everyday Life*, but this line of thought also appears throughout his body of work. His analysis centers on the assertion that one of the most neglected but fundamental manifestations of a space's impact upon the body consists of the rhythmic patterns one experiences though the course of one's everyday experience. He claims that "the surroundings of bodies, be they in nature or in a social setting, are also *bundles, bouquets, garlands* of rhythms, to which it is necessary to listen in order to grasp the natural or produced ensembles" (Lefebvre 2004, 20). Such rhythms reveal the sequential nature of one's movements and, subsequently, the quality of the thoughts, habits, and senses these movements prompt. Bodies constantly move, and this temporal extension consists of differentiated moments, ebbs and flows of reactions prompted by new locations and modes of bodily extension. Thus, the "bundles" of different relations between thought and habit, and different relationships and reactions, accrue over time, forming overlapping or, as Tsing might assert, "polyphonic" rhythms. For him, the production of space does not occur in a single instance, but comes to be constituted by rhythmic iterations of the mutual affects of bodies within spaces, or as he claims "through the mediation of rhythms . . . an animated space comes into being which is an extension of the space of bodies" (Lefebvre 1992, 207). The rhythmic properties of such affects constitutes a record of the quality of such movements—the ebb and flow of the affects produced by the relations one senses throughout the course of one's experience. Exploring the social and political implications of the rhythmic patterns of such movements through space reveals important yet underacknowledged characteristics of city life.

Despite the seeming focus on the individual in this account, Lefebvre emphasizes that affective rhythms come to be produced by much more than one's immediate environment. Siegworth and Gardiner stress that,

> almost like music, certainly like rhythm, the event-full (and always more-than-human) movement from moment to moment undulates (as the substantial link between monads is itself a monad)—like the infinity of water particles that gets re-cast from one wave to the next, or like the smallest dancing specks of dust, caught in a certain angle of light, rising, falling, and hovering against a dark backdrop. "The specter of undulatory movements (with or without trajectories) extends," writes Lefebvre, "indefinitely, even infinitely, from the macro to

the micro, from corpuscular movements to the movements of metagalaxies." (Seigworth and Gardiner 2004, 142)

The imprint of many environments with many scales constantly sculpts, to different extents, the individual rhythmic experience. The body, in and of itself, according to Lefebvre, is subject to contradictory rhythms—both cyclical and linear, "combining the cycles of time, need and desire with the linearites of gesture, perambulation, prehension and the manipulation of things—the handling of both material and abstract tools" (Lefebvre 1992, 203). He claims that linear rhythms characterize capitalist expe-rience, as relentless cycles of accumulation push the individual toward the next task, while he characterizes cyclical rhythms as indicative of nature and recreation. Yet, due to these contrasting modes of quality, individuals never experience a unitary sense of the rhythms that surround them. Rhythms are always becoming something new and clashing against each other. And he emphasizes that rhythm need not manifest itself as unchanging repetition. He notes that "We should not separate repetitive praxis from creative praxis. There are several types of repetition. . . . The stereotypes mechanical repetition of gestures and signals differs from the rhythmed and periodic starting and restarting which characterizes vital activities" (Lefebvre and Trebitsch 2002, 239). Thus, rhythm might not only manifest itself in similarity and repetition, according to Lefebvre, but also can constitute a powerful constituent in the phenomenology of creative praxis, as Deleuze and Sennett observe in their understanding of the radical implications of craft.

Although he doesn't use this term, Lefebvre implies that the cre-ative possibilities that lie within the combination of such linear and cyclical rhythms constitute a third type of "developmental" rhythm that characterizes creative practice. This third possibility lies between the cyclical and the linear, in that these rhythms do form recursive loops, but these loops are not uniform—with each iteration they change and develop like linear rhythms. I want to stress this third understanding because Lefebvre's presentation of only two forms does not allow for the possibilities contained in other areas of his work. As will become increasingly apparent as my argument progresses, Lefebvre's concept of the many possibilities for resistance in the capitalist city cannot be ade-quately described through this dualistic description. Cyclical rhythms, by definition, do not change, yet Lefebvre suggests the possibility of groups engaging in the collective transformation of capitalist space through some form of rhythmic activity that offers a contrast to the linear rhythms encouraged by capitalist space This transformation does not seem to be adequately subsumed under either form that Lefebvre discusses here. Although I will not undertake my interpretation of Lefebvre's account of such creative appropriation of space until later in this chapter, it is important to highlight this lacuna in the concept with which he constructs this account before I actually engage in this task.

Simply because bodily practice contains the potentiality to inspire creative, rhythmic affects does not mean that individuals will notice such vague prompts and indications. Lefebvre suggests that, for the most part in contemporary society, "most people ignore their body and misunderstand it." They rhythms that the body senses are ignored or misinterpreted. What then is needed to use the complex and cryptic rhythms. In reaction to this lack of bodily awareness he asserts the need for

> [a] kind of pedagogy of the body, its rhythms a kind of teaching will fill the enormous gap. But such unpleasant words: pedagogy, teaching, fill! Of course the body cannot be appropriated with speech, and references to language fall on their own at the appropriate moment. What is needed is a practice, addressed to lived experience to lead it to the level of the perceived world. How can we reeducate bodies for spaces? (Lefebvre 2014, 34)

Such a pedagogy of the body constitutes an education through movement itself. Verbal instructions, or reading, to Lefebvre, cannot by themselves open the body to the rhythms that surround it. One's everyday production of space occurs within the constraints of the actual space through which one moves—and thus Lefebvre focuses on how the spatial constraints of urban formations structure one's experience, and ultimately form a pedagogy of the body that imprints social structures upon individuals without their conscious participation. And Lefebvre stresses that such a pedagogy of the body happens whether we choose to engage in it or not—as we move, our body changes, learns, and adapts, cultivating patterns of response that mold the entirely of our perception.

One can see the importance to Lefebvre of such a pedagogy of the body when he analyzes architecture in terms of not simply the conscious symbolism buildings express, but also through their tendency to prompt certain directions and styles of movement in those who dwell among them. Of course, buildings reference particular historical sources, express concrete political ideas, and contain powerful symbols. But this did not exhaust the "meaning" of buildings for Lefebvre. Stanek notes that "Lefebvre suggests that architecture be thought of not as text but as 'texture': architecture as 'archi-texture' would include strong points, nexuses or nodes in the 'populated area and the associated networks in which it is set down, as part of a particular production of space'"(Stanek 2011, 203–204). This description of architecture in terms of its texture focuses attention upon how space constitutes a background filter through which one experiences everyday life. Lefebvre's use of the concept of texture of a space, like Berlant's use of the concept of infrastructure, suggests how a building or landscape sculpts the affective background of everyday actions, a background that can be sensed as affects that structure the quality of one's experience.

For Lefebvre, texture constitutes the bridge concept that links architecture, rhythm, and the macro environment. Architecture as texture suggests how spaces structure the spatial and temporal quality of the actions of those who move through them. This can be seen when he analyzes specific spaces:

> When formal elements become part of *texture* they diversify, introducing both repetition and difference. They articulate the whole and conversely the mustering by the whole of its component elements. For example, the capitals of a Romanesque cloister differ, but they do so within the limits permitted by a model. They break space up and give it rhythm. (Lefebvre 1992, 150)

Here, one can see the rhythmanalytic method being practiced. Lefebvre reads the textures and rhythms of a space—how the possible trajectories of a body through that space constitute a spatial and temporal pattern set by the architecture of the space. Just as a fugue is comprised of winding patterns of notes, a building composes and choreographs movement. Yet he does not limit such analysis to single buildings. He also argues that landscapes and larger environments possess textures that can be sensed. Lefebvre claims, "What is inscribed and projected [in the city] is not only a far order, a social whole, a mode of production, a general code, it is also a time, rather times, rhythms. The city is heard as much as music as it is read as discursive writing" (Lefebvre, Kofman, and Lebas 1996a,

109). The rhythms of the city, or the affects that one senses through one's movements through the various architectures of the city (both in terms of buildings, neighborhoods, and the entire urban landscape) over time, form patterns that possess implications for one's identity and perception. Some cities possess textures that encourage flowing, smooth movement, yet such flow can deaden the perception of difference as one encounter leads quickly to the next in a blur of perception. Some cities possess textures that are jarring and disjointed, reflecting the existence of wildly different districts existing in close proximity. As one travels from one area to the next (oftentimes transgressing unmarked yet distinct borders), one can exist in an almost-different city with its own patterns of movement, population, and unstated neighborhood norms. Of course, such urban textures are not immutable or invariable constraints on city dwellers. They are produced by the interactions of autonomous individuals and their surroundings, which consist of concrete (both literally and figuratively) structures and the individuals who move through them. Two individuals might experience much different affective senses of the texture of the same urban space. But in the long run, Lefebvre suggests, the texture of a city does constitute a persistent infrastructure (to use Berlant's term for an affective environment) that subtly sculpts one's perception of one's urban environment and the experiences and relationships that one undergoes within it.

Despite the diversity of the city in both its temporal and spatial qualities, one particular characteristic, according to Lefebvre, stands out so clearly that it defines the urban. He notes that the greater the urbanity of the space is, the more concentrated are the people, ideas, and thus rhythms of the space. He describes how "urban space gathers crowds, products in the market, acts and symbols. It concentrates these and accumulates them. To say urban space is to say centrality and it does not matter whether they are actual or merely possible" (Lefebvre 1992, 101). Centralities are not merely physical concentrations of buildings or wide-open urban plazas, but the interactions of individuals and ideas with these spaces. And because centralities force together so many differences, they cannot remain stable. He notes that "the essential aspect of the urban phenomenon is its centrality, but a centrality that is understood in conjunction with the dialectal movement that creates or destroys it. The fact that any point can become central is the meaning of urban space-time" (Lefebvre 2003, 116). Notice how he emphasizes that centrality can occur anywhere—empty spaces with wide-open design may become transformed by concentrations of people. Thus, centrality for Lefebvre constitutes a principle rather than any specific design characteristic or urban space. Centrality can happen anywhere, although certain architectural qualities might encourage or discourage this phenomenon. More importantly, centrality, to Lefebvre, constitutes both a physical space and the normative core of city life. Centralities can be centrally located within a city, in the case of, for instance, a city square or urban mall. But more importantly, they are spaces where people gather and experience difference, and thus they can be found in any location within the urban landscape. A centrally located space might contain a moment of centrality, and then this moment, due to the "dialectical movement" that Lefebvre mentions as destructive of such encounters, can fade away—a crowd, or a discussion, can form in a space and then disperse. What is important to remember is that centrality for Lefebvre possesses a double meaning of both a space and a type of encounter between individuals, and encouraging centrality can play a role in cities acting as environments that generate radical political potential.

Although Lefebvre celebrates the centrality that often occurs in cities, he also identifies how capital accumulation deleteriously sculpts urban spaces, including centralities. Lefebvre notes that "the commodity prevails over everything. (Social) space and (social) time, dominated by exchanges, become the time and space of markets; although not being things but including rhythms, they enter into products" (Lefebvre 2004, 6). He asserts that the consequences of the imprinting of commodity rhythms upon urban space are multiple and profound. The logic of the market has overwhelmed the normative potential of centrality and transformed urban spaces, especially centralities, into spaces that propagate the rhythmic qualities of exchange. Lefebvre emphasizes that "the city and urban reality are related to use value. Exchange value and the generalization of commodities by industrialization tend to destroy it to subordinating the city and urban reality which are refugees of use value, the origins of a virtual predominance and revalorization of use" (Lefebvre, Kofman, and Lebas 1996a, 67–68). Lefebvre refers to such central spaces as "instrumental," "impersonal," and notes "the great empty spaces of the state and the military plazas that resemble parade grounds . . . commercial centers packed tight with commodities, money and cars" (Lefebvre 1992, 50–51). Sennett posits a similar preponderance of "abstract," or perhaps a better word for his characterization might be "absent" qualities as the dominant characteristic of capitalist space. This emphasis upon absence of quality within spaces can be seen in his description of the grid-layout of most contemporary city streets. He states, "Here is where the grid found its place. It was a space of economic competition to be played upon like a chessboard. It was a space of neutrality, a neutrality achieved by denying the environment any value of its own" (Sennett 1992, 55). Notice here how the "neutrality" by which Sennett describes the urban grid robs the environment of any qualitative value, or, to put it in terms used by the Marxist Lefebvre, any use value. The value of such spaces, in fact, lies in their neutrality, their seeming absence of restraint, and their easy replication across space and time. The grid allows for maximal rational movement and interchange—forcing movement across a wide area, yet quantifying and restricting the directions that movement can take. It is abstract in that it is imposed upon multiple locations, offering quantitative legibility across time and space. While any space can be subject to abstraction, the abstraction of spatial centralities heralds a particularly troubling manifestation of this phenomenon due to spatial centrality's potentials to foster encounters characterized by centrality. What is important to remember is that the supposed neutrality and absence of abstract spaces in fact play an important role in the propagation of capitalist worldviews—for such spaces, seeming neutrality actually molds places and the bodies that move through them into vehicles for commodity exchange and thus capital accumulation.

All of these designations emphasize the uniformity within these environments, but, to Lefebvre, it is not simply allowing free movement that defines such spaces. Instead, he argues, the primary quality of an abstract space is that, "coinciding neither with the abstraction of the sign, nor with that of the concept, it operates negatively. Abstract space relates negatively to that which perceives and underpins it—namely, the historical and religio-political spheres. It also relates negatively to something which it carries within itself and which seeks to emerge from it: a differential space-time" (Lefebvre 1992, 50). What Lefebvre means by defining abstract space negatively is that, while it can take many forms, for example, the open plaza or the kitschy shopping mall, its primary function is to negate the multiplicity and differentiation embodied in the Mediterranean urban form. As Stanek emphasizes, abstraction to Lefebvre should be thought of as an "active abstraction" (Stanek 2011, 148) that can take many forms and adapt to new variations of spatial practice. And, of course, it must, because abstract space, as Lefebvre points out, "carries within itself" and "is based on" differential space.

Commodities constantly move and interact—prompting encounters that result in unpredictable affects. Abstract spaces both facilitate and control such affects, channeling them into abstract exchanges that can be reproduced in various locations. And from these qualities one can see the challenge of reproducing abstract spaces—they cannot be static yet they must reproduce uniformity.

But Lefebvre stresses that abstract space develops dialectically and thus the formation of centralities also results in the formation of peripheral areas. He observes how "the interaction of a center and a periphery reveal the importance of a new social political and cultural sphere—urban society" (Lefebvre 1968, 123). To him, peripherality does not connote a purely spatial designation, but is instead an indication of social stratification. The marginalized of urban society tend to be pushed out to the outskirts of the city. Such capitalist control can never be flawlessly maintained, as the center is not only divided from the periphery but is dependent on the periphery. As city life increasingly gathers individuals together, it also pushes some segments of the population and its functions out to the periphery of urban space. Labor and waste, the nonmarket inputs and outputs of capital, are shunted off to the outskirts of cities. Urban centers thrive on difference, according to Lefebvre, but only a particular type of difference that facilitates capital accumulation. He refers to the exclusion of noncapitalist functions from urban areas as segregation. This terminology might seem confusing, in that segregation is often associated with the protection of racial and religious homogeneity within cities, but Lefebvre goes out of his way to note that

> difference is incomparable with segregation, which caricatures it. When we speak of difference, we speak of relationships, and therefore proximity relations that are conceived and perceived, and inserted in a twofold space-time order: near and distant. Separation and segregation break this relationship. They constitute a totalitarian order, whose strategic goal is to break own concrete totality to break the urban. Segregation complicates and destroys complexity. They constitute a totalitarian order whose strategic goal is to break down concrete totality, to break the urban. (Lefebvre 2003, 133)

Segregation, to Lefebvre, constitutes the forced division of the "totality" of the city, and thus, undermine the process of smooth capital flow that characterized the ideal capitalist urban form. Capital depends upon workers, yet their dwellings are increasingly forced to move away from close proximity to their workplaces. Stanek notes that "Lefebvre read Engels's account of Manchester as a double moment of disclosure and concealment: while the misery of the workers' districts was shrouded from the view of the upper class, the spatial segregation manifested in the social relations of the city—above all the contradiction between the proletariat and the bourgeois" (Stanek 2011, 148).[3] The concealment of the qualities of daily life within the workers' residential district comes in conjunction with the clear setting of a contentious boundary between the bourgeois residential and industrial districts.

More importantly, segregation between centralities and peripheries not only obscures the reality of life within the specific districts, but conceals the relationships within the urban enclaves that comprise the "totality" of the urban environment. In a sense, they fetishize (in the sense of Marx's understanding of commodity fetishization) the abstract urban center, concealing the necessary interrelationships that must occur for the city to act as a vehicle for capital accumulation. Because of this disintegration of the relationships that comprise the totality of the city, urban dwellers' experience comes to be fragmented. Lefebvre explains that

> here is a daily life well-divided into fragments: work, trans-
> port, private life leisure. Analytical separation has isolated
> them as ingredients and chemical elements, as raw materials
> (whereas they are the outcome of a long history and imply
> an appropriation of materiality). It is not finished. Here is
> the dismembered and disassociated human being. (Lefebvre,
> Kofman, and Lebas 1996a, 143)[4]

This reification of urban space is felt as experiential reification—the fragmentation and thus naturalization of what are, in reality, the inter-connected aspects of urban life. It is important to remember that this fragmentation does not lead to difference as Lefebvre understands it. Urban segregation results in casting the city dwellers' experience as "homogeneous yet at the same time broken up into fragments" (Lefeb-vre 1992, 113). Such discontinuous yet monotonous social aesthetics of experience render attempts to discern the connections between different districts of a city and the social forces these districts represent nearly impossible. Besides the loss of the tendency to perceive the relationships one experiences as a totality, existence in such urban forms discourages individuals from perceiving the importance and possible meanings of affect at all. Butler argues that Lefebvre drew upon the thought of Bachelard to explain what he called the "'loss of affect' . . . that accompanied the rise of technological modernism in the urban context" (Butler 2012, 124). As urban space increasingly compounds the fragmentation of experience, Lefebvre contends, the rhythms of daily life come to be more and more obscured. People do not perceive the many instances of segregation and separation because either they occur too quickly or they represent mere iterations of the same. Rhythmanalysis becomes all the more difficult when individuals can neither intellectually know nor effectively sense the separations that constitute the capitalist abstract city. As any possible individuality or use value comes to be evacuated from their experience they become more desensitized to the qualities of their surroundings. This loss of affect further cements the seemingly universal and unchangeable nature of their surroundings, making critique and resistance all the more unlikely.

Despite the prevailing presence of capitalist urban textures resulting from segregation and the propagation of abstract centralities, Lefebvre claims that the experience of affects that might prompt resistance can never be fully eliminated from any space. For example, although one's job, family life, or hobbies and other enjoyment might not change, one experiences them in different sequences. Even if the sequences might remain the same, in that the routines of a particular day might be experienced in the same order every time that day occurs, the changes from one institution and environment become more frequent. One experiences the juxtaposition between work and home, between different neighborhoods, more diverse entertainments, during a particular day in an urban environment, presenting more possibilities to consider comparison, contrast, different rules of behavior, different perspectives. Lefebvre claims that such potential clashes lead to the necessity of innovation and rethinking, as routines are harder to keep and norms are more easily challenged. And while the innovations urban dwellers undertake seem episodic and fragmented, they are all accompanied by a general sense of the increased "pace" or rhythm of urban life. He describes the rhythmic roots of everyday urban crisis and creativity by explaining:

> All becoming irregular (or if one wants, all deregulation, though this word has taken on an official sense) of rhythms

produces antagonistic effects. It *throws out of order* and disrupts; it is symptomatic of a disruption that is generally profound, lesional and no longer functional. It can also produce a lacuna, a hole in time, to be filled by an invention, a creation. That only happens, individually or socially, by passing through a *crisis*. Disruptions and crises always have origins and effects of rhythms: those of institutions, of growth, of the population, of exchanges or work, therefore those which make or express the complexity of present societies. (Lefebvre 2004, 44)

Lefebvre here clearly ties crisis not only to creativity, but, more importantly, to the experience of rhythm—crises are felt as disruptions in rhythm before they are comprehended. In terms of the urban landscape, where crises of the city are involved, urban landscapes that prompt choppy movement can indicate a number of larger social phenomena— uncontrolled growth, ethnic segregation, precarious labor—whereby any manifestation of the capitalist landscape produces resonances that one can feel as one undertakes one's daily activities. Such rhythms, and the movements that produce them, represent the "loosening" of linear rhythms and abstract centralities.[5] Furthermore, such disruptive rhythms can express more than one phenomenon and can shift and transmute with little warning. The ambiguity of such rhythms does not render them useless. Lefebvre sees them as invitations, although they are not always accepted, to engage in larger investigations into how one's daily experience is molded by larger social structures.

Because urban rhythms come to be produced by a multiplicity of phenomena, different rhythms produce different affects, and consequently different effects upon the possibility for creativity. Through taking on a perspective of "hydrodynamics," Lefebvre claims that theorists can begin to distinguish between "great movements, vast rhythms, immense wages—these all collide and 'interfere' with one another," and "lesser movements" that "interpenetrate." He emphasizes that "we could say that any social locus could only be property understood by taking two kinds of determinations into account: on the one hand that locus would be mobilized, carried forward and sometimes smashed apart by major tendencies, those tendencies which 'interfere' with one another; on the other hand, it would be penetrated by, and shot through with the weaker tendencies characteristic of networks and pathways" (Lefebvre 1992, 87). Here, one can see Lefebvre laying out the concepts that drive the process of rhythmanalysis in an urban setting and establishing the distinction between rhythms that "interfere" with each other, causing tension, disruption, and questioning, and rhythms that "penetrate" and build upon the potentialities and tendencies inherent within their presence.

Lefebvre explicitly ties radical political activity to particular rhythms produced by efforts that loosen the controlled environment of abstract space. He states, "Liberty is born in a reserved space and time, sometimes, wide sometimes narrow; occasionally reduces by the results of dressage to an unoccupied lacuna. Creative activity as distinct from productive activity proceeds from the liberty and individuality that unfurl only in conditions that are external to them" (Lefebvre 2004, 43). He goes on to tie his concepts of inhabitation and appropriation to rhythm, stating:

> Through a certain use of time the citizen resists the state. A struggle for appropriation is therefore unleashed in which rhythms play a major role. Through them civil, and therefore time, seeks to and succeeds in withdrawing itself from linear unirhythmic, measuring/measured state time. Thus public space, the space of representation, becomes "spontaneously" a place for walks and encounters, intrigues, diplomacy deals and negotiations—it theatralises itself. Thus the time and the rhythms of the people who occupy this paces are linked back to space. (Lefebvre 2004, 96)

Notice in this quote how Lefebvre intertwines the temporal dimensions of rhythm with the spatial dimensions of the public. The rhythms encouraged by particular places encourage their users to undertake new movements, gestures, and relationships, which subsequently modify the original space. These new uses then prompt new rhythms. Lefebvre advocates actions to "defend ourselves at all times from the bards of conditioning—and reverse their rhythms" (Merrifield 2017, 87).Thus, the rhythmic properties of space constitute an important and undervalued method of imposing capitalist power, and thus, new rhythms must be encouraged through new spaces in order to break the power of everyday conditioning.

In sum, Lefebvre's rhythmanalysis of the city allows me to establish numerous links between his work and the political theory of salvage described thus far. Lefebvre's contention that "the city is heard as much as music as it is read as discursive writing" invokes the theorists of affect I discussed in chapter 2. The sensed background texture revealed through rhythmanalysis constitutes what Berlant would call the infrastructure of society. This rhythmic infrastructure reflects the spatial and temporal dynamics of the social processes that sculpt the contours of one's environment. Lefebvre contends that the sensed rhythms of the city can alert individuals to crises and contradictions even though they do not realize the specific origins of these affects. The challenge, according to both Lefebvre and the theorists of craftwork I discussed in the last chapter, remains to embrace and not reject these chaotic and contingent affects. Just like the craftworker, rhythmanalysis suggests that acute attention and even surrender to the affects constitute the first steps in "repairing" the crises and disruptions that one senses. This process of repair begins by searching for the potential causes of the contingent affects one senses and then following them, much as a craftsperson with a honed habit of material consciousness follows the grain of a piece of wood, following the indications suggested by these affects into new realms of investigation and action.

The felt rhythms of the capitalist city are the product of the real tensions and segregation of the city. As capital seeks to transform as many spaces as possible into those characterized by what Lefebvre would deem as abstract centrality, it pushes surplus spaces and populations to the peripheries, which is where salvage grows. Yet capital both creates and destroys, and as the old abstract centralities wane in their importance for accumulation, new areas become ripe for exploitative transformation. The squats, informal communities, and occupations that practice salvage as part of their activism constitute spaces that represent "ideorhythmic" islands challenging oncoming waves of capitalist abstraction, and are themselves activated by the rhythms of segregated capitalist development. As capitalist urban planners rearrange the city to facilitate the flow of capital, certain activities and those who engage in them are pushed to the peripheries. Dumps, populations engaged in contingent labor, informal economic activity are all pushed to the outskirts of the cities. Such districts possess their own textures, in sharp contrast to the abstract centralities characteristic of capitalist urban planning. They are areas where salvage often occurs in both the productive and reproductive activity, such as childrearing, of the residents. They can never be eliminated, because centralities depend upon them as necessary depositories of everything that must be discarded for their functioning. Salvage spaces in the periphery will always constitute the "other" of capitalist space, and thus represent a challenge, merely by their existence, to efforts made by capitalist urban planners to transform cities into spaces completely devoted to capital accumulation.

Before entering into a discussion of how Lefebvre interprets the political potential of such spaces, I want to connect his analysis of capitalism's spatial structuring of urban space to my previous discussion. Abstract space robs individuals of their ability to sense the city's affective infrastructure. Abstract spaces dedicated only to facilitating exchange value lead to individuals sensing affects "dull with anxiety" (Stewart 2007, 50–51), a phrase Katherine Stewart uses to describe the experience of everyday life under capitalism. Furthermore, the deadening repetition of one stopgap solution after the next both creates false hope in those who experience it and fragments attempts to make connections between the various aspect of one's life. Segregation abets such cruel optimism by facilitating the disjunctures between the spatial and temporal textures of one's experience. Even if one primarily spends most of one's life in similar spaces containing similar people, traveling within an urban environment crisscrossed by the borders that enforce segregated enclaves produces repetitious affects that obscure the connections between these enclaves and their surroundings. Lefebvre's understanding adds concrete situational detail to the account of capitalist infrastructure I discussed in chapter 2. Using his work, it becomes clear that it is not simply life in capitalism that produces such infrastructure, but everyday experience in the capitalist city, with its abstraction and segregation, that results in the experience of such affects, and their depoliticizing consequences.

Liberated Salvage Space

Lefebvre's understanding of how the spatial tensions of the capitalist city create possibilities for resistance constitutes the beginning of my exploration of how everyday acts of salvage can lead to anticapitalist politics. Lefebvre begins to translate his understanding of how the textures and rhythms that city dwellers experience in their movements through capitalist landscapes by deploying the concept of *détournement*. This term was popularized by Situationists such as Guy Debord to describe their acts of subverting familiar spaces, items, and practices. Playful repurposings of the familiar in ways that made them unfamiliar were meant to "rock people out of their slumbering torpor, out of their modern passivity, monkey-wrenching received meaning in bourgeois reality, reveling in collective feats of resistance and action of lampooning" (Merrifield 2011, 27).[6] Lefebvre emphasizes that acts of *détournement* represent a moment of scrambling preconceived usages of space by "repurposing" (Lefebvre 2014, 97) them in ways that were not previously accepted or even conceived. He emphasizes that these "repurposings" should not be thought of as instrumental interventions—they are unstable, and constitute a process of invention and reinvention. He claims:

> [A]t the moment of *détournement* new aspirations appear, transposing the earlier form whenever it reveals its limitations in the face of new practices and languages. At a given moment, *détournement* exhausts itself and the form that has been used collapses, either because something new has been created or because the decline overwhelms its creative capacity. (Lefebvre 2014, 98)[7]

Lefebvre goes on to contrast *détournement* to both domination and appropriation (a term that will be discussed more thoroughly in the next section) and links its specifically to the process of non-instrumental creation. Others use the concept of *détournement* to highlight the playful, ephemeral repurposing of public spaces and buildings during urban occupations. She states that the workers who occupied the Hôtel de Ville during the1871 Commune

> were not "at home" in the Center of Paris; they were occupying enemy territory. . . . Such an occupation, however brief, provides an example of what the Situationists have called a *détournement*—using the elements or terrain of the dominant social order to one's own ends, for a transformed purpose: integrating actual or past productions into a superior construction of milieu. (Ross 2008, 42)[8]

Although the business of the commune was obviously deadly serious and taken as a direct challenge to the state's authority, Ross's use of *détournement* to describe the actual practice of the Communards emphasizes how the struggle for power was intertwined with experimentation, and, though it seems strange to deem such serious and even tragic events in this way, play, for, even though the acts of *détournement* undertaken by the Communards were not undertaken by choice, their creative, spontaneous, and ultimately subversive uses of space took on a playful form as described by Lefebvre.

Despite the subversive power of festival, such activities seem like week reeds upon which to build a political strategy that might lead to the radical transformation of society. Festivals, while subversive and disruptive of capitalist divisions of space, are not constructive in either a physical or political sense. Furthermore, festive, playful repurposing of space constitutes a temporary intervention, which might not leave behind a significant or permanent impact. Such festivals, while intense, rarely leave anything behind, and can hardly be thought of as craftwork. But Lefebvre employs another concept to describe spatial activities that both undermine capitalist reifications of the city and contain the possibility of developing new spaces that would support longer lasting and more coherent political activity. As I have previously noted, the main concept that Lefebvre uses to describe his political urban strategy is that of inhabitation or appropriation—remember that he states that the dialectical tension of segregated capitalist space leads to "struggles for appropriation." To appropriate or inhabit[9] a place (a concept Lefebvre first articulates in his *Critique of Everyday Life*, but which appears throughout his corpus) is, in a superficial sense, to make it one's own. As opposed to the everyday routines that accompany what he refers to as habitat, inhabiting a space comprises a process whereby individuals simultaneously mold and are molded by spaces. Inhabitation, he asserts, is the result of a process of playing in a space. He states, "To inhabit, again finds its place over habitat. The quality which is promoted presents and represents as playful" (Lefebvre, Kofman, and Lebas 1996a, 172). Inhabiting transforms a space into one that allows for the creation of use values as opposed to facilitating exchange value. Before the onset of capitalist urban modernization, inhabiting constituted an everyday necessity and flowed from the quotidian demands of existence—one used space in ways that responded to one's needs, and in the process that space came to exhibit the imprint of those uses. But as Butler states, once daily life became saturated with and constructed by commodities, due to what Lefebvre terms the onset of "controlled consumption . . . the every-day . . . spatially and experimentally transformed by a form of ordering that has reduced the disparate elements of inhabitance to the functional requires of what Lefebvre terms the 'habitat'"(Butler 2012, 105). From this, one can see that, whereas this understanding of inhabiting a space describes a process whereby individuals undertake small interventions within their immediate environments only to mitigate them immediately, in fact he asserts that inhabiting a space can initiate a process that lifts individuals away from their everyday frustrations and deposits them in larger moral and political realms. Those who inhabit an abstract space undertake activities expressive of developmental rhythms that slowly modify the space in a way that expresses their own interests and desires, not simply those helpful to capitalist accumulation. Like craftworkers, they tinker with the space, experimenting with new uses until they find one that "fits" within the constraints of the space and its users. The enactment of spatial activity embodying "use" as opposed to exchange value, even in the most quotidian contexts, for Lefebvre constitutes the potential jumping-off point for larger reinterpretations of and resistance against capitalist space.

It seems from the previous description that appropriation constitutes an act undertaken in one's immediate environment, such as one's house, one's street, and perhaps one's neighborhood. But Stanek stresses that individual acts of appropriation will not suffice, and thus, "It became clear to Lefebvre that the appropriation of space cannot be thought of limited to an individual home or private apartment but must address the urban scale. . . . In this perspective, appropriation needs to be thought of as not only multiscalar but also straddling multiplicities of time" (Stanek 2011, 118). A neighborhood, a city, and even country can be "appropriated" through continued acts of transformation and communication between dwellers of different locations. As individuals travel, and modify their routes and destinations, within even the most meticulously planned city, they will, if they can, leave the imprint of their actions and thus appropriate space in a way that both respects their own uses and other uses of that space. Stanek argues that appropriation also forges a connection between the community to "inhabit" the history of the space. Or in other words, when appropriating a space individuals not only transform it to be amenable to their various uses, but also modify it in a way that forges a connection between themselves and the past of their community through symbolic spaces such as monuments, public spaces, and other environments that evoke historical connection and demonstrate past uses of the space.

The question now becomes, What characteristics does an inhabited or appropriated space possess? Simply modifying a controlled space in a way that satisfies personal desires does not necessarily lead to radical politics. It might seem that spaces defined by their unique use value cannot in fact share any qualities, in that each individual and community will shape each space according to their unique circumstances and desire. But, in fact, Lefebvre claims, these appropriated, inhabited spaces do exhibit some common elements, most notably their flexibility and oneness to appropriation. Perhaps ironically, Lefebvre asserts that inhabited spaces that are adapted by groups to their specific needs do not permanently retain the shapes produced by these adapted uses. Lefebvre notes that the main "move" of those inhabiting a space is to "produce differences in an undifferentiated space" (Stanek 2011, 143). This remains true of both the spatial and symbolic characteristics of such spaces. As Lefebvre stresses in both his theoretical writings and his concrete suggestions for urban design, an inhabited space "produces multiple spatial configurations open to individual designs" (Stanek 2011, 210).[10] Thus, appropriated spaces constitute more fully an environment productive of a practice of becoming than a space representing any particular use. For Lefebvre, appropriating a space represents entering into a possible relationship with a space that will necessarily transform itself—and thus the appropriation does not represent an end point but instead an inducement to a particular "pedagogy of the body" that allows for constant adaptation to use, as opposed to the transformation of the body into a mere vehicle for exchange and consumption.

Although the city has been classically understood as the epitome of settlement, with its agglomerations of buildings and infrastructure that last for centuries, Lefebvre advocates for a "nomadic" understanding of the liberated city. He desires a society where

> the enthusiasm for the ephemeral and nomadic, the fascination with incessant departures, will supplant the earlier sense of rootedness in the home, the traditional attachment to the place of birth. . . . Whether from above or from below, this would be the end of both habiting and the urban as sites of bundled oppositions as centers. (Lefebvre 2003, 95)

He suggests that urbanity, perhaps ironically, should encourage nomadism, and thus multiple acts of appropriation, as people move from centrality to centrality. In his interpretation of the New Babylon plan, Lefebvre, perhaps in a fit of enthusiasm, describes this ideal city as "a camp for nomads on a planetary scale," in which "efficiency, production, competition and individualism are to be replaced by appreciation for a sense of adventure, exploration, disorientation, cooperation and mass creativity"(Stanek 2011, 220).[11] With this valorization of nomadism, it becomes clear that inhabitation, for Lefebvre, is not meant to constitute isolated, single activities but comes to be seen as a way of life—a way of life that should be encouraged by one's environment. Spatial appropriation, in this interpretation, does not end in an inhabited home, neighborhood, or even city. Appropriation is meant to expand and grow in scale while moving from location to location—as differing combinations of people and spaces occur through these movements, they appropriate these spaces according to the new combinations of their perceived usage of that space.

Lefebvre claims that even the most sculpted city spaces exhibit the potential for people to appropriate them as they see fit. People sit and eat their lunch on the monumental steps leading to the gilded doors of financial institutions. Vendors sell their food on streets meant to convey workers quickly from office to train. Punk teenagers hang out in the foyers of government buildings. And, if less frequently, activists occupy plazas, construct encampments, and collectively dream of different worlds. Lefebvre sees the potential for these inhabitations to overflow their original confinements, as the increasing need of capital to circulate commodities and workers ever faster forces ever newer combinations of people into unfamiliar places. Such activities exhibit "progressive" rhythms, as I call them. And, most importantly, salvage can also be seen as possessing these progressive rhythms, in that it displays playful development of the plastic potentials of experience. Such playful development of salvage embodies the same form as the development of concrete utopias, and salvage can act as a tool to generate these impulses to radical political critique and action. Thus, the capitalist dynamic of increasing circulation actually sets in motion a dynamic that increases the possibility of urban centrality and undermines abstract space. This nomadic tendency accompanies the tendency to desire self-management because the process of appropriation is a playful process that originates in small, everyday acts of adjustment, experimentation, and improvisation. Skateboarders and merchants occupy different parts of a public space—they might clash but they most likely will negotiate a spatial compromise that allows for both. Although such everyday, small negotiations seem far from political, Lefebvre contends that they inculcate habits, expectations, and practices of autonomy, tolerance, and a general view that space should be for the use of those who inhabit it. The diverse members of a space come to see themselves as co-inhabitants of the space, and begin to partially define themselves by this identity.[12] As the expectation of inhabitation builds in one space, Lefebvre sees people potentially carrying this expectations to other parts of the city as they visit them. And of course, as the enforcers of capitalist space push back against these inhabitations, the identification that people possess toward these spaces comes to be strengthened, and people fall back upon them as the only thing that can unite them in the face of capitalist power that is imposed not upon a factory but upon the entire city.

For Lefebvre, the activity of appropriation also often leads to self-management of these spaces, or what he refers to as *autogestion*. In his writings on the Paris Commune, the May 1968 uprisings, and especially in his submission for the "New Belgrade Urban Structural Improvement" competition in 1986, this plan called for the creation of multiple "nodes of structural intensity" that would encourage repeated acts of spatial appropriation. According to the plan, these multiple centers, which constitute environments that do not force any particular manifestation of inhabitation, instead would encourage citizens to collectively rethink their spatial environments by providing relatively open and flexible spaces where habitual practices and interpretations would be disrupted by new combinations of people engaging in new combinations of practices.[13] To Lefebvre and his collaborators, these "nodes" would maximize the urban qualities of the city—the plasticity and diversity by which he defines centrality. Because these spaces are spatially open and free from municipal control, the appropriation he sees occurring comes about through the citizens themselves, negotiating with each other to find mutually satisfactory accommodations and collective practices. The proposal goes so far as to define urbanity by these collective acts of spatial appropriation, stating, "It is impossible to string together an urban-ism whose ideology is fundamentally opposed to the self-management of the city, space and time" (Bitter and Weber 2009, 85). He also emphasizes that autogestion functions as a radical critical activity, undermining the reification encouraged by capitalist abstract space. He states that autogestion, or self-management, "radically contests the existing order from the world of the commodity and the power of money to the power of the state" (Lefebvre 2009, 148). Thus, urbanity, for Lefebvre, possesses a political import. To him, it is also appropriate to self-govern, and this represents a further expression of his underlying insight not only that particular spatial environments possess the potential to encourage particular ideas and attitudes but also that particular uses of space can act as powerful tactics in efforts at liberation from capitalist oppression.

Salvage as Anticapitalist Inhabitation

Until this point, my argument has led to revealing Lefebvre's account of how the spatial contradictions of the capitalist city manifest themselves in affective textures that might prompt subversive uses of space. While I have demonstrated that such spatial tactics are at the core of Lefebvre's radical urban politics, and suggested the many overlaps of Lefebvre's understanding with my previous argument, especially in terms of the importance of rhythmic affects experienced in everyday life in the for-mulation of radical political activity, I have not made any direct mention of salvage activity within Lefebvre's corpus. Such references do exist, though, and pointing them out not only helps to establish a concrete connection between Lefebvre and a political theory of salvage, but aids in identifying how salvage within the city becomes explicitly political.

To begin, Lefebvre notes how the inevitable waste of capitalist accumulation must also be segregated from areas of production and reproduction. He states that "the phenomenon of segregation must be analyzed according to various indices and criteria: ecological (shanty towns, slums, the rot in the heart of the city)" (Lefebvre, Kofman, and Lebas 1996a, 140). Thus, spaces inhabited by surplus materials, such as garbage dumps, and surplus people, such as slums, constitute a necessary part of capitalist production that must be externalized and thus segre-gated. This process of forced segregation constitutes an unending activity within the capitalist city that results in a mutually reinforcing culture of exclusion. Fredericks observes that "governmental techniques which render unruly slum spaces unlawful define and enforce aesthetic norms to produce specific images of modernity and legitimize the displacements of those deemed 'polluting' or lacking a proper 'citizen culture' as unfit to belong in the city"(Fredericks 2018, 20). He goes on to observe that whole cultures and communities develop around these excluded zones of waste and that "garbage disposal requires not just places that are discardable, but also disposable people to accomplish the task" (Fred-ericks 2018, 21). Thus, the inevitable cleansing that accompanies the production of abstract spaces also produces the "waste" areas from which salvage springs. Furthermore, the technologies of exclusion, both spatial and social, that reinforce this segregation imposing the isolation and thus inescapable inhabitation of ruined landscapes that forces people to salvage. If there is no grocery store in one's neighborhood, one must reclaim the land in order to grow food. If the electrical grid does not extend to one's house, then one must salvage a generator or jury-rig a pirate connection to distant power lines. As long as the "spatial fix" as David Harvey calls it, plays a role in the strategies of contemporary capital accumulation, a phenomenon that leads investors to frequently abandon spaces to find new activities for profit, there will be landscapes of neglect and ruin. As traditional resources and forms of labor disappear from such spaces, residents turn to salvage. And while salvage springs from the actions of capital, capital cannot abide it as it challenges the segregations that enable its existence.

As I have said before, Lefebvre identifies efforts to undermine abstract capitalist space as inhabitation, and it is through this concept that he makes his most direct connection between his larger spatial theory and salvage. I introduced this chapter with an example citing how Lefebvre suggests that individuals might play with their urban space, appropriating leftover, discarded landscapes through building informal communities. He states:

> The vast shanty towns of Latin America (*favelas, barrios, ranchos*) manifest a social life far more intense than the bourgeois districts of the cities. . . . Their poverty not with-standing, these districts sometimes so effectively order their space—houses, walls, public spaces—as to elicit a nervous admiration. *Appropriation* of a remarkable high order is to be found here. The spontaneous architecture and planning ("wild" forms, according to a would-be elegant terminology) prove greatly superior to the organization of space by specialists who effectively translate the social order into territorial reality with or without direct orders from economic and political authorities. The result—on the ground—is an extraordinary spatial duality. . . . Duality means contradiction and conflict; a conflict of this kind eventuates either in the emergence of unforeseen differences or in its own absorption. (Lefebvre 1992, 374)

While Lefebvre here praises the effectiveness of the spatial arrange-ments of these neighborhoods he also notes their "wild" forms and the "contradiction and conflict" that produces "unforeseen differences" in space, and the interactions of individuals within this space. These sal-vaged landscapes not only constitute reflections of the individuals who construct them but also take on playful lives of their own and lead to surprising and challenging new interactions among residents. They inspire constant tinkering, reformulation, and experimentation. The "repurposing" characteristic of inhabitation does not constitute a conscious effort meant to shock a complacent population or challenge authority within a controlled space, but instead embodies a constant practice of spatial relation. To say that salvage might be a manifestation of playful inhabitation emphasizes the constant call to reformulation, often prompted by conflict and competition, that accompanies instability. In salvaged neighborhoods, it is also the material instability of the spaces, the need for constant repair, the unexpected juxtaposition of items and materials out of which the most mundane spaces are constructed, the constant efforts to find new supplies of resources with which to maintain one's existence that all result in the necessity to repurpose and play with one's space. And although Lefebvre offers only a brief mention of this salvaged environment and does not emphasize the unstable, contingent material inducements to play that exist in salvaged neighborhoods, my interpreting salvaged informal communities as examples of spatial inhabitation falls well within his articulation of the concept. More importantly, attempting to understand not simply salvaged barrios but, through extension, the other salvaged spaces most frequently linked to political activity, that is, occupations and squats, helps to illuminate the dynamics of existence in such spaces in a way that further highlights their political potential.

Whereas Lefebvre explicitly mentions the existence of salvaged peripheral neighborhoods as prime examples of spatial appropriation, he also offers another, less obvious example with even more provocative implications for a political theory of salvage. The autonomous construction of salvaged buildings and even entire communities establishes "ideorythmic" zones that stand in stark contrast to capitalist centralities, and when urban planners attempt "urban renewal"–based plans of gentrification, these communities resist. As I have noted, one can find such defensive actions in salvage cites in barrios all across Latin America, occupied factories in Argentina, and squatted buildings in metropolises such as London and Berlin. Lefebvre's work points to other more expansive, and, one can say, even aggressive forms of inhabitation of ruined, peripheral landscapes, which can thought of as possessing political implications. Remember that Lefebvre discusses how the "hydrodynamic" spatial forces within a city produce contradictions and slippages that undermine efforts to sculpt the city into a rationalized, uniform zone of capital accumulation. He discusses how uses of space can interfere with each other, for example, how a collection of people relaxing in a public square might disrupt the flow of people in and out of businesses. He also states that capitalist spaces can be "penetrated by and shot through with weaker characteristics of network and pathways" (Lefebvre 1992, 160). Whereas this description is certainly provocative, the exact implications and physical manifestation of such "penetrations" remains to be seen. Yet in other works Lefebvre and scholars who write on his work suggest how such penetrations, which might seem to be only manifestations of aggressive capitalist reconstruction as spaces dedicated to use are aggressively transformed into spaces of exchange, also in fact can be assertions of use and inhabitation that transgress the boundaries set by capitalist urban planning.

For example, in the introduction to *Architecture of Enjoyment*, Stanek presents the work of Lefebvre's student Mario Graviria, which focuses on the inhabitation of modernist public housing estates in Spain. These estates were designed according to modernist principles—segregated from city centers, consisting of uniform apartment buildings, rationalized, square city blocks, and lacking adequate facilities for recreation and education. Despite its lack of resources both by design and by its segregation from the city center, Graviria notes "[t]he intensity of urban life in these estates, which was based on a 'spontaneous urbanism' differing from that foreseen by the planners and yet 'well understood by some street vendors who change positions according to times of the day and days of the week" (Lefebvre 2014, xxi). One of the primary means by which that Graviria maps this spontaneous urban intensity is by tracing the ways in which the inhabitants of the community collectively build new routes of movement over the grid imposed upon them by urban planners. Like the "activity lines" that guide the foraging of mushroom pickers, as described by Tsing, new paths emerge in the city, especially in its northeastern and western areas. These lines reflect the inhabitants' actual uses of the space—resembling arteries that represent the actual flow of life within the abstract landscape—meant to maximize the movement of people. They are formed not by planned intervention, but through the residents' affective sense of the most useful connections between the different parts of their neighborhoods—avoiding difficulties both physical and social (for instance, avoiding authorities) while being guided by repeated feelings of flow. These pathways emerge through rhythmic interventions, where groups of people recursively respond to the moments of others in in a collective negotiation that reacts to, and ultimately undermines the rules of the built environment. And because of this estate's segregation from the center of Madrid and its relative neglect by municipal authorities, the appropriation of this space did not, at least initially, arouse the ire of the planners and government that imposed the plan. The peripheral status of the estate allows for the creation, at least spatially, of a hetero-topia of use—a space outside the realm of exchange value that reflects the daily uses and desires of the inhabitants and not its role within the large urban system of capital accumulation.

Now I want to present a picture of a similar, yet more intensely abandoned, landscape: twenty-first-century Detroit, Michigan, a city where ruins abound as a consequence of deindustrialization, abandonment by its white population, and persistent financial control by the state that have left large parts of the city bereft of population and city services. During the city's heyday in the early and mid-twentieth century, it was paradigm of modernist development—wide streets arranged in grids traversed by multiple superhighways meant to facilitate quick and easy access from the city's center to its many suburbs. But as industries left and large portions of the city were virtually abandoned by the munic-ipal government, the citizens themselves began to impose their own usages and pathways of movement upon the grid that no longer served their purposes. Just as in the estates studied by Graviria, the residents inhabited a landscape that was ill-suited to their uses, forcing them to carve pathways with their daily movement over streets designed to ferry workers in their cars to factories, parks, and schools. Such "desire lines"[14] carved by collective appropriation once again, were facilitated by neglect, but in the case of Detroit were accompanied by a much more profound abandonment of the peripheral areas of the city. While Detroit's downtown gains boutique hotels and new sports arenas, the residents of the city's outlying neighborhoods collectively salvage their environments through long, rhythmic processes of self-management of the spaces in which they live their daily lives. These "desire lines" or the "informal paths that people wear through the grass instead of following the formal paths laid for them by building and landscape designers"(Parkinson 2012, 78) represent the accumulated, collective voyages of urban nomads following the paths that their bodies created through interaction with their environment. They are geographies of affect, where senses created by a body's relationship with its surroundings suggested paths of movement, not observation of urban design created by others. These paths embody the actual use values of the residents as they reclaim their spaces from the neglect to which they were subjected by the capitalist economy.

In both of these examples, individuals have engaged in spontaneous incursions into spaces abandoned by capital. What remains significant about such actions is that the people salvaged not particular buildings or items, but the spaces themselves. In both the Spanish estate and in Detroit, individuals have used their bodies to forge new uses for what had been deemed useless and, more importantly, to transgress the boundaries and rethink the flows of movement imposed by "rational" urban planning. Such desire lines connect spaces that were not meant to be connected. The boundaries between individual property lines and zones proscribed for particular activities such as living and commerce, come to be scrambled. Even though these desire lines usually crop up within peripheral areas not subject to intense monitoring by authorities, they still contain the imprint of capitalist urban planning. Both the neighborhoods of Detroit and the Gran San Bla Estate were designed to be organized by the straight lines, roads, and property boundaries characteristic of capitalist cities. Thus, such desire lines not only reconfigure one space but aggressively challenge the arrangement and status of many places, the places that capitalist planning attempts to segregate and rationalize. Such desire lines can transcend larger boundaries, not simply within peripheral districts but between them. Of course, such spontaneously constructed paths are more likely to be challenged and destroyed by authorities than simple inhabitations of abstract space such as sitting on the steps of a public building, and thus they constitute provocations, challenges to capitalists' spatial segregation. Even though such unorganized subversions of capitalist spatial arrangement do not originate with organized political groups, they nonetheless result in political consequences. Unlike constructing a salvaged structure or foraging for materials in an abandoned lot or landfill, desire lines challenge the exclusions and boundaries that Lefebvre identifies as the core of the production of abstract space. Through imprinting spatial uses that reflect the needs of particular communities engaged in particular activities on landscapes meant to facilitate movement and segregate activities, these actions confront and undermine the core of the capitalist logic of space. They create new, challenging textures in spaces that previously contributed to the deadening of city dwellers' perceptions of ideorhythmic and thus challenging affects. They represent a further example of a pedagogy of the body through which urban salvage can spark more pronounced political resistance.

The City as the Landscape of Salvage?

Lefebvre, through both his explanation of the microfoundations of inhabiting urban spaces and his observations concerning the macro political economic tendencies that produce peripheral salvage spaces, gives us the "where" of a political theory of salvage. Yet, in many ways, his identification of spatial tendencies within capitalist cities that produce radical contestation relies too much upon space itself as an activating agent for politics. He helps us to understand how salvage becomes political salvage, but these spatial dynamics that can lead to salvage inhabitation cannot be regarded as the only cause or even prime agent of such political salvage. I will now raise questions concerning Lefebvre's work that will not only highlight his overreliance upon space itself to prompt anticapitalist attitudes and actions, but will open the door to further argument regarding how political salvage can play a powerful role in contemporary anticapitalist resistance.

As increasing segregation and abstraction within urban spaces lead more and more stakeholders to demand a "right to the city," it is important to understand how Lefebvre's work demonstrates that salvage activities can act as an important expression of that right. Whereas Lefebvre often talks about the origins of such demands in the repression people experience in their daily efforts to inhabit public spaces—the signs prohibiting sitting on steps and the harassment members of marginalized communities feel in certain areas of cities, a political theory of salvage suggests that a similar everyday prompting to spatial appropriation might be trying to find usable parts within a pile of rubbish and then, perhaps, to use those parts to repair a wall, faucet, or bicycle. Furthermore, as Lefebvre sees these small acts of appropriation facing increasing official resistance, greater defiance to repression and defense of appropriated spaces by groups develops, so too with the communities that protect the squats, informal communities, and public squares they have salvaged. Finally, as Lefebvre sees appropriation generating affiliation and solidarity with place that replaces sole identification with factory or possession, thus rendering the city as potent a cause around which to organize as class, salvaged spaces act as a potent manifestation of the connection to a space that might unify a people in both challenging efforts to undermine their collective appropriation and also challenging the underlying capitalist social dynamics that caused governments in the first place to organize cities based on the model of abstract urban design.

But despite the fact that Lefebvre's work can be generally linked to my discussion of salvage by examining his concept of appropriation, and his discussion of the capitalist city can be used to deconstruct the spatial dialectics that constitute the macro geography that creates the spaces with potential for salvage, his vision relies too heavily on the concept of self-organization. He sees the spatial dynamics of cities themselves as nearly independent causal factors that will inspire the excluded to engage in acts of spatial appropriation exhibiting *autogestion* and other horizontal forms of organization. Such rosy assumptions about the power of the city to generate radical political activity act on both the micro and macro levels. In terms of the macro, Lefebvre assumes that the necessities for constant capital accumulation will generate constant production of difference within the city. Both the destruction and reconstruction of centralities, he assumes, will create tension, as vulnerable populations are forced out of their previously undesirable areas by the application of acts of "accumulation by dispossession." Furthermore, as these populations are shuffled into new forgotten urban zones they continue to be excluded from both old and new districts in which capital is being invested. While this dynamic certainly creates tensions and even resentments, there is no guarantee that these will break out in resistance and other forms of political activity. Some type of catalyst remains necessary to build this dissatisfaction into action. Even if urban resistance and subversive festival does erupt, too often these revolts remain isolated and temporary. For Lefebvre, in many ways, such characteristics remain the attractive qualities of such actions—their chaotic subversion and unpredictability constitute a powerful tactic for subverting the reified, quantitative repressions of capitalist space. But as we can see from the long-term consequences of both the Paris Commune and the May 1968 uprisings (events he sees as prime examples of radical appropriation of space), such momentary eruptions might shine brightly for a moment, but they leave behind very little permanent change. If salvage not only comes about due to the tensions Lefebvre identifies as stemming from the spatial dynamics of the capitalist city, but also constitutes a political practice that can generate meaningful and radical social change, it must be situated within a political theory that overcomes the short-comings of Lefebvre's understanding of the formation of viable political subjects. *Autogestion* is not a political group, nor is the city a political actor, although Lefebvre tends to portray them both as such. While the solution to this problem does not necessarily lie in the formation of a traditional political party to foster a political basis for these principles, stronger organizational forms remain necessary to translate Lefebvre's vision into an actual body capable of achieving radical political change

Similar political lacunae can be seen within micro assumptions inherent in Lefebvre's political thought. When discussing how appropria-tion leads to self-management, he does not provide any account of how groups might form or how they might be sustained. In my analysis of craftwork, I identify habits, rituals, and spaces that help individuals both cultivate and maintain the practice of political salvage. If Lefebvre identi-fies the salvage-based construction of informal communities as exemplary manifestations of appropriation, and I claim that such salvage practices can be thought of as "crafts of the poor," which are thus amenable to intensification through the conscious adoption of certain habits within certain types of groups in certain spaces, then appropriation should also be seen as able to be cultivated and intensified. Remember, I identify the political/normative core of salvage as plural anticapitalist becoming, and thus spatial appropriation can be seen as another practice of becoming. Yet, just as not all acts of salvage exhibit this political ethos, neither do all acts of the transformation of space. It is the repeated practice of such spatial transformation that constitutes the best chance for participants to adopt this attitude. Furthermore, the plasticity at the core of becoming also lies at the core of *autogestion* in that self-management constitutes cooperative acts of groups transforming spaces and thus themselves. The core principle of such commonplace building cannot lie outside of the group but must come from within the group itself. Thus, thinking of *autogestion* as a craft and example of collective metis endows it with a set of concrete practices that might increase the possibility of its continued existence and improvement. Self-management requires many technical tools, depending on the particular endeavor, but to ensure that it both begins and continues it also requires the generation of the ethos of plural becoming at the core of this practice. Thinking of spatial appropriation through the framework of salvage as a potential "craft of the poor" can help to fill this conceptual gap. And with the understanding of inhabi-tation fleshed out by such a presentation of the actual skills involved in this practice, one can get a better picture of the enabling conditions for sustained and meaningful inhabitation and how inhabitation can gain political potency and resilience.

So, at this point I have attempted to articulate both the how of political salvage (the rhythmic process that alternates between the expansive affects of love and the inward effects of depression) and the where (the segregated waste areas of cities). But the "where" of salvage possesses another layer that must be addressed. While the city is the landscape of salvage, Lefebvre's understanding of rhythmanalysis and everyday life points to a smaller scale upon which to focus analysis. It is important to note Lefebvre's references to salvaged spaces such as informal communities because it endows my, up to this point, focus on micro practice and phenomenology to expand into a macro sociological context. Yet, the question that is begged by linking Lefebvre's work to a political theory of salvage is how do we fit the assertion that "radical workshops" can play an important role in encouraging political salvage with the more concrete and contemporary analysis given in this chapter. Lefebvre can play an important role by discussing exactly how capitalism abets spaces of salvage and how recent movements of resistance that employ salvage fit into a larger theory for reclaiming the "right to the city," but he does not discuss, on the micro level of tactics and organization, how particular spaces might play a role in building salvage resistance. The next chapter will begin to discuss these questions and imagine how the specific spatial designs of "radical workshops" might aid in building spaces of political salvage.

Chapter 5

Choreographing Anticapitalist Salvage

Introduction

In the last chapter, I argued that the politics of salvage can be enabled by the spatial dynamics of the capitalist city. This chapter will explore how the microgeography of salvage spaces can both enable and hinder political salvage—especially the process of plural becoming and the undermining of reification that I discussed in chapters 2 and 3. Whereas space constituted a main theme in the discussion of salvage and urban space in chapter 4, I did not discuss the specifics of the landscape within which political salvage occurs—the arrangement of the tents, tables, and open spaces within the Occupy camps, the patterns of walls and corridors within squats, and the patterns of street design and building construction within informal communities. Yet analyzing these spaces remains paramount for a political theory of salvage. Salvage landscapes are by their nature chaotic, unforeseen, confounding topographies and geographies. Salvagers do not choose the items they find. In some ways the materials choose the person, calling out with strange, vague, and confusing affects that suggest potentialities rather than certainties concerning their use, strength, and appropriateness for a particular project. Salvagers must search with their hands and feel the minute contours of their materials. Thus, the spatial and temporal characteristics of salvage landscapes, as I suggested earlier, act as interlocutors of encounter that produce their own affects. When one interacts with another person, one's focus is drawn to the substance of the speech one hears and utters; one the other hand, when one interacts with a physical landscape one focuses on the particularities of affect one feels through movement and touch. The microgeography and felt particularities of spaces constitute the "text" one must interpret and negotiate when one salvages, and understanding the dynamics of such a process can aid in deepening its potentiality for becoming an anticapitalist politics.

When one picks up an item, turns it over, presses it between one's hands, even bangs it with a hammer in order to assess what it is and what it might be able to do, the theorists of vibrant matter stress that that item might "push back" in ways that express an indeterminate agency. Spaces also possess their own vibrancy in their ability to make us duck, look around their corners, jump, and move our bodies in specific ways in which we might have otherwise not moved them. They possess textures that subtly encourage a pedagogy of the body. And because individuals experience affect through the body, the fact that spaces move bodies means that they constitute particularly powerful, if not always acknowledged, influence upon affect. Many social theorists have recently begun to analyze how spaces move bodies in everyday life, calling this mode of inquiry "choreography." Just as choreographers move dancers, spaces move people. Space influences not only the direction of the motions expressed by those within them but also the way they hold their bodies, use their limbs, and direct their senses. Like the individual styles of different choreographers, some spaces are restrictive and some allow for more improvisation. While some have noticed that the general choreography of spaces containing the activities I have identified as instances of political salvage plays a role in the creation and sustenance of these actions (while not specifically using the term *choreography*), very few have examined how the specific design characteristics of these spaces contributes to the mobilization or diminution of affect so important to salvage. More importantly, and perhaps because such musings on spatial design seem, at first glance, to be addressing the most quotidian and superficial of topics, their importance for understanding how salvage might become a political act has not been recognized.

I will begin this chapter by discussing how the spaces of Occupy London and Occupy Wall Street choreographed the movement, gestures, and activity of the activists and others who dwelt in them, and how the designs of these spaces both activated and hindered the political potential of the individuals who used them, particularly their potential as it related to political salvage. I next examine a number of contemporary authors who claim that the choreography of spaces can encourage anticapitalist becoming. I will end the chapter by using the insights gained from my conceptual and empirical examination of choreography to theorize how the spaces of political salvage might be designed to intensify this political promise. I claim that the problems caused by divisions present in New York and London—divisions that can be observed in many efforts of political salvage—might have been managed through more deft choreography of the spaces. The rhythm that I identified as essential for becoming, and that already manifests itself in the unplanned, everyday practice of salvage, might be more deeply embedded by adding certain design elements within these spaces. Furthermore, I argue that the consequences of salvage might be better integrated with the political goals of these movements if more attention were devoted to choreography. The counter-reification and plasticity encouraged through engaging in salvage are more likely to be translated into the political goals of activists if they undertake their activism in spaces that choreograph particular rhythmic movements.

My focus on anticapitalist choreography's relationship to political salvage is intended to make another point beyond any practical benefit such geographic thinking might contribute to the sustenance and political efficacy of activist groups. One of the most vexing issues confronting the political Left was inflamed by criticism of the lack of structure, leadership, and focus during Occupy Wall Street and other, related anticapitalist occupations of public spaces. Defenders of horizontalism claimed that attempting to impose organization and a unified focus would have not only lessened the impact of the protests, but undermined their core purpose—to act as spaces where individuals could autonomously direct and maintain their lives, in stark contrast to undergoing the discipline, control, and inequality they experienced in their daily existence. Critics maintained that while the goals of equality, horizontality, and spontaneity were laudable, when faced with repression by the state the movements embodying these goals were rendered impotent by the absence of coordinated response and their inability to act quickly in the face of official retaliation, and thus were easily crushed. I maintain that the choreography of collective democratic becoming can play the role of a "weak" organizational principal and can be used to strengthen the resilience and increase the longevity of movements employing political salvage. While I do not claim that such choreography can completely overcome the "tyranny of structurelessness" (Freeman 1972), it can serve to counteract that tendency. Choreography does not attempt to impose any particular ideology or goal, but does represent a structure that can unify diverse occupations and encourage them to form the federated networks that constitute the substance of inhabitation and becoming. It represents a "weak structure" that accentuates spatial tendencies already present in many iterations of political salvage and represents a median position between the advocates of traditional party structures and fully self-organizing political movements.

Spaces of Salvage Occupation

Although both critics and supporters of Occupy Wall Street have emphasized its spontaneous, nonheirarchical, and chaotic development, the geography of the encampment actually manifested an identifiable, consistent, spatial structure, even though its development was inadvertent. This geography subtly encouraged particular paths of movement through the encampment, although not in a way that complemented the stated political goals of most of the participants. When occupied, the encampment in Zuccotti Park was divided into two sections, with a pedestrian pathway acting as the border between them (Fig. 5.1). While various areas/activity centers were scattered around the park, as one can see, the lower, western end of the park contained mainly sleeping bags and shelters, and also medical, comfort, and social areas, while the eastern and northern sections contained the assembly, art, and, media outreach spaces. Divisions also reflected particular social, economic, and racial characteristics. The western end of the park was occupied by more individuals marginalized by their economic status and racial background, and

> appeared on one level to be more organized: the tents located there were generally larger, providing accommodation for sizable groups and they were clustered together in such a way that starting at the sides of the kitchen, two clear walkways stretched down to the edges of the park. (the 99% et al. 2012, 62)[1]

The eastern end of the park (closer to busy Broadway and Wall Street) was inhabited by more educated and affluent individuals, constituting

> an impassable rats nest of small single occupancy tents. Though two parallel walkways existed on either side, they

were at points considerably narrower and more twisting than those at the western end. Despite this appearance of packed chaos, the eastern end of the park was home to most of the major organized activities in the square, including the media desk, the live feed video center and the library. (the 99% et al. 2012, 62)[2]

The two halves of the park, as is clear, not only contained two different communities, but also subtly reflected two different understandings of the political function of the encampment itself: the eastern half tended to be inhabited by those with a more reformist bent who wished to pursue concrete economic goals such as striking debt or restoring banking regulation. Those on the western end tended to value the maintenance of the camp as their highest goal, including issues that they saw as threats to the camp—police brutality, antiracism, and homeless advocacy. Thus, ironically, although the camp was meant to act as a microcosm of society where all could autonomously govern their community through consensus, it actually was rife with many of the same divisions and segregations lamented by theorists such as Lefebvre as indicative of reified capitalist space. Furthermore, it spatially embodied the capitalist division of labor the activists meant to question, and therefore undermined a potentially powerful generator of the "experimental micropolitics," which Connolly states encourages anticapitalist becoming.

The segregation was matched by the modes of interaction between the occupiers and passersby on the street. For example, the western end, which was characterized by less instrumental, overtly political action, acted as the area of the park where the least traditional forms of expression and interaction occurred between camp and pedestrians. It was the location of the "sacred space"—centered on a single tree surrounded by benches—where campers led yoga classes that would entice passersby, where electricity-generating bicycles were available for pedestrians to stop, pedal, and thus take a turn powering the camp, and, perhaps most intriguing, where people could deposit pizza boxes (pizzas were ordered from nearby pizzerias by supporters from all over the world) upon which they wrote messages expressive of their economic hardships and political ideals. The wall where the boxes were deposited became space "that attracted many tourists and photographers [and] also served as a space for public reclaiming of symbols" (Writers for the 99% et al. 2012, 129), such as American flags. This "quotidian" form of protest inspired con-

Zuccotti Park Occupied

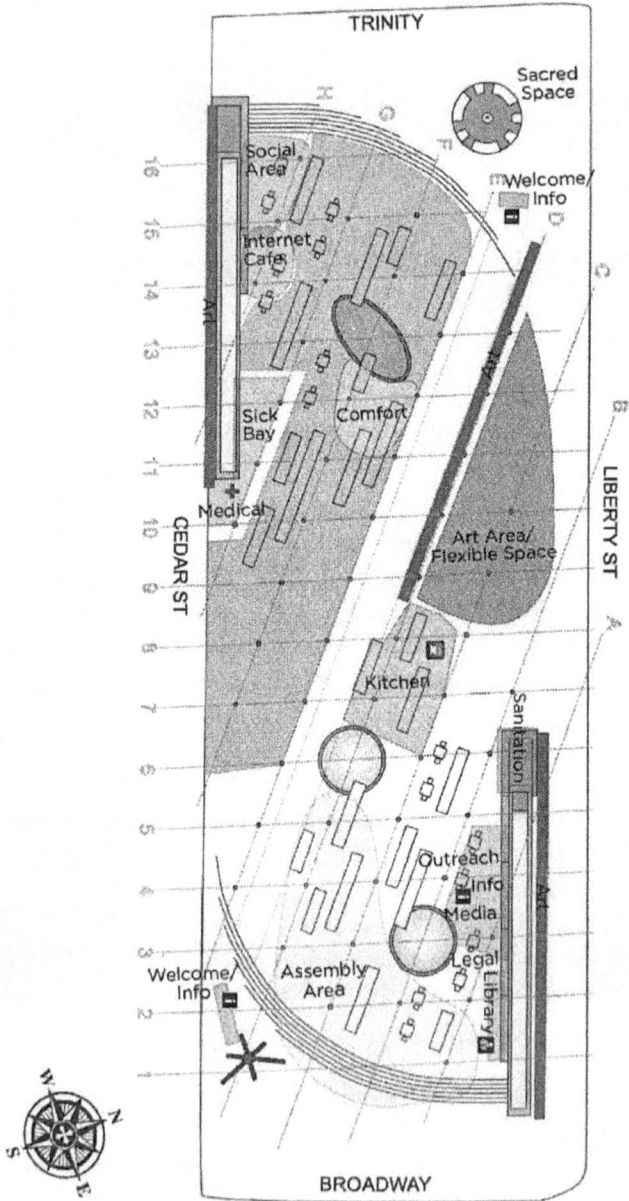

Figure 5.1. Zuccotti Park occupied, with activity. Writers for the 99% et al., *Occupying Wall Street* (2012). Fair use.

versation, connection, expression, and personal connection. The eastern end of the park, bordering Broadway, also led to interactions between street and camp, but these interactions often took the form of debate and emphatic expression. The physical topography of this end encouraged such spirited expression due to the fact that "the sidewalk running alongside Broadway sat elevated above the rest of Zuccotti Park, which lay at the bottom of stairs on the sidewalk's edge, created a backdrop effect that displayed the whole eastern half of the park, making it photogenic and a site of interviews" (the 99% et al. 2012, 130). Thus it acted as a mini amphitheater, with a dramatic backdrop that encouraged projection, volume and other dramatic forms of expression, including the occasional confession from the repentant financial worker seeking absolution (ibid., 131). What remains most fascinating in the context of the physical divisions of the encampment is that such dramatic forms of expression were in stark contrast to the "quotidian" forms expressed on the opposite side.

Others claimed that while interactions between citizens and activists were frequent at the beginning of the occupation, both on the borders of the encampment and throughout its center, as the action progressed these encounters occurred less frequently. One of the reasons for this was that the increasing police presence increased the separation between the park and the street through the erection of barricades. But another explanation was that as the occupation grew, so did the number of tents and other structures, making pedestrians' ability to pass through the park smoothly and without blockage nearly impossible. This not only decreased the number of citizens passing through the park, but also cramped the movement of activists, increasingly isolating them in particular places. One observer, sympathetic to the goals of the activists, expressed frustration over the decreasing "looseness" of the space by stating, "[A]fter a few week of cheek-by-jowl tents, I began to question how long the occupation would preclude the general use of the plaza. The balance had shifted" (Shiffman et al. 2012, 349). Instead of the park allowing general citizens to move through it and thus interact with the activists, it had become an "encampment of the few to the exclusion of the many" (348), and thus encounters between activists and citizens became less frequent. The physical barriers that developed between the interior of the encampment and the rest of the city can also be traced back to the different forms of interaction on the edge of the park, where police barricades transformed what was once a porous boundary into a concrete border.

The divisions within the park were actually concretized by the OWS Town Planning and Architecture Working Group, who took as their charge to design the space to be both livable and sustainable. As the encampment became more populated and carried on for a longer time, more and more functions and activists came to be crammed into a finite space. This group observed that "as the occupation continued, structures became more dense and sophisticated creating a labyrinth of clustered settlements, winding pathways and mounds of buildings" (Bolton et al. 2013, 148). In order to make the site, in their eyes, more legible, they officially demarcated the central, diagonal pathway that led from one corner of the park to the other, demarcating official areas and creating access to important services such as first aid. In essence, they attempted to rationalize the park. They described how they used their professional urban planning skills to rationally re-plan the encampment, stating, "[T]he Manhattan grid had exerted its discursive power on liberated Zucotti Park" (ibid., 150).

The members of the planning committee asserted, though, that such rationalization did not inhibit what they referred to as the "carnivalesque" characteristics. They argue that:

> It would be a mistake to depict Manhattanism as a monolithic, deterministic system that simply crushed and tamed OWS. Even as the grid enlisted OWS, OWS enlisted the grid (and the urban planning practices that it implies) in the service of making their encampment a survivable and sustainable one. . . . It spurred a flowering of artistic expression, viewable on a horizontal pedestrian plane in a formerly drab vacuum surrounded by vertically enclosed corporate towers. In Zuccotti Park more than any space we had previously seen in New York City one could be weird, strange, and other. OWS has created a carnival that recognized the need to sustain the very carnality of the revelers. As a spectacle, performative space and heterotopias Liberty Square became kind of an organized and non corporate Times square. (Bolton et al. 2013, 152)

It is certainly true that OWS set the stage for the individuals who participated to enjoy a carnivalesque environment that allowed them to be "weird, strange and other." And if one imagines OWS purely as a heterotopia dedicated to encouraging self-expression and weirdness, then attempting to imbue the space with permanence as a contrast to the surrounding streets makes sense. But their account not only does not discuss the possibilities for interaction between groups of activists and general citizens, but seems to have officially instantiated the divide between the different areas of the park and, by extension, their different populations, activities, and political perspectives. Furthermore, their design in fact intensified spatial divisions between the individual activities with the park—which, although they seem minor due to the close proximity among activists within the camp's cramped borders, were quite significant between the eastern and western parts of the park and their distinct racial, class, and activity focuses. If one of the main criticisms of the encampment was that it balkanized into divisions based on class, profession, and race, attempts to instantiate even a modified plan based on the abstract space of the Manhattan grid seem to have undermined the potentialities for critical becoming nascent within the encampment.

A similar division, based upon inadvertent spatial separation, also occurred during Occupy London. This separation came about not between two distinct sections of the encampment but two distinct encampments. The main encampment was constructed on the property of St. Paul's Cathedral in Central London, yet when this became too crowded and too frequently subjected to control and repression by the Metropolitan Police, another encampment was founded in Finsbury Square, just north of the City of London. While at first all of the activities associated with these encampments, such as internal communication and decision making, confrontation with authorities, maintenance of the encampment (of which salvage played an important role) occurred at St. Paul's, eventually many of the processes associated with the physical needs, such as rest and eating, of activists were relocated to Finsbury. Halverson contrasts the two spaces as embodying two distinct experiences of the flow of time—St. Paul's with its confrontation, swirling encounters, and activism representing a moment of rupture, while Finsbury, on the other hand

> seemed less oriented to the moment of rupture as seen at St Paul's, and more oriented towards the cyclical time of everyday life. Holloway contrasts the "intensity" of moments of rupture to the "gentler time" of creating new social relations in everyday life. The latter is a rupture that is based not on a particular moment, "the temporality of rage and rave," but on "the temporality of patient creation." This is the temporality of cyclical rhythms of everyday life that Lefebvre understood as a "non-accumulative process." (Halvorsen 2015, 412)

According to Halvorsen (who participated as an activist in Occupy London), Finsbury facilitated "at least initially, a more close-knit community in which people were more aware of each other and the different everyday tasks that needed doing" (ibid). One of these everyday tasks was recycling and salvage. In contrast to this space of sustenance, support, and easy exchange between individuals, Halverson describes a situation in St. Paul that, as the encampment became more crowded, raucous, and torn by rupture, tended to put off more and more long-term occupiers, who retreated to Finsbury. Just as there was a division between activism and reproduction, between longer-term residents and others participating for only a limited time, another division manifested itself in Occupy London, which resulted in a division of space.

The significance of the above is that it demonstrates that occupations of public space require spaces dedicated to both moments of time—spaces for calm respite, sustenance, and recovery; and spaces dedicated to challenging the prevaling political order. Yet these two usages of space and the temporalities they encourage do not rest easily together. Halverson argues that "[t]his dual function seems central to understanding the taking of space yet I demonstrate that in the case of Occupy London the relationship between the two functions can often be antagonistic and perhaps provides a more difficult challenge" (Halvorsen 2015, 408) than many, including Fiegenbaum, whom I cited earlier, suppose. Halvorsen does not propose a solution to this problem and only endeavors to highlight it. He does point out that "most concerning, this article has demonstrated an under-valorisation of everyday practices of social reproduction and care, in comparison to the desire to take space for high-energy 'political' work" (415). This suggests that activists who attempt to occupy space must always remember to include spaces dedicated to such "depressive" and recuperative activities, but fails to suggest how such activities might be integrated within the more active, political spaces that produce loving affects, as I described them in chapter 2, in those who dwell in them. Simple inclusion of these spaces and the activities they foster merely establishes another degree of segregation, and separation, between the people who engage in them. One might argue that recuperative activities need to be separated from activism, community building, and the challenging encounters that such endeavors necessitate, Yet if, these spaces are truly meant to be "laboratories of the insurrectionary imagination," then segregating populations and activities that might contribute to the rethinking of the division of labor and building the habits that encourage critical becoming circumscribes their radical potentialities.

Identifying the spatial divisions present in Occupy London and Occupy Wall Street does not mean that these divisions were unbridgeable or that other iterations of Occupy did not manage to bridge tensions originating in identity and space to better or lesser extents. For example, Stravrides recounts that Occupied Syntagma Square was comprised of micro squares, each of which "had its own group of people who lived there for some days, in their tents people who focused their actions and their micro-urban environment on a specific task: a children's playground a free reading and mediation area" (Stavrides 2016, 166). He goes on to relate how "differences in space arrangement choices and media of expression were more than apparent" (167), yet these different spaces dedicated to different uses and populated by different people still managed to engage in acts of "space commoning." He claims that "in place of a public space that was routinely shaped by the intersection of incessant pedestrian flows directed to the underground station's entrance, a rich common space was created in the heart of Athens" (168). The commoning of this space as undertaken by the free interaction of participants traveling from space to space, combining and dissolving intermediary spaces, according to Stavrides, not only resulted in a coherent, vibrant, resilient public encampment, but also allowed for the diverse population to engage in common political activity, most notably, in his estimation, the massive protests held on June 28–29, 2011.

Yet despite this picture of unity constructed from diversity, divisions still remained within the camps, some of them spatial. A few days before the unity of the protest, an observer reports tensions rising within the camp. Antagonism rose due to the presence of fascists who erected a tent within the encampment. Calls to eject this particular tent, according to a contemporaneous account by a fellow occupier, "extended to somehow proposing yesterday that ALL tents should be evacuated by Syntagma because 'we do not know who is in them and it is a security concern" (Anonymous 2011).[3] In addition to this cleavage, this observer reports continuing tension between immigrants and native Greeks within the park, necessitating a "day against racism" where immigrants in the general assembly "[has] to respond to a Greek guy who said that 'we like you as people and we want you to live well but we don't want so many immigrants here'"(Anonymous 2011). It is not my intention to contradict Stavrides's account, but simply to offer a different perspective, which suggests in addition to commoning of space, like the other occupy encampments, Syntagma Square possessed its own spatial and racial tensions, divisions that seemed to both reinforce each other and encourage interaction and mutual becoming between participants.

While, of course, the arrangement of the camp did not cause the racial and class divisions that persisted in the encampments, what this example demonstrates is that activist spaces containing diverse populations engaging in diverse activities with no seeming impediment to their interaction might still contain divisions that become emphasized by their spatial arrangement. If salvage constitutes a part of such activist encampments yet is not integrated with other activities, its political potential becomes extremely circumscribed. I don't want to claim that any radical occupation of public space that does not either include or fully integrate salvage should be considered unsuccessful or not sufficiently radical. It is simply that those political activities will not encourage the anticapitalist becoming that I identify as the embryonic political potential within everyday acts of salvage. The spatial arrangements of the encampments undermined the political potential lying embryonic within the activities, especially that of salvage, that participants undertook in the encampment.

Anticapitalist Choreography

What makes these observations concerning the spatial arrangement of these Occupy encampments so notable is that they run contrary to many understandings of the role urban space plays within political theory. Many have theorized that urban spaces encourage diverse encounters between citizens due to the fact that urban geographies contain so many different people, ideas, and spaces packed into a limited area. Political theorists have surmised that such internal diversity leads to the adoption of beneficial civic virtues such as tolerance, skills in deliberation, and a greater appreciation of the public in general. A primary example of this view can be seen in Iris Marion Young's influential claim that everyday city life encourages ideal "normative" citizen relationships that counteract both the isolation of liberal individualism and the coercion of communitarian collectivism. She states, "By city life I mean a form of social relations which I define as the being together of strangers. In the city persons and groups interact within spaces and institutions they all experience themselves as belonging to, but without those interactions dissolving into unity of commonness" (Young and Allen 2011, 237). She considers such "difference without exclusion"[4] to be the underlying principle of a democratic polity, stating, "[I]f city politics is to be democratic and not dominated by the point of view of one group, it must be a politics that takes account and provides voice for the different groups that swell together in the city without forming community" (227). Young claims that once citizens become accustomed to inhabiting urban spaces with others who don't necessarily adhere to their particular worldview, they will more likely be amenable to engage in relationships of "affinity" (172) wherein individuals challenge, share, and create policy and collective action together without demanding conformity to a narrow definition of political membership. Young goes on to suggest that urban spaces encourage the frequent meeting of an ever-shifting congeries of individuals because "city dwellers frequently venture beyond such familiar enclaves, however to the more open public of politics, commerce and festivals, where strangers meet and interact" (237).[5] This exposure to individuals who possess widely different racial, ethnic, and class identities causes city dwellers to become accustomed to otherness, and thus more likely to question their own understandings of themselves. She claims that these functionally diverse spaces must also exhibit another quality, that of eroticism, or, "attraction to the other, the pleasure and excitement of being drawn out of one's secure routine to encounter the novel, strange and surprising" (239). As is clear from this quote, she claims that city life not only accustoms individuals to difference, but can stoke the desire to encounter such difference. Thus, she regards her ethic of urban citizenship as able to motivate individuals to expand this ethic and advocate for the urban design policies, such as building public spaces, desegregating neighborhoods, and supporting dense development, that flow from its embrace

Yet, as my previous examples show, such unmediated encounters with difference possess an equal chance of resulting in tension, rejection, and thus segregation.[6] Despite their successes in both maintaining their encampments and engaging in political activity, both Occupy Wall Street and Occupy London continued to exhibit social cleavages, even with their diverse participants and open layouts. Multiple criticism of how the encampments reflected racial, educational, gendered, and other differences appears in accounts of these actions. Although not as prominent, many of these accounts suggest that these demographic separations corresponded to and reinforced spatial divisions based on particular activities, especially the political and the recreative. The maintenance activities, many of which were based in salvage, such as building basic infrastructure, procuring food, and cleaning the spaces, were spatially segregated and thus undertaken more frequently by certain groups of activists that became more defined and insular, and consequently these people found themselves only partially integrated into the entirety of the collective experience of the camp. While all aspects of the encampments were discussed in the general assemblies, greater experiential, and thus affective, overlaps, resonances, and possible becoming might have occurred if these encounters with people and material were more integrated. The style of integration most effective to such becoming, as discussed in chapter 3, with its rhythmic development, does not necessarily flow simply from people working together. The development of relationships embodying tolerance and "affinity," which Young hypothesizes results from the raw experience of urban diversity, actually can depend, as we saw in chapter 3, upon a particular aesthetic form. Furthermore, the "affinity" that Young deems to be the result of interaction within public space seems distinct from the becoming that I have identified as the result of undertaking collective political salvage. Affinity implies affection and similarity, while mutual becoming need not be based on either liking or sameness. Finally, while such developments certainly occurred during the Occupy encampments, they occurred without planning or intervention, and the question remains whether the promise of such haphazard experiences can become more regularized. OWS, with its conscious adoption of an urban grid-like geography, might have actually inhibited the aesthetics of such becoming by discouraging the flow from one activity to the next through the divisions that so many describe within the park.

During my discussion of the rhythm of anticapitalist becoming in chapter 3, I presented two figures that acted as visual representation of the spatial and temporal dynamics productive of such experiences. While these diagrams were not meant to be taken literally, they did highlight the fact that becoming, because of its affective dimensions, remains profoundly shaped by the actual experience of the body, especially its embeddedness within space and time. Thus, the figures not only represent aesthetic qualities such as distinction with connection and rhythmic development, but also suggest actual design qualities for spaces that might aid and structure experiences of becoming. These figures particularly highlight the roles that different modes of affect play during encounters with difference that lead to becoming. Young's desired outcomes from urban life, those of "attraction" and "affinity," constitute experiences that clearly can be interpreted as affects, but Dewey's School and the Deleuze's Baroque House suggest that becoming best occurs primarily through a certain form. One potent enabling condition of becoming is the experience of rhythmic alternation between affects of "love" and "depression" that encourage openness and observation. And thus, while the public urban spaces Young applauds certainly seem to encourage affects similar to those described as loving, they do not encourage the depressive affects so important to this understanding of becoming and, by extension, political salvage. This insight is important not simply for my argument, but also for Young's, in that the "relational difference" she so values risks falling apart into the rejection of difference without some sort of mediating factor; publicity as she describes it does not necessarily lead to more tolerance and "affection" for others. A more complex form of public space would be necessary to encourage both Young's view and the common becoming that occurs through the collective inhabitation of space that I see as occurring through political salvage.

This suggestion, that spaces that encourage more complex gestures and sequences of movement might aid in the facilitation of what I have called the affective rhythms of resistance and the radical becoming that such experience can encourage, has recently become explicitly embraced by a number of theorists. For example, Derek McCormack has suggested that space can "choreograph" individuals' movement through it and sculpt interactions between group members in a way that encourages their propensity to experience anticapitalist becoming. These moves toward envisioning a choreography of becoming do not rely upon encouraging a specific sequence of substantive encounters that lead participants to know a discrete set of facts. Nor do they lead to the type of civic virtues, such as "affinity," outlined by Young in her account of the political benefits of urban diversity. Instead, they rely upon "particular attention to the affective qualities of these spaces combined with a commitment to experimenting with different ways of becoming attuned to these qualities" (McCormack 2014, 3). McCormack's emphasis upon "experimenting" with different modes of attunement points toward his affinity to understandings of rhythmic becoming and the rhythmic alternation between different modes of affect that it entails.[7] He mentions both Lefebvre and Dewey as inspirations for his effort to discover how rhythm might serve the process of "experimenting with experience," or, in other words, how different qualities of one's sensed existence might possess unforeseen and surprising implications for how one thinks, believes, and lives, just as Connolly suggests in his account of anticapitalist becoming.

But effective choreography, according to McCormack, cannot simply consist of experiencing different forms of rhythm. He specifies his understanding by claiming that "experimenting with experience" requires rhythmic patterns of repeated movement—encounter, sensing the affects created by this movement, consciously experimenting with these movements, and then rhythmically repeating the process in light of the modifications one previously undertook. He describes this process, using Deleuze's concept of the refrain:

> [T]he refrain names the durational mattering of which affective spacetimes are composed. Refrains have a territorializing function: that is they draw together blocks of space time from the chaos of the world, generating a certain expressive consistency through the repetition of practices, techniques, and habits. These territories are not necessarily demarcated or delineated however: they can be affective complexes, "hazy, atmospheric" but sensed nevertheless, as intensities of feeling in and through the movement of bodies. (McCormack 2014, 7)

Thus, for McCormack, it is not the concrete space that necessarily matters. Rather, the aim of moving through a particular space with its particular repertoire of encounters is to create a refrain, sensed as an atmosphere, that achieves an "expressive consistency" that might then be transported to other situations. Such refrains are not contained within individuals and are not expressive of certain personality traits or sets of habits, characteristics, or virtues. They represent basic frameworks that develop through long experimental improvisations. In a sense, they act as maps, an important concept for both Dewey's classroom and Deleuze's Baroque House, created by the interaction of the actor and the choreographed space, revealing the pattern of their particular experiment with experience.[8] Because they always encounter transversal resonances through the stream of experiences, these refrains constantly generate new affects. The choreography comprising such refrains represents moments of quasi-intentionality and returning and reattunement, wherein individuals consciously engage in a process of opening themselves up to a predetermined beginning without a predetermined end. Such refrains constitute patterns of consistence that are noticed and consciously modified. They establish the rhythmic pattern of action and reflection indicative of craft.

McCormack contends that one of the most important skills required for this process of experimenting with experience lies in "learning to be affected by affective space-times." He outlines an operation that can be aided by thoughtful choreography that both stimulates and does not overwhelm, especially to those who have been robbed of their propensity to acknowledge and respond to quality—an experience described by theorists of the deadening aesthetics of capitalism. Such a conscious choreography of the body might stoke the appreciation of affect. This appreciation can only be encouraged through actual movements that open the body to new and surprising movements that produce affects far afield from the repetitious, deadening infrastructure characteristic of everyday capitalist experience. He stresses that there are many different types of rhythms—flowing, promiscuous staccato, chaotic and lyrical. It is those experiences that combine all of these rhythms in reiterated yet distinct patterns that produce the most productive experimenting with experience. McCormack emphasizes that one can never know which affects will wake the body's affective capacities and lead to further experimentation, and thus following the patterns of rhythm and reacting to them with an open and loving perspective, interspersed with depressive and introspective periods of recuperation. McCormack's work demonstrates that the experience of experimenting, no matter where it leads and however seemingly insignificant, can play a role in the process of learning to be affected and the transformational possibilities of the cultivation of such skills. Yet such experiments are best practiced not only in environments that ensure diversity of affective experiences, but also in environments characterized by locations that produce distinct affects so that experimenters might fully sense their unique qualities and with spaces that encourage connection between these distinct domains.

Despite McCormack's desire to consciously choreograph experimenting with experience through the sculpting of spaces productive of the emergence of distinct refrains, he describes his ambitions for choreographing experimenting with experience not as a set of specific instructions for a grand ballet of movement but instead

> [a] modest diagram for facilitating what Stephen Bottoms and Matthew Goulsih call "small acts of repair" in everyday spacetimes. These small acts of repair offer opportunities for intervening in and reworking, however modest a scale

> economies and ecologies of value and for differentiating tra-
> jectories of thinking and moving. (McCormack 2014, 202)

This quote highlights the partial, groping, and necessarily reiterative nature of the ambitions of choreography—while breaching the subject of its potential consequences for radical politics. Slow, modest repairs of ecologies of individual movements through environments constitute the objects of choreography—rituals that allow people to experiment with arranging and rearranging their encounters. Justin McGuirk describes something similarly modest when he identifies what he calls a trend of "weak architecture." Such an architecture does not attempt to choreo-graph every movement of its users or impart specific ideas, ideologies, symbols, or even affects upon its inhabitants. Instead of trying to inspire particular social relations, weak architecture "however create[s] the channels for those social relations to occur naturally, they can create lines of communication and transport link" (McGuirk 2014, 28).[9] All of these limited spatial strategies to encourage individuals to become more acclimated to the promise of difference, while not cast specifically in terms of becoming, do point toward how weak spatial design structures can create environments that encourage aspects of what my account of becoming encouraged through political salvage requires.

To give a concrete example, an emphasis upon "weak" choreography was expressed by participants in Thomas Hirshorn's Gramsci Monument, yet in a more explicitly political and critical context. Yasmil Raymond, the "instillation ambassador" of the monument, whose job was to intro-duce visitors to the monument and answer their questions, wrote in her journal about one seminar hosted on the site:

> [T]he seminar . . . started with Gramsci's term "spontaneous philosophy": which stands as a straightforward defense of the vernacular. When thinking of the role of the vernacular in recent examples of contemporary dance the name Yvonne Rainer comes to mind. The energized body of the subaltern has been a recurring motif in her recent choreographies granting the leading rose to concentration and endurance of what I like to think as methods of recuperation that return ownership to the body of the dancer. In dance as in other forms of art the immediacy of the vernacular no doubt remains a latent force field for resistance. (Hirschhorn 2015, 256)

Such modest repairs, or recuperations, constitute a powerful tool for reworking the affective trajectories of thinking and the creation of values—processes that, for the most part, go unnoticed yet are profoundly shaped by social and economic forces. The result constitutes the return of the "ownership" of the body, which, although a seemingly inward and individualized result, actually constitutes a powerful phenomenon in light of the reification and alienation of affect that results from everyday existence in capitalism. Remember, the affective infrastructures of capitalism sculpt the body and its habits that squash the contingent, unruly, and creative potentialities that we sense. Dance, when organized around creative and developmental choreographies,[10] assists participants in loosening habits and thus being able to sense the affects that capitalist habits obscure, thus allowing the "reappropriation" of the body.[11] While not completely spontaneous, in that the practice was initiated and encouraged by activists at the Gramsci Monument the choreography did not consist of a list of movements that were to be undertaken in a particular order. Instead, the participants were encouraged to undertake a spontaneous somatic "philosophy" whereby their bodies interrogated their own subtle precognitive tendencies and styles of interaction with space and other bodies. The dancerss "performances"[12] were experimenting with how their everyday movement constitutes an unacknowledged background texture that plays a role in the formation of their conscious thought. Through movement, this affective texture came to the foreground and was then able to be somatically interrogated by being led by the spontaneously generated, novel movements and affects produced by the interactions of their bodies with others'.

McCormack also outlines the radical political potentiality of refrains when he discusses a movement exercise designed to "open up the possibilities" for rethinking the relationship between the choreographic and the geographic, and, subsequently, the individual and their larger social and political existence. He states that experimenting with experience is meant to "repair everyday spacetimes," but how might this undermine, for example, the forms of affective reification and alienation that I discussed in chapter 2? He does this by designing a choreographed experiment meant to both invoke and undermine the board game Monopoly. He describes the game by stating:

> Monopoly in its current form is a perfect diagram for the reproduction of capitalist value. Accumulate sites, build property

and collect rent. And continue, around and around until you dominate. . . . In some ways what emerged through our experiment . . . is a specific game that short-circuits the axes of Monopoly foregrounding how movement between events creates opportunities for generating universes of value that are not defined by site-specific capital accumulation. The work in the dance studio becomes an eventful space time within which to devise a machine for making more of the value of geographies distributed across and between bodies in process. (McCormack 2014, 202)

Instead of the endless, deadening recurrence of commodity accumulation represented through the traditional design of this game, McCormack envisions his "anti-Monopoly" as retraining individuals to experience rounds of expansive, creative, embodied cartographic becoming. These experiments that are not defined by "site-specific capitalist accumulation" transgress not only the physical boundaries between individual acts of production but also individuals and commodities. Through weaving connections through movements that connect the reified granules that comprise capitalist experience, participants can start to "repair" their connection to the totality their surroundings. Such repairs are experiments because they are based on affect—the experience of the dance produces sensed possibilities of connection, not definite causal links. Each person's place within the totality of capitalist society is both unique and changing, and the exercise results in awakening one's perception to these resonances, rather than providing a concrete guide that indicates distinct paths of cause and effect. Experimenting with experience, while meant to reaffirm the relationship between sensed affect of experience and its larger geographic environment, more importantly constitutes a subversive activity when one of the main ways capitalism operates to maintain its legitimacy is to sculpt the body in a way that legitimizes it existence.

A final example of such choreography, which places its anticapitalist intentions in the foreground, can be seen in Senselab, a philosophic, spatial experiment founded by Brian Massumi and Erin Manning. In this space (which is not a particular space at all, but instead a series of spatial events in various locations), Massumi and other discuss philosophy while consciously arranging themselves and their space in a way meant to prompt multiple affective resonances. In their book *Thought in the Act*, Manning and Massumi describe in detail many experiments undertaken in the Senselab, but I would like to specifically explore their recounting of the experiment *Dancing with the Virtual*. In the exercise, participants were required to bring "something essential to his or her practice as an offering to the group: an object, a material, a keyword a conceptual formula, a technique system," a ritual they referred to as "the (im)material potluck." Everyone was then required to read the same selection from a philosophical text, and they would begin the activity through "plenaries" where groups would discuss key concepts. In order to activate affective resonances between individuals, the text, and the other individuals, they engaged in what they call "conceptual speed dating," where participants moved around another group of seated participants with whom they discussed how the passage related to the objects they held.[13] These individual conversations are not simply infused with each other but infused with the items or symbols each of the participants brings to symbolize their occupation and thus express the affective senses that one receives when conceptualizing and somatically enacting these activities. The choreographed movements create felt contrasts and new affects, stoking interest and establishing resonant refractions between ideas, methods, and individual perceptions. During this "conceptual speed dating," they occasionally introduce random, unexpected actors they call "free radicals," who act as "trickster figures" that disrupt and rearrange spatial relations periodically to ensure that no atmosphere becomes stale and thus inadvertently productive of further refractions. Choreographic experiments and tactics such as these engage in the same experimenting with experience as that described by McCormack and encourage the critical becoming envisioned by Connolly.

The exercise creates a controlled dynamic of convergence and divergence—encouraging modulation and refraction without uncontrolled chaos—regularized movement between different elements and not the staccato repetition of the same, which characterized the affect of cruel optimism. They refer to the choreographic principle they employ in this exercise as "dilating" the moment—an activity they see as providing an affective atmosphere that might "remodulate relational potentials that over spill the present." Such an exercise suspends "the 'chunking,' which suspends the crystallization of pragmatic presuppositions and precipitous launching into the most prepared and accessible action paths. This involves a certain amount of disorientation and that can be painful. Even so it's still a joy of a kind because it's intense, it's vital" (Massumi 2015, 141). Manning and Massumi emphasize that such disorientation remains important to break the affective atmosphere of rhythmic reification propagated by capitalism. They also argues that Senselab's experiments were meant to interact with and perhaps counteract "capitalist capture, to invent new lines of flight or reinforce existing ones, for a lived glimpse of a non capitalist economy" (Manning and Massumi 2014, 123). They go on to describe how "polyrhythmic attuning of mutually composing autonomous activities that collectively resist definitive capitalist capture and affirms value in terms that cannot be quantified" (ibid.) affirms the importance of the way the uniformity of capital affect can capture even the most diverse experiences and values, transforming them into iterations of the commodity—the reified quick fix that overcomes cruel optimism. Anticapitalism, to them, is the allowing of oneself to move or be moved into other zones of life value, challenging the borders set up by the economy. Massumi claims that

> it's in response to that problem that at the Senselab we have been exploring concepts like technique of relation, gift, tweaking and modulation, conviviality, processional proposition and lure. And we're doing this within the wider perspective of anti-capitalist struggle. . . . What does an anti-capitalist affective politics look like that moves the global relational field in other directions? All I can say is that to improvise that kind of politics we have to take seriously the qualitative-relations working of the field we are in, we have to accept our immersion in it and see ourselves as working immanently to that field as work to move from within towards one of its constitutive limits and over the tipping point. (Massumi 2015, 139–40)

The recognition of the fact that moving the relational field can be aided by moving the body is one of the fundamental insights of Senselab. The choreography of such movements sets the stage for the possibility of crossing such boundaries of value and forging new connections. The impermanence of the experiments of Senselab, according to its founders, constitutes one of its advantages, as such interventions can be inserted within spaces characterized by the divided, controlled daily life of capitalism. Others have taken up these insights and undertaken affective interventions in the form of art installations and other gatherings that attempt to initiate spaces that create choreographies embodying a politics of affect,[14] and such attempts point the way toward fighting the cruel optimism that subtly traps people in the everyday rhythms that undergird the experiences of capitalism.

I want to emphasize that the weak architecture of radical choreography I discuss here need not be thought of as an imposition from above. Instead, it can be viewed as a self-imposed "enabling constraint that helps participants to practice the craft of political salvage. Constructing a salvage space, whether a *favela*, squat or occupation with a choreography that encourages "experimenting with experience" constitutes an act of autonomy, *autogestion*, and self-organization. One cannot simply choose to adopt habits, but one can choose to undertake the somatic rituals that allow one to cultivate them. Such is the animating spirit of this understanding of choreography. By choosing to establish a space choreographed as a radical workshop, one chooses to try to encourage experimentation. Whether experimentation will actually occur, and the specific paths this experiment might take, cannot be determined before the experiment actually occurs. All that activists can do is to establish the conditions that increase the likelihood that such experimentation, becoming, and cultivation of anticapitalist consciousness will come to fruition.

Tactics of Anticapitalist Choreography— Corridors and Thresholds

McCormack's and Manning and Massumi's experiments in anticapitalist choreography are all rhythmic in multiple ways—they involve the repeating of refrains that are constituted by internal differentiations of modes of encounter—reception, activity, analysis, communication, etc. Furthermore, refrains produced by such experiments must develop through movement within the entirety of diverse ecologies and involve the material and the nonmaterial, the human and nonhuman. Effective choreography in this context comprises the subtle management of such differences to open the individual to the affects created by their movements, to encourage widespread movements, and to foster the rhythmic modulation of the spatial and temporal aspects of the encounters in a way that facilitates becoming. Managing the rhythm of experiencing and experimenting with such difference requires concrete spatial tactics that modify the effects individuals experience as they move through spaces. I will now discuss two of these spatial tactics, which I consider fundamental to fostering such spaces of anticapitalist becoming, and their implications for a political theory of salvage.

The first goal of such choreographic management lies in stimulating interest in affective difference itself. Simply because the possibilities for moving various ways in a space exist does not mean people will in fact take advantage of these possible trajectories. Senses, even if perceived, need not be followed. Sennett suggests that the most effective methods for drawing attention to physical objects are emphasis or discontinuity. While emphasis often relies upon exaggeration of a common pattern, that does not lend itself well to encouraging interest in difference. McCormack recognizes this, while understanding that too much dif-ference experienced too quickly might lead to its rejection, and thus he emphasizes the importance of transitional spaces that can facilitate encounters with difference. He names such spaces corridors. Entering one space characterized by one particular milieu or activity and directly entering into a completely different milieu, with a diametrically opposite layout composed of wildly different individuals and encounters, remains an experience too jarring to actually stimulate interest. Yet McCormack contends that a corridor leading between two distinct environments, a corridor that allows for the mingling of diverse encounters without one predominant atmosphere, can create a "sense of anticipation" and a "joyful disturbance"[15] in a relatively neutral zone that inspires individuals' interest in the unknown and different. He states that a corridor "is a space of and for mingled bodies. As zones of transition corridors generate perturbations by virtue of the mundane, transitory presence of passers through" (McCormack 2014, 32). Whereas the typical understanding of this architectural structure usually takes the form of a long, wide, clear space (such as an open hallway or even a boulevard), this conception of a corridor emphasizes the obstacles that one might face while traversing such an area. While obstructions are present in the form of others in such corridors, they still allow for movement through them. Thus, corridors are stimulating without overwhelming, enticing movement in general without requiring any one movement or activity. While corridors possess certain qualities of the public, in the sense that for them to work they must allow for relatively free access, this openness is always qualified by the characteristic and number of spaces connected by the corridor. It is important to mention that in McCormack's understanding not all passages are corridors. A pathway between two similar spaces constitutes a different mode of transition than a corridor that connects two diverse spaces—yet each always represents a lull and temporary shift in quality between one space and another.

An example of this conception of the corridor that choreographically stimulates "experimenting with experience" can be seen in Sennett's discussion of the Athenian Agora, but he complicates and defines the brief discussion of the corridor presented by McCormack. The Agora, although packed with many people engaged in many activities, was not a site of chaos. Instead, "[T]hose who could participate found in the Agora many discrete distinct activities occurring at once" (Sennett 1996, 54). Thus, the experience of this space was an experience of difference, but not uncontrolled difference. People moved through the Agora and were spatially presented with the opportunity to participate in a limited number of disparate civic activities. For example, "by strolling from group to group, a person could find out what was happening in the city and discuss it" (Sennett 1996, 55), and, alternately, observe the proceedings of the court, where, because it was designed with an open roof and low walls (perhaps three feet high, notes Sennett), "from the outside anyone could look in, and jurors and people passing by could discuss the formal arguments" (ibid). Thus, the Agora acted as a space of observation or participation, and thus presented the Athenian with multiple modes of stimuli just like a corridor. It is important to emphasize that the corridor-like qualities of the Agora came not simply from the crowded central area where Athenians could "bump" into each other while crossing the open space, but also through the contrast between the bustle of the central area and the focused possibilities for observation within the law courts. It was not just many people that Athenians might encounter in their travels through the Agora, but different activities—informal conversation and the formal activity of the courts. The experience of a variety of activities is the essence of a corridor as McCormack conceptualizes it. If the Agora had been only an open space filled with people, while many different conversations could have been heard, it would have been only the specific activity of informal talk that would have been contained within the area, which would not have possessed the same stimulating effect as an area containing many activities.

Such activities/contrasts/connections were further heightened by the fact that the Agora was located next to the Pnyx, a connection that, in the context of my discussion, caused the combined area to further act as a corridor, yet, once again, not in the way that most people think about such spaces. In the Pnyx, citizens sat and listened to carefully crafted speeches that followed an orderly procedure, persuaded by logic and rhetoric.[16] If the Agora was the space of plurality and activity, the Pnyx was the space of inward thought. Sennett contends that while both spaces were necessary for the functioning of Athenian democracy, both prompted a sense of inadequacy in users and thus prompted somatic desires and affects contrary to those spaces. He describes that

> [t]he Athenian Agora and Pnyx were urban spaces in which citizens felt bodily insufficiency, the ancient Agora stimulated people physically at the price of depriving them of coherent speech with others; the Pnyx provided continuity in speech and so gave the community experiences of narrative logic, at the price of rendering people vulnerable to the rhetorical stimulation of words. The stones of the Agora and Pnyx put people in a state of flux, each of the two centers a source of dissatisfaction, the other could resolve only by around dissatisfactions of its own. In the dual-centered city, people know incompleteness in their bodily experiences. . . . Intense civic bonds arose from the very play of displacement, people cared strongly about one another in spaces which did not fully satisfy their bodily needs. (Sennett 1996, 371)

This rhythmic contrast between different bodily modes such as activity and passivity, diversity and focus, in Sennett's estimation, constitutes one of primary constituents of the care (which does not necessarily imply affection, but instead, their interest in each other) that linked citizens each other.[17] While the Agora acted as a corridor that stimulated interest by contrast, the general contrast of the Agora and the Pnyx further stimulated interest, but in this case in a different form of bodily comportment. The rhythmic interplay between the focus required by the Pnyx (a focus that might result in manipulation by skilled orators) and the stimulating freedom of movement of the Agora (which might have resulted in a feeling of inadequacy due to the superficiality of one's involvement in what one observed) pulled individuals into the contrasting space of the entire geography. Thus, the Athenians' heightened sensitivity to both those around them and the general politics of the city. Their daily lives were structured by the refrain of alternation between the modes and affects of both the Pnyx and the Agora, each of them offering a unique perspective on the city and both together comprising a spatial machine that encouraged, in embryonic form, the affective receptiveness and experiential refrains necessary for "experimenting with experience."

While corridors stoke interest in the different affects and rhythms of one's daily life that might otherwise easily be brushed aside and ignored, they also represent the potential to overwhelm, alienate, and confuse any individual who hopes to use their body as a sensory tool for the spaces around them. Many architects and urban theorists who explore how design elements of spaces can encourage individuals to engage in particular movements, adopt specific bodily stature and enact distinct gestures, offer strategies helpful to solving this problem of the choreography of affect. One of the most prominent design elements they employ is that of the threshold—a liminal space between two distinct areas that encourages individuals to modulate the pace and direction of their movement between them. Stavrides, while not employing the language of affect, yet while still invoking the concept of liminality and pause, describes corridors as facilitating "the suspension of a previous identity and the preparation for a new one" (Stavrides 2019, 7). He also identifies them with the "civility" and "modesty" that comes through slowly approaching an unfamiliar person or situation. He emphasizes that when introducing oneself to another one "hides in order to reveal" (108) in new situations so as to not overwhelm the new person, and that the physical space of the threshold encourages such concealment. He also characterizes thresholds as physical inducements to "postponement" (109). One might inquire concerning the difference between a threshold and a corridor. While a corridor is a space of flow and locomotion, containing diverse, constantly changing, and even chaotic elements and rhythms, a threshold is a space that, while connecting two distinct places, allows for cessation of movement and waiting.

Yet despite the distancing and concealing spatial inducements provided by thresholds they do not only function as inhibitors. Stavrides argues that thresholds play a double role in both delaying and facilitating movement. He emphasizes that the distances created by thresholds are meant to be "crossed and crossed again." Each crossing, he claims,

> creates interpretations of crossing actions. The effort needed to cross the distance is itself turned into the measure of this distance. Therefore, distance corresponds to different forms of body-environmental relations. These different relations are recorded by the body's senses in their effort to estimate, cross and use spaces. (Stavrides 2019, 114)

Stavrides emphasizes here the porous nature of thresholds, and how they act as zones of transition that do not simply allow the experience of being alone among others, but instead constitute the opportunity to reflect, assimilate, and even choose whether or not to enter environments that embody the different modes of affect and movement described by McCormack. Their different modes of rhythmic affect are best assimilated not as an onslaught or chaos, if they are truly to be objects of experimentation. If they can be somehow isolated and experienced in their individuality, then refrains of response and development can better develop. It is not that thresholds encourage individuals to complete their becoming but instead to modulate and play a role in its development. A threshold allows a person to sense that their transformation might be spinning out of control or too much to handle and thus to assimilate. It might allow those who sense stagnation to choose to enter an environment that comprises more diverse and strange encounters.[18] Thresholds constitute a point of possible agency—although the moves that they enable might not turn out, especially in the short run, to lead to a welcome or expected outcome. But in the long run thresholds facilitate the modulation of the rhythm of becoming—its management, so that it develops at a pace and direction that not only produce new equilibrium, "consummations," or any of the other terms I have been using to describe the resolutions or ways of establishing some type of growth and influence over the course of events that one encounters in one's life (see figure 5.2).

Sennett's examination of thresholds reaches its most sophisticated form in his discussion of the stoa that surrounded the Agora in ancient Athens. Stoa were long structures that consisted of two distinct architectural features. Individual rooms were located in the back of the stoa where individuals could meet privately, eat, or discuss with acquaintances. In front of this succession of rooms was a long colonnade that acted as a transition area between the privacy of the individual rooms and the chaotic public space of the Agora. Sennett notes that the colonnade acted as a "transition space," where "he [sic] could retreat yet keep in touch with the square" (Lecuyer et al. 1998, 19). He goes on to describe how even though the rooms of the stoa were private they were open, leading to a situation in which "people would not recline with their back turned into an open colonnade. However other people did not intrude though they could perfectly well see within. When a man moved toward the unwalled side facing the Agora he could be noticed and approached" (Sennett 1996, 50). Thus, the stoa represent a nearly

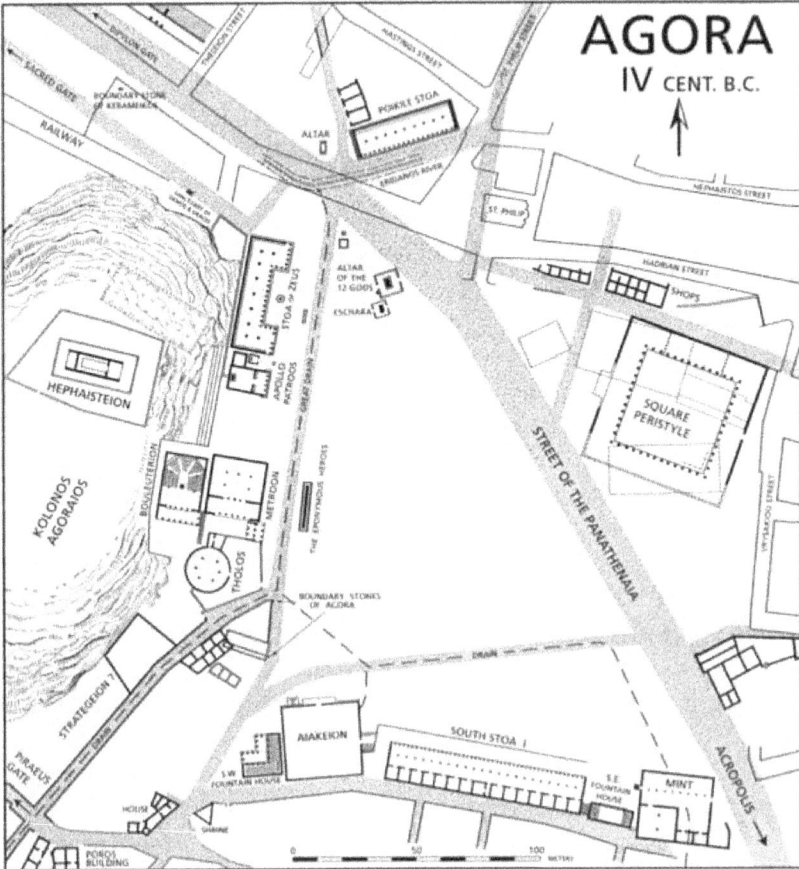

Figure 5.2. Athenian Agora. Lecuyer et al., *Raoul Wallenberg Lecture*, 1998. fair use.

paradigmatic example of the multiple choreographies of thresholds. They were membranous areas of diffraction due to the openness of the colonnades; many people would stroll through them, and their diversity was ensured by the chaotic, exciting, and constantly changing population of the Agora. They were also areas of respite, where individuals could retreat from the Agora corridor to reflect upon and recover from the strange, exciting, and occasionally upsetting encounters they experienced there. They could even retreat further into the private rooms, for near-disconnection from the chaos of the square. Yet even these walled-off areas were not completely isolated from the colonnade—their openness always afforded the possibility of reengagement.

Stavrides observes a similar spatial dynamic occurring during the time of the Syntagma occupation in Athens. In describing one of the many satellite occupations that occurred in other parks, he claims that "the park's porous perimeter is defined by spatial arrangements that acquire the characteristics of a threshold rather than those of a boundary" (Stavrides 2019, 231).[19] The threshold-like boundary of the park slowed down movement, leading to rest, repose, transition, and reflection. In all of these examples, thresholds choreographed the modulation of the rhythms between different spaces. They play the role of zones where individuals can modify their movements in ways that allow for slow mutations of their somatic stances in a way that facilitates the change between one rhythmic environment and another. Although these theorists do not strictly cast the utility of thresholds in this affective modality, such spaces, because they act particularly on the body and its spatiotemporal qualities, the implications for the sensed rhythm experienced by those entering thresholds, and thus choreography in the sense presented by McCormack, embody potentialities that could be cultivated by activists to strengthen their movements

Perhaps the most dramatic suggestion of how architecture might encourage experimenting with experience can be seen in the contention that architecture itself should move. In that way, an entire building might take on the characteristics of a threshold. Many such contemporary imaginings of "nomadic" architecture come from those who study protest camps, linking the choreography to nomad craftwork that I introduced in chapter 3. Feigenbaum and her co-authors in *Protest Camps* refer to the mobile "nomadic" architecture of tents and encampments characteristic of the movements they study. They link this ability of camps to move themselves to their tendency to act as "laboratories of insurrectionary imagination"; as new encounters lead to new affects that resonate with new tendencies and potentialities, protesters can dismantle the camps and reestablish them to address other problems and experience new encounters.[20] Sennett lauds spaces displaying design characteristics that encourage critical becoming, such as the Kara-za theater designed by Tadao Ando—a structure designed to literally be dismantled and moved after each performance much like a nomadic tent. Sennett claims that "portability has an important political dimension. Meetings through the city can be organized under common physical conditions. Portability serves a certain equality of discourse" (Lecuyer et al. 1998, 28). Sennett frames the principal utility of such a portable theater in terms of the possibility of its use in contributing to the diminishment of segregation in cities, stating that "as Ando has understood, a portable community meeting place might at least provide common ground in a fragmented city. . . . A portable political architecture therefore suggests a way of sharing political activity without unifying it" (Lecuyer et al. 1998, 43). Sennett's observation that a portable political architecture might act as a space that choreographs individuals mutually encountering yet not unifying around settled goals or identities suggests that such a nomadic theater might act as a portable corridor or threshold, depending on its use. It is impossible to reform settled urban space overnight—and such urban space is rife with the segregation and abstractions described by Lefebvre. But a mobile theater, which brings together people who might not usually encounter one another, could not simply provide a shared experience, but might encourage the contrast, and thus the intensified interest in new affect, provided through the transition provided by corridors and the modulation provided by thresholds. Such mobile spaces might act as corridors that bring individuals into contact with people and experiences not present within their segregated neighborhood. Yet they might also offer the modulation, respite, and transition provided by thresholds. Furthermore, a mobile architecture might provide a space of repose and then refraction, allowing individuals to temporarily retreat from their everyday environments, where they allow affects to slowly seep into their experience and try to tease out the multiple polyrhythmic resonances that might propel them in new directions.

Not only might whole buildings take on nomadic forms, but so might spaces themselves, with mobile "internal architecture" where walls and other design elements move and develop according to the shifting desires and potentialities of the inhabitants. An example of such internal nomadism is the Mietskaserne squat in Berlin which consisted of a number of interconnected buildings. Observers highlight the internal flexibility of the architecture, with the "permeability" of the buildings constantly increasing in order to suit the wishes of the inhabitants. In the Mietskaserne, "walls were removed in order to increase the size of social spaces including kitchens while stairwells were created to produce a new geography of movement through the buildings now interconnected and held together by a network of doors, passageways, courtyards and vestibules" (Vasudevan 2017, 137). The specific configuration of rooms constantly changed according to the developmental path of the squat and its inhabitants. It is important to stress how this internal nomadism is actualized through salvage. The frequent rearrangements of rooms, walls, and corridors, which were jury-rigged salvage construction in the first place, allowed for easy reconfiguration. Each time the squatters constructed a new internal geography, they simply scavenged for new materials and repaired and reconstructed the already existing structures. Through frequent salvage they combined thresholds and corridors, and, thus intermingled, affective environments of love and depression can be rearranged to form long strings of mutually developing refrains that constitute a never-ending symphony of becoming through movement and autonomous choreography.

All of the examples above intensify and specify the spatial qualities of the "radical workshop" I discussed in chapter 3. They entourage rhythmic movement by incorporating the corridor and threshold. Yet this rhythmic movement is not haphazard: it is not the general, unstructured encounter with difference described by Iris Young in her paean to urban diversity. Thresholds and corridors encourage different types of "connections" between an internally differentiated spaces. Corridors represent the open, expansive "love"-like movement that opens individuals to their surroundings—think of Walt Whitman's rambles through the streets of Brooklyn invoked by Hardt and Negri's account of love. And thresholds allow for the reflection and shelter invoked in Berlant's understanding of depression. Such choreography doesn't proscribe, it enables, in that it presents opportunities and inducements for individuals to intensify the aspects of experiences upon which they would like to focus at a particular moment. Whereas capitalist infrastructures act as compulsions to constant frenetic movement, radical choreography encourages rhythmic experimenting that allows for critical interrogation of the affects felt through the body. Such critical interrogation constitutes the foundation for liquid, plural becoming. Therefore, choreography in the mode about which I have been speaking here can act a powerful inducement to cultivating the craft of salvage and intensifying its political possibilities.

Radical Choreography: Neighborhood Labyrinths

The choreographic principles articulated by McCormack, and their embodiment in actual environments, such as the Athenian Agora, that are meant to instigate experimenting with experience, while they possess political import, might seem of little consequence to the actual instances of political salvage I have previously examined. Although Both McCormack and Massumi claim that choreography can be used to spark anticapitalist political action, their experiments with experience do not directly confront entrenched political power. Yet some of the same principles of affective choreography I have been discussing operate in the *favelas* that surround many Latin American cities, and these spatial geographies, according to some, play an important role in their ability to resist state control and foster autonomous, horizontal, and even anticapitalist social relations. Raul Zibechi argues that the *favelas* outside of Santiago, Chile, possess topographies that intensify their ability to defend themselves from government efforts to forcefully invade, relocate, and eventually destroy them. More importantly for this argument, he claims that the geography of salvaged informal neighborhood facilitates "the fusion of individual lives" (Zibechi 2012, 222). Yet he emphasizes that this fusion does not take the form of creating cultural or political uniformity, due to the spatial dispersion of the *favelas*, which he contrasts to concentration. He claims that "the dispersed city opens itself up to difference, but it is a difference rooted in social ties of a communitarian character (going beyond the traditional meaning of community). In any case, the territory enables a convergence of difference with communitarian ties that may turn—particularly during moments of rebellion—into an exclusive (and exclusionary) political unity" (68). In the previous description, notice that Zibechi uses both the words *convergence* and *fusion*. Convergence implies encounter but not necessarily a subsumption of one element to another. The fusion of individuals in a community might lead to a similarity of viewpoints and identity, but convergence only suggests the interaction and concentration within the same space without unity. Of course, connections, or "fusions," can occur due to convergence, but this word suggests connection of a temporary and fluid quality. Thus, Zibechi's description of the relationships encouraged by the neighborhood geography suggest both unity and difference, and thus a community that exists in a state of continual change and reinvention.

He describes how dispersion manifests itself both within and between homes. As opposed to apartments with small functional rooms, the *favela* dwellers build dwellings with "a large, central family area." In these units, single-story dwellings dominate, as opposed to large modernist apartment blocks "spread out generously" (Zibechi 2012, 69). Despite the preponderance of distinct single-family homes, the geography of the informal neighborhood does not encourage disconnection or privatism. One particular informal neighborhood called Zañartu, upon which Zibechi comments is divided into single-family homes, yet interconnected. According to another observer, it is "grouped in fourteen lots, where it is not easy to distinguish between the private, the communal and the public. They are juxtaposed domains infiltrating each other. The population is unstable. Family constantly come and go" (Skewes 2005, 104). The interconnecting passageways are further demarcated by the residences, each facilitating a different pace and category of movement. The different spaces are

> interconnected by passages that represent a true capillary system that allows both open and hidden movement. One of these passages, used by residents and neighbors, runs parallel to the open sewer that marks the northern boundary of the shantytown. The other is for "acquaintances" and although this passage ends halfway along, it has a private shortcut that connects it to the previous one. Residents know shortcuts, passageways and other hidden nooks that turn the shantytown into a real labyrinth. These shortcuts facilitate interaction between neighbors and, for those who need it, a quick exit. (Skewes 2005, 108)

These "capillary" internal structures have established different possibilities for different rhythms of internal movement. The *favela* does not simply contain dwellings and passages, but "the main passage, on the other hand, serves as a meeting place for collective meetings and games" (Skewes 2005, 11). The various "nodes" of the capillary system do not solely consist of residential dwellings, but also spaces of gathering that form autonomously in reaction to the needs and movements of the dwellers themselves. Thus, the neighborhood contains both corridor-like and threshold-like areas. The connections between the spaces act as corridors that stoke one's perception of new affects while the nodes themselves allow for introspection and retreat indicative of thresholds. Both movement and repose (with their concurrent loving and depressive affects) are choreographed by such a web-like geography. This structure, by its very nature, displays corridors and thresholds. The numerous cramped connections that stoke affective sensitivity while the numerous nodes can provide both respite and the ability to safely observe, like thresholds. Thus, the geography of the neighborhood contains differentiated yet connected areas that are both hivelike due to their individual cells yet contiguous due to their porous borders, and can often possess many of the choreographic qualities that McCormack identifies as encouraging "experimenting with experience."

Not only are the boundaries between individual homes and spaces within the informal neighborhood porous, but the border demarcating the inside and the outside of the community permits movement and penetration. Although the labyrinthine internal structure of the neighborhood remains opaque to most outsiders, its porous threshold-like borders allow for tentative access from the outside. As one observer reports:

> The image of a labyrinth as a self-contained unit is misleading. . . . An example of this are objects transported from the outside as stolen goods and returned as merchandise. The design must, therefore, provide the facilities to make these operations possible. For this reason, intermediate zones are established between the exterior and the interior. Such zones (sidewalks, passageways) cushion the traffic from outside, so that towards the interior the actors can accommodate themselves as best suits them. (Skewes 2005, 107)

Zañartu and other informal neighborhoods possess a complex, dispersed yet connected internal architecture containing many corridors that facilitate movement and thresholds that provide the opportunity for modulating movement. Thresholds that "cushion" movement between inside and outside and various passages between spaces that form a complex capillary systems of connections demonstrate the various rhythms of movement established by the *favela* dwellers. The internal structures of neighborhoods show, once again, that centralities that facilitate becoming cannot be open and featureless but instead exhibit a distinct yet flexible structure.

Zibechi also observes that a logic of dispersion affects the relationship between spaces of dwelling and spaces of work in the *favela*. In El Alto, Bolivia, he recounts how much production takes place in the home with these individual sites loosely unified in confederation, sometimes with a single "owner," who also gives aid and other forms of non-wage assistance to the families in his or her production network. There is very little division of labor and workers control production times and practice with the frequent rotation of the different tasks, moving between individual production spaces within the community, including the task of salvage. Yet, he claims that despite this frequent task rotation between different sites of production he observes that individuals develop patterns and habits of cooperation, mutual aid, and even resistance to incursions by state authorities within this jumbled, collectively accreted "postmodern Baroque" social environment. He observes that "the same logic of dispersion that we saw in the territorial construction of habitat operates in production." This pattern, he asserts, "is an internal logic in which the sectors involved adjust their way of life by establishing a different relationship to territory" (Zibechi 2012, 73), where families and thus micro units of production deploy themselves in a way that is both separate yet interconnected. They "adjust" not simply how they interact with each other, but how they produce, altering their methods, developing their skills, and even what they mean to produce, due in part to the dispersed landscape of the neighborhood and the encounters of production between both individuals and their landscape that this dispersal enables.

Perhaps most importantly for this argument is the observation that, because of the salvaged nature of the neighborhood, residents face the constant need to adapt, repair, and accommodate new residents and materials. The internally dispersed structure of the neighborhood constantly changes in line with the continually changing needs and desires of the dwellers:

> The boundaries of this occupied terrain are adapted to the needs of the user. It is perhaps in this regard that the predominance that use values acquire over those of change manifests itself with greatest emphasis. The residents have the option to accommodate the boundaries of their lots to the tasks that ensure their daily lives. (Skewes 2005, 110)

As is clear from this description, although not explicitly articulated, the salvaged construction of the *favela* contributes to its transformation. Both the space and the individuals within the space undergo constant rounds of inhabitation, as their space, their community, and their own identities become different from what they were before. Zibechi makes a similar point when he states: "In terms of production the neighborhoods becomes like one large factory or *maquilla*. As in other poor parts of the continent the people do not invent something new here without first fixing or improving something that already exists" (Zibechi 2012, 245).

With the entire community acting as a factory that reproduces its own conditions of material existence, and with the only material available to them that which mainstream society considers waste, the neighborhood/*maquilla* can be thought of as a factory of salvage. The things that already exist that the *favela* dwellers collectively undertake to "fix and improve" consist of discarded and broken items. Furthermore, because the entire neighborhood participates in this salvage production and reproduction, constructing and repairing a wide variety of items to address their various needs, the participants in the neighborhood/ *maquilla* engage in numerous types of labor. The salvaged nature of the materials they use further contributes to the necessity of engaging in "plastic" production that confounds the capitalist division of labor. As they attempt to fix their plumbing, grow food, scavenge for bike parts, the members of the neighborhood/*maquilla* use what they can find to fulfill numerous tasks. Within the geography of their dispersed neighborhood, the corridors and thresholds are constantly shifting due to the need to repair and the opportunities provided by new scavenged material. The *favela/maquilla* constantly produces and reproduces itself in ways that its dwellers cannot predetermine, nomadically shifting its internal geography and its outer boundaries when it expands and contracts as both oppor-tunities and obstacles present themselves due to the materials they find. Thus, the spatial qualities of the neighborhood/*maquilla* that Zibechi and others identify as constitutive of its anticapitalist geography come to be intensified by the salvaged nature of its construction and maintenance.

One final design feature of Zañartu and other informal neighborhoods merits commentary. The other examples of the spatial choreography of salvage that I have offered, from the Athenian Agora to Senselab, were not specifically designed as spaces that might act as sites of protest or resistance. *Favelas*, by their very nature, constitute sites of resistance where segregated populations forgotten by authorities claw out the means to live from what is discarded by others. Although sometimes ignored and sometimes tolerated, the mere fact of their existence separates them from the institutions that structure capitalist society. The inner labyrin-thine structure of the neighborhood contributes to the residents' ability to defend it by creating an inner structure, known only to themselves, that remains inscrutable to those on the outside. The citizens themselves become partially inscrutable to each other, donning alternative identities or "masks" that obscure their previous selves from the other residents. As the neighborhood dwellers inhabit and become inhabited by the neighborhood's capillary labyrinth, they become something other, and:

> In effect, becoming part of the shanty town implies suspending one's citizenship. Inside there are no complete names, identity cards, nor the rights habitually consecrated by the Constitution

and the laws. People become known by their nicknames and become part of the cycles that affect the residential collective; from a celebration to a fire from a funeral to a break in all are incidents from which none of the residents escapes. (Skewes 2005, 107)

With the donning of these "sociable masks" that facilitate neighborhood life, they develop a secret language for negotiating the landscape of the neighborhood, but it is a language that does not consist of words; instead, communication occurs through the physical senses. As Zibechi describes it, the landscape of the neighborhood and the masks it encourages its residents to don "facilitate[s] social control through acoustic, visual and olfactory means, contributing to the formation of a porous environment" (Zibechi 2012, 222). The residents, in essence, communicate through their senses. They learn visual cues, both warn and invite through sounds, and become wary due to smells. The residents come to be able to "read" the senses that others are experiencing, and communicate by conveying the quality of their experience through affects. They become like Deleuzian "wolf packs" bound by mutual affects and using an autonomously formed language to convey these affects such as danger, change, and mutual accommodation. But more importantly, this language constitutes a form of communication only to the neighborhood dwellers, a language that aids in their mutual defense. Skewes reports that communication based on sense creates "a dynamic that makes the exercise of self-protection possible. Whistles, barks, and a whole range of sounds make it possible to keep alert a population that knows itself to be vulnerable" (Skewes 2005, 108). The whistles and barks, an autonomously formed language that conveys the affects produced by intrusion and danger, are an offshoot of the communication of affects that take root due to the internal structure of the neighborhood. The community and its space become like a single, yet constantly changing and porous, organism that responds nonverbally to changes in its state of equilibrium, especially when facing threats from the outside. The constantly metamorphosing architecture and population of the neighborhood facilitates a metamorphosing vocabulary of affects that provides both a weak unity between residents and a secret language that can be employed against invaders. Thus, the architecture of the informal community itself represents a *metis*-built weapon of the weak.

While some of the terms used in Zibechi's description of *favela* environments might seem incompatible with the choreography, due to the fact that no particular choreographer exists to design the *favela*, in fact this description can be fruitfully interpreted through this theoretical lens. First of all, remember that Zibechi casts the "social control" about which he speaks in terms of the dual logic of dispersion—diversity that coalesces through internal negotiation into patterns of cooperation. This manifests itself in terms of a landscape that is differentiated and porous, lacking rational order, and filled with constantly shifting individuals and activities. The ability to negotiate such twisted and shifting landscapes comes not only through the establishment of focal points, thresholds where people might attempt to orient themselves and take stock of the changes around them, but also through social control that employs vague, possibly confusing yet definitely resonating and refracting "acoustic, visual and olfactory means." This observation begs the question, in the context of this argument, of how such a reliance upon sensory input relates to choreography that explicitly acknowledges the role of affective sense. What social control in this context means can be fruitfully understood using the logic of dispersion. In other words, the neighborhood encourages the coming together of the separate elements of the community in encounters led not by predetermined plan but through physical senses, smell, hearing, and, although it is not specifically mentioned, affective sense. *Favela* dwellers cooperatively build affiliations and common actions based on the different combinations, encounters, and relationships that come about through the porosity of their environment. They sense the possibilities created by the numerous and diverse encounters they experience, and experiment with, reorient themselves to, and retreat from these encounters into individual houses, reorienting themselves in relation to towers and other markers. All of these movements are negotiated, at least partially, by affect-based communication and other choreographic markers encouraged by the dispersed landscape and facilitated by the numerous corridors and thresholds of the neighborhood's labyrinthine environment. The rhythms created by different movements through these areas—some abetting connection, like corridors, some stressing individuation, and some representing thresholds whereon residents both maintain distance from encounters and yet establish a general orientation toward their entire neighborhood, using lookout posts and other markers to facilitate their perception of distinctions and estimate the balance of the entire community beyond individual encounters.

In introducing the above example, I hope to demonstrate actual landscapes that choreograph movement using corridors and thresholds. These landscapes, while internally differentiated, encourage the distinct styles of movement between their distinct zones (and the activities practiced within them) indicative of the spatial inducements to choreography identified and practiced by McCormack and Massumi in their experiments. The spontaneous, salvaged architecture of the informal community represents unconscious examples that allow for the "experimenting" with experience that encourages plastic, plural becoming. Furthermore, it points the way toward envisioning an activist choreography that might overcome the divisions I identified in Occupy Wall Street and London. While not suf-ficient in itself to bring about radical political transformation, existence in such environments, especially when paired with political activities similar to the ones I have discussed earlier, such as squats, occupations, and informal communities, intensifies the possibilities for becoming, which have already been engendered by such activities. They suggest how activists might maximize the potency inherent within the affective infrastructure created through salvage, while more fully integrating this infrastructure with activism. Furthermore, when such activities include salvage, as they often do, the political potential inherent in these acts of resistance comes to be even more heightened. It is to this, the specific intersection of salvage with the choreographic/political insights I have been stressing, that I now turn.

The Choreography of Anticapitalist Salvage

I would now like to shift attention back to the central theme of this work and discuss how the choreographic design elements and the exam-ples of choreographed spaces of becoming might be used to deepen the potential for becoming that already exists in salvage landscapes. I will discuss how the anticapitalist choreographic experiments with which I began this chapter can be intensified through the integration of salvage practices, and then how the anticapitalist qualities of the *favela* geography might be enhanced by accentuating the nascent choreographic qualities it already possesses. To begin to make such connections between salvage and anticapitalist choreography, I would like to emphasize that in many ways spaces of salvage, especially spaces where people forage, act like corridors. Corridors, remember, are spaces of passage and diversity. They are ever-changing and increase the possibility of presenting unintended encounters. Thus, corridors have the potential to foment the experience of contrasting encounters and thereby to inspire interest and attention, the same way that salvage spaces contain contrasting, confusing, yet provocative encounters. More specifically, the act of "foraging," that is, looking for items while observing the patterns within a broken environment, in places where individuals are led by their senses to find possibly useful materials and where they are propelled in new directions of interest and action by what they find. The difference between how McCormack describes corridors and how I am describing "salvage" corridors of foraging lies in the fact that the difference in encounters involves interactions with vibrant human and nonhuman "actors." As one attempts to scavenge, one "bumps into" things one was not expecting and senses brief, affective "glimpses" into what they might be used for, and comes to notice small indications in one item or part of the environment that suggest what might be hidden within another part. Just like the Athenian Agora, the pulsating plethora of confusing, upsetting, and exciting encounters that fling one's consciousness and sense of self in various directions, salvage forces one to think about items in different ways, to pay close attention to the contours of one's landscape (if one hopes to negotiate its many eddies and currents), and to develop habits that can take advantage of, and not be overwhelmed by, such difference.

Whereas the scavenging aspect of salvage involves being thrust forward like a corridor, the repair component acts as a threshold. When one repairs, one must slow down, reflect, actually attempt to implement the possibilities indicated by the senses and produced by interactions that came about through scavenging. One must peer into other activities, the realm where the item to be repaired will actually be used, and thus dwell in two "realms" of activity itself—scavenging and that activity. Furthermore, repair, as I have stressed before, can be greatly aided if it occurs in a workshop, where those engaged in repair can discuss their individual projects, collaborate, or merely watch others who are engaged in interesting projects. Craftworkers are not necessarily forced into final decisions or rigid timelines when they work in a workshop, such as there was within the Pnyx or as exist in a factory—one can participate as one wishes, as a tinkerer or an experimenter. The threshold modulates the speed and pace of movement between these two realms, and thus helps to establish a rhythm of tinkering, as one adjusts the salvaged item, using trial and error. The presence of thresholds implies the dispersal of different spaces dedicated to different activities within a space—the number of thresholds corresponding to the number of activities. This is the importance of the internal differentiation of spaces implied by the choreography of experimenting with experience.

Although many of these design characteristics are present to various extents within cites of political salvage, as I have shown with my previous discussion of informal neighborhoods, such experiences of critical anticapitalist becoming might be intensified, if the tools of choreography were consciously applied to these salvage spaces. Thus, the question arises of how might the spaces I discussed earlier—Senselab and the neighborhood discussed by Zibechi, be thought of as models for a space that integrates salvage? First of all, in the context of Senselab—the encounters that it encourages, especially in the conceptual speed dating exercise, are exclusively between individuals. Although each individual brings a material "offering" representing their work, the interactions between people and the mediating or "triangulating" element (the minor concept used to introduce refraction as a "differentiating exchange," as Sennett would put it, between two individuals), constitute the primary benefit of the encounters between individuals. What if the conceptual speed dating, in addition to involving bodies in different locations and interactions with different objects, wrenched from their original context and thus approximating salvage? What if participants were asked to use objects in different and seemingly inappropriate ways, such as tightening a screw with a wooden paint brush, or constructing a chair from sponges. The need to examine, prod, pull, and generally test and thus sense the potential of these materials and their possible alternative uses would add a further dimension to the resonances created by the exercise. Furthermore, attempting to use items in ways for which they are not intended—by experimenting with how they might be joined together or how striking one with another might produce a particular sound or feel—might further produce resonances that could contribute to the democratic becoming of the individuals. If these material encounters were paired with immaterial ones—conceptual speed dating intermingled with material speed dating, using the refrain of corridor, threshold, activity to guide the arrangement—in an attempt to solve problems or embody concepts with items brought as "offerings" to symbolize different practices and methodology, their vibrancy might better resonate with the philosophical encounters and vice versa, and might increase the possibility of counteracting the "capitalist capture," which they describe as enveloping our daily affective experience.

A further example of how salvage might be integrated with Senelab experiments could be seen when the experiment *Propositions for Thought in Act* was retooled from occurring at one site to inhabiting one that embodied the idea, "drop the site: let the site be the city as a whole" (Manning and Massumi 2014, 139). One part of this exercise was entitled *The Mi(d)st* when a comment was generated from an iteration of conceptual speed dating that occurred in a forested area outside Montreal concerning the "captivating ephemerality" of the mist that rose from the lake. This ephemerality was then materially embodied by stretching a hundred-meter length of mosquito netting across a lake to represent this concept, creating a "play across surfaces," with the reflection on the surface of the lake meant to embody ephemerality and the "interpenetration of process and event" (143), which spurred other installations into choreographing invitations for participants to engage in different moments (crawling, running) that would then recursively be integrated into further philosophic reflection. This use of netting to choreograph interactions was then transported to a neighborhood within the city limits where the exercise was undertaken, where it was mostly met with confusion and suspicion by denizens of the neighborhood. Whether or not their transportation of a choreographic intervention was successful in an urban setting, what this installation did not include was any attempt to experiment with materials. Therefore, introducing salvage into this experiment raised questions such as what materials were used to embody "ephemerality" and "play across surfaces" and then to formulate assessments in terms of the resonances they created. What if the materials were taken from the surroundings of the forest or the neighborhood where it was installed? The potential resonances might have been not only intensified but diversified, to include items related to the area and the landscape itself, if the experiment were expanded. In essence, the choreographic tools of corridors and thresholds might have both linked these areas and allowed for the modulation of movement between them, which might have led to greater possibilities for rhythmic becoming.

In terms of Zibechi's portrayal of the *favela* as a space of anticapitalist becoming through experimenting with experience, salvage already plays an important role, at least pragmatically—the buildings, pathways, and infrastructure in these communities are built from and maintained with detritus collected by their poor inhabitants. Zibechi's work suggests that such "postmodern baroque" architecture leads to dispersion within the community that both maintains the autonomy of the families and yet allows for the "social control" to bind them enough to resist incursions by the state. But such spontaneous dispersion might not always occur—and the same applies to the presence of corridor- and threshold-like spaces in the neighborhood. One thing that might encourage the propagation of such spaces would be the conscious inclusion of a salvage workshop within the informal community. While salvage certainly represents a nearly omnipresent activity in such spaces, the inclusion of a dedicated space where individuals might share techniques and materials, practice social rituals of salvage, and thus hone their salvage craft might help residents to hone their salvage skills. Furthermore, the conscious acknowledgment and even celebration of salvage construction might lead to the introduction of such practices into other, less "informal" contexts and segregated spaces and thereby increase the number of spaces that encourage everyday experiences of radical becoming.

One can see an example of the conscious implementation of salvage practice in the Quina Monoroy housing development in Santiago, Chile.[21] There, housing units are given to residents "half-completed," with one, vertical half of the three-story structure built with concrete walls, and the other half left "open" yet easily built upon by the residents themselves. Thus, all of the individual dwellings have one similar concrete half and another uniquely inhabited and constructed half built from cheap and salvaged material. While this design was largely conceived as a cost-cutting measure, it has resulted in a flourishing community of mutual aid and autonomous design. Yet, if a communal workshop, where residents might borrow tools, take and store found materials, discuss and practice techniques, were established in the neighborhood, the salvage practice and autonomous, self-directed design elements might be even more widely distributed. Despite the fact that not everyone uses salvage in this development, Quina Monoroy not only constitutes a neighborhood where salvage constitutes a conscious part of the design, but demonstrates how more formal housing and communities might be designed with informal qualities. It represents an example, both for informal and traditional neighborhoods, of how salvage can be "instituted" in a way that encourages the practice without undermining the autonomy and spontaneity that constitute the normative core and political potential of the practice.

Furthermore, understanding and acknowledging the anticapitalist political potential of such design principles might act as a general regulative guideline for the construction of informal neighborhoods. As I have noted, often the porous neighborhood border offers both resistance and the opportunity to be traversed, by acting as a corridor. Zibechi also emphasizes that bricolage and dispersion of this type is counterpoised against areas of observation and centralization in the informal neighborhoods, creating threshold-like spaces that for the modulating of movements that could enhance the space's choreography of critical becoming. Yet, such diversification might produce an overabundance of either corridor, threshold, or unitary spaces, and thus simply keeping in mind the different types of spaces and trying to balance them could both maintain the ability of the space to enable an affective infrastructure characterized by the rhythms of resistance and allow for autonomous salvaged modification within that space. Simply knowing that *favelas* need not take any specific form, but should try to balance the particular design elements that often occur without conscious design represents a regulated spatial ideal rather than a predetermined plan. And this simple acknowledgment could constitute part of the shared knowledge passed from community to community that constitutes part of the salvage craft, which, if practiced, might maximize the political potentialities of such spaces.

Such weak yet conscious salvage choreography could have benefited Occupy Wall Street and London, both of which, while possessing most if not all of the characteristics of urban public spaces that Young and Jacobs believe enhance the production of tolerance and other civic virtues, and exhibiting the pronounced internal pluralism and experimentation that Connolly describes in his account of the "micropractices of the everyday," embodied the segregation and division of labor that they hoped to overcome. This theory of choreography suggests that, instead of insisting on further mixing and dismantling boundaries within these spaces in an attempt to force more and diverse encounters, one must maintain and even accentuate spatial differences, along with adding membranous boundaries (for example, a curtain or a low wall) and threshold spaces. This would encourage participants to better modulate the rhythms of their movements, giving them the opportunity to gain confidence and enter Agora-like spaces and to retreat when overwhelmed by difference. In this instance, the space of the assembly might be understood as a Pnyx, encouraging listening and occasional, directed participation, while the rest of the encampment may be thought of as an Agora. Yet, with the Planning Committee's efforts to "rationalize" the space, the disruptive, creative reformulations that stem from collective becoming were effectively negated. What was needed were threshold spaces and borders that facilitated movement and allowed for the tempering of the participants' movements. These choreographic design elements should have been part of the constitutions of the camp—while there can be no one "map" of a salvage encampment, due to the specificity of the site and the materials available to construct the camp, there can be design guidelines, beyond simply efficiency and legibility, which were the principles that motivated the members of the Planning Committee. And while Occupy London established a space in Finsbury where salvage constituted a conscious element of the camp's maintenance and reproduction design, Occupy Wall Street designated no such space. The establishment of a salvage workshop might have indicated a threshold for vibrant materiality—where the participants in the encampment, as part of their diverse tasks, might have played a role in the becoming of the camp. The sanitation working group that was tasked with recycling might have spawned a salvaging or scavenging working group, with its own area in which to oversee its own operations. The same thing might have been established for repairs—a workshop in an accessible space that might have fulfilled the role of a salvage threshold, thereby encouraging "tinkering" and experimentation. The process of construction by salvage encourages a bricolage, postmodern baroque aesthetic within a secretive, labyrinthine layout—a salvage space that might truly transform the encampment into a "laboratory of insurrectionary imagination," which could have maximized the possibilities for plural becoming and thus subversion of capitalist ideology within the participants.

One might ask whether or not any of these spaces encouraging choreography could have been added to such a constrained space as Occupy Wall Street, with its hard borders, such as sidewalks and streets, and active attempts by police to arrest its growth. But the same constraints faced the participants in Occupy London, who reacted to spatial limitations by establishing a satellite encampment at Finsbury Square. As I stated before, this second encampment, although it acted as a space of respite where many of the activities that supported maintenance of the encampment occurred, did not constitute a true corridor because of its separateness; its role as a retreat from the contestation and tension of the St. Paul's encampment furthered segregation, as opposed to stoking interest. Yet its existence points toward the ability of such encampments to choreograph their becoming through the establishment of separate areas that act as corridors—the connections between such distinct spaces need not be physical. Remember, refrains are relationships, and if a rhythm of travel were established between distinct areas—scavenging corridors and repairing thresholds—constituting a routine of participants moving through areas of affective love and depression, then the possibilities for building refrains of becoming existed even if the actual areas embodying such affective landscapes were separate from the main encampments.

Consciously choreographing salvage spaces to maximize the possibility of anticapitalist becoming might seem antithetical to anarchist-inspired, horizontally governed political forms such as Occupy, squats, and informal neighborhoods. But, as Graeber discusses when discussing Occupy, anarchism is not a lack of rules and procedures, it is simply a lack of hierarchy.[22] Thus, providing practices or, better said, traditions that can be implemented by participants without leaders forcing them to do so is not outside of the anarchist, networked ethos of these types of political action. Furthermore, by providing a weak, spatial structure for such political activities, as opposed to a strong, substantive unifying element, they split the difference between those who criticize Occupy and similar actions and those who maintain that any efforts to standardize these actions would rob them of their horizontalism and potential for autonomous political creativity. Thus, a political theory of salvage, as I am articulating it, would not lead to "parties of salvage" with leaders choreographing the layout of camps in a way that they saw fit due to their expertise, but instead, habits and practices that are passed on from one group to another, as was done in artisan workshops.

Chapter 6

Salvage and the Politics of the Commons

Introduction

Before I discussed choreographed salvage "laboratories of insurrectionary imagination" in the last chapter, I claimed that the spatial contradictions of the capitalist city often constitute a powerful stimulus for those engaged in salvage to engage in radical political resistance. Modern cities, facing pressures to increase their competitive advantage, undergo spatial segregation whereby populations less central to the processes of accumulation come to be pushed to the periphery to make way for abstract centers dedicated to the free flow of goods and ideas. The residents of such marginal areas and buildings attempt to salvage and protect these spaces, so that, Lefebvre suggests, they often come together in self-administering communities. The informal neighborhoods, squats, and Occupations that the poor establish in order to survive on the periphery either block plans for redevelopment or face redevelopment themselves, as peripheries come to be viewed as potential centers for capital accumulation.

But is defense really all there is to the politics of salvage? Are the communities that form in them merely dedicated to the spaces themselves and to local issues? Can one say anything in general about the political goals, strategies, and tactics of salvage political actors in terms of larger social and political trends? How might political salvage come to be seen as a persistent tactic that activists use within their movements or that constitutes a part of a more permanent political formation? It seems difficult to imagine a "political party of salvage," and the groups that do engage in such actions are disparate, local, and autonomous, political formations that seem to defy the logic of coordination and permanence inherent in the concept of a party. If this is true, then, is there anything definitive to be said about the actual political strategy and organization of a political theory of salvage?

One way of linking a political-organizational form to salvage has been introduced by Anna Lowenhaupt Tsing in her claim that salvage groups can be said to be united through a "latent commons" that shared ownership and community without the assistance of public institutions. For Tsing, who originated this concept, the latent commons constitutes a potential relationship between the matsutake mushroom pickers, who see themselves as mutually supportive of each others' goals, and the space in which they operate, inasmuch as see their picking-grounds as shared and mutually administered. She interprets the commons as latent because it only infrequently coalesces and, when it does, remains undeveloped and precarious. But simply because a political theory of the commons does not immediately flow from the practice of salvage does not mean that this activity does not possess political potentialities that can be interpreted through the concept of the commons. Various political actors have engaged in salvage while creating common social formations. Such examples are manifestations of the commons acting as the animating concept of syndicalist, anarcho-communist, and various other manifestations of horizontal-mutualist political movements throughout the rise and triumph of capitalism.

As I have said before, theorists such as Tsing are skeptical of the political promise of the commons. But what if the very qualities that convince Tsing of the inappropriateness of designating the commons as a base for political action constitute the link between it and the political tradition of the commons that I previously invoked? For example, when one looks to the characteristics of plural becoming articulated by William Connolly, it is this very lack of complete human control, along with the presence of divergent ecologies, that allows for the surprising and novel relationships between humans, their environment, and themselves that comprises this phenomenon. Furthermore, whereas Tsing cautions that the thin, unstable relationships of the commons constitute a weak foundation for political action, syndicalists and anarchists would highlight these characteristics as advantageous building blocks for horizontal, self-governing relationships. The fact that the salvage commons exists within the interstices of the formal legal structure seems to establish a salutary contrast to the formal and abstract legal regime that characterizes capitalist development, and thus opens the door to practices of *autogestion* that Lefebvre suggests can flow from spatial inhabitation and subsequently undermine abstract capitalist space. Although it would be inappropriate to affiliate the commons that flows from salvage with a particular movement such as syndicalism, I think it is safe to claim that salvage remains much more pregnant with strategic political possibility than Tsing deems it to be.

While I have previously claimed that salvage represents an activity that diverges from capitalist production and is tied to a distinct political principle—that of Connolly's politics of plural becoming[1]—these assertions say very little concerning the practical political actions, groups, and strategies that might constitute a political theory of salvage. By focusing on the principle of the commons, both the relationships around which one would constitute such groups, and the value that would define their goals inasmuch as that they would attempt to establish and defend the commons, I hope to give further weight to envisioning the possibilities of a political theory of salvage. And with the posting of the commons as the political manifestation of salvage, I further hope to counteract both salvage pessimists and Left pessimists in general who deny the possibility of effective radical political action in the face of hegemonic capitalism.

Before linking the commons to salvage, I first must offer a definition of the commons. In general, the commons both lies between and combines the concepts of private and public. Whereas private goods are exclusively owned and controlled by individuals and public goods are owned and controlled by governments and other institutions, common goods are owned and administered by the groups that use them. Using this as a baseline definition, I begin the chapter by exploring the conceptual constituents of the commons, focusing on how various contemporary theorists emphasize that common property and the groups that administer it are not simply diverse—in that they are united by the space or property they commonly own—but also that they constantly enter into relationships of exchange and modification with each other, becoming something different than they were before. Next, I will explore how one of the most prominent portrayals of the political import of the commons, that of Michael Hardt and Antonio Negri, relates to salvage—specifically, their claim that salvage represents a prime example of biopolitical production. I will end by asserting that my understanding of political salvage might help to conceptualize how the "multitude,"

Hardt and Negri's preferred Left political formation, might produce a revolutionary commons. In exploring this linkage, my understanding gains power as it conceives these disconnected efforts as belonging to a larger political agent, that is, the multitude. Salvage can be seen as producing the same political affects as the multitude and thus possibly constituting part of this larger coalition of forces. Not only does Hardt and Negri's understanding benefit by the addition of this phenomenon to its own "movement of movements," but also, more generally, my vision of choreographed "radical workshops" demonstrates how the nodes of the multitude might be cultivated and maintained by establishing "weak" architectures and political structures, which can be thought of as existing as something between a crowd and a party. Thus, I challenge one of the most powerful Left arguments, against not only Hardt and Negri's understanding but also autonomous and horizontal political movements in general, which is that they naively embody a "new Proudhounism" that assumes that the multitude will self-organize without the aid of elites or party structure.

Rebirth of the Commons

Despite the claims made in Garrett Hardin's influential article "Tragedy of the Commons" (Hardin 1968), the social formation of the commons continues to manifest itself, in many resilient forms. Economist Elinor Ostrom's work presents the best-known rebuttal to Hardin's argument by revealing qualities of common management and ownership that counteract the tendencies toward shirking so often identified with manifestations of non-private ownership. Whether it concerns lobster beds in Maine, where fishermen maintain rules that govern the size of allowable catches and prohibitions against collecting pregnant females, or rural communities in sub-Saharan Africa that collectively both maintain and share their herds of cattle, she identifies the characteristics that have allowed various forms of the commons to thrive, such as clearly defined boundaries, low-cost conflict resolution, graduated sanctions, and effective monitoring as necessary to motivate participation and hold together the diversely motivated individuals found in any common formation (Wall 2017, 29–31).[2] She contends that such practices strike a balance between the unity necessary to hold the commons together and an autonomy that respects the unique motivations and skills of each of the participants.

Ostrom also articulates a further quality of successful commons that directly contradicts the image of the commons as unstable and isolated, namely, the need for any group maintaining a commons to work with other groups. As Wall contends,

> she argued . . . that commons need to be part of nested enterprises, i.e. they work within wider systems. . . . So, a commons might be part of a river estuary, which might be part of a larger region, and so on. Environments are not discrete islands and even islands are influenced by weather systems and oceans. Despite Ostrom's emphasis on boundaries, common property systems may overlap with inter-communing occurring between different communities. There must, there-fore, be ways of negotiating the links between interlocking commons. (Wall 2017, 32)

Thus, successful commons are necessarily political, in that they must engage in larger forms of decision making and coordination in order to influence their larger social environment. Isolated commons cannot survive; instead, they must form networks of mutual aid and debate. Thus, Wall asserts, Ostrom's work not only points toward the practices that lead to well-maintained common holdings, but also contains the nascent seed of a political formation upon which they might be based.

The commons has been theorized not simply in terms of shared property, but also as "non market webs of interdependence—creating stable infrastructures for the diffusing of risk, resilience and opportunity within webs of placed and embodied relationships between human and on going human creatures" (Reid and Taylor 2010, 37). In this expanded definition it is important to unpack the meaning of "placed," "embodied" relationships and "human and on going human creatures."[3] To begin, even when a commons is not centered around a piece of land, the common, reciprocal relationships between commoners occur in a place. Relationships are always embodied and spatially located, and thus while the commons is not necessarily a place, it always involves relationships with places. But by decentering the material in understanding the com-mons the above quote emphasizes that the commons represents a type of relationship between people and things.[4] To emphasize the multiplicity of relationships within the commons, Reid and Taylor never refer only to the "commons" but instead coin the phrase "body-place-commons."

> [H]uman beings emerge from the interplay of diverse yet overlapping forms of bioaesthetic, growth grounded in a body-earth hinge of changing persons and places. Today the face of human hinges on the claim, a necessarily political one that human life requires a lifeworld facilitating the ability to weave levels and facets of reality into integrative coherence such that the earth recovers its generative status as a place, not merely economic space. (Reid and Taylor 2010, 157)

The commons, in this understanding constitutes a pulsating, shifting assemblage even when it involves a fixed piece of land, because the relationships, understandings, and practices used to maintain that land must undergo constant renegotiation. This understanding expands the conceptualization of the commons and points toward the possibility of common relationships forming through a variety of manifestations of body-place-commons, not simply around pieces of land. Furthermore, it points toward the relationships formed through common ownership of land or things persisting and transforming even after the original locus of the common relationship no longer exists. If the commons constitutes a relational form as opposed to a mode of ownership, the relations originally established can migrate to focus on new constellations as one aspect of the body-place-commons undergoes transformation.

The necessity of communicating and forming relationships with real, ever-changing matrices of "human and non human creatures" results in assemblages united not by the commonality of the group's members. Hardt and Negri assert instead that "no, the common has nothing to do with sameness. Instead, in struggle, different social groups interact as singularities and are enlightened, inspired, and transformed by their exchange with each other" (Hardt and Negri 2012, 90). Reid and Taylor express a similar understanding when they suggest that commoning requires the ability to "kilter multiple knowledges," giving the commons "elective affinities with democracy, empowerment and tolerance" (Reid and Taylor 2010, 167).[5] Their use of the word *kilter* constitutes an important choice that emphasizes the provisional, fragile, and partial nature of the bonds holding together relationships in the commons. To employ kiltering as a solution might take the form of ramming an ill-fitting plug into a hole or taping two pieces together in a bond that will not last. "Kiltered" solutions, as defined by Reid and Taylor, are solutions that are bound to fail and break. Thus, the shared solutions, outlooks, and strategies that constitute the commons do not last—something that is known and even cheered by participants. The impermanence of the "kiltered" connections preserves the differences among the individual elements and does not require them to permanently adopt one identity. The commons is a bricolage of loosely pasted-together-yet-independent pieces that necessarily requires constant maintenance.

This "kiltering" can be seen as a form of repair that shares many similarities to salvage. Just as the use during salvage of found parts that never quite work as one might hope leads to constant tinkering, with its attendant rhythm of sense, action, evaluation, and sensing again for new possibilities, efforts to collectively maintain a common object by a diverse group will most likely lead to a process whose form and a rhythm possess many similarities to those I have described as characterizing salvage craft. The use of the word *kiltering* also implies that such repairs constitute contingent, fragile interventions that even when successful do not last for long periods of time. "Kiltering" necessitates embracing the arts of failure discussed by the activists who constructed the "disobedient objects" they use in their protests. It suggests the experimental, frustrating rhythmic process of activity, disappointment, and reflection I described as employed by salvagers.

Despite the local origins of common practices such as the maintenance of a single field, project, or building, Reid and Taylor argue that the kiltered, patchwork relationships and practices comprising such assemblages lay the groundwork for reimagining the scale of participants' understanding of the commons relevant to their well-being. They suppose that embracing the plasticity of the body-place-commons might lead to "a rescaling and reclaiming of social being that pivots on the very complex temporalities and spatialities of *re-inhabitation—rebuilding* infrastructures of embodied being, in a particular places, in sedimented and emergent dependencies within ecological matrices and *given* limits of the nonhuman surround and placed histories" (Reid and Taylor 2010, 4). The rescaling for which they advocate occurs across multiple levels. For them, the commons entails coming to think of one's body being constituted by the common substance of one's environment; thus, the body is rescaled and comes to be seen as exceeding one's simple corporeality. One's temporal scale is also expanded, in that one's past and future come to be seen as an integral part of one's present. And perhaps most importantly, the commons, despite its localizations, flows from the immediate to the global. While grounded in particular places and practices, the commons, for Reid and Taylor, is better described as an ethos that influences one's political practices and conception of oneself.

The plastic and diverse constitution of the commons necessitates it being thought of as much as a process as a place or a group. As aforementioned, Reid and Taylor characterize the process as involving the constant formation, maintenance, and "kiltering" of the commons—a cluster of activities that they use to construct their idea of "participatory reason."[6] Lest the word *reason* be interpreted as a purely cognitive process, such reason must be predicated on opening oneself to the affects prompted by one's interactions with one's environment. It is only through the close observation of and active experimentation on environments that the perception of not just a single cause, but multiple causes of change are produced within a particular commons.[7] Through participatory reason, one not only discovers what causes changes within one's environment but gains the general ability and propensity to seek multiple origins for the phenomenon they seek to understand. Thus, they claim that engaging in participatory reason will frequently guide its practitioners to inquiries that lead beyond the borders of their body-place-commons. Such expansive investigations prompt questioning of the boundaries of the original commons itself, and thus lead to nomadic, and frequently recalibrated, common relationships.

Even though Reid and Taylor characterize the process of maintaining the relationships of the commons as participatory reason, it does not mean that they envision this process as solely comprised of rational calculation. Because such "kiltering" relies on educated guesses concerning potential recalibration of the commons and depends upon not simply observations of fact but interpretations of value, they and other theorists of the commons stress that commoning relies upon participants' employment of affect. Hardt and Negri express this by stating that "becoming common is a continuous activity guided by the reason, will, and desire . . . which itself must undergo an education of its knowledge and political affects" (Hardt and Negri 2012, 64). Thus, participation in the commons prompts not simply an education in the details of how to maintain one's common property, but a more general education in the perception of affects. Such an education should comprise not simply general knowledge of the expansiveness and multiplicity of affects inherent within every commons, but, presumably (and this observation constitutes an outgrowth of my earlier interest in affect), enhancement of the ability to sense particular affects produced by the interventions of the commoner's participatory reason. This is why Reid and Taylor maintain that such a democratic process of maintaining the commons "requires fluency—the ability to flow easily from one perspective to another in order to ensure that a question is deliberated upon in an open ended and egalitarian way" (Reid and Taylor 2010, 13). The use of the verb *flow* should not be taken as mere rhetoric—it demonstrates the importance of the spatial and temporal dynamics of participatory reason. Shared affects can indicate equivalencies between people and things that are sensed before they are known. Such flow aids in building relationships and endows them with sensed energy and momentum, which helps to sustain and deepen the process.

Yet this fluency rarely manifests itself as a completely smooth and fluid process—especially due to the many different manifestations of kiltering—i.e., between different people, between people and the vibrant commons itself, and between different levels of the commons. Such complex efforts will necessarily result in stops and starts and divergent, surprising redirections of affiliation. Reid and Taylor acknowledge this when they argue that "the key characteristic of body-place-commons is the power to kilter heterogeneous temporalities of the cyclic, linear and arrhythmic temporalities with spatialities that are rerecursive, planar, topological and so forth and that integrate sedimentary forms of retention with capacities of protention toward the unexpected, new or the maddeningly or wonderfully same-old" (Reid and Taylor 2010, 90). As is clear from this quote, Reid and Taylor see the creation and maintenance of the commons in profoundly spatial and temporal terms. Furthermore, their highlighting of the "protention toward the unexpected," or, as they state elsewhere, the "folded ontology" of the commons that lets loose "ruly and unruly generative matrices" (Reid and Taylor 2010, 167), demonstrates their belief that maintaining commoning will necessarily result in unstable relationships between commoners and commons, as the recursive cycles of maintenance and reproduction never repeat in exactly the same ways. In light of the internal becomings let loose by such a process, the rhythm itself, its peaks and valleys, trajectories and surprises, reveals important qualities of the body-place-commons. Yet those qualities also represent the difficulties inherent in a filtering process that involves periods of both flowing, loving connection and depressive failure. Mastering the habits that allow one to effectively use their sense of such rhythms to guide their participatory reason can be thought of as the craft required to build the commons.

Not everyone sees commoning as a promising basis for a Left politics. Berlant, upon whom I drew extensively to describe capitalist affective infrastructure, believes that understandings of the political commons embody universalist tendencies and thus result in "political fantasies" that create a false "shared substance of our social being." Instead, Berlant, insists that to avoid the commons falling into the same universalist, and thus ultimately regressive, tendencies the concept should be imagined as "incoherent" and as a process of "unlearning." They invoke the commons as a relationship that consists of "being close without being joined and without mistaking the other's flesh for one's own or any object world as identical to oneself. Non sovereignty is not here, in the dissolution of a boundary it's the experience of an affect, of being receptive, in real time" (Berlant 2016, 402). This "positive version of dispossession" results in a tendency to "retrain affective practical being, and in particular in its power to dishabituate through unlearning the overskilled sensorum that is so quick to adapt to a damaged life with a straight and not a queer face" (Berlant 2016, 399). One can truly grasp the ambivalence of their position through these two statements. On the one hand, the commons represents a type of unlearning and dispossession—a state she exemplifies by exploring Emerson's walks through Boston Common, where he went to feel a sense of being alone with others, to lose his chaotic particularity of his thoughts and desires and to "submit to being dispossessed of the property in the self by the immediacy of a nature that dissolves the attachment to sovereignty and instrumentality" (Berlant 2016, 400). Yet they claim that with the dissolving of the self comes acute sensitivity to affect and an appreciation, if partial and ambivalent, of the possibilities for constructing a new sense of relationship with one's environment. Such sentiments suggest an understanding of the commons as the action of commoning, a relationship to the possibility that exists within one's environment whereby one allows one's sense of possibility to flow not from particular interests or personal desire but instead from the nascent possibilities in one's surroundings. Perhaps ironically, they recommend separation from and proximity to others to cultivate such an attitude, which produces common openness, receptivity, and willingness to be undone, as opposed to common ideas, interests, identity, or even property.

It seems that Berlant presents their ambivalent understanding of commoning in order to fully acknowledge the difficulties created for the successful achievement of any Left project resulting from destruction wrought by capitalism. The coming undone that she envisions as the core of commoning is the coming undone that must occur when all possibilities seem inadequate to repair the increasingly vast wasteland, both material and cultural, created by capital. All of the provisional possibilities she sees as a product of her "positive version of dispossession" are tinged with the somber realization of the dire situation in which the world currently exists. They claim that "the better power of the commons is to point to a way to view what's broken in sociality, the difficulty of convening a world conjointly, although it is inconvenient and hard, and to offer incitements to imagining a livable provisional life." They go on to explain that her interpretation aims "to extend the commons concept's pedagogy of learning to live with messed up yet shared and ongoing infrastructures of experience" (Berlant 2016, 395). They specifically claim that the unlearning indicative of commoning "acknowledges a broken world and the survival ethics of a transformational infrastructure. This involves using the spaces of alterity with ambivalence" (399). Such a pedagogy, for them, suggests the possession of the same sense of provisionality as Reid and Taylor's understanding of commoning as "kiltering." When she states that "what remains of our pedagogy of unlearning is to build affective infrastructures that admit the work of desire as the work of an aspiration ambivalence . . . [which] holds out the prospect of a world worth attaching to that's something other than an old hope's bitter echo" (414) they embrace the provisionality and experimentation of kiltering. But even the provisional, kiltering, and participatory reason envisioned by Reid and Taylor entails not simply unlearning, but the formation of (perhaps temporary and provisional) communities and acts of resistance. Berlant is right to emphasize the affective promise of the commons—the act of working together in diverse groups that assemble around projects and not identities or values does "decenter" participants in a way that opens them to sensing new and vibrant affects, propelling them forward by drawing upon energies and resonances that come from their environment and not from their preexisting selves. But claiming that such "decentering" results primarily in "unlearning" and not at least the possibility of the creation and maintenance of fragile common projects and "aspirational ambivalence" concerning the ability of groups to manage their broken landscapes does not fully encapsulate the promise of the other understandings of commoning that I have been advocating.[8] Although their understanding of commoning as a modest and partial reaction to contemporary political challenges to the Left seems to be the only realistic response, the other theorists I cite do not fall into the "political fantasy" of universalism or shared political substance. Acts of kiltering are not the same as grand creations of political sovereignty. And a commons characterized by diverse participants and constantly in need of repair and maintenance need not devolve into false hope, and, thus, the recreation of individuation and forms of desire that ultimately end up supporting the formation of capitalist subjects.

This humility, apparent when one faces the challenges of a broken world without resorting to false, and ultimately self-defeating, visions of political universality but instead characterizes commoning as a process of participatory reason, displays many similarities to my previous characterizations of salvage. Thinking of the commons as an act of salvage might help to sway skeptics such as Berlant and, therefore, I would argue that these examples of "experimenting with experience" in laboratories of insurrectionary imagination, and, more generally, my equation of salvage spaces with workshops, do in fact represent manifestations of the "provisional life" Berlant equates with the commons. Understanding the process of building common relationships and maintaining common land and objects as a unique type of participatory, or even communicative reason,[9] helps to shed light on the indeterminate nature of the kiltering process, just as the nature of salvage becoming leads to autonomous development of land and community. Furthermore, as Reid and Taylor suggest, the participatory reason productive of commoning involves dialog with both human and material actors. Finally, their understanding of body-place-commons, when interpreted as salvage, stresses that the process of kiltering relationships between these three elements might use elements taken from what one finds in the immediate environment to repair rips in the fabric of the commons. In fact, searching for seemingly waste material, whether that material be physical or semiotic, constitutes a deep example of the "kiltering" necessary for the maintenance of body-place-commons. When dealing with a limited scope of material within a possible commons, one must "kilter." When the poor construct their commons, their knack, or *metis*, constitutes the packet of skills they must use to maintain the relationships between themselves and their environment that hold their community together.

Even if one remains skeptical that these theorists of the commons can play a salutary role in contemporary Left politics, one further perspective should at least partially persuade skeptics: mainly, the existence of textual evidence that Marx himself did not reject the commons as a useful political category. In letters responding to Russian communist

Vera Zasulich, Marx speculates that anticapitalist movements need not originate solely in factories populated by exploited workers, but also within communal settlements such as those present among peasants. In good historical-materialist fashion, he indicates in these letters that specific circumstances of economic development in particular times and places contain their own contradictions and political potentials. As summarized by Teador Shanin, Marx opined that "the fact that the Russian commune was relatively advanced in type, being based not on kinship but on locality and its 'dual nature represented by 'individual' as well as 'communal land' ownership, offered the possibility of two different roads to development" (Shanin 1983, 16). This communal aspect, based not on shared identity but instead on "locality" or the actual maintenance of common land, represents a sharply different attitude toward property and others than the individualism and privatism of capitalism. Moreover, the less-structured division between labor and local autonomy within the Russian communes (in the form of decisions made by an assembly of heads of households) mirrors many of the humanistic and developmental norms present in Marx's early work. Even the localism that seems to undermine the universality of Marx's vision of working-class politics does not constitute an insurmountable obstacle to affective organization. Marx notes that, while in prerevolutionary Russia individual communes were organized into governmental units, or *volosts*, he recommends instead the establishment of "'*une assemblée de paysans*' which is chosen by the communes themselves, and capable of serving as an economic and administrative institution for the protection of the interests of those communes" (ibid., 66). Thus, Marx clearly opens the door to the commons acting as the social foundation on which a revolutionary political movement might form.[10] He suggests that that various places manifest various forms and levels of development of capitalism, and thus differing forms of resistance to these circumstances are called for. Furthermore, as Ross suggests of the Paris Commune, in circumstances characterized by "the collapse of the labor market" and the "growth of the informal economy," the economic practices of Russian peasants in their communities that encouraged mutual aid, horizonality, and the establishment of common forms of ownership can be seen as the correlates of many of the salvage communities I have been discussing.

Another argument can be found within Marx's work that uses the concept of the commons to further both the conceptualization of and revolutionary advocacy for communism. A frequently heard critique of

Marx centers around the fact that his theoretical work does not contain any strong advocacy for political democracy. Yet in his *The Civil War in France*, Marx clearly admires the self-government and administration instituted by the Communards. Yet, as I said before, the Commune, for Marx, was not a form of "prefigurative politics" in that he imagined such a form to act as a model for governance of communities or production after the revolution. Marx was clear in stating that any adequate manifestation of actual communism cannot simply take the form of a bourgeois state appropriated by workers and administered for the advancement of the working class. He states that "the working class cannot simply lay hold on the ready-made state-machinery and wield it for their own purpose. The political instrument of their enslavement cannot serve as the political instrument of their emancipation" (Shanin 1983, 83). Instead, he saw the Commune as an exercise in breaking free not simply from a particular manifestation of the state, but from bourgeois understandings of the state and politics itself. According to Shanin, Marx claimed, "What is needed is not simply political emancipation but emancipation from politics, understood as a particularized set of activities, occasions and institutions. This is why Marx hails the Commune as a "revolution against the state itself" (86). Ross makes a similar point when she refers to the Commune as a "working laboratory of political invention" (Ross 2016, 11), emphasizing the fact that the breakdown of the division of labor embraced by the Communards led to new understandings of what the political could be.[11] The widespread participation of regular Parisians in the governance the Commune, and its "universal object of participation" not simply concerning the government but all social and economic activities within Paris, constituted a necessary experience to break away from understanding politics as something politicians do in the government, and instead to view society itself as a commonly held and administered field. This universal commons, and not simply overthrowing the state or occupying a factory, to Marx constitutes the social experience necessary that opens the door to determining what form communism might actually take. Thus, a conception of the commons that I have been advancing here can be seen, at various points, within Marx himself. While I remain agnostic about whether such writings represent the "true" Marx, it is clear from the preceding that his writings are much more sensitive to particular social and historical contexts than many assume. Even in the absence of what most would call the "working class," or even capitalist relations of production, political potentialities that can lay the ground toward communism do exist. Of course, these writings should not be taken to conclude that Marx somehow abandoned the working class as an important, if not the most important, revolutionary agent. Instead, it shows that he was open to a diverse, contextual understanding of revolutionary politics that included other formations besides the industrial working class.

The definitions of the commons that I have been emphasizing, comprising internal diversity, plasticity, the need for "kiltering," and participation, create a particularly useful guide to understanding the commons as springing from salvage. Although Tsing feels that the lack of formal structure, as well as the plasticity and instability, of the salvage commons, makes it a fragile and thus untrustworthy base for radical political organization, according to Reid and Taylor (and, as we shall see to a greater extent soon, Hardt and Negri), it is these very characteristics that identify good candidates for establishing the commons. They accept the constantly shifting, internally diverse, and contingent nature of the commons as comprising the very factors that encourage the "revolutionary becoming" they see as undermining capitalist life. For Reid and Taylor, the fact that these assemblages do not constitute "exclusive enclaves" renders them amenable to expansion and rescaling and thus might, potentially, lead individuals who see themselves as isolated to embrace a wider acceptance of their own intertwining in the body-place-commons. And while Tsing laments the fact that "every collaboration makes room for some and leaves out others," others read this as allowing for the local, particular, and experimental "participatory reason" by which commoners manage their common property. Berlant is also correct to envision the project of commoning as ambivalent, although she does go too far in this regard. Furthermore, her insight that commoning constitutes a form of "unlearning" particularly appropriate to dealing with the challenges of a broken world provides a provocative and direct link between commoning and salvage. Yet her insistence that commoning can only result in an "aspirational ambivalence" that results in opening participants to provisional affective possibilities stands in contrast to the "insurrectionary imagination" and "participatory reason" envisioned as the product of other forms of commoning I have described. Although my specific translation of the commons into a political grouping will not occur until I analyze Hardt and Negri's understanding of the multitude, at this point I want to stress that the general characteristics of the commons that Tsing and others see as antipolitical are used by some to base their political understandings of the commons.

Finally, I hope it is clear at this point that my presentation of the commons not only encompasses many affinities with my interpretation of political salvage, but also that likening salvage to understandings of the political commons might lead to new understandings of how the commons can act as a generator of anticapitalist becoming. Reid and Taylor's understanding of the commons as relationships of body-place-commons stresses the materiality and embodiment of the commons. Even though a commons is built around a community and relationships, the fact that all individuals have bodies in places grounds the process of commoning. The qualitative affect of the body-place-commons can be sensed, and thus repairing this vibrant matrix requires that attention be paid to the "shimmering" vibrant affects that surround all of its relationships. The constant process of "kiltering" such relationships uses many of the same skills as salvage, in that one must constantly modify one's surroundings and oneself, using the tools and materials that are at hand, to maintain the fragile balance of the commons. When the poor form the body-place-commons, the likelihood of "kiltering" taking the form of trying to fit found items (and found people) into contexts which they were not "designed" to fit, this dynamic becomes all the more pronounced. That salvage leads not simply to a "latent commons" but instead can be linked to more robust understandings such as Hardt and Negri's and Reid and Taylor's constitutes one of the most powerful arguments that the scavenging and repairing undertaken by the poor can be used to construct a robust political theory.

Commons Biopolitics

Having discussed recent theorizations of the commons, I want to focus on what is perhaps the best-known political theory relying on the concept of the commons, that of Hardt and Negri. I do this to both link the concept of salvage to a vibrant, contemporary political theory that articulates a vision of an anticapitalist collective political agent and to show how salvage challenges this theory. Although ever since their groundbreaking *Empire* they have invoked themes similar to those discussed above, in their works *Commonwealth* and *Assembly* they explicitly argue that the commons constitutes the social formation from which their preferred revolutionary political agent, the multitude, originates. Similar to classical Marxism, they argue that radical political agents develop in the context of new forms of production that produce contradictions within themselves. The new macroeconomic force upon which they focus they name "immaterial production." What they mean by this is that commodities come to be increasingly immaterial as information technology allows companies to sell more services that provide affects and relationships, as opposed to material things. The cultural values, ideas, and desires toward which companies shift their attention cannot be designed by engineers or delivered in kits with instructions—they are the product of common, creative interaction between groups of people. Authentic meanings cannot be constructed by marketing executives, but instead are the product of the autonomous interaction of people. For example, the popular memes and compelling personal content monetized by Facebook cannot be mass produced and instead are created through the efforts, and most importantly the symbols and affects, of the users themselves. As the use of communications technologies increases, both in terms of production and consumption, the individual codes, values, and affects produced through individual interactions become fundamental to capitalist accumulation.

Hardt and Negri call this increasing reliance upon technologies that propagate communication and affect biopolitical production. The prefix *bio* stresses that through this process of production the bodies of interacting people, their language, their emotions, and their ideas become the factories that produce value. Such interactions cannot be forced and are facilitated by sharing and mutually modifying ideas. They also cannot be easily contained through property classifications such as patenting that attempt to exclude others from use. Thus, biopolitical production occurs within and produces the commons. Hardt and Negri state:

> Bioplitical production takes place and can only take place on the terrain of the common. Ideas, images and codes are produced not by a lone genius or even by a master with supporting apprentices[12] but by a wide network of cooperating producers. Labor tends to be increasingly autonomous from capitalist command and thus capital's mechanisms of expropriation and control become fetters that obstruct productivity. Biopolitical production is an orchestra keeping the beat without a conductor, and it would fall silent if anyone were to step onto the podium. (Hardt and Negri 2009, 173)

This mode of production is aided by the proliferation of new types of subjectivity that emerge from increasingly neoliberal policies—pressures to constantly "market" oneself, build one's "brand," and mold oneself to the dictates of the global economy result in human bodies and consciousness taking on the attributes of contemporary capitalism itself: its liquidity, communicative relationality, and its performative nature. Thus, the biopolitical commons plays the role that the factory did in classical Marxism, due to the fact that it constitutes the site of production and value extraction in contemporary capitalism.

It is important to emphasize that Hardt and Negri do not believe that the communicative and symbolic nature of biopolitical production somehow replaces material production—instead, it transforms it while creating whole new categories of material and immaterial commodities. They argue that the rise of biopolitical production "means, of course not that the production of material goods, such as automobiles and steel, is disappearing or even declining in quantity but rather than their value is increasingly dependent on and subordinated to immaterial factors of goods" (132).[13] Thus, the value of a car is not simply that it can transport a person from point A to B, but that it expresses that person's personality and represents to the world the ideas and values that the consumer wants to project to others.[14] Furthermore, as more and more everyday items, such as cars and dishwashers, collect data on users, both the software that collects this data and its analysis are constructed using software created through processes of biopolitical production.[15] Thus, biopolitical production, while not the exclusive form of modern capitalism, comes to take on a larger and larger role in more and more areas of industry.

The assertion that the commons acts as the site of biopolitical production raises serious questions concerning the exact "means" that manufacture the commodities. Even when capitalists provide offices for creative workers, the languages, codes values, and ideas that they use as their tools come about through the common fund of culture that no one person owns or controls. This leads Hardt and Negri to explain that

> rather than providing cooperation, we could even say that capital expropriates cooperation as a central element of exploiting biopolitical labor-power. This expropriation takes place not so much from the individual worker (because cooperation already implies a collectivity) but more clearly from the field

of social labor, operating on the level of information flows, communication networks, social codes linguistic innovation, and practices of affects. (140)

They claim that biopolitical expropriation takes the form of rent,[16] with the capitalist expropriating value from processes external to its own operation. This rentier's economy produced through expropriation of the commons explains the prevalence of finance, the sector of the economy that engages in "capturing and expropriating the value created at a level far abstracted from the labor process" (Hardt and Negri 2009, 142). Such privatization and financialization of the commons—as water resources, cultural artifacts, and even the future of college students through financing their higher education in return for a percentage of their future earnings—represents a new enclosure movement, where instead of common land being forcefully transformed into a commodity, now culture itself comes to be surrounded by the fences of finance.

Simply because biopolitical production involves common forms of labor it does not mean that capitalists do not try to discipline workers and extract more value, even if those methods differ from traditional forms of capitalist control. And despite the innovative nature of these forms of control, Hardt and Negri argue, these efforts lead to their own internal tensions and contractions. For example, they suggest that although biopolitical production thrives on the cooperative creation of value and culture, capitalists still attempt to monitor and intensify such labor. But the monitoring of labor and forcing of relationships undermines the sincere and unforced communication that must occur to form and develop common ideas and values, and the enclosure of culture by commerce robs workers of many of the potential "tools" they might use to make more value. Furthermore, bioplotical production encourages temporary work and constant mobility of labor, which both increases the creative potentialities of such workers through the enabling of new encounters and creative interactions and also further immiserates workers through increasing competition and reducing stability. These contradictory characteristics of biopolitical labor point toward crisis tendencies within the economy.[17] When viewed in this light biopolitical production creates contradictions that spawn the seeds of its own resistance.

They also claim that the communicative networks upon which biopolitical production depends thrive in the metropolis, yet the city

234 / The Political Theory of Salvage

itself also constitutes a space rife with contradictions that can undermine such production. They state, "The metropolis is site of biopolitical production . . . languages, images, knowledges, affects, codes, habits" (Hardt and Negri 2009, 250). This is because modern cities represent to them a concentration of workers, cultures, and ideas that spur the common creativity and collaboration that lies at the core of biopolitical production. It is not simply the presence of such urban diversity that convinces Hardt and Negri, but its constant, flowing, undulation. They state, "The metropolis . . . is a place of unpredictable encounters among singularities, with not only those you do not know but also those who come from elsewhere, with different cultures, languages, knowledge, mentalities" (252). Hardt and Negri view the affective experience produced by the city as an important tool for biopolitical production. Capitalists look at the intense and shifting affective landscape of urban life as a field to be cultivated and thus monetized. Furthermore, such efforts at the commodification of urban affects can lead to the confluence of forces within a particular space that lead to simultaneous manifestations of resistance, festive becoming, and abstract control, which produces political action within that space. They see that both the affects produced through the micro encounters of biopolitical production and the macro trends that result from the macrospatial dynamics of the capitalist city can lead to the affects upon which the development of a more active and coherent multitude depends. Hardt and Negri's emphasis upon the unique affective environment of the city highlights the fact that the commons-created styles, cultures, and modes of life, all embodying certain rhythms of the city, represent both future commodities and tools for resistance to capital.

Hardt and Negri make a further point that raises particularly provocative questions concerning the linkage of biopolitical production to a political theory of salvage. In their discussion of how biopolitical production creates value within the commons that capitalists later extract for profit, they mention salvage as one possible manifestation of this process. They state that

> the many forms of cooperative social production constitute another face of extraction, a face that helps compose together many of the others. Anna Tsing, for example, following the trails of wild mushroom pickers in Oregon to the sale in Japan, recognized the ability of capital to capture value that

is produced autonomously. "this is what I call 'salvage' that is, taking advantage of value produced without capitalist control." "Salvage" is indeed an excellent description of how capital captures and extracts value produced in the relationships of social production and social life. (Hardt and Negri 2017, 169)

Hardt and Negri's linkage of Tsing's understanding of salvage to biopolitical production, while representing an endorsement of Tsing's views, also represents a challenge, or at least a modification, to her understanding of the latent commons. If the salvage commons represents a powerful iteration of biopolitical production, then, at least in Hardt and Negri's view, the potentiality within such forms of production to produce the commons seems stronger than the description of the latent commons provided by Tsing. Of course, the formation of the salvage commons is never guaranteed—no one can force people to join together and salvage, but if there are macropolitical economic forces encouraging such activity, then one can see another powerful route that leads to its formation.

Describing salvage as a site of biopolitical production also implies that it is subject to the contradictions cited by Hardt and Negri. Capital does attempt to expropriate salvage, not simply through purchasing what is salvaged such as the plastic scavengers of the Rio landfill, but also through purchasing the autonomous sites of salvage production such as squats and favelas. Furthermore, because biopolitical production within the commons encourages precarious and itinerant work, salvage communities that depend upon familiarity with their landscapes can simply not undertake salvage labors with the same effectiveness without managing their own time, and thus the itinerancy demanded by capital, the booms and busts, not only undermines the ability to salvage, but can result in aggressive resistance to control—think of the valuation of "freedom" and working for oneself that Tsing reports as articulated by so many salvagers of the matsutake.[18] Finally, the biopolitical impetus to nomadism flies in the face of the deep rootedness of many salvage communities. Remember Lefebvre's assertion that salvage communities such as favelas constitute particularly intensified manifestations of habitation. These constructed commons come about through the autonomous labors of their residents, and thus when capitalists attempt to either appropriate the land upon which these communities reside, or attempt to regulate these communities, denying them the right to autonomously manage what they have created or charging them for resources that they have salvaged themselves, they face particularly strong resistance. Those engaged in salvage can even unwittingly add value to spaces through their improvements and innovations, as can be seen when squats and poor neighborhoods become the object of gentrification—the cultural cachet of salvaged spaces becomes desirable and the urban trends they originate become the object of corporate exploitation. All of these tensions can lead to a desire for autonomy for the culture, time, and place of political salvage communities—as they embrace and defend the commons that they helped create. In their view, the squats, informal communities, and occupations that I have defined as examples of political salvage all express the potential for a type of unalienated, common, biopolitical production that results in cultural, temporal, and spatial commons that represent the normative core and political potential of salvage.

Salvaging the Multitude

Hardt and Negri go beyond simply stating that biopolitical production, of which salvage is an example, constitutes a contradictory social and economic phenomenon that both depends on and destroys the commons. They also claim that a new political agent has, slowly and provisionally, come into existence, prompted by these contradictions, that they call the multitude. Just as their analysis of biopolitical power finds its methodology in Marx, the political agent they see as emerging from the contradictions they identify to challenge capitalism exhibits many characteristics of the labor process from which it springs. If Marx identifies the proletariat as springing from the capitalist workplace and finding its consciousness of a class "in itself" due to its concentration within large factories, the multitude also exhibits many characteristics of the commons from which it springs. Yet because the commons represents a much more heterogeneous social formation than the proletariat, organized around the creation and maintenance of a wide range of shared social and physical objects, it might seem difficult to imagine the possibility of identifying any concrete political formation finding its genesis in such a situation. Hardt and Negri begin to lend specificity to their understanding by stating that the multitude can be defined as the body of the poor who labor in biopolitical production. Their understanding of the concept of "the poor" remains highly idiosyncratic. They claim:

> The poverty of the multitude, then, seen from this perspective does not refer to its misery or deprivation or even its lack, but instead names a production of social subjectivity that results in a radically plural and open body politic, opposed to both the individualism and the exclusive, unified social body of property. The poor in other words refers not to those who have nothing but to the wide multiplicity of all those who are inserted into the mechanism of social production regardless of social order or property. (Hardt and Negri 2009, 40–41)[19]

Notice that this definition is much broader than the classic Marxist understanding and shares much with those who advocate conceptualizing Left politics through what they call the plebeian political tradition[20] that envisions radical political movements as inclusive of more than proletarians. It is the poor who are most subject to the contradictions of biopolitical production and thus, like Marx, this political formation finds it roots firmly within the contradictions of the concrete relations of production of a particular society.

Although the numbers of those who operate on the periphery of capitalist labor have varied across history, Hardt and Negri claim that such comparisons are particularly relevant today because

> in different ways, in various contexts around the world, as modes of life and work characterized by mobility, flexibility and precarity are ever more severely imposed by capitalist regimes of production, wage laborers and the poor are no longer subjected to qualitative different conditions but are both absorbed equally into the multitude of producers. The poor whether they receive wages or not are located no longer only at the historical origin or the geographical borders of capitalist production but increasingly at its heart. (Hardt and Negri 2009, 55)

The fact that labor is contingent and mobile does not negate the centrality of exploitation in capitalism, but, as we saw earlier, Hardt and Negri emphasize that within the regime of biopolitical labor exploitation is often transformed into expropriation. Expropriated value need not be produced under the watchful eye of Marx's Mr. Moneybags described in Volume One of *Capital*, constantly trying to squeeze absolute and relative surplus value out of workers protected by the "veil" of the factory walls. Expropriation, in Hardt and Negri's account, happens after the product is produced, or need not involve the process of production at all. In such production, workers sometimes work at home, sometimes work in a factory, and even sometimes work in public. They work to produce ideas, data, and norms when they don't even realize they are working, and sometimes they don't work at all. This is not to say that the multiplicity of the poor are not exploited in the way traditional Marxists describe, it is simply that they are also excluded from consistent participation in this process, and thus exclusion is layered onto their exploitation. Even those rich in resources might be poor in terms of their time and space—with itinerancy and nomadism forcing them into increasing possibilities for precarity, and the common, cultural, and affective resources they create, even when they are not formally working, stripped from them.

With such a weak thread of commonality between its individual members, how does the multitude of the poor come into existence? For Hardt and Negri, this primarily occurs not through conscious, hierarchical effort by a vanguard party but through self-organization. They claim that "the multitude is the result of a process of political constitution, although whereas the people is formed as a unity by a hegemonic power standing above the plural social field, the multitude is formed through articulation on the plane of immanence without hegemony" (Hardt and Negri 2009, 169). The fact that such self-organization cannot occur with the efficiency or thoroughness of traditional organizing strategy does not trouble Hardt and Negri. They laud such seeming haphazardness as protective of the horizontality, fluidity, and creativity of the multitude, stating, "The multitude is a form of political organization that on the one hand emphasizes the multiplicity of social singularities in struggle, and on the other seeks to coordinate their common actions and maintain their equality in horizontal organizational structures" (110).[21] While Hardt and Negri describe the general character of the multitude in terms of both diversity and coherence, the particular form the multitude takes within a particular struggle constantly changes as individuals undergo processes of both organization and becoming in a mutual reinforcing rhythm. They claim that "the multitude is composed through the encounters of singularities within the common . . . the process of articulation accomplished in insurrectional intersections does not simply couple identities like links in a chain but transforms singularities in a process of liberation that establishes the common among them" (350). This process of organization, which can be seen as a form of common becoming, occurs on both the individual and collective level—groups both coalesce and disintegrate, alternating between times of rest and activity. Furthermore, individuals go through periods of confusion, internal debate, and rest that lead to moments of activity and self-integration. Thus, they see the multitude as the political correlate of the commons—both diffuse yet cooperating, a political formation that both grows from the commons and represents the rhythmic development and transformation of the multitude through common struggle.

While they offer general characteristics of what they see as the form of the multitude, it is more important for my argument to ana-lyze how they see the multitude's self-organization as rooted in specific forms of everyday existence. One can see this emphasis on the everyday when they argue that "if one can realistically establish the capacities for self-organization and cooperation in people's daily lives, in their work, or more generally in social production, then the political capacity of the multitudes ceases to be a question" (Hardt and Negri 2009, 176). The nascent seeds of such capacities lie within biopolitical production itself—and as the contradictions within this form of production mount, some of those subject to its disciplines attempt to regain what they are robbed of—the means of their production, which in this case does not lie within a factory, but within their own autonomous cooperative activity. As biopolitical workers are increasingly called upon to creatively produce ideas and affects, they come into contact with more and more individuals engaged in similar tasks. As they communicate and collabo-rate, they make more and more connections and increase the potential scope of the multitude itself. And as they increasingly realize that they all are subject to the same forces of capitalist biopolitical expropriation, the chances increase of their forming the collective identity based on resistance to these economic forces.

The everyday exercise of such biopolitical reason, Hardt and Negri stress, does not exclusively involve cognitive and cultural activities under-taken by the "creative class" and thus their reliance on this concept does not circumscribe the possible scope of the membership of the multitude. They instead stress that biopolitical reason is not characterized by the production of particular types of products, but by a particular bundle of skills and propensities. Hardt and Negri make this clear through their supposition that a Deweyan understanding of habit plays an important role in explaining how the exercise of biopolitical reason can play a role in the formation of the multitude. Although they later replace the concept of habit with that of *dispositif*, the former concept illuminates characteristics of biopolitical reason and its relationship to the constitution of the multitude, both underplayed through viewing such practices solely through this Foucauldian lens, and more closely ties Hardt and Negri's conception to my previous argument. When they begin their discussion of habit they state, "We can already recognize a concept of the multitude emerging from this pragmatic notion of habit" (Hardt and Negri 2004, 198). They invoke this concept because it emphasizes the interaction of the individual and the social in the process of individual development, a process they claim is both "produced and productive, created and creative—an ontology of social practice in common" (ibid.). Thus, in the context of biopolitical reason, habit describes the personal characteristics necessary for engaging in this process—one does not simply adopt this practice, but one slowly develops the habits necessary for this process, through both learning and creation. While Hardt and Negri praise Dewey for his position that habit should be regarded as both passive and active, individual and social, they ultimately claim that it should be eclipsed by the concept of performance in describing the creative becoming of the multitude. They claim that understanding biopolitical reason in terms of habit limits this procedure to describing the "reproducing or reform the modern social bodies" (Hardt and Negri 2004, 200). This brief criticism seems to highlight a belief that the conception of habit can only describe the formation of types of relationships between individuals, and not the aspects of the deep desires of individualism themselves. They contrast the formation of habit to Queer politics, which they laud as subversive of identity in general, even though they acknowledge the flexibility of habit in Dewey's understanding. This criticism seems strange in light of the fact that, as I suggested earlier in chapter 3, Dewey grounds his understanding of habit within the body, and thus it is not merely an expression of the "modern social body." This understanding of habit lies at the core of Dewey's account of thinking, which, for him, results in the type of transformation and becoming that undermines any fixed identity, the very characteristic Hardt and Negri claim Queer politics possesses in opposition to the pragmatist notion of habit. This understanding of the importance of habit in the formation of the multitude, especially "queer" habits of transformation and becoming, demonstrates that, for Hardt and Negri, the production of the multitude depends not on the undertaking of any particular task but instead the propagation of the unique habits and *dispositifs* of biopolitical reason.

When thinking of the multitude as not only a self-organizing political formation, but also one that is grounded not in shared identity but shared habits, another possible linkage to my discussion of salvage becomes clearer. Furthermore, I want to stress that this linkage is not simply one of similarity—in that both Hardt and Negri's understanding of the multitude and my understanding of salvage stress that both such practices (if the formation of the multitude is understood as a practice) are more likely to effectively occur if undertaken by those who possess certain habits. Thinking of the formation of the multitude as a "craft of the poor" allows me speculate on how habits of becoming encouraged by salvage might make it more likely that the multitude could come into existence. The habits of biopolitical reason, while definitely nascent within biopolitical production, constitute weak reeds upon which to build the radical commons that lies at the core of the multitude, just as commons's "kiltered" fragility will end in failure more often than not. Thus, if practitioners choose to engage in the conscious cultivation and practice of these habits by constructing choreographed salvage spaces that are integrated with their political activities, then the commons they attempt to build will be stronger and more likely to generate anticapitalist consciousness. Furthermore, the habits they cultivate in these spaces might flow into other environments where the multitude might grow, and thus the plastic, radical becoming that I say is possible through participation in radical salvage workshops might more likely grow into a widelyspread political ethic. It is important to stress that in emphasizing the possibility for consciously integrating salvage practices within the political program of the multitude, I am merely suggesting the accentuation of trends and phenomena that are already present within contemporary political economy. Hardt and Negri's account of biopolitical production is not a normative stance but instead an empirical description of a powerful developmental trend in contemporary capitalism. Therefore, hypothesizing that the conscious embrace of salvage practices might further strengthen and propagate the multitude constitutes merely identifying further conditions of possibility for this political phenomenon.

Tactics of the Salvage Multitude

Identifying salvage as an important generator of the habits of the multitude does not illuminate the political consequences of viewing political salvage as a manifestation of Hardt and Negri's political theory. To fully engage in this task, one must begin by analyzing the actual political strategies and activities Hardt and Negri see the multitude undertaking. David Graeber provides a detailed and compelling description of his understanding of how the multitude relates to the actualities of contemporary activism. He emphasizes that the multitude does not lack organization and structure, even though it cannot be likened to a traditional party or political organization, and should not be thought of as a chaotic mob. He suggests instead

> that if one wishes to understand the difference between the old-fashioned leftist concept of "the masses," and the newer notion of "multitude," one might best consider the difference between the unorganized crowd—a mass of undifferentiated individuals, subject to all the rumors, panics, and passion so endlessly documented by crowd psychologists—and the self-organized crowd conducting a mass action. The latter is at once made up of endless cell-like affinity groups, but crosscut by networks of comms units, medics, performers, legal observers, support groups and media liaisons, ranged by the degree of risk they are willing to endure and level of training or preparation. These groups are usually themselves organized into "slices" and "clusters" and at the same time with each cell highlighting only one particular aspect of multiple political identities as a basis for affinity for this particular action: queer activists from Cleveland, autonomous Marxists, pagans, Wobblies, punk rockers from LA and animal rights activists from New Jersey. There are very few ways in which the "mass" and the "multitude" are the same. (Graeber 2009, 372)

The equation of the multitude with "cell-like affinity groups" in the above description should not surprise anyone familiar with Hardt and Negri's account of the multitude. What remains most notable concerning the above description are the multiple, crosscutting, developing, and disintegrating relationships between the different activists. While the members of the "cell" or "affinity group" often share unity of identity, each action of the multitude, as Graeber describes it, also exhibits multiple encounters between different affinity groups, coalescing around "slices" or "clusters" who have united for a particular action. Furthermore, crosscutting networks of activists from multiple cells who have chosen to undertake specific tasks, such as security, communication, defense, disrupt the unity of these cells and clusters by facilitating encounters among people of different cells engaging in common action. Such disruptions, because they all occur in the context of a common action, according to Graeber, can lead to mutual anticapitalist becoming, difficult as it is, as each encounter challenges individuals by not simply exposing them to difference, but by challenging them to work together in their activism with people who embody different ideals, practices, and backgrounds. This demonstrates how the multitude exhibits both unity and difference—local cells temporarily coalesce into larger assemblages during political action. But the insight taken from my discussion of political salvage is that habits cultivated through the choreography of radical workshops can help to further "bind" the members of the multitude and encourage their construction of activist spaces and attempts to further radical political change. Such habits help to sustain the rhythmic, sometimes difficult process of common becoming that lies at the core of multitude and assists the "nodes" "slices" and "clusters" that constitute the network in both developing and persisting.

I want to discuss another aspect of the above description: its portrayal of the spatial field of the multitude. If depicted as a topographical map, Graeber's description would not simply constitute a number of islands or cells, united with each other into larger masses and crosscut by networks of activists dedicated to specified tasks. Due to the constant occurrence of unplanned encounters in reaction to political circumstances and the becoming that they prompt, a more accurate rendering would be that of the surface of a river as it flows downstream—each turn of its banks, fallen tree trunk, and rainstorm causing new flows and eddies, and disruptive undercurrents. Thus, the web of the relations is constantly re-spun and adjusted in light of the rhythmic tensions, waves, and movements produced during its development. Because of this constant becoming, one might say there was an aesthetics of the multitude, and as it, possibly, develops into a more coherent, if temporary, unity, a rhythm of encounter and retreat—as individuals come to participate in challenging encounters with others, even when engaged in common action, they become tired and drained, and thus need to retreat within their own affinity group. I emphasize this to note the existence of both weak structures and anticapitalist becoming within such a social formation. In fact, both structure and becoming should be seen as mutually reinforcing. Acknowledging the aesthetics of the experience of politics within the multitude adds not only more depth to describing the experience of working within such groups, but highlights structural dynamics that are not adequately understood by its advocates.

Yet what about those who claim that because structures such as the multitude lack any formal and hierarchical organization they are doomed to break apart because of the internal tensions inherent in movements characterized by the "tyranny of structurelessness"? Can a political formation exist for longer than an instant that displays the horizontalism, autonomy, and fluidity of individual manifestations of the multitude? Many contemporary authors have argued so, claiming that only through strong, hierarchical organizations such as parties might any revolutionary project be accomplished. For example, Jodi Dean remains critical of "amorphous" political formations such as Occupy Wall Street, which Hardt and Negri, especially in their *Declaration*, identify as an exemplary manifestation of the politics of the multitude. Curiously, though, when Dean articulates her understanding of the function of a revolutionary party, it becomes clear that that there is much more room for dialog between the two conceptions than one might initially think. Dean's vision of a revolutionary party strays far from the "traditional" understanding of a vanguard party. She focuses not on the necessity for intellectuals to impose structure or knowledge on the formless working class, but instead upon "affects the party generates and unconscious processes it mobilizes." She goes on to state that the proper role of the contemporary party should not be seen as to "represent the interests of the working class . . . rather the function of the party is to hold open a gap in our setting so as to enable a collective desire for collectivity" (Dean 2016, 5). This invocation of the results of participation in the party as resulting in desires and affects should clearly invoke not only Hardt and Negri's focus on the *dispositifs* of biopolitical reason upon which the multitude is formed, but also my previous discussion of the importance of affect to the practice of political salvage. Although Dean takes issue with the lack of leadership in political forms such as the multitude, she does not dismiss the importance of such eruptions of dissent. She emphasizes, "The question that emerges from these experience is how they might endure and extend how the momentary discharge of equality that crowds unleash might become the basis for a new process of political composition" (25). Therefore, her problem with multitude-like political formations does not lie in their lack of specific policies and the diversity of tactics, but instead the self-organization of such forms. Without some type of hierarchical leadership, she fears, Occupy-type actions will either fall apart through dissipation of energy or internal dissension, or not be able to withstand attacks from more organized forces.

While Dean's understanding of the party might have similar goals to that of the multitude, it remains clear that she envisions party leaders and organizers as actively recruiting members of the party and encouraging certain attitudes and teaching certain skills to members once they have joined. In contrast, Hardt and Negri do not envision a party and its staff acting as the vehicle of organizing, but the metropolis itself. They state that "the politics of the metropolis is the organization of encounters. Its task it to promote joyful encounters, make them repeat and minimize infelicitous encounters" (Hardt and Negri 2009, 256). They go on to specify that such an organization (and presumably the individuals who undertake this task, perhaps organizers) needs to display an openness to alterity, the ability to decide when to withdraw from destructive relationships, and knowledge of how to transform confrontational encounters into joyful ones. For them, the city represents the political space that Dean feels must be occupied by the party, and the organization of encounters constitutes the correlate for the functions the party organizer would undertake. As to whether there could, or should, be "organizers" of the multitude, Hardt and Negri do not say. On the one hand, the city itself presents a plethora of potentially joyful encounters that might lead to plural becoming. It seems that they imply such encounters simply need to be tweaked or rejected, and such skills come to be developed in the exercise of biopolitical reason during particular struggles.

Such a reliance on the city itself as a generator of the multitude could be interpreted as falling prey to the same optimism concerning the politically generative powers of the city as that displayed by Lefebvre, which I discussed in chapter 4. While Hardt and Negri do claim that "joyful encounters" that lead to the formation of the multitude need to be promoted, they do not give any thorough account of the details of such a "politics of the metropolis." The concepts that I have been articulating throughout this work, of salvage as a craft, radical workshops, the choreography of salvage spaces, can act as powerful manifestations of such a politics. Such a politics might consist in identifying sites of salvage that are under threat of capitalist capture through appropriation or continued exploitation and giving them some of the tools that I have identified as the formalization of techniques and phenomena in which they already engage. Thus, if a political theory of salvage were integrated with the politics of the multitude, then Hardt and Negri's account might more forcefully rebut the critics of autonomous politics, such as Dean.

One final objection that Dean voices concerning horizontal political formations such as the multitude concerns what she sees as their necessarily local character. To counter what she sees as this inward-looking tendency within recent horizontal political revolts, she claims that the party acts as "an affective infrastructure that enlarges the world." And when she uses the word *affective* in the previous sentence, she specifically refers to her understanding of the role of radical parties not as "ideology, program, leadership or organizational structure" but instead "in terms of the dynamics of feeling [it] mobilizes" (Dean 2016, 210). While this assertion by Dean links her understanding of the functions of a party to my earlier discussion of the affects mobilized by political salvage, it does raise the issue of how such localized manifestations as Hardt and Negri's political agent can transcend their particularized struggles. Hardt and Negri address this point by observing that horizontalist struggles that claim to presage larger mobilization of the multitude have tended to "find support and inspiration in federalist models. Small groups and communities find ways to connect with one another and to create common projects not by renouncing but by expressing their differences. Federalism is thus a motor of composition" (Hardt and Negri 2012, 50). By describing the federated nature of the relationships of these groups as "a motor of composition" they emphasize that the local-federated relationships between groups are not simply based upon mutual interests. They claim that local groups, when participating in the federated multitude, undergo transformative encounters with each other, just as individuals experience in their smaller-scale rebellions. Thus, it is not simply interests that are reconciled in these federations, but new interests come to be constituted—not permanently or completely, but within the context of the larger encounter.

With the understanding that manifestations of political salvage can act as a site of the constitution of the multitude, one can easily imagine how such sites might act as nodes in the federated structure that Hardt and Negri imagine. Not only can they fuel the propagation of habits that contribute to individuals resisting capitalism in any of the various actions members of the multitude might take in many different geographical location, but they might easily coalesce around larger political actions and goals, if such consolidation were understood to be temporary and in reaction to serious threats or political opportunities. Hardt and Negri's suggestion that the city constitutes the "organization of encounters" can be thought of as a nod to the type of conscious choreography of radical salvage workshops that I outlined earlier, but simply saying that the city in and of itself will organize encounters echoes the overreliance upon urban space in and of itself to result in the encouragement of certain political attitudes. The weak structure embodied in choreographed radical salvage workshops provides a concrete, experiential mechanism for the encouragement of the habits that Hardt and Negri believe will be created simply by participation in biopolitical production. Thus, the choreography that will assist political salvage in capitalizing upon its political promise might also help other nodes of the multitude. While salvage itself constitutes an exemplary manifestation of the liquidity that is also an animating practice of the multitude, choreographing the affects that lead to becoming in other sites of the multitude could play an important role in both propagating and maintaining its existence.

Objectives of the Salvage Multitude

Having sketched out the possibilitity of imagining political salvage as a manifestation multitude—open to tactical leadership yet strategically developed through horizontal becoming, composed of both small affinity groups while crosscut by specialists, encouraging affects that lead to a "collective desire for collectivity" and a federated structure of not simply aggregation but mutual becoming—at this point, the question arises regarding what types of political actions the multitude undertakes and how this activity might relate to political salvage. Thus, now I want to demonstrate that the modes of political salvage I have discussed throughout the book—occupations, squats, and informal neighborhoods—have engaged in many of these tactics. Through this discussion the concrete implications of a political theory of salvage become much clearer. Furthermore, this discussion will, hopefully, illuminate many of the pitfalls and challenges that a political theory of salvage might face due to the qualities of contemporary capitalism. I do not claim that the tactics discussed here will, in and of themselves, lead to revolution and the transformation of capitalist society. Contemporary capitalism is too resilient and fungible to fall prey to a simple list of actions that groups practicing political salvage might take. Thus, acknowledging these challenges will not only help improve anticapitalist practice but also prepare us (we who advocate for a political theory of salvage) for the difficult road ahead—one of constantly "kiltering" our fragile salvaged political movements in a way that reacts to the shifting capitalist landscape around us.

As I have emphasized, Hardt and Negri believe that the capitalist metropolis acts as the primary environment in which biopolitical production can lead to resistance and thus the formation of the multitude. Because the metropolis is defined by fluidity, connection, and communication, one of the primary ways that revolt by the multitude occurs has been to block such flows. They relate how the Argentinian *Piqueteros* protesting unemployment, Bolivians in 2003 in El Alto battling against privatization of common resources such as water, and the Parisan *Banlieusands* revolting against discrimination and segregation all engaged in "blocking the mobility of the metropolis" by "blocking streets, obstructing traffic and bringing the metropolis to a halt" (Hardt and Negri 2009, 259). Due to the fact that biopolitical production does not occur in a specific location, but throughout the entirety of the metropolis itself, and the fact that the workers who undertake biopolitical production frequently do not hold full-time positions, it is the goal of the multitude to "strike" against the entire city. Occupations might impede the flow of people and commerce in the financial district of a city, while squats and *favelas* might block the gentrification of a neighborhood. And this one simple blockage can undermine the flow of people and capital throughout the entire metropolitan area, especially if it occurs in a strategically important area, as it did in El Alto, or in any of the recent occupations in New York, Athens, or Cairo. Even if such blockages cannot affect the commerce in an entire city, Hardt and Negri claim that these rebellions can possess implications beyond their immediate environment because of the fact that they not only exist in the metropolis but, by their very nature, protest "against" the current form of the metropolis and its "pathologies and corruptions." The outbreaks, thus, despite their seeming amorphousness and lack of objective, in fact aim to disrupt the space of biopolitical production and draw upon the new "proletariat" who undertake biopolitical production.[22]

Such blocking does not manifest itself simply in terms of impeding the mobility of capital, but also in terms of violent indignation, which some call riots but Hardt and Negri instead refer to as *jacqueries*—a term that dates to the fourteenth century—thus invoking the tradition of food riots, urban uprisings, and other spontaneous outbreaks of indignation. Although most interpret such actions in terms of violence, destruction, and singular demands, instead Hardt and Negri claim that "although in *jacqueries* organization arises as a set of singular demands, there is always a pressure to make common the action of the multitude, and this organizational initiative most often takes the form of construction and reproduction of informal networks" (Hardt and Negri 2009, 238). They also claim that rebellion increases the intensity of struggle and often extends it to incorporate other struggles. The manner in which such intensification and expansion often occurs, they claim, is not through conscious planning and organization, but the diffusion of the common culture and affects that develops through struggle. They observe that, often

> [t]he common antagonism and common wealth of the exploited and expropriated are translated into common conduct, habits and performativity. Any time you enter into a region where there is a strong revolt forming you are immediately struck by the common manners of dress, gestures and modes of relating and communicating. Jean Genet, for example, remarked that what characterized the Black Panthers was primary a *style*— not just the vocabulary, the Afros, and the clothes but also a way of walking, a manner of holding their bodies, a physical presence. (Hardt and Negri 2004, 212–13)

The revolt, in this case, led to new common networks, styles, and affects (note the reference to "a way of walking" and "manner of holding their bodies"). The revolt was not simply about destruction, but the creation of new revolutionary styles (cultural styles, styles of affect) that could be transferred to many particular struggles. In many ways, the contemporary Black Lives Matter revolts take on a similar form,[23] with bursts of outrage leading to the articulation of demands for more concrete political reform. These revolts mobilized not simply those within communities that suffered particular injustices, but created phrases, styles, and even a quasi "uniform" that were later codified into a formal organization. The linkage between this recent uprising and Hardt and Negri's understanding of the multitude was not simply through the spontaneity of its occurrence, but reflected the spontaneous creation of styles of protest along with particular affects.

Hardt and Negri assert that in addition to these *jacqueries* and blockades, another political tactic often employed by the multitude is the "social strike." In an economic environment of temporary work, diffuse corporations, and free production of the common, which is then expropriated, the only effective mode of strike is that of the social or "general" strike. They emphasize, "When cooperative production comes to invest all of social life, when the working day expands to include all waking (and even sleeping) hours, and when the productive capacities of all workers seem to be caught in the networks of command, on the one hand, it seems impossible to carve a space for independent action, which is required to 'go on strike'" (Hardt and Negri 2017, 242). Because of this, a contemporary social strike must involve "a refusal of the extraction of value in its various forms. . . . Blocking the capitalist apparatuses to capture value while fortifying the cooperative relationships of social production and reproduction" (Hardt and Negri 2017, 243). Such an expansive social strike would encompass actions such as refusal to pay debt and participate in the creation of monetized data (through extraction portals such as Facebook), in addition to a refusal to work.

Although a social strike would render the extraction of the commons impossible, it would not end the production of the commons—it would in fact withdraw to protect and reform the commons in a place where capital could not reach. This is their final description of the political tactics of the multitude, that of exodus. They state that the "exodus attempts to withdraw from the dominant institutions and establish in miniature new social relationships" (Hardt and Negri 2017, 274). Such an exodus, while frequently concrete and spatial, involving taking over spaces, making them common, and defending them against efforts by the state and capital to reestablish patterns of appropriation and state administration, need not take this form.[24] Instead, they emphasize an exodus from the "relationship with capital and from capitalist relations of production"—in other words, moving away and reestablishing new relationships in the commons (an example of this would be joining communities of open-sourced software use and maintaining as opposed to purchasing such software). Exodus follows the social strike—it is not simply movement, but movement to establish anew—not simply leaving a factory but occupying it to launch it as a place of community and production, not simply blocking the city but establishing an autonomous neighborhood distribution point for common resources and amenities.

All of these political tactics spring from the unique characteristics of the multitude. Exodus, the social strike, and blocking reflect the multitude's constitution within biopolitical production in the commons. They represent autonomous actions that either defend or expand the commons, and reflect the internal diversity, horizontalism, and constantly developing nature of the multitude. But this does not mean that Hardt and Negri recommend the avoidance of all institutional politics. In addition to strategies reflective of the multitude, they also foresee politics of what they call "antagonistic reformism" that attempt to modify institutions from within and "hegemonic strategies" that seek to take power. They emphasize, in fact, that of the three strategies, "it is not a matter of debating which of these three is correct, but rather finding ways to weave them together (Hardt and Negri 2017, 274). Weaving such strategies together might entail efforts to ensure that "the taking of power, by electoral or other means, must serve to open space for autonomous and figurative practices on an ever-larger scale. Similarly practices of exodus must find ways to complement and further projects of both antagonistic reform and taking power" (278). For example, institutional reforms would allow for and encourage the establishment of cooperative production and commonly held land, while blocking and social strikes would serve to pressure institutions to end individual acts of expression and expropriation. No matter the combination of individual political actions reflective of the three general strategies, the goal would be to further the propagation of the commons.

With the articulation of these political tactics of the multitude we can more clearly see what salvage political tactics might entail, what challenges they face and how the establishment of sites of salvage could aid in sustaining such tactics. I have argued that blocking, exodus, the social strike, and even the *jacquerie* might be seen as shared modes of resistance and defense of these cites of political salvage. For example, the *jacquerie* that blocks the circulation that occurs in an abstract centrality might last longer and be more resilient if paired and integrated with a site of salvage, such as we saw, at least partially, in Occupy London. Furthermore, exodus, although based in movement, still requires occasional rests for recuperation, and establishing radical salvage workshops could aid in this process. Once again, these tactics should not be seen as plans that must be followed, but instead as tools in a common tool kit that can be used to generate salvage-based manifestations of the multitude. But with informal neighborhoods engaging in blockading actions, Occupy encampments acting as bases for *jacqueries* and encouraging social strikes, and urban squats representing the exodus of populations from urban life, one can see that these tactics already constitute a common script used by those undertaking acts of political salvage. The social strike, due to the fact that it entails the withdrawal of participation in the formal economy, often results in communities needing to autonomously maintain their basic infrastructure, which often entails salvage. By understanding the possibilities of how salvage can play a role in these tactics of the multitude, the political significance of this activity is made even more apparent. Furthermore, political salvage involves unique actions and habits and generates particular affects and political potentialities, and if these are integrated into the conception of the multitude, the multitude can only benefit from the association.

Another benefit of thinking of the commons in terms of salvage, as I have repeatedly stressed, is that salvage represents not simply encounters between people, but encounters between people and vibrant matter. The objects that constitute the material aspect of salvage are things that possess heightened qualities of plasticity—salvage environments have been abandoned and thus lack supervision, control, and order. They are confused, jumbled, and internally diverse—lacking the categorical and rational design of most spaces within modern capitalist society. They pulsate in ways that grab one's attention and require one's acute attunement to sense in ways that more structured and settled environments do not. Thus, salvage spaces represent particularly heightened examples of what Bennett refers to as "vibrant matter." Such vibrancy produces possibilities for both excitement and confusion as individuals attempt to interact with an unknown landscape. To use the Spinozan terms so frequently used by Hardt and Negri, perhaps a person's encounter will induce affective joy and the ability to increase one's affective potentialities, and perhaps sadness, if these encounters isolate and limit one's ability to affect ones surroundings. But what remains important to stress is that salvage represents a form of encounter that reproduces the consequences of Hardt and Negri's account of the commons in a terrain that they do not discuss, that of materiality itself. When Hardt and Negri state that they see the politics of the metropolis as the organizing of encounters, they regard the metropolis only in terms of its characteristic concentration of people and ideas, and not the material space of the metropolis as a producer of encounter and subsequent affects that might result in the production of the commons. But while "abstract spaces," as noted by Lefebvre, induce encounters that produce and reinforce commodification and reification, spaces on the periphery of the urban, segregated landscape, that, while performing the necessary function of containing the excess population and material detritus produced through the production process, remain outside this heightened capitalist abstraction and present the likelihood of the possibly creative, possibly harmful but always vibrant encounters that Hardt and Negri nearly exclusively describe in defining the commons in terms of encounters between people, ideas, and culture. Salvage represents the mixture of materiality and immateriality of Reid and Taylor's "body-place-commons" and when paired with the political vision of Hardt and Negri such an understanding allows for a more expansive understanding of the commons and its political potentiality.

With this discussion of the relationship between salvage and the tactics of the multitude we can better see how the potential for the propagation of political salvage might be strengthened through its integration with a political formation such as the multitude. For example, in salving spaces using the discarded material that they find in those spaces and others like them, matsutake pickers are subject to the same contradictory dynamics of biopolitical production as other practitioners of this activity. Tsing recommends leaning into these trends, discussing how efforts at Satoyama forest management in Japan, where foragers maintain wastelands for matsutake foraging with the support of buyers and government officials, represent efforts to maximize the value that salvage landscapes can provide for capitalists. She argues that "matsutake help peasant forests remain in the working landscape. With high prices, the mushroom salves alone pay the taxes for the land and support its maintenance (Tsing 2015, 262). She also relates that in 2008 matsutake foraging was officially integrated into one U.S. Forest Service district's plan for forest management. Yet she concedes that logging companies constantly thwart the matsutake pickers' effort to use the land, and that "it is amazing to me that foresters listen to such complaints at all" (Tsing et al. 2017, 202). More frequent than fragile compromises between huge logging interests and foragers are the simple purchase and enclosure of land in the western United States,[25] or, as one sees in contemporary Brazil, the complete decimation of forests.[26] The understanding of salvage as integrated within the larger capitalist system, as described by Tsing, does not take account of the contradictions inherent in a noncapitalist form of accumulation's existing within capitalism. Salvage, because of its tendency to lead to becoming, represents a constant threat to the reification that molds the everyday experience of contemporary life. Salvage, while not always manifesting a threat, represents an always-possible threat of building the commons in a way that stands in opposition to, rather than residing within, the capitalist system.

254 / The Political Theory of Salvage

I assert that as logging companies continue to advocate for exclusive use of the land and the practices, skills, habits, and affects that these foragers create in common through their communication, the "translation" (Tsing 2015, 254) of difference she sees as constitutive of the latent commons comes to be expropriated and stilted. The prospects for such compromises in urban settings seem to be even less likely, as is evinced by Millar's account of how the salvagers with whom she lived and worked were ejected from the landfill that acted as their environment of the commons. When efforts to form common salvage turn out to be successful, as informal neighborhoods begin to act as functioning neighborhoods, squats come to be desirable and popular locations in which to work and play, and occupations come to be permanent encampments, as opposed to momentary protests, they will be subject to expropriation and repression. And, as opposed to the fragile detente between workers in the commons and capitalists described by Tsing, biopolitical workers are just as likely to face the painful contradictions and expropriations described by Hardt and Negri. Thus, exodus, blocking, and the social strike might result from the development of the salvage commons described by Tsing, specifically if this site of salvage were to take inspiration from other radical sites that constitute the multitude. Furthermore, if the participants construct a choreographed "radical salvage workshop" as part of their efforts, the possibility that they might cultivate the habits of radical anticapitalist becoming would be more likely. As mentioned, Hardt and Negri themselves think of salvage as simply a mode of extraction of value created outside of capitalism, instead of a mode of the production of the multitude. But in fact, salvage can play an important part in constituting the multitude that they see as the most promising group that might resist capitalism itself.

In conclusion, I want to stress that political salvage as I have explained it can be fruitfully interpreted as both a manifestation and an augmentation of Hardt and Negri's multitude. The examples I have given show that salvage does often not result simply in translation and interpretation, but in resistance and critique. The protests that often accompany salvage are not simply those of raw resistance, but articulate an ethos strongly antithetical to contemporary capitalism. Even more importantly, the subjectivity created through salvage shares much with the subjectivity identified by Hardt and Negri as constitutive of the multitude. But the political theory of salvage should be seen as more than simply an addition to an already adequate theory. The activity of salvage, due to its necessary materiality, challenges and expands upon the productive base upon which they ground their theory. The vibrant materiality of salvage constitutes a correlate of the creative communication Hardt and Negri posit as the foundation of biopolitical production. Both salvage and free communication at the core of biopolitical production result in creative, surprising becoming. And with the inclusion of salvage within the realm of activities productive of the multitude, this political formation comes to be increasingly relevant to an understanding of contemporary radical politics.

Conclusion

Activist and Marxist theorist Grace Lee Boggs lived a large part of her life in the city of Detroit, dying there in 2015 at the age of one hundred. After her husband, the noted union agitator and communist James Boggs, died in 1993, she shifted her attention to more seemingly prosaic concerns when she founded the Boggs Center in 1995. The Detroit of 1993, as it does today, suffered from intensive disinvestment and deindustrialization. Many of its once-grand buildings lie abandoned, its poverty rate rests well above the average for both the state of Michigan and the United States in general, and its residents suffer from high rates of sickness and death due to both their lack of access to health care and their proximity to toxic pollutants left behind in the city by the corporations that abandoned it. Yet when Boggs surveyed this ruined broken landscape, she did not despair, instead arguing that "Detroit is a city of Hope rather than a city of Despair. Thousands of vacant lots and abandoned houses provide not only the space to begin anew but also the incentive to create innovate ways of making our living—ways that nurture our productive, cooperative and caring selves" (Boggs, Kurashige, and Glover 2012, 105). This is the spirit in which I approached this book. That salvage, while not offering a political panacea that will immediately bring about the downfall of capitalism, does offer a strategy of hope and transformation that represents a possible way out of the social and political waste of our current situation.

The activities of the Boggs Center focus on community development, but not development as it is conceptualized by most nonprofits and governmental agencies. As an example of the new types of community the Boggs Center attempts to encourage, she cites the Detroit Summer program. This program was designed to occupy young people during their vacation from schools. But instead of classroom instruction or basketball leagues, Boggs recounts, "We engaged them in community building activities with the same audacity with which the civil rights moment engaged them in segregation activities forty years ago; planting community gardens, recycling waste, organizing neighborhood arts and health festivals, rehabilitating houses and painting public murals" (Boggs, Kurashige, and Glover 2012, 112–13). The pedagogic program and community-building philosophy of the school combines physical forms of work with workshops and intergenerational dialogues on how to rebuild Detroit, thus further expanding the minds and imaginations of the young, old and in-between" (113). In these two descriptions, although she does not specifically use the word *salvage*, it is clear that finding discarded material and repairing useful parts of what they find comprise an important activity in these endeavors. The students who participate in Detroit Summer rehabilitate houses, reclaim abandoned land for community gardens, recycle, and establish workshops in which to build and repair the tools they need to undertake these practices. I have devoted the bulk of this study to closely examining how the rehabilitation, reclaiming, and recycling that Boggs briefly mentions as a part of the program she founded play important and unacknowledged roles in encouraging the community building that the program she started was meant to foster. To Boggs, these daily activities remain unexamined, most likely due to their familiarity—recycling, tinkering, repairing, and scavenging comprise daily activities of the poor in cities like Detroit. But by offering the perhaps excessive analysis in the previous pages, I hope to suggest methods of intensifying the political implications that Boggs and the participants in her programs have formulated themselves. I am not telling people to salvage, or even suggesting that salvage possesses a politics that these salvagers have not already articulated to some extent; I am merely filling in gaps and connecting this increasingly prevalent practice to strains of theory and politics with which it possesses affinities, and through this connection I am suggesting possibilities for deepening the practice.

One result of connecting projects like Detroit Summer to a political theory of salvage is to highlight a missing aspect of Boggs's account—the resistance to such autonomous "laboratories of insurrectionary imagination" mounted by the forces of neoliberalism. One program in particular that she mentions places this lacuna in stark relief: the Catherine Ferguson Academy. Boggs praises this public school not only for the fact that it demonstrated great success in educating young single mothers who otherwise would most likely not have graduated from high school, but also for the fact that it undertook the salvage and community-building activities she sees as representing the promise of Detroit. The students engaged in active learning, in which they planted reclaimed fields and practiced animal husbandry in a barn they built themselves, in part using reclaimed material. But, as had happened in Flint, once the state of Michigan appointed an emergency manager to resolve the bankruptcy the city leaders could supposedly have resolved themselves, this unelected administrator started selling off public resources, including CFA. The students resisted, occupying the school and many were arrested. The emergency manager reversed his decision only later, in order to convert the school into a public charter, which eventually closed.[1] Like so many of the experiments in community that Boggs praised, the CFA fell prey to the very forces of capital flight and neoliberalism that it was meant to address, at least in miniature. Furthermore, the small, autonomous farms built of salvaged land that Boggs so strongly praises soon faced competition from large, corporate urban agriculture firms that not only produced food but were meant to serve as "development hubs" that would entice outside investment and raise real estate prices in the neighborhoods where they were located.[2] I introduce these examples to emphasize that salvage projects do not exist in a vacuum. Whereas Boggs stresses the creative and experimental nature of these endeavors, she does not address the resistance and co-optation they face. Acts of resistance, such as those undertaken by the students of the CFA, constitute a necessary activity, just as important as the experimentation and maintenance of the common community advocated by Boggs.

It is in that spirit of resistance that I offer one concluding example, or perhaps better yet in this specific context, image that represents the ethos of a political theory of salvage. Science fiction author China Mieville sits on the editorial board of the journal *Salvage*, which I cited in chapter 1 as an example of "salvage pessimism." But perhaps, in Mieville's case, this designation is unfair. I base this assessment not primarily on his published fiction or his political writings, but instead on a post from his personal blog that he entitles "Rejected Pitch." In this post, he recounts an idea for a limited-edition comic set in "Flinton, Michigan," a once-prosperous industrial town that has been abandoned by the corporations that were the foundation of its livelihood. All that is left in Flinton are the workers and the ruins of the factories in which

260 / The Political Theory of Salvage

they worked. When they realize that they have been abandoned by the
political and economic actors in whom they had previously placed their
trust, these workers decide that the only way they can defend what is
left of their livelihoods is to build a powered superhero suit with which
a group of workers (the suit does not contain one person, but instead is
remotely controlled by a collective) might fight the forces of global capital.
When they decide to seek revenge on the CEO of the company that
abandoned Flinton, one worker exclaims: "Capitalists are a superstitious
cowardly lot. . . . This fucker put our town out with the trash, threw
us on the scrap heap. Well, the scrap heap's got up, and it's coming for
him" (Mieville 2011). They name their salvaged superhero Scrap Iron
Man, and undertake missions all over the world to defend the workers
and the towns that have been abandoned by capital.

While the image of a salvaged superhero (see figure C.1) pum-
meling indifferent CEOs provides me with close-to-sublime emotional
gratification as someone who has worked in Flint for more than a decade,
such flights of fancy might seem either useless or indulgent in a work
that purports to engage in serious political thinking. But I do think it
is important to provide an image such as this. The idea of a superhero
made of scrap iron does not seem so outlandish when one looks at protesters in Hong Kong and New York with their salvaged gas masks and
improvised armor. In a sense, Scrap Iron Man can be seen as a "concrete
utopia"[3] in that the story and image are based in so many real world
circumstances. It emphasizes that salvage is not simply a practice that
results in plasticity and becoming, but a weapon of the weak whereby
those with little political agency, at least according to traditional metrics
of this ability, weld their *metis* to sculpt a "weapon of the weak" with
which to fight, and then stealthily retreat back into their labyrinthine,
salvaged neighborhoods—spaces too forgotten and ignored to be subject
to high levels of capitalist control. Such clashes between salvage and
capital are increasingly frequent. As demonstrated by the instances of
Catherine Ferguson Academy and the Heidelberg Project about which I
spoke earlier, the spaces of salvage represent barriers to the capitalist propagation of abstract space. The jumbled, contingent geographies produced
through salvage stand in the way of the neatly ordered, discernible, and
surveilled spaces of capitalist urbanity. And although such spaces can be
salvaged because they are peripheral, they often do not stay peripheral
for long, both because capital searches for new spaces of accumulation
and because nomadic salvagers undertake incursions of inhabitation in
the cracks that form in abstract space.

Figure C.1. Scrap Iron Man. Mieville, "Rejectamentalist Manifesto," 2011.

Although a political theory of salvage (or any political theory) does not constitute a clear and certain path to social transformation, it does offer a number of important contributions that might identify the conditions that have led to the manifestation of what I have called political salvage and highlight the potentialities present within this activity that, with the proper cultivation, might intensify the radical political consequences of this action. So when Boggs states that cities that have borne the brunt of deindustrialization constitute cites of hope and not despair, I see my political theory of salvage as helping to pinpoint the specific strategy that could better transform these hopes into effective actions. Furthermore, to identify salvage as a strategy for concretizing political hope in difficult circumstances also highlights the fact that this will not be an easy hope to fulfill. Salvage, the repair it envisions (and thus the failures it will inevitably entail) and the construction of "kiltered" communities of commons in which it might result, will necessitate constant maintenance and recalibration. Because contemporary capitalism has embraced a "spatial fix," as David Harvey terms it, to overcome the challenges of capital accumulation, spaces both of development and of destruction constantly shift. What has been deemed a peripheral waste area where communities might salvage with relatively little interference quickly can become a site of reinvestment and thus dispossession. One of the primary ways to comprehend political salvage as a craft is to emphasize its procedural and incremental nature. As more people engage in political salvage its victories cannot be measured purely in the length of its existence or the number of salvage cites that are identified as such. Instead, even though seemingly defeated and discredited, as in the case of a program of the Boggs center such as the Catherine Ferguson Academy, the habits gained and perspectives changed through acts of salvage persist in the activists. The long-term hope produced by salvage and the habits that sustain the practice of that hope outlast the sense of failure that accompanies short-term defeats, and can even act as the "depressive" moments from which new short-term hope is born.

Furthermore, despite the growing ubiquity of political salvage, I should not be understood as arguing that this practice represents the most powerful or most frequently employed strategy undertaken by those resisting capitalism. Salvage is just one of many activities that possesses the potential to generate anticapitalist consciousness and action. It should be seen as a complementary strategy that can be applied in multiple contexts beyond those I have described in this work. Furthermore, recent history has shown that salvage politics, such as that exemplified by the Occupy protests, have worked in coalitions with more traditional political groups and movements. For example, labor unions in the United States have formed coalitions with Occupy encampments, whereby they have donated needed supplies and the participants in these encampments have joined picket lines and supported other labor-friendly activities.[4] Participants in squats have undertaken homeless and rent control advocacy and *favela* dwellers have constituted large blocs of voters for left-wing candidates in Brazil and Venezuela.[5] Especially when seen as a site for the sustenance of the multitude, salvage should be taken as a part, rather than the totality, of an anticapitalist politics. It is one piece of a larger puzzle, and not an all-encompassing strategy of resistance.

The exact form that future integrations of salvage with activism might take will of course depend upon specific circumstances. But the examples I have cited throughout this work give indications of how such politics might manifest itself. For example, the factory occupations that occurred throughout Argentina point toward a strategy of further refurbishments of abandoned workplaces and sites of production. Unions and other institutions might provide resources and suggest rough schemas of choreography for laid-off workers from a community to occupy and salvage. Furthermore, unions might reestablish their practice of encouraging worker co-op housing, as they did in cities such as New York in the 1930s, but instead of building the larger modernist towers of the Hillman Houses located on the Lower East Side and other well-known developments, they might supply the tools and knowledge for enabling workers to build their own salvaged housing in the sort of half-completed "weak architecture" frames outlined by McGuirk. If salvage were integrated into the other political activities of more traditional political and activist institutions, then the possibility that its practitioners could experience episodes of anticapitalist becoming might be increased. With such becoming, as Connolly asserts, a new relationship to politics, and especially to democracy, might be encouraged. Furthermore, the plasticity that flows from salvage, which one adopts as an attitude toward the world and oneself might also affect one's views toward the institutions in which one participates. Thus, unions and even political parties that adopt strategies of salvage might be more open to joining new assemblages and thus able to constitute nodes in the multitude. While none of these suggestions constitute certainties, the political theory of salvage suggests undertaking and examining their possibilities.

Even though engaging in political salvage will not overthrow capitalism in and of itself, it is important to remember its unique contributions to contemporary radical activism. First, salvage concentrates affect. Those engaged it in must use things they do not choose, and thus must rely upon their sense of how an object will behave. Salvage landscapes surprise those who forage in them, and repaired items operate in unexpected ways. Such confusion and surprise leave salvagers with nothing but the affects they experience to evaluate their next steps—hunches take over for thorough evaluation. Such vibrant, and even perhaps disturbing affects possess the power to awaken qualitative senses that have been deadened by the "anesthetic" existence in abstract spaces. Salvage is uniquely able to break through the reified, repetitious infrastructure that constitutes the contemporary "cruel optimism." Identifying skills, spaces, and communities that intensify the practice of salvage increase its anticapitalist potential. While political salvage, as expressed through occupations, squats, and informal communities, should not be taken as a replacement for more traditional movement strategies, it does offer something that these forms of politics cannot, and might thus augment other strategies.

The hope that Grace Lee Boggs expressed concerning Detroit is the hope of salvage. While it is impossible to precisely define the affects that accompany hope, it is safe to say that they are expansive. To use affective categories I invoked earlier, hope is love for the future in all of its unpredictable messiness. It is expansive, gushing, and propulsive. Such intense affects always present the possibility of overwhelming those who sense them, and, perhaps ironically, depression, when understood as an affect, constitutes an important part of sustaining hope. As my experience in Occupy Flint revealed, engaging in politics from the base of a salvaged landscape does often prompt rhythmic alternation between depression and love, and the hope that such existence inspires takes on this dual character. If a political theory of salvage manifests itself as a type of hope, it is certainly a pragmatic hope, a "real utopia" that can inspire action while focusing those who engage in it upon the true, messy, broken nature of their surroundings.

Notes

Introduction

1. Although there are many terms for such self-built, popular communities, such as slums, shantytowns, and barrios, in this work, unless referring to a specific location where a specific term has become standard(such as the *favelas* of Brazil) I will use the term *informal neighborhoods* or *communities*.

2. Personal communication with author.

3. The above contention that the activists who participated in Occupy Flint were attempting to radically rethink local government begs the question of who these activists were and whether or not every participant in Occupy Flint was dedicated to the same goal. As with many Occupy encampments, the identities, political backgrounds, and aspirations of the activists were diverse. Not all harbored such radical intentions, and initially most did not—they participated out of a deep sense of grievance and vague notion that U.S. politics and economics should be organized differently. Despite this heterogeneity, a core of well-known, seasoned Flint activists continually pushed the participants to engage in more radical critique of capitalism and imagine more racial goals for the encampment. Mark Bray (2013) describes something similar in his account of Occupy Wall Street when he claims that many of the anticapitalist, anarchist organizers of the event eschewed overtly articulating their radical goals so as to not alienate those possessing more traditional political identifications. Instead, he claims that they hoped that both the collective governing and maintaining of the occupation and their efforts to subtly widen the scope of the political discussion within the encampment would act as a vehicle for "translating anarchy" into a form that could be more easily digested by those unfamiliar or uncomfortable with the concept. Many of the examples of radical political activity that I will discuss in this work will exhibit a similar strategy—that by engaging in the practice, salvage-laced activism can play an important role in "translating" radical ideas that will be more palatable to novice activists and low-commitment participants.

4. Jodi Dean makes such a claim when she states, "[T]he general assembly was a primary organizational form during the Occupy Movement" (Dean 2016, 2).

5. For perhaps the best-known account of the "artisan" virtues as articulated in the popular imaginary see *Shopcraft as Soulcraft: An Inquiry into the Value of Work* (Crawford 2010).

6. I will frequently highlight the difference between salvage undertaken by those with resources and those without in this work in order to highlight not only the difficulties, but the promise of salvage being interpreted as a craft of the poor. Investing the poor with particular "potentialities" might seem as though I am somehow romanticizing the poor and their lack of resources. I want to emphasize that just because salvage as a "craft of the poor" can be distinguished from simply looking for old things and using them in new ways and that salvage undertaken by the poor possesses a nascent political potential, this does not mean that all salvage undertaken by the poor constitutes only a possibility that has been actualized under particular conditions. Poverty might be an enabling state to those who integrate politics with salvage, but it in and of itself does not guarantee such activity.

7. One branch of current "salvage" scholarship, focusing on how the neoliberal retreat from the provision of infrastructure such as garbage and sanitation, has spawned both creative modification and struggle around these services. See *Garbage Citizenship* for a discussion of political struggles in Dakar. The book describes what it calls "salvage infrastructures" and describes one such example, stating that "in Dakar, this has bred infrastructures of salvage bricolage even within the core of urban public services. These systems underscore that infrastructures are processural—they are constantly undergoing innovating processes of care and refabrications by the bodies and system of society they are built upon" (Fredericks 2018, 17). For more on salvage infrastructures in Ghana see (Chalfin 2014, 2017). Examples of reclaimed spaces in parts of the developing world I do not cover range far and wide, and can be seen in places as diverse as the West Bank (Berger 2018) and South Africa (Gebrekidan and Onishi 2019).

8. In this sense I act in the mode of the "pearl diver" as articulated by Hanna Arendt. As Buck-Morss describes, Arendt conceives the pearl diver as someone who

> descends to the bottom of the sea not to excavate the bottom and bring it to light, but to pry loose the rich and the strange, the pearls and the coral in the depths and to carry them to the surface. Thinking delves into the depths of the past—but not in order to resuscitate it the way it was and to contribute to the renewal of extinct ages. What guides this thinking is the conviction that although the living is subject to the ruin of the time the process of decay is at the same

time a process of crystallization in that the depths of the sea, into which sinks and it dissolves what once was alive some things "suffer a sea-change" and survive in new crystallized forms and shapes that remain immune to the elements. (Buck-Morss 1989, 51)

9. For an account of the connections between Occupy Flint and the later water justice movement in Flint see *Flint Fights Back: Environmental Justice and Democracy in the Flint Water Crisis* (Pauli 2019).

Chapter 1. Salvage and Politics

1. Mark Fisher states something similar when he claims that ruined landscapes in particular possess the power to inspire eerie feelings that can lead to critical attitudes toward capitalism. He claims that ruins conjure the "failure of presence" and prompt questions pertaining to:

what disappeared. What kinds of being created these structures? How were they similar to use, and how were they different. . . . Confronted with Easter Island or Stonehenge, it is hard not to speculate about what the relics of our culture will look like when the semiotic systems in which they are currently embedded have fallen away. (Fisher 2017, 63)

2. A term he borrows from the artist Kurt Schwitters, see Williams 2011, 37–38.

3. His invocation of "what can be sold back to the suppliers" refers to a previous discussion of the industrial scrappers of ships in South Asia, but can also be seen as a critique of Tsing's understanding of salvage capitalism discussed in the introduction.

4. Beyond the theorists I have mentioned, there are very few extended discussions of what a politics based in practice of salvage might look like. On the other hand there are many "Left pessimists," as I call them, who share with salvage pessimists an understanding that traditional Left strategies have lost their efficacy and ability to inspire. See see Zerzan 2015, 1994; Dupont 2009; Stengers 2009; and Traverso 2017.

5. David Giles in his "Anatomy of a Dumpster" reports a similar feeling of creativity and liberation expressed by those living off refuse in American cities, especially in Seattle, where he did his fieldwork. He states, "Dumpster divers sometimes contrast for instance their initial gut hesitations at dumpster diving with expressions of subsequent liberation, accomplishment and joyful transgression at successfully living on the left overs" (Giles 2014, 107).

6. It is interesting to contrast this, if not hopeful at least not despondent, view to Davis's work, *Planet of Slums* where he devotes entire chapters to the hellish landscape he sees lying within the world's informal communities (Davis 2007). He expresses similar general sentiments in "Who Will Build the Ark": "Since most of history's giant trees have already been cut down, a new ark will have to be constructed out of the materials that a departed humanity finds at hand in insurgent communities, pirate technologies, bootlegged media, rebel science and forgotten utopias" (Davis 2018, 202).

7. Hazan also emphasizes the importance of salvage, in this case through the construction of barricades, and other improvised structures during the Paris Commune. He states, "Improvised powder workshops were constructed. . . . Bullets were founded in sewing thimbles and in the Faubourg du Temple: even a cannon was built" (Hazan 2015, 88).

8. The classic anthropological work on the distinction between dichotomous concepts such as valued/disdained and clean/dirty is Mary Douglass's *Purity and Danger: An Analysis of the Concepts of Pollution and Taboo* (1966). I find the value of Thompson's work is that it confounds the hard division of purity-valued and imagines a much more fluid and dynamic relationship between these concepts.

9. The example of pallets remains particularly significant to the author. After college, as a VISTA (Volunteers in Service to America) volunteer in Tucson, Arizona, I was assigned to assist with a program that salvaged used but usable building materials and distributed them to those in need. One of the most vexing repurposing assignments I was given was attempting to find a use for dozens of heavy pallets donated by the Grumman Corporation that had been used to transport missile parts. They were finally used in the construction of fencing required in order for a needy family to receive a service dog—the agency would not place one of their dogs in a house without a fenced-in yard.

10. In another example, in Rome, "to bring greater national attention to their plight about a hundred Kurds created an improvised settlement called 'cartonia,' built entirely of recycled cardboard and other found materials which they located in a park in sight of the Colosseum. In this cobbled-together village the Kurds set up a restaurant, a tea room, a barbershop and a store for provisions" (Franck and Stevens 2012, 201).

11. For DIY City Services see Grant et al. 2006, 462–69, and for internet see Grossman 2017.

12. A similar salvage phenomenon can be seen outside the public toilets of Ghana, where "craft porticoes, called 'ghettos, from the detritus of zinc roofing, worn canoes, nets and plastic sheeting. Bridging work, leisure, survival and social reproduction, ghettos enable multifunctional congregation. Built on unoccupied or unclaimed land next to established structures, they host an array of activities—cooking, eating and drinking, napping, conversation, singing, Bible study, and card playing" (Chalfin 2014, 105).

13. The phrase "seeing like a state" I draw from Scott 1999.

14. Numerous instances of such state resistance to salvage, especially examples in Latin America, are outlined in McGuirk 2014.

15. For example, see the Heidelberg project in Detroit, where artist Tyree Guyton transformed an entire street of abandoned houses into a salvaged art environment by adorning the structures with found items (Herron et al. 2007). Another example of "salvaged" art that embodies a political ethos can be seen in "zines"—small publications usually reproduced through photocopies and other nontraditional methods. Zines have been a staple of DIY, anarchist communities since the 1980s, and use salvage in their collage-like design, and in their production. The practice of producing zines has been developed into a larger cultural and political perspective called by practitioners "zine theory," which emphasizes many of the political values I claim are suggested by salvage practice. For a good appraisal of "zine theory" see Duncombe 2017. The website crimethink embodies this nexus of creativity, activism, DIY, and thus salvage. For an excellent example, see the instruction provided by the website Crimethink. org for constructing "Spiders of Mutual Aid," large puppets first seen at 2017 May Day rallies in Seattle, Washington, using salvaged pieces of chicken wire covered in papier maché all mounted on abandoned, salvaged shopping carts (Crimethink 2017).

16. Accusing Occupy activists of being "filthy" constituted a major theme in the mainstream media and among elected officials (Liboiron 2012).

17. In his *Waste Away: Living and Working in an American Landfill*, Joshua Reno describes something similar when he interprets the experience of his co-workers at the landfill when they reclaim discarded objects. He states, "Lucky finds and clever repairs interrupt the dreamlike, phantasmic ways in which subjects and objects ordinarily relate to each other within consumer capitalism" (Reno 2016, 102).

18. Hardt and Negri also emphasize the political import of the affects produced by participation in the recent occupations of public space that involved salvage. They state, "Tahir Square, Rothschild Boulevard, the occupied Wisconsin Statehouse and Syntagma Square are all obviously characterized by intense affects. Affects are expressed in those sights, but more importantly they are produced and trained" (Hardt and Negri 2012, 32).

19. She states of her own experience during fieldwork in the landfill, "But then I saw it. A gap between burlap sacks, rarely a couple of feet wide led all the way to the unloading zone. I was standing in the middle of this rain. During all the times I had trekked back and forth between loading trucks and my partially filled sacks I had never realized that I was following a passage way that was marked off and respected by *catadores* . . . it was like looking at one of those magic eye posters whose hidden image had suddenly come into view" (Millar 2018, 14).

20. Reno, in his *Waste Away*, relates his own experience with the sensed potentialities of interacting with waste when he worked in a Michigan landfill. His description, though, does not fully convey the novelty of encounters with waste. He recounts how during a day at work he encountered a discarded toy, the type of which he owned when he was a child. Encountering this toy triggered a rush of memories and a desire to possess it, despite the fact that such taking was against company policy. He relates, "There is an element of uncanny serendipity involved in acquiring estranged commodities as when the exact thing one needs or desires just happens to arrive in one of the waste loads" (Reno 2016, 119). Whereas the term *uncanny serendipity* conveys the vague, pregnant potentialities he experienced when encountering the toy (bringing it home, reliving important memories, talking about the toy with others), stating that the object was "the exact thing one needs and desires," to my mind, neglects the originality and contingency of the desire. He did not simply possess a latent desire he somehow discovered when ran across the toy. The desire itself was created through his encounter with the object. It was the transaction between two bodies, one human and one nonhuman, that created the desire, not an object fulfilling a preexisting desire. The "uncanniness" he sensed was not simply the fulfillment of a desire but the potentiality of an unknown and developing desire within himself. Because the dump "estranges" commodities from their usual webs of relationships, it constitutes an ecology pregnant with such possibilities, encounters, and desires.

21. We can see this in the requirements demanded by companies that owners cannot repair their own computers, farm equipment, and other items that they own. This has spawned a "right to repair" movement that would outlaw such contracts. See BBC News 2019.

22. I am indebted to an anonymous reviewer for this point.

23. A similar common structure was built by the sanitation workers of Dakar, who used it as a base of their political operations in their struggles against neoliberal austerity. Fredericks describes it as "an old abandoned building by a neighborhood association, which they transformed into an imaginative headquarters where they bided time in between shifts and held union meetings. With all manner of reclaimed objects meticulously placed about—mats to lay on, and old radio, a fan that limped along, and old map of the United States—it struck me as a kind of secret fort, a hideaway for those who knew something mysterious and special" (Fredericks 2018, 93).

24. Even in arguments that assert the "Hobbesian" chaotic and authoritarian nature of salvage environments, relationships of cooperation can show through. For example, Brenda Chalfin in her article "'Wastelandia': Infrastructure and the Commonwealth of Waste in Urban Ghana" suggests that the salvage-constructed toilet structure around which a community developed "is not a common in the sense advocated by Hardt and Negri . . . Wastelandia's

sprawling public toilet facility is wholly a private enterprise. It was conceived and built and is managed by a single individual, let us call him M" (Chalfin 2017, 652). She claims that this individual established a "covenant" with users "in which he stood as the ultimate sovereign helm" (Chalfin 2017, 655). But Chalfin provides much evidence of a community characterized not by absolute sovereignty backed by violence and fear, which Hobbes describes, but instead one involving negotiations and compromises made by the "owner" of Wastelandia, prompted by the autonomous interventions of the users. For example she relates how "the teen-age boys who squatted on the hostel's unroofed third story pursued infrastructural experiments of their own. Away from their mothers, sisters and younger siblings on the second floor and not obliged to pay like the men living in the fully served ground floor bunk room they constructed their own roofed shelters" (Chalfin 2017, 660). If "M" truly exercised the absolute sovereignty described by Hobbes, it is hard to see him allowing for such freeloading and independent modification of the infrastructure. At times her account wavers from this absolutist interpretation, instead describing the squatting she observed as "at once reiterating the infrastructural logic of M's rule while refuting his claims to absolute authority" (ibid). I choose to emphasize the subversive nature of these salvaged squats and thus see such activity as an instance of autonomous salvage commoning within a controlled, already salvaged landscape.

25. scott crow describes a similar phenomenon occurring in New Orleans in the wake of Hurricane Katrina. He recounts how mutual aid efforts that were started as reactions to immediate needs that were not being met by officialdom developed into radical experiments in decommodification, local democracy, and the development of the commons. See crow, Cleaver, and Clark 2014.

Chapter 2. Sense, Becoming, and Political Salvage

1. Not all who adhere to a "vibrant" understanding of the nonhuman believe that such environments offer the potential to lead to novel actions and new interpretations of one's environment. According to Mark Fisher, such suppositions concerning the productive use encounters with the agency of the nonhuman environment merely recapitulate flawed understandings of human intentionality. He argues that "new materialists such as Bennett accept that the distinction between human beings and the natural world is no longer tenable, but they construe this to mean that many of the features previously ascribed only to human beings are actually distributed throughout nature" (Fisher 2017, 84).

2. Although he does not use the word *affect*, John Dewey describes something very similar when he talks about the "pre logical" "sensed" unity of what he calls a situation. Alexander recounts Dewey's description of a situation by stating, "Situations . . . are primarily organized, active, lived, experiences

unified by a pre-logical or pre-analytical qualitative unity which gives them their continuity and sense . . . they are spatio-temporal, organically unified and developmental: they have diversified parts and phases and they are both immediate and mediated (Alexander 1987, 104–10).

3. Dewey's understanding of the "sense" one experiences of a situation also mirrors the language of affect employed by Bennet, and by Stewart. He states, "Empirically, things are poignant, tragic, beautiful, humorous, settled, disturbed, comfortable, annoying, barren, harsh, consoling, splendid, fearful and are such immediately and in their own right and behalf" (Dewey and Hook 2008). I discuss Dewey here, despite the fact that he is not an important influence upon the modern theorists of affect I discuss, because his work will play an important role in the next chapter.

4. The constant movement of bodies within constantly mobile environments have led some to describe the sensed affects one one's experience as revealing the contours of "a mobile ontology in which movement is primary as a foundational condition of being, space, subjects and power, helps us to imagine the constituent relationality of the world in a new way" (Sheller 2018, 9). Such an ontology calls upon us "to detect the relations, resonances, connections, continuities and disruptions that organize the world into ongoing yet temporary mobile formations" (Sheller 2018, 10).

5. Silvia Federici expresses the same understanding of the body as a receptor, especially of potentiality, albeit in the process of criticizing theorists of performativity such as Judith Butler, who she sees as focusing too heavily on the discursive constitution of the body. She states, "There is something that we have lost in our insistence on the body as something socially constructed and performative. The view of the body as a social (discursive) production has hidden the fact that our body is a receptacle of powers, capacities and resistances that have been developed in a long process of coevolution with our natural environment as well as integration of practices that have made it a natural limit to exploitation" (Federici 2020, 119).

6. Clara Fischer states of this indelible relationship between affect and emotion, "Dewey thus rejects the apparent reduction of emotions to mere physical feeling-states lacking in cognition, and resists the atomistic treatment of individual processes involved in the emotional experience itself" (Fischer 2016, 821).

7. Thrift goes so far as to say that "affect does not require a subject" (Thrift and Amin 2013, 46). While this is true to the extent that matter, in its unavoidable relation with other matter, does possess the vitality that Bennett claims, there is always a subject, at least in the form of a body, that constitutes the locus of unique situations, and thus there is always the sense produced by the affect of this situation.

8. Stengers describes something similar when she examines the manner in which the anarchist activist Starhawk advocates activists opening themselves

to the "non-human" that fundamentally contributes to "collective becoming they experiment." She relates how when Starhawk "writes about the Goddess as an empowering presence, and about rituals as a matter of experimentation by which to learn how to invoke and convoke her in different situations, or about magic as a craft for transforming conscious awareness, the point is clearly not a matter of belief in some supernatural power. . . . The point is an achievement that cannot be reduced to general purely human categories, an achievement which demands that humans do not feel themselves as masters of the situation, as responsible for what is achieved" (Stengers and Bennett 2010, 22). What Stengers takes from Starhawk, and what I would emphasize, is how activists are often carried away by senses that they cannot describe and that they feel constitute autonomous forces outside their conscious wills.

9. Tsing uses strikingly similar language, that of a "fever" to describe the, passionate, propulsive affects when mushroom pickers often feel a compulsion to undertake their scavenging. She relates how "[p]ickers describe their eagerness to get into the forest as a 'fever.' Sometimes, they say they didn't plan to do but the fever catches you. In the heat of the fever one picks in the rain or snow, even at night with lights" (Tsing 2015, 242).

10. I get the term "ecology of practice" from Massumi 2015.

11. For another interpretation that sees the contemporary condition through its qualities of incessant change, dislocation, and, "liquidity," see Bauman 2000.

12. Berlant alternately describes the allure of affective passions such as cruel optimism as being "unspoken" or in other words, not articulable. Yet they claim this lack of semantic content does not lessen the attraction of such passions. They argue, "But many more sustaining relations than the normative ones go on without saying, because they provide relatable rhythms" (Berlant 2011a, 686). The importance of understanding how the rhythmic qualities of affect can both impede and enable radical politics, and how the rhythmic affects accompanying the practice of salvage will become important to the argument, will be discussed in chapter 3.

13. Other theorists describe similar affects produced through capitalist existence and behaviors that often accompany them. Eve Sedgwick, in her essay "Paranoid Reading and Reparative Reading, or, You're So Paranoid, You Probably Think This Essay Is About You," discusses the political and existential perspective she sees adopted by so many academics as "paranoid." This way of being in the world does not only find expression through the behavior of academics, but it can act as a potent example of an attitude particularly prevalent in our time of neoliberal capitalism. She claims that the paranoiac's primary goal remains to avoid negative affects and to make sure there "are no bad surprises" (Sedgwick 2003, 130). This relationship to affect, she argues, has profoundly conservative and depoliticizing implications. She states, "In a paranoid view it is more dangerous for the frustrations of reifications imposed by powerful institutions and

identities ever to be unanticipated than to be challenged" (Sedgwick 2003, 133). The affects accompanying such constant vigilance, while certainly not joyful or empowering in the Deleuzian sense of acting in a way that complexifies and compounds a body, does provide comfort. Sedgwick states that this effort to "minimize negative affect and maximize positive affect," ironically, leads to a situation where "the mushrooming self-confirming strength of a monopolistic strategy of anticipating negative affect can have the effect of entirely blocking the potentially operative goal of seeking positive affect" (Sedgwick 2003, 136–37). Thus, the paranoid mode acts as a circumscribing type of cruel optimism in that it does provide individuals with a feeling of agency and control, but only in terms of an affect of repetitive anticipation.

14. Like the theorists described above, Deleuze interprets disempowerment and the diminishment of agency as rooted in the spatial and temporal characteristics of the capitalist landscape. Furthermore, these spatial and temporal characteristics produce affects that obscure the individual's ability to discern the wider field of capitalist social relationships. Such "continual monitoring" and the disappearing of "differentiated" institutions such as school and work constitute a regime of what he calls "control." The control comes through the "modulation" between calm and excitement, equilibrium and trauma, the inability to distinguish between these different periods and the activities and interpretations required to negotiate these ecologies of practice. Overall, Deleuze claims that capitalist controls manifest themselves as "modulation like a self-transmuting, molding continually changing form one moment to the next" (Deleuze 1997, 178–79). Thus, the obscuring, ideology-like consequences of control originate not from the particularity of the tasks or inhibitions required by a particular institution, but from their spatial and temporal arrangement. To control someone is to keep them off guard, to randomly modify the spaces and times that one needs to exhibit certain behaviors or possess certain permissions. "Disciplinary man produces energy in discrete amounts," he claims, "while control man undulates among a continuous range of different orbits" (Deleuze 1997, 180). Such undulations not only constantly disturb one's balance and sense of the expected, but they cannot be perceived in their individuality, due to being experienced as merely an incomprehensible smear of affects. Although he does not place his understanding of control in the context of reification and alienation as I have, his focus on the "differentiation" of institutions, and the disjointed experiential rhythms of "equilibrium and trauma" certainly points toward an elective affinity between his thoughts and more traditional Marxist thought.

15. It is important to emphasize that none of the theorists I will be discussing interpret love as a romantic relationship between two people—the common understanding of this concept in contemporary culture. In fact, Reid and Taylor suggest that such an understanding consists of "two decontextualized selves discovering each other in the mini-social contract" that "functions as the

ontological anchor for liberal democratic ideology." Love bolsters capitalism, for Reid and Taylor because such "an intimate event seems to solve, but actually covers up, the constitutive contradiction of possessive liberalism—it cannot explain the grounds for solidarity except by an endless regression of 'free contracts among atomistic individuals'" (Reid and Taylor 2010, 86–87).

16. Berlant expresses discomfort with Hardt and Negri's appropriation of love for politics. They state, "[L]ove allows one to want something, to want a world amid the noise of the ambivalence and anxiety about having and losing that merely wanting an object generates, even when the object is a political one. But I would rather begin my thought looking at the whole field of what it takes to sustain an attachment to the world. The ambitions and capacities of love would be magnetized to attachment, but other modes of relating would be to the ones involving proximity, solidarity, collegiality, friendship, the light touch and intermittent ones, and then the hatred, aversions, and not caring the pleasures of the city; to be proximate without a plan" (Berlant 2011a, 687). It will soon become clear that I am sympathetic to the argument that an affective, political love can and should be augmented with other "modes of relating" and metrics of "proximity." But I do wonder whether Berlant's "pleasures of the city" and the state of being "proximate without a plan" cannot also be observed in Hardt and Negri's invocation of Walt Whitman. As an expression of this love, Whitman's rambles through the city, the attachments he forged through fleeting encounters, do seem to conform to the state of being "proximate without a plan" she describes here.

17. I want to emphasize that Berlant's political interpretation of depression, through its use of terms such as *stretching out*, *splits off*, and *atmosphere* not only indicates that they understand this phenomenon in terms of affect and not emotion, but also clearly differentiates them from many other recent interpretations of how depression and despair might constitute a Left politics. For example, in the recent work *Left-Wing Melancholia: Marxism, History and Memory*, Enzo Traverso when discussing the political efficacy of mourning in reaction to a Left political tradition seemingly ruined by the fall of communism, seems to be employing a similar strategy to Berlant in their mutual employment of a seemingly "negative" emotional stance to spur a Left revival. But when Traverso discusses what he calls "the transformative effect of loss" that comes from the "work of mourning," he discusses how such work stimulates action in a "conscious and self-reflexive way" (Traverso 2017, 28) solely through the employment of memory. He goes on to valorize a "melancholia consisting in a kind of epistemological posture: a historical and allegorical insight into both society and history that tries to grasp the origins of . . . sorrow and collect the objects and images of a past waiting for redemption" (Traverso 2017, 48). This construction of a conscious, epistemological understanding of mourning clearly differs from the "atmosphere" of depression described by Berlant.

18. Such a focus on the importance of affect and everyday encounters to radical politics has led to criticism by those advocating for more traditional forms of activism and social change. A recent example of such skepticism can be found in Nick Srnicek's and Alex Williams's *Inventing the Future: Postcapitalism and a World Without Work*. They argue that shifting focus away from what most deem to be the substance of activism (e.g., parties, interests, and institutions) constitutes "folk politics" that will never be able to constitute a politics powerful or effective enough to confront the enormous power of capital. They state:

> [A]t its heart, folk politics is the guiding intuition that immediacy is always better and often more authentic, with the corollary being a deep suspicion of abstraction and mediation. . . . In terms of spatial immediacy, folk politics privileges the local and the site of authenticity . . . habitually chooses the small over the large . . . favors projects that are unscalable beyond a small community, and often rejects the project of hegemony, valuing withdrawal or exit rather than building a broad counter-hegemony. . . . In terms of conceptual immediacy there is a preference of the everyday over the structural, valorizing personal experience over systematic thinking, for feeling over thinking, and emphasizing individual suffering or the sensation of enthusiasm and anger experienced during political actions (Srnicek and Williams 2016, 11).

I counter this position by claiming that the possibility that affective love would prompt "feverish" excursion into wider and more varied contexts lessens the propensity for a politics focused on the everyday to remain as hermetic as Srnicek and Williams claim.

Chapter 3. The Craft of Salvage

1. Others have argued for the threatening and destabilizing nature of nomads in the eyes of the state. Cowan highlights this by stating that "tents and nomadic camping practices have a long history of disobedience, challenging the idea that established or settled architectures should dominate how we live This is why travelers caravans, carnivals and other mobile ways of life and work are often seen as threatening" (Flood and Grindon 2014, 39).

2. Metallurgy constitutes one of the examples ancient Greeks used to exemplify *metis*. They described the blacksmith-god Hephaestus through "his distinctive characteristic of being endowed with a double and divergent orientation. In order to dominate shifting, fluid power such as fire, wind and minerals with which the blacksmith must cope with the intelligence and *metis* of

Hephaestus must be even more mobile and polymorphic than these" (Detienne and Vernant 1991, 273). Notice in this description the use of the words *mobile* and *polymorphic*. The mobile nature of Hephaestus clearly resembles the itinerant of Deleuze's description of the blacksmith-nomad, while the hybrid nature of Hephaestus alludes to the Greek propensity to liken the blacksmith to the crab, with its joints that move in many directions, and the seal, which is a hybrid of land and sea animals (Detienne and Vernant 1991, 273–75).

3. I use this phrase in conscious reference to Scott's book of the same name (Scott 1987).

4. David Graber also sees peasant practice as a "weapon of the weak" while explicitly tying this mode of existence to anarchist political potential. He states, "While anarchism as a movement tended to be very strongly rooted in mass organizing of the industrial proletariat, anarchists also tended to draw inspiration from existing modes of practice, notably on the part of peasants, skilled artisans or even to some degree outlaws, hobos, vagabonds and other who lived by their wits—in other words those who might be considered at least to some degree autonomous elements. People with experience of non alienated production" (Graeber 2009, 213).

5. This understanding that craftwork was best practiced in workshops undermines criticisms that Sennett's valorization of the artisan remains too rooted in individualism to be useful for a radical politics. An example of such criticism can be seen when Jodi Dean states, "Sennett wants to shore up the individual. . . . More to the point with his emphasis of life narratives, useful-ness and craftsmanship Sennett increases the burden on the individual form. Instead of building up the collective and solidarity that might relieve some of the demands placed on individuals his suggestions continue the turn in and on the individual, as if the cultural anchor were nothing more than the fetish to be held onto as we nevertheless acknowledge the impossibility of the command to individuate" (Dean 2016, 43–44).

6. I discuss how the design of Dewey's schoolroom facilitates affect-based development of connective meaning in Kosnoski 2010.

7. This term has been used to describe many fugitive spaces established by activists that encourage experiences of time that undermine reified capitalist experience. For example, one group of activists claims that the "squat model could have been borrowed from philosopher Roland Barthes and his ideal of an idiorhythmic community. . . . A community where each person can live at their own pace . . . contra common rhythms. Contrarily the idiorhythmic community must be able to make room for the desires and routines of each person. . . . This is how each of us, little by little, weaves our routine and familiar world from which we draw strength to face the outside world. By moving in, the person forges their singularity and pace, and keeps the injunctions of theirs and the rules of social life at arms length" (Kollective 2014, 73).

8. For an example of squats instituting skill-sharing workshops in Berlin see Vasudevan 2017, 136.

Chapter 4. Salvage and the City

1. See Matta-Clark, Smithson, and Koolhaas, *Shrinking Cities* (Ostfildern-Ruit, Germany, and New York: Hatje Cantz, 2006) for analysis of deindustrialization in cities such as Detroit, Leipzig, Manchester, and Ivanova.

2. It is not that the poor do not squat in rural areas, but often this "squatting" takes the form of indigenous people defending their land, not actively taking land that was once subject to capitalist property relations. The political aspect of salvage most frequently comes through resistance to it—and salvaging in lands that do not play prominent roles in the capitalist economy are often spaces where individuals are free to salvage. Furthermore, not all squatting is salvaging, in that pristine lands can be foraged, but salvage foraging only occurs in broken landscapes, or landscapes that have been damaged through rounds of capitalist accumulation.

3. Hardt and Negri engage in a similar analysis of the intensification of segregation that accompanies the growth of urban centrality, in their discussion of the residential *banlieues* located on the outskirts of many French cities. They state that "the emblematic space of the precarious working in the European context is the poor metropolitan periphery, the *banlieue*. The *banlieusands* traverse all the frontiers of the city just to make a living every day, and a larger number of them participate during their lifetimes in massive continental and intercontinental migrations—and yet their movement is subject constantly to a complex set of obstacles, detained by the police and the hierarchies of property on the subway, in the streets and the shopping centers, and throughout the city. The *banlieusands* are socially excluded at the same time that they are completely within the processes of economic and social production (Hardt and Negri 2009, 245).

4. Tuan, from a non-Marxist perspective, makes a very similar observation when he states, "in contrast, modern life tends to be compartmentalized. In modern society, spatial organization is not able, nor was it ever intended to exemplify a total world view" (2001, 113).

5. Frank and Stevens claim that urban space, by its very nature, always possesses the possibility to become "loose" and thus be used in ways that designers never intended. They claim that these spaces often inflict a virus-like effect upon other spaces with "the potential of space to become loose may live in its relationship to other spaces. When the edge is porous one can see and move easily between space and easily straddle the barriers between them" (Franck and Stevens 2012, 9). Therefore, loose spaces, when found (and they are often

hidden, if not physically, then psychically, outside the habitual routines of most urban dwellers), can spread as individuals salvage them, transforming the spaces and themselves into what otherwise might not have been.

6. Merrifield goes on claim that "squatting and occupying buildings and streets are classic examples of *détournement*, as are graffiti and free associate art (Merrifield 2011, 27). Such assertions directly link this concepts to the examples of political salvage, which I will discuss later in this chapter.

7. Halverson also notes that ephemerality constitutes an important characteristic of Lefebvre's concept of the moment, and ties this concept to *détournement*. He notes in his study of Occupy London that taking space is often framed as a moment of rupture. He then invokes Lefebvre's understanding of the moment to describe the event, defining this concept as "'the attempt to achieve the total realization of a possibility,' which he often associated with the festival." These attempts to maximize the possibilities of experience "have both a duration and an intensity, from which they organize time and space, pushing back the boundaries of what was previously considered possible" (Halvorsen 2015, 406). In fact, instances of *détournement* can often lead to moments as creative reuses and displacements of familiar spaces. Symbols can also manifest the deepest possibilities of a particular situation. Halvorsen also notes the ephemerality of moments, further tying this concept to that of playful *détournement*. He notes that "the moment is destined to fail, and is both 'alienating and alienated.' If the moment is a festival then Lefebvre states it is 'a tragic festival'"(Halvorsen 2015, 407).

8. Ross also claims a similar importance for play and festival during the 1968 May Paris uprisings—yet she posits that the *détournement* occurred not simply within space, but also time. She argues, "The festival or pleasure of the clime of those days was not the residue that remains when politics has been subtracted, but it is in fact part and parcel of the concrete political action itself. . . . May and June . . . had a temporality all their own made up of sudden accelerations and immediate effects; the sensation that meditations and delays had all disappeared. Not only did time move faster than the forced time of bureaucracies it also surpassed the slow careful temporality that governs calculation. When the effect of one's action infinitely supersede one's expectations, or when a local initiative is met with impromptu echoes from a hundred different places all at once, space compresses and time goes faster" (Ross 2002, 102). Notice here how she links the repurposed sense of space creating linkages from "hundreds" of locations separated by the separations of the state-capitalist city, so that a new sense of time that supersedes "calculation" comes to be experienced by participants in the political festival.

9. Stanek emphasizes the grammatical distinction between inhabiting and habitat, stressing "Lefebvre's distinction between *habiter* (to inhabit) ("an activity a situation") and habitat (a morphological description)" (Stanek 2011, 83). Inhabitation connotes an active process undertaken by an individual, while a habitat

suggests a process, concretized in space but not consisting solely of space, but also involving practices, codes, meanings, and other people. This distinction between *habiter* as a verb and *habitat* as a noun helps to distinguish between the various translations of *habiter* as inhabit and habitate, or habitation, as in this passage.

10. David Harvey ties the qualities of appropriated spaces that I am articulating, spaces that do not simply allow for the chosen uses of a community but the fact that these spaces will be open to future uses and thus flexible, to the concept of heterotopia. He states, "Lefebvre, however fashioned an alternative view of heterotopia [to Foucault's usage of the term] He understood heterotopic as spaces of difference, of anomie, and of potential transformation, but he embedded them in a dialectical conception of urbanization" (Harvey 2009, 162). Lefebvre posited a permanent tension between rationalized abstract space and heterotopias, and not as an alternative to such spaces to stress the constant change and disruption inherent in the concept. Harvey goes on to state, "The differences captured within the hetertopic spaces . . . are about potentially transformative relations with all other spaces" (ibid.). Thus, appropriation of one space acts as a catalyst for the appropriation of other spaces, especially in in environments dominated by capitalist abstraction. Appropriation constitutes a heterotopia not simply because its fluidity stands in stark contrast to the strictures of abstract space, but also because such spaces propagate difference.

11. Lefebvre's understanding of the promise of New Babylon is predicated on the radical transformation of society through the end of capitalist relations of production. It is clearly utopian in many senses, although Lefebvre does believe its encouragement of multiple and ever-changing centralities finds its roots in the material contradictions of actual urban spaces. For a perhaps more concrete and immediate model of nomadism as embodying the politics of spatial appropriation I turn to Paul Routledge's account of the activist group People's Global Action. He describes how:

> PGA also organized activist caravans. These are buses of activists from various struggles around the world, which visit social movement struggles in countries other than their own. . . . Rather than being forms of political tourism, the PGA caravans are organized in order for activists from different struggles and countries to communicate with one another, exchange information, share experience and tactics, participate in various solidarity demonstrations, rallies and direct actions, and attempt to draw new movements into the convergence (Routledge, 2003, 340).

In essence this caravan represents a nomadic centrality that moves from concrete space to concrete space in an effort to facilitate communication and the formation of trans-national solidarities. These new combinations of activists constitute new appropriations that result in centralities that represent a combination of the use values desired by the local community and those of the visiting activists that scramble previously understood notions of identity, scale and locality.

12. Harvey goes so far as to argue that Lefebvre replaced the working class as the most likely revolutionary agent with urban dwellers. Harvey states, "In invoking the 'working class' as the agent of revolutionary change through his text, Lefebvre was tacitly suggesting that the revolutionary working class was constituted out of urban rather than exclusively factory workers. This he later observed, is a very different kind of class formation—fragmented and divided, multiple in its aims and needs, more often itinerant, disorganized and fluid rather than solidly implanted" (Harvey 2013, xiii).

13. Lefebvre's desire for an urban landscape that connected multiple centralities also embodies Harvey's desire to encourage political processes that "work across different scales" and "find ways to 'telescope in' the political insights and actions of another" (Harvey 2009, 229). The actions and political programs generated in one centrality, if it is connected with others, always possesses the potentiality to become an issue across a number of centralities, urban areas, and then perhaps nations.

14. For the concept of "desire lines" see Anonymous, "Streets With No Name" (2009).

Chapter 5. Choreographing Anticapitalist Salvage

1. Other participants noticed this difference, with one account relating, "We along with others, observed a growing difference between the sides of the park: participants and activities more directly connected to OWS were located on the east side, while people more engaged in just enjoying the opportunities offered were on the west side. Or as one person walking by was heard to comment, the punks are on this side the political science majors are on the other side" (Shiffman et al. 2012, 16).

2. This division based on profession also manifested itself in terms of spatial segregation in terms of race. "A young Latino occupier, David, described the Northeast side of the park as full of well-educated and mainly white people, including a sleep camp calling itself "Upper East Side Sacks." Meanwhile, Zuccotti's southwest side was "all black and Latino." "The divisions were just like New York City," David noted (the 99% et al. 2012, 64).

3. Such concerns were also voiced by participants in OWS, with one stating that "soon individual camping tents filled the park, densely covering not only the Southwest area, but also much of the previously open territory to the North and East. These privatized environments undermine the collectivism of the movement and its efforts at self-policing" (Massey and Snyder 2012).

4. She also refers to this principle as "relational difference" (Young and Allen 2011, 172), where others play a fundamental, if not mutually identical, role in the fulfillment of their goals and constitution of their subjectivity and thus form a basis for cooperation and democratic contestation.

5. In describing city life as such, Young draws on urban theorists such as Jane Jacobs, who states, "The tolerance, the room for great differences among neighbors—differences that often go far deeper than differences in color—which are possible and normal in intensely urban life, but which are so foreign to suburbs and pseudo suburbs, are possible and normal only when streets of great cities have built in equipment allowing strangers to dwell in peace together on civilized but essentially dignified and reserved terms" (Jacobs 1992, 73).

6. Young's supposition that exposure to diversity in urban settings will most likely result in greater tolerance and understanding of others has been contradicted by many accounts. Perhaps the most well-known is Lyn H. Lofland, *A World of Strangers: Order and Action in Urban Public Space* (1973). In this book Lofland stresses how city life can alienate urban dwellers from each other and circumscribe their awareness of spatial possibility.

7. Stavrides also describes the choreography of urban space not in terms of the rigid control of bodily movement, but as a method for training the body to open up to and explore the possibilities for different relationships to space. He claims, "Choreography conducts an anatomical investigation not of the body but of movement" (2019, 103).

8. Massumi expresses a similar aspiration in his desire to choreograph encounters that would result in "diagrams" facilitating critical becoming. He states that his approach creates the "opportunity for a kind of choreographic thinking which I define not as the imposition of a choreographic score, but as the creation of tools that enable the mobile diagram of speciations to come to the fore—a kind of incipient diagrammatic praxis" (Massumi 2015, 123). Once again, notice that he claims that the benefit of such choreography would be not the imposition of norms or virtues but instead the cultivation of "tools" and a "mobile diagram" much like a refrain—which allows for praxis—or experimenting with experience indicative of critical becoming.

9. Similarly, the architects who designed the salvage refurbishment of the Witznize Briquette Factory in Borna, Germany, state their intention as "like a bricoleur, we create design strategies that can cope with incompleteness and can transform a situation of multiplicity of styles and expectations into a plea-sure." They go on to state their goal as the creation of a "specific indeterminate architecture" (Matta-Clark, Smithson, and Koolhaas 2006, 136).

10. A specific example of such "developmental" or "weak" choreography within the world of dance can be seen Susan Leigh Foster's "contract improvisa-tion." This practice choreography constituted a type of guerrilla dance, wherein participants undertook their movements in public, undertaking a journey through

the streets guided by their spontaneous reactions to the environments through which they moved and the individuals they encountered. She notes that this practice is

> deftly situated between art, sport and sociality contact improvisation functioned throughout the Seventies as both aesthetic and social initiative. As dance it contented[okay?] the boundaries between pedestrian and art movement . . . claiming that its cultivation of agility and spontaneity could make of life a dance. It promoted egalitarian access and interaction with the form constructing many opportunities for success while avoiding hierarchies of evaluation. And it offered an intriguing new experience of subjectivity wherein dancers became defined by the contact between them. (Foster 2002, 132)

She goes on to state that the dancers "developed a spectacular bodily responsiveness" and a "shared sensibility for public interaction contact provided a focus for group activities and it also served as a model for communal living and sharing, group decision making and the sharing of power" (133).

11. Silvia Federici expresses something similar when she praises the radical potentialities for "reappropriating" the body from its capitalist discipline that comes about through dance:

> Dance is central to this reappropriation. In essence the act of dancing is an exploration, a divination of what a body can do; of its capacities, its languages its articulations of the strivings of our being. I have come to believe that there is a philosophy in dancing, for dance mimics the process by which we relate to the world, connect with other bodies, transform ourselves and the space around us. From dance we learn that matter is not stupid, it is not blind it is not mechanical but has it rhythms it is language and it is self activated and self organizing. (Federici 2020, 119)

12. Foster is highly critical of Judith Butler's well-known account of the importance of performativity in the construction of identity. She states, "Butler preserves the distinction between verbal and non-verbal acts. Her performativity provides no framework for the analysis of bodily movement" (Foster 2002, 138). Federici takes a similar tack in her criticism of a purely discursive description of performativity—in forgetting the powers of the body to act as a receptor of potentialities, many miss its powers as a site of resistance and tool for social criticism. She states, "There is something we have lost in our insistence on the body as something socially constructed and performative. The view of the body as a social (discursive) production has hidden the fact that our body is a

receptacle of powers, capacities and resistances that have been developed in a long process of coevolution with our natural environment as well as intergenerational practices that have made it a natural limit to exploitation" (Federici 2020, 119). Although her assertion that the body constitutes a "natural limit to exploitation" seems to imply that she believes the body to possess a universal, even metaphysical capacity for resistance, her insistence that its powers "have been developed in a long process" of encounter with both the natural and social world clearly aligns with my discussion of habit.

13. They describe this practice by stating:

> [T]ake half the group and classify them as "posts" their job is to sit or stand or lie in position in a circular formation at the edges of the room. The other half are "flows." As in speed dating, the flows move from one post to another, clockwise, at timed intervals. Next find what Deleuze and Guattari call a "minor" concept—a concept that activates the philosophical web of a text without drawing attention to itself as a special term. For Dancing the Virtual, the minor concept chosen was "terminus" found in William James's philosophy. It refers to the tendency orienting the unfolding of an event as it senses its potential completing and follows itself to culmination. . . . For conceptual speed dating the group is given the term, as well as a passage or page number to start from. At five minute intervals, the flows move from one post to another trying to sort out the concept. The force of the exercise plays itself out not only in the working through of the concept in parts but perhaps even more so in the moving-forward to the next pairing where a discussion takes up again, already infused with the previous conversation. (Manning and Massumi 2014, 97)

14. One final example of a quasi-artistic experience of critical choreography is the exhibit *The Phantom Public*. In this exhibit, the movement of visitors is tracked with radio frequency identification markers inserted in their tickets, and their various interactions with the space and with others trigger various visual and auditory stimuli, including maps, graphs, and other information concerning the space projected on floors and ceilings. This is meant to "devise an entirely new rhythm that depends, minute after minute, on the visitors' own attitudes through the whole 2,500 sq. meters of the show. At every moment the compound behavior of the *Phantom* depends upon the visitor's number, they spread across the space their interactions with one another and with the exhibit" (Latour and Weibel 2005, 218). The larger point of the exhibit, its creators explain, was to give the visitors a sense of their effect upon their interaction with the exhibit. They hope to endow their visitors with "a strong impression, as if he or she were inside a vibrating milieu of shifting consistency. Sometimes it weighs

very heavily as a sort of suffocating presence; at other times on the contrary, it 'breathes,' easily allowing participants to connect with others and to express themselves with greater freedom" (220). The exhibit engages in "launching a series of rules that might have some traceable consequences—or might not. In watching puzzled, some of the effects [and possibly affects] generated by our black box, we are actually imitating rather closely some of the most puzzling features of political production" (221). Thus, the exhibits hopes to recreate the vague, pulsating senses of our own impact upon the larger phantom public, and how distant political phenomena produce vague affects in ourselves.

15. In a similar discussion of the stimulating effects of corridors, Sheller states that "[i]n contrast to privileging efficient flows of traffic and unfettered mobility whether for the fast-moving pedestrian or the rush-hour automobile commuter, we might argue that there are vital frictions that take place within the uneven terrains of corporeal mobilities, for example as diverse people pass on a sidewalk as they mix slow and pause for social encounters of conviviality or conflict" (Sheller 2018, 56). Such "vital frictions," of course, occur at different intensities, especially when the space contains diverse inhabitants.

16. Peter Sloterdijk articulates a similar interpretation of the "atmosphere" of the Pnyx when he states, "[D]emocracy is based on the proto-architectonic ability to build waiting rooms, [not?] to mention the proto-political ability to disarm citizens" (Latour and Weibel 2005, 944).

17. Sloterdijk similarly highlights the importance of this contrast in Athenian democracy when he discusses how these two spaces encouraged a "combination of actor and spectator" (Latour and Weibel 2005, 948).

18. Franck and Stevens contrast what they see as the tendency of "skating" between locations in streets or corridors to "threshold spaces which are comfortable and expansive" that "can also facilitate a range of more relaxed behavior. Thresholds are designed to make the transition between inside and outside gradual and leisurely" (Franck and Stevens 2012, 84).

19. Stavrides also claims that the boundary thresholds of the occupied parks in Athens encouraged new forms of threshold communities. He relates that "space commoning the reappropriated square involved the production and use of in-between spaces. Common spaces emerge as threshold spaces, spaces not demarcated by defining perimeter. Whereas public space bears the mark of a prevailing authority that defines it common space is opened space, space in a process of opening toward 'newcomers.'" Common spaces are porous spaces in movement, space passages (Stavrides 2019, 220). I will discuss the political formation of the "common" in much greater detail in the next chapter. At this point all that is necessary to note is how thresholds can also act as settings for the formation of relationships and even community.

20. It could be said that the Occupy Sandy movement—the effort to engage in mutual aid after Hurricane Sandy in New York—was an example of an encampment "moving." As I stated before in my discussion of "disaster

communism," many participants in Occupy Wall Street participated in this effort, and a type of "encampment" was set up in a church in Brooklyn that acted as a base of operations and community-gathering space. One activist described this "encampment" by stating:

> I volunteered with Occupy Sandy after the storm hit at The Church of St. Luke and St. Matthew in Clinton Hill, where the organizers of Occupy Sandy set up camp. Each day, hundreds of volunteers came by. Some went to Coney Island, The Rockaways, or Red Hook to figure out what residents needed. Some showed up with cars and vans full of donated food, clothing, and supplies to distribute. Some stayed at the church to coordinate volunteers and donations. And some sat and listened to the stories of residents who lost everything—giving hugs, shedding tears with them, and offering words of comfort. (Huang 2015)

Notice here how the church acted not simply as a depot for supplies, but also as a meeting place where people shared stories and affection.

21. For a thorough discussion of this community see McGuirk 2014, 80–89.

22. This description can be found in Graeber 2013.

Chapter 6. Salvage and the Politics of the Commons

1. As I stated before, Connolly defines plural becoming in terms of practices and what he calls a "political ethos." Connolly has not linked the principle of the commons to his work, nor do I claim that he would make such an assertion—that the politics of becoming is also a politics of the commons. What I want to do is to use his work as an intermediary between salvage and the commons. I want to state that salvage is a type of becoming, with its attendant political possibilities. One of those possibilities, the linkage of salvage to becoming, is a politics of the commons.

2. Some leftists misinterpret the presence of such organizational norms within well-functioning commons as the necessity for the commons to be protected by state-sanctioned property rights. For example, Desai states, "The commons were defined by complex institutional arrangements which provided rights to some sets of users and explicitly excluded others The earth, culture and language or even our genetic inheritance are only open to corporate predation to the extent that they are not protected by regimes of property rights. . . . [P]rotecting them requires creating rules of access. . . . [T]here is no alternative to state enforcement." She goes on to state, "The abolition of property" which the

"new communists of the commons" such as Hardt and Negri (about whom I will speak in this chapter), "would only lead to the sort of free-for-all that Hardin, not to mention Hobbes, feared, a sort of state of nature in which the powerful would be able to appropriate at the expense of the weak" (Desai 2011, 215). While it is true that within the regime of the state securing property rights for sites of the commons does offer protection from capitalist appropriation and state intervention, this says nothing of the internal workings of the commons, which depend on noninstitutional norms such as mutual reciprocity and negotiation. Finally, while many iterations of the commons might depend on formalizing their property rights, this constitutes a survival tactic for existence within capitalism, not a characteristic necessary for their existence as common social formations as such. Thus, Desai's reliance on Hardin's understanding without any mention of Ostrom's deep empirical work on the actual workings of the commons underplays the radical potential of the inner workings of such groups.

3. Other theorists, such as Hardt and Negri, argue that "the task of the commoner, then, is not only to provide access to the fields and rivers so that the poor can feed themselves, but also to create a means for the free exchange of ideas, images, codes, music, and information" (2012, 89).

4. One provocative historical example of "commoning" can be seen in radical political movements during the English Civil War. As Hill notes, "If we see the New Model Army as a short-lived school of political democracy, commons wastes and forests were longer-lasting though less intensive schools in economic democracy" (1984, 128).

5. Other theorists of the commons refer to this necessity as "translation." Stavrides gives an example of such translation by recounting that "around a collective kitchen's pot, at the benches of an occupied square and during the long sleepless nights in front of the popular barricades of Oaxaca Commune, common space was weaved through acts of translation that created common stakes, new shared habits and views and new common dreams" (2016, 43).

6. Harvey also characterizes the commons as more a process of building a type of relationship than a specific type of organization. He states, "The common is not to be construed, therefore as a particular kind of thing, asset or even social process, but as an unstable and malleable social relation between a particular self-defined social group and those aspects of its actually existing or yet-to-be-created social and/or physical environment deemed crucial to its life or livelihood. There is in effect a social process of *commoning*" (2013, 73).

7. Due to the lack of any unifying values or identities and the emphasis upon a process that, by design, will result in temporary solutions, the commons itself becomes an even more important node of convergence for the group. Such common spaces both hold the commons together and encourage the encounters that prompt translations of difference that lead to change and becoming. As

Stavrides notes, "Common space may take the form of a meeting ground, an area in which expansive circuits of encounter intersect" (2016, 56).

8. I thoroughly acknowledge that Berlant would most likely characterize this project as expressing a "naive" hope in the possible, yet provisional positive promise of the commons. Yet, in this essay I would assert that she expresses, or at least approaches, many of the themes, if not the general tenor, of the salvage pessimists that I discuss in chapter 1.

9. Here, I consciously invoke Habermas's understanding of this concept, but without the metaphysical justification and in a much less formal and rule-bound manifestation (Meter 2017, 153).

10. Theorists such as Martin Breaugh who use the Commune as an example of what they call "plebeian" politics would most likely disagree with my assessment of the compatibility of Marx's work with any commons-based understanding of revolutionary politics,. Those like him who use the commons as an example of such plebeian politics bristle at attempts to reconcile more plural understandings of revolutionary classes with Marx's work. Marx's positive assessment of the Russian commune should allay fears that communism and the political actors advocating for the end of capitalism need only stem from one particular social and economic environment. See Breaugh 2013.

11. Some might be scathingly critical of the supposition that Marx was anything but hostile to a radical politics based in the common. Desai emphasizes that what she deems the "new communists of the common" deny the possibility of any "general organization of labor in society" because she believes it leads to "petty bourgeois fantasies about doing away with any overall coordination of the economy, fantasies that also rest, in effect, on accepting market coordination" (2011, 214). While I will dwell upon this in more detail later, I would emphasize that such a focus on the commons and its local roots need not exclude coordination, just the hierarchical coordination typical of Soviet economic policy.

12. My earlier discussion of the creativity of the workshop should belie this stereotypical image of the practices of artisans.

13. David Graeber makes a similar point concerning the imbrication of "material" and "immaterial" labor, but does so to claim that such a distinction never made sense—that capitalist production was always a combination of both. He argues, "One could after all go back and ask whether it ever really made sense to think of commodities as objects whose value was simply the product of factory labor in the first place. What ever happened to all those dandies, bohemians, and *flaneurs* in the 19th century, not to mention newsboys, street musicians, and purveyors of patent medicines? Were they just window-dressing? Actually, what about window dressing (an art famously promoted by L. Frank Baum, the creator of the Wizard of Oz books)? Wasn't the creation of value always in this sense a collective undertaking?" (2008, 7). I believe that while Graeber does make an important point concerning the necessary co-presence

of the material and the immaterial in all labor, this does not exclude the possibility of particular historical periods leaning toward one ideal/typical mode of production or the other.

14. Desai states that the creative class and petit bourgeoisie that she interprets as the core of Hardt and Negri's account of biopolitical production produce merely "fictitious capital" (2011, 217) and thus organizing based on such workers cannot truly attack the core of capitalist value production. What Hardt and Negri emphasize here is that traditional material production is increasingly intertwined with what Desai dismisses as "unproductive labor" (unproductive of value). Are the individuals who produce the code for the navigation systems of contemporary automobiles not engaged in the production of value? Desai's argument (which is admittedly somewhat dated) would seem to suggest this.

15. For an account of how everyday household items are increasingly used to collect personal data see Zuboff 2019.

16. The increasing prominence of rent in contemporary capitalism comes mostly through its increasing reliance on "accumulation by dispossession," as described by David Harvey. He argues that as traditional forms of capital accumulation become less lucrative as the rate of profit declines, capitalists, in league with governments, try to find new activities and spaces for profit. They do this by forcefully transforming what was public into what was private—this can take the form of land, activities, or services. For example, instead of free public education, school becomes a pay service enterprise. These fees are rents—payments for necessities, such as schools, roads, and parks, that once came from the public coffers. For the concept of "accumulation by dispossession" and its relationship to rents, see Harvey 2018.

17. Graeber, once again, questions the utility of Hardt and Negri's definition of biopolitical or immaterial labor, this time as a basis for conceptualizing modern forms of resistance. He claims that many adherents of this concept, including Negri, invoke it because they see it describing the normative potentials lying fallow within contemporary capitalist labor. He claims they harbor the supposition that "we are already living under communism, if only we come to realize it" (Graber 2008, 13). Instead, Graeber sees his supposition that production has always included both the material and the immaterial heralds another political potentiality. He argues,

> [W]ould it not be better to, as I suggested earlier, reexamine the past in the light of the present? Perhaps communism has always been with us. We are just trained not to see it. Perhaps everyday forms of communism are really—as Kropotkin in his own way suggested in Mutual Aid, even though even he was never willing to realize the full implications of what he was saying—the basis for most significant forms of human achievement, even those ordinarily attributed to

capitalism. If we can extricate ourselves from the shackles of fashion, the need to constantly say that whatever is happening now is necessarily unique and unprecedented (and thus, in a sense, unchanging, since everything apparently must always be this way) we might be able to grasp history as a field of permanent possibility, in which there is no particular reason we can't at least try to begin building a redemptive future at any time. (Graber 2008, 16).

Graeber's point remains particularly provocative for my argument in light of my use of craftwork and peasant *metis* as concrete models of the plural becoming indicative of salvage. Thus, I see Graeber's intervention here as productively expanding on Hardt and Negri's account in that he links the tradition of peasant *metis* to contemporary biopolitical production. Both forms of human action embody a type of common, participatory reason based on creativity, improvisation, and even craftiness. That biopolitical production might embody a form of *metis* that is not new but simply an iteration of a longstanding tradition does not negate its usefulness as an analytic category.

18. As I noted in the first chapter, Tsing sees salvage spaces as not contradictory but as complementary to traditional forms of capitalist accumulation, and thus, it would seem safe to say, the geography of contemporary capitalism. She calls these spaces "pericapitalist" (Tsing 2015, 21) and interprets them as providing resources that fit well within global capitalist supply chains, although their method of accumulation remains outside of the logic of exploitation of labor power. Yet even Tsing's account of matsutake foragers notes tensions between the foragers and the managers of the public lands upon which they forage. It stands to reason that as public lands become both more scarce and subject to capitalist exploitation (many public lands are leased to companies for resource extraction) the tensions will become more pronounced and salvagers will experience greater difficulties in undertaking their role as "pericapitalists." Such tensions evoke the dynamic recounted by Mylar in her account of the Rio dump—although the salvagers play a temporary role in their local economy, such relationships have a tendency toward tenuousness. Thus, Tsing's understanding of a relatively smooth relationship between salvage and capitalism seems somewhat optimistic, even when such salvage efforts are not tied to political resistance, such as in the cases about which I am speaking. I would argue that such official attempts to control or eliminate salvage possess the potentiality to transform into political resistance.

19. Poverty manifesting itself as more of an existential condition that might apply to those who possess material resources and that could generate radical politics has been a theme explored by other writers, especially Walter Benjamin. He states in his essay "Poverty and Experience" that, after World War I, "a completely new poverty has descended on mankind." This new poverty

was grounded not in lack of resources but spoke of a "poverty of experience" brought about by a lack of ability to either assimilate or communicate the rush of experiences brought about by the dislocations of changing technology and the horrors of war. He goes on to claim that this new poverty brings about a desire for a new "barbarism." He asks, "What does poverty of experience do for the barbarian? It forces him to start from scratch; to make a new start; to make a little go a long way, to begin with a little and build up further, looking neither left nor right" (Benjamin and Jennings 1999, 734). My interpretation of the premise of Benjamin's description of poverty lies in his vacillation between the "new" start that the barbarian takes using nothing, a "tabula rasa," and the barbarians' use of something to make "a little go a long way." He seems to resolve this ambiguity later in the essay through his discussion of the housing that would be appropriate to this poverty-induced barbarism, which he claims is informed by a stark modernism bereft of ornamentation, particularly adorned with smooth, glass walls, "to which nothing can be fixed."(Benjamin and Jennings 1999, 736) He particularly invokes the architecture of Le Corbusier and Adolph Loos. What remains particularly relevant for this argument, that poverty constitutes a condition of political salvage seen as a "craft of the poor," are the aesthetic differences between these two architects. While Le Corbusier is known for his imposing glass facades, Loos was known for simpler if unadorned aesthetic. As Sennett notes, his own house was built with very few resources, forcing him to often salvage. He claims that Loos's "lack of money often combined with the aesthetics of simplicity" (Sennett 2008, 257), and that he had to "respond positively to the difficulties he encountered. . . . [N]ecessity stimulated his sense of form" (258). His lack of materials, his inability to construct simply anywhere, and his episodic work schedule became part of the building itself, and, at least to Sennett, resulted in many design innovations and aesthetic triumphs absent in the "perfect buildings" built by the wealthy. Thus, although Benjamin implies that the barbarism prompted by poverty manifests itself as a desire to begin anew with nothing, it can also be interpreted as the need to begin again salvaging in the detritus that surrounds us.

20. For an account of the "plebeian" political tradition and its similarities to and differences from classical Marxism see Breaugh 2013.

21. Critics of Hardt and Negri often miss this point: that the multitude is not confined to the "creative class" or small-scale production by the "petit bourgeois." For example, Desai states, "The deluded individualism of the new petty bourgeois concept of itself as creative class leads the new communists [such as Hardt and Negri]to defer and deny any possibility of a 'general organization of labor in society'" (Desai 2011, 220). Her emphasis on radicals advocating for "the general organization of labor in society" relies on what Desai claims is "historically necessary in a society whose productive capacity had come to rest on large scale production." She goes on to claim, "This is why Marx and

Engels so resolutely opposed anarchist tendencies and so scathingly criticized petty bourgeois fantasies about doing away with any overall coordination of the economy, fantasies that also rested in effect on accepting market coordination" (Desai 2011, 214). Her claim that any truly radical movement must envision the coordination of "large scale production" and thus the network nature of the multitude could only result in small groups with "anarchist" orientations that could never work together not only misunderstands the concept of the multitude but contemporary capitalist production itself. Contemporary global capitalism, although increasingly concentrated in ownership, is increasingly decentralized in production. Just in time production organized around numerous shifting sub-contractors. The networked nature of the multitude with its numerous nodes of resistance responding to specific struggles reflects this. Whereas Desai sees this emphasis upon local networked resistance as reflecting a desire for autonomous worker-controlled shops competing with each other, and thus a reflection of "Proudhounism," the localism and network-based organizing of the multitude instead reflects this new form of production. In terms of what might happen "after the revolution" or, in other words, the vision of production desired by the multitude, once the centralized ownership and influence of a particular firm is dissolved within an industry, there is nothing stopping the various sites of production that were once under direct or indirect control of a certain firm from coordinating with each other.

22. For a similar account this contemporary manifestation of political activism see the notion of "blockadia" (Klein 2014).

23. BLM has, at least in one instance, established a salvaged protest camp in Seattle, Washington, known by many as CHAZ, the Capitol Hill Autonomous Zone (Golden 2020).

24. Feigenbaum and the other authors of *Protest Camps* claim that "Hardt and Negri argue against territorializing strategies of placemaking, which they associate with nationalism. Hardt and Negri's nomads, it is reasonably safe to assume are not building camps" (Feigenbaum, Frenzel, and McCurdy 2013, 189). But it is clear in numerous places in various texts that Hardt and Negri see no contradiction between exodus, nomadism, and grounding the protest and constitution of the multitude in particular spaces. To give one example, they state that "today's movements of the subordinated do appropriate the spaces in which they live and they do produce the wealth they want—and this is really a new characteristic of social and class struggle—they have no propensity to divide either in terms of individual or corporate interest; instead they accumulate diverse collective desire" (Hardt and Negri 2017, 237–38). Thus, they are not averse to particular places, simply to particular interests, identities, and desires that are often associated with particular spaces. Exodus will result not in the avoidance of protest spaces, but new types of spaces. Furthermore, nomads do

establish camps; it is simply that they occasionally move these camps in reaction to new goals and desires.

25. See Turkewitz 2019.

26. See Alves 2019.

Conclusion

1. See Wells 2014.

2. See Perkins 2017.

3. My use of the term *concrete utopia* here comes from Ernst Bloch, who attempted to shift the traditional Marxist animosity toward utopia into a more materialist, dialectical concept that would not raise such ire on the Left. He claims that concrete utopias are not mere idealistic creations of a better world, but flow from actual conditions. Many have used this term and other similar terms to describe the nascent, hopeful, actual potentialities for radical political transformation contained within political failures. For example, Ross states:

> By granting pre-capitalist societies an exemplary status or by investing them with uncommon significance, they may in turn offer ideas that can be appropriated, in the strong sense of the word favored by Henri Lefebvre. They become "anticipatory designs," "novae," in the words of Ernst Bloch, or "exemplary suggestions" to borrow a phrase from Peter Linebaugh. The fact that in Iceland after the twelfth century, wealth and power did accumulate in the hands of a few as the edifice of a state came into being is of little importance to Morris as is the "failure" of the commune—in both cases, for those who lived it, a type of liberty and a network of solidarity were realized and out of local defeat there may well come a prototype for future social revolution. (Ross 2016, 76)

4. For an example of this during Occupy Oakland see Balderson 2012.

5. For an example of *favela* dwellers playing a decisive role in the maintenance of the Chavez and the subsequent "Bolivarian" regime in Venezuela see Ciccariello-Maher 2016.

Works Cited

Alves, Lise. "Over 1.3 Million Hectares of Forests Disappeared in Brazil in 2018." *The Rio Times*, April 28, 2019. https://riotimesonline.com/brazil-news/rio-politics/over-1-3-million-hectares-of-forests-disappeared-in-brazil-in-2018/.

Anonymous. "Streets with No Name." *SweetJuniper* (blog). 2009. http://www.sweet-juniper.com/2009/06/streets-with-no-name.html.

Anonymous. "Updates from the Greek Squares and People's Assemblies" *Mute*, July 1, 2011. http://www.metamute.org/community/your-posts/updates-greek-squares-and-peoples-assemblies.

Balderson, Bill. "Occupy Oakland and the Labor Movement." *New Politics* (blog), 2012. https://newpol.org/issue_post/occupy-oakland-and-labor-movement/.

Ballantyne, Andrew. *Deleuze & Guattari for Architects*. Routledge, 2007.

Barlow, Maude, and Tony Clarke. "The Struggle for Latin America's Water." NACLA, September 25, 2007. https://nacla.org/article/struggle-latin-america%27s-water.

Beaumont, Matthew, and Gregory Dart, editors. *Restless Cities*. Verso, 2010.

Benjamin, Walter. *Illuminations: Essays and Reflections*, edited by Hannah Arendt, translated by Harry Zohn. Schocken Books, 1969.

———.*Selected Writings Volume 2: 1927–1934*, edited by Walter Jennings. Harvard UP, 1999.

Bennett, Jane. *Vibrant Matter: A Political Ecology of Things*. Duke UP, 2010.

Berger, Yotam. "Israel Demolishes Protest Shacks Built by Palestinian Activists Near Khan Al-Ahmar." *Haaretz*, September 13, 2018. https://www.haaretz.com/israel-news/.premium-israeli-forces-demolish-protest-shacks-built-near-khan-al-ahmar-1.6468956.

Berlant, Lauren. *Cruel Optimism*. Duke UP, 2011.

———. "The Commons: Infrastructures for Troubling Times" *Environment and Planning D: Society and Space*, vol. 34, no. 3, 2016, pp. 393–419.

Bignall, Simone, Sean Bowden, and Paul Patton, editors. *Deleuze and Pragmatism*. Routledge, 2017.

Bitter, Sabine, and Helmut Weber. *Autogestion, or Henri Lefebvre in New* Belgrad, edited by Jeff Derksen. Sternberg Press and Fillip Editions, 2009.

Blumenkranz, Carla, Keith Gessen, Mark Greif, Sarah Leonard, and Sarah Resnick, editors. *Occupy!: Scenes from Occupied America.* Verso, 2011.

Boggs, Grace Lee, Scott Kurashige, and Danny Glover. *The Next American Revolution: Sustainable Activism for the Twenty-First Century,* foreword by Danny Glover, afterword by Immanuel Wallerstein. U of California P, 2012.

Bolton, Matthew, Stephen Froese, and Alex Jeffrey. "This Space Is Occupied!: The Politics of Occupy Wall Street's Expeditionary Architecture and De-Gentrifying Urbanism." In *Occupying Political Science: The Occupy Wall Street Movement from New York to the World,* edited by Emily Welty, Matthew Bolton, Meghana Nayak, and Christopher Malone. Palgrave Macmillan, 2013, pp. 135–61.

Boyte, Harry C. *Commonwealth: A Return to Citizen Politics.* Free Press, 1989.

———. *Awakening Democracy through Public Work: Pedagogies of Empowerment.* Vanderbilt UP. 2018.

———, and Nancy N. Kari. *Building America: The Democratic Promise of Public Work.* Temple UP, 1996.

Bray, Mark. *Translating Anarchy: The Anarchism of Occupy Wall Street.* Zero Books 2013.

Breaugh, Martin. *The Plebeian Experience: A Discontinuous History of Political Freedom,* translated by Lazer Lederhendler. Columbia UP, 2013.

Buck-Morss, Susan. *The Dialectics of Seeing: Walter Benjamin and the Arcades Project.* The MIT P, 1989.

Butler, Chris. *Henri Lefebvre: Spatial Politics, Everyday Life and the Right to the City.* Routledge-Cavendish, 2012.

Butler, Judith. *Senses of the Subject.* Fordham UP. 2015.

———. *Notes toward a Performative Theory of Assembly,* reprint edition. Harvard UP, 2018.

Casarino, Cesare. *In Praise of the Common: A Conversation on Philosophy and Politics.* U of Minnesota P, 2009.

Chalfin, Brenda. "Public Things, Excremental Politics, and the Infrastructure of Bare Life in Ghana's City of Tema." *American Ethnologist,* vol. 41, no. 1, 2014, pp. 92–109.

———. "'Wastelandia': Infrastructure and the Commonwealth of Waste in Urban Ghana." *Ethnos,* vol. 82, no. 4, 2017, pp. 648–71.

Chari, Anita. *A Political Economy of the Senses: Neoliberalism, Reification, Critique.* Columbia UP, 2015.

Ciccariello-Maher, George. *Building the Commune: Radical Democracy in Venezuela.* Verso, 2016.

Clough, Patricia Ticineto, and Jean Halley, editors. *The Affective Turn: Theorizing the Social.* Duke UP, 2007.

Clover, Joshua. *Riot. Strike. Riot: The New Era of Uprisings.* Verso, 2016.

Coles, Romand. *Visionary Pragmatism: Radical and Ecological Democracy in Neoliberal Times.* Duke UP, 2016.

Collective, Mauvaise Troupe. *The Zad and NoTAV: Territorial Struggles and the Making of a New Political Intelligence,* translated by Kristin Ross. Verso, 2018.

Connolly, William E. *Neuropolitics: Thinking, Culture, Speed.* U of Minnesota P, 2002.

———. *Pluralism.* Duke UP, 2005.

———. *Capitalism and Christianity, American Style.* Duke UP, 2008.

———. *A World of Becoming.* Duke UP, 2011.

———. *The Fragility of Things: Self-Organizing Processes, Neoliberal Fantasies, and Democratic Activism.* Duke UP, 2013.

Crary, Jonathan. *24/7: Late Capitalism and the Ends of Sleep.* Verso, 2014.

Crawford, Matthew B. *Shop Class as Soulcraft: An Inquiry into the Value of Work,* reprint edition. Penguin, 2010.

Crimethink Collective. "The Spiders of Mutual Aid: Solidarity and Direct Action—A Report and How-To Guide From May Day in Portland Oregon." 2017. https://crimethinc.com/2017/05/03/the-spiders-of-mutual-aid-solidarity-and-direct-action-a report-and-how-to-guide-from-may-day-in-portland-oregon.

crow, scott. *Black Flags and Windmills: Hope, Anarchy and the Common Ground Collective.* AK Press, 2014.

Damasio, Antonio. *The Feeling of What Happens: Body and Emotion in the Making of Consciousness.* Mariner Books, 2000.

Danisch, Robert, editor. *Recovering Overlooked Pragmatists in Communication: Extending the Living Conversation about Pragmatism and Rhetoric.* Palgrave Macmillan, 2020.

Davis, Mike. "Learning from Tijuana." *Grand Street,* vol. 14, 1996, pp. 33–36.

———. *Planet of Slums,* reprint edition. Verso, 2007.

———. *Old Gods, New Enigmas: Marx's Lost Theory.* Verso, 2018.

Dawson, Ashley. *Extreme Cities: The Peril and Promise of Urban Life in the Age of Climate Change.* Verso, 2017.

Dean, Jodi. "Communicative Capitalism: Circulation and the Foreclosure of Politics." *Cultural Politics,* vol. 1, no. 1, 2005, pp. 51–74.

———. *Crowds and Party.* Verso, 2016.

Deleuze, Gilles. *The Fold: Leibniz and the Baroque.* U of Minnesota P, 1992.

———. *Difference and Repetition,* translated by Paul Patton, revised ed. Columbia UP, 1995.

———. *Negotiations 1972–1990,* translated by Martin Joughin, revised edition. Columbia UP, 1997.

———. *Spinoza: Practical Philosophy,* translated by Robert Hurley. City Lights, 2001.

————, and Felix Guattari. *A Thousand Plateaus: Capitalism and Schizophrenia*, translated by Brian Massumi, 2nd edition. U of Minnesota P, 1987.

Detienne, Marcel, and Jean-Pierre Vernant. *Cunning Intelligence in Greek Culture and Society*, translated by Janet Lloyd. U of Chicago P. 1991.

Dewey, John. *The Middle Works of John Dewey, 1899–1924, Vol. 1: Essays on School and Society, 1899–1901*, edited by Jo Ann Boydston. Southern Illinois UP, 1983.

————. *The Later Works of John Dewey, Volume 8, 1925–1953: 1933, Essays and How We Think, Revised Edition*, edited by Jo Ann Boydston. Southern Illinois UP, 1986.

————. *The Later Works of John Dewey, Volume 5, 1925–1953: 1929–1930, Essays, The Sources of a Science of Education, Individualism, Old and New, And . . .* , edited by Jo Ann Boydston. Southern Illinois UP, 2008a.

————. *The Later Works of John Dewey, Volume 10, 1925–1953: 1934, Art as Experience*, edited by Jo Ann Boydston. Southern Illinois UP, 2008b.

————. *The Middle Works of John Dewey, Volume 9, 1899–1924: Democracy and Education, 1916*, edited by Jo Ann Boydston. Southern Illinois UP, 2008c.

————. *The Later Works of John Dewey, Volume 1, 1925–1953: 1925, Experience and Nature*, edited by Jo Ann Boydston. Southern Illinois UP, 2008d.

Diouf, M., and R. Fredericks, editors. *The Arts of Citizenship in African Cities: Infrastructures and Spaces of Belonging*. Palgrave Macmillan, 2014.

Duncombe, Stephen. *Notes From the Underground: Zines and the Politics of Alternative Culture.* Microcosm, 2017.

Dupont, Monsieur. *Nihilist Communism: A Critique of Optimism in the Far Left*. Ardent Press, 2009.

Ehrenreich, Barbara. *Dancing in the Streets: A History of Collective Joy*. Metropolitan Books, 2007.

Escobar, Arturo. *Designs for the Pluriverse: Radical Interdependence, Autonomy, and the Making of Worlds*. Duke UP, 2018.

Evans, Sara M., and Harry C. Boyte. *Free Spaces: The Sources of Democratic Change in America*. U of Chicago P, 1992.

Fairfield, Paul, James Scott Johnston, Tom Rockmore, James A. Good, Jim Garrison, Barry Allen, Joseph Margolis et al. *John Dewey and Continental Philosophy*. Southern Illinois UP, 2010.

Federici, Silvia. *Beyond the Periphery of the Skin: Rethinking, Remaking, and Reclaiming the Body in Contemporary Capitalism*. PM Press, 2020.

Feigenbaum, Anna, Fabian Frenzel, and Patrick McCurdy. *Protest Camps*. Zed Books, 2013.

Finnegan, William. "Leasing the Rain." *The New Yorker*, April 1, 2002. https://www.newyorker.com/magazine/2002/04/08/leasing-the-rain.

Fischer, Clara. "Feminist Philosophy, Pragmatism, and the 'Turn to Affect': A Genealogical Critique." *Hypatia*, vol. 31, no. 4, 2016, pp. 810–26.

Fisher, Mark. *The Weird and the Eerie*. Repeater, 2017.

Flood, Catherine, and Gavin Grindon. *Disobedient Objects*. V & A Publishing, 2014.

Foster, Susan Leigh. "Walking and Other Choreographic Tactics: Danced Inventions of Theatricality and Performativity." *SubStance*, vol. 31, no. 2/3, 2002, pp. 125.

Franck, Karen, and Quentin Stevens, editors. *Loose Space: Possibility and Diversity in Urban Life*. Routledge, 2012.

Fredericks, Rosalind. *Garbage Citizenship: Vital Infrastructures of Labor in Dakar, Senegal*. Duke UP, 2018.

Freeman, Jo. "The Tyranny of Stucturelessness." 1972. https://www.jofreeman. com/joreen/tyranny.htm.

Garrett, Bradley. *Explore Everything: Place-Hacking the City*. Verso, 2013.

Gebrekidan, Selam, and Norimitsu Onishi. "In South Africa's Fabled Wine Country, White and Black Battle Over Land." *The New York Times*, March 9, 2019, World.

Giles, David Boarder. "The Anatomy of a Dumpster: Abject Capital and the Looking Glass of Value." *Social Text*, vol. 32, no. 1(118), 2014, pp. 93–113.

Golden, Hallie. "Seattle Protesters Take over City Blocks to Create Police-Free 'Autonomous Zone.'" *The Guardian*, June 12, 2020, U.S. news.

Goonewardena, Kanishka, Stefan Kipfer, Richard Milgrom, and Christian Schmid. *Space, Difference, Everyday Life: Reading Henri Lefebvre*. Routledge, 2008.

Graeber, David. "The Sadness of Post-Workerism." Libcom.Org., 2008. http:// libcom.org/library/sadness-post-workerism.

———. *Direct Action: An Ethnography*. AK Press, 2009.

———. *Debt: The First 5,000 Years*, reprint edition. Melville House, 2012.

———. *The Democracy Project: A History, a Crisis, a Movement*. Spiegel & Grau, 2013.

Hailey, Charlie. *Camps: A Guide to 21st-Century Space*. The MIT P, 2009.

Halberstam, Jack. *The Queer Art of Failure*. Duke UP. 2011.

Halvorsen, Sam. "Taking Space: Moments of Rupture and Everyday Life in Occupy London." *Antipode*, vol.47, no. 2, 2015, pp. 401–17.

Hardin, Garrett. "The Tragedy of the Commons." *Science*, 162, Dec. 1968, pp. 1243–48.

Hardt, Michael, and Antonio Negri. *Empire*. Harvard UP, 2001.

———. *Multitude: War and Democracy in the Age of Empire*. Penguin, 2004.

———. *Commonwealth*. Belknap Press, 2009.

———. *Declaration*. Argo-Navis, 2012.

———. *Assembly*. Oxford UP, 2017.

Harvey, David. *Paris, Capital of Modernity*. Routledge, 2005.

———. *Cosmopolitanism and the Geographies of Freedom*. Columbia UP, 2009.

———. *Rebel Cities: From the Right to the City to the Urban Revolution*. Verso, 2013.

Hazan, Eric. *A History of the Barricade*. Verso, 2015a.

———. *A History of the Barricade*. Verso, 2015b.

Hill, Christopher. *The World Turned Upside Down: Radical Ideas During the English Revolution*. Penguin, 1984.

Hirschhorn, Thomas. *Thomas Hirschhorn: Gramsci Monument*. Dia Art Foundation, in association with Koenig Books, 2015.

Huang, Kerry. "Inside Story: What Occupy Sandy's Disaster Relief Model Taught Me about Organizing to Meet Our Neighborhoods' Greatest Needs." *Ioby* (blog), July 16, 2015. https://www.ioby.org/blog/inside-story-what-occupy-sandys-disaster-relief-model-taught-me-about-organizing-to-meet-our-neighborhoods-greatest-needs.

"Indonesia Plans to Move Capital from Jakarta." April 29, 2019. https://www.aljazeera.com/news/2019/04/indonesia-plans-move-capital-jakarta-1904291 54834438.html.

Jackson, Shannon. *Lines of Activity: Performance, Historiography, Hull-House Domesticity*. U of Michigan P, 2000.

Jacobs, Jane. *The Death and Life of Great American Cities*, reissue edition. Vintage, 1992.

"Jewish Community Center—Data, Photos & Plans." WikiArquitectura. https://en.wikiarquitectura.com/building/jewish-community-center/. Accessed August 12, 2019.

Klein, Naomi. *This Changes Everything: Capitalism vs. The Climate*. Simon and Schuster, 2014.

Kohlstedt, Kurt. "Least Resistance: How Desire Paths Can Lead to Better Design." *99% Invisible* (blog), January 26, 2016. https://99percentinvisible.org/article/least-resistance-desire-paths-can-lead-better-design/.

Kollective, Squatting Europe, editors. *The Squatters' Movement in Europe: Commons and Autonomy as Alternatives to Capitalism*. Pluto Press, 2014.

Konings, Martijn. *The Emotional Logic of Capitalism: What Progressives Have Missed*. Stanford UP, 2015.

Kosnoski, Jason. *John Dewey and the Habits of Ethical Life: The Aesthetics of Political Organizing in a Liquid World*. Lexington Books, 2010.

Lahiji, Nadir, editor. *Architecture Against the Post-Political: Essays in Reclaiming the Critical Project*. Routledge, 2014.

Latour, Bruno, and Peter Weibel, editors. *Making Things Public: Atmospheres of Democracy*. The MIT P, 2005.

Lazar, Sian. *El Alto, Rebel City: Self and Citizenship in Andean Bolivia*. Duke UP, 2008.

Lecuyer, Annette W., Robert Levit A., Richard Sennett, and Robert A. Levit. *1998 Raoul Wallenberg Lecture*. U of Michigan, 1998.

Lefebvre, Henri. *The Explosion Marxism And The French Upheaval*. Modern Reader Paperback, 1968.

————. *The Production of Space*, translated by Donald Nicholson-Smith. Wiley-Blackwell, 1992.

————. *The Urban Revolution*. U of Minnesota P, 2003.

————. *Rhythmanalysis: Space, Time, and Everyday Life*. Continuum, 2004.

————. *State, Space, World: Selected Essays*, edited by Stuart Elden and Neil Brenner, translated by Gerald Moore. U of Minnesota P, 2009.

————. *Toward an Architecture of Enjoyment*, edited by Łukasz Stanek, translated by Robert Bononno. U of Minnesota P, 2014.

————, Eleonore Kofman, and Elizabeth Lebas, eds. *Writing on Cities*. Wiley-Blackwell, 1996.

————, and Michel Trebitsch. *Critique of Everyday Life, Volume II*, translated by John Moore, complete numbers starting with 1. Verso, 2002.

Lepik, Andres, and Barry Bergdoll. *Small Scale, Big Change: New Architectures of Social Engagement*. The Museum of Modern Art, New York, 2010.

Liboiron, Max. "Tactics of Waste, Dirt, and Discard in the Occupy Movement." *Social Movement Studies*, vol. 11, no. 3–4, 2012, pp. 393–401.

Linebaugh, Peter. *The Magna Carta Manifesto: Liberties and Commons for All*. U of California P.

Lofland, Lyn H. *A World of Strangers: Order and Action in Urban Public Space*, reprint. Waveland Press, 1985.

Lordon, Frederic. *Willing Slaves of Capital: Spinoza and Marx on Desire*, reprint. Verso, 2014.

Manning, Erin, and Brian Massumi. *Thought in the Act: Passages in the Ecology of Experience*. U of Minnesota P, 2014.

Massey, Jonathan, and Brett Snyder. "Mapping Liberty Plaza." *Places Journal*, September 2012. https://placesjournal.org/article/mapping-liberty-plaza/.

Massumi, Brian. *Semblance and Event (Technologies of Lived Abstraction): Activist Philosophy and the Occurrent Arts*, reprint. MIT Press, 2013.

————. *Politics of Affect*. Polity, 2015.

Matta-Clark, Gordon, Robert Smithson, and Rem Koolhaas. *Shrinking Cities: Volume 2: Interventions*, edited by Robert Fishman. Hatje Cantz, 2006.

McCormack, Derek P. *Refrains for Moving Bodies: Experience and Experiment in Affective Spaces*. Duke UP, 2014.

McGuirk, Justin. *Radical Cities: Across Latin America in Search of a New Architecture*. Verso, 2014.

McKay, George, editor. *DiY Culture: Party and Protest in Nineties' Britain*. Verso, 1998.

McKee, Yates. *Strike Art: Contemporary Art and the Post-Occupy Condition*, reprint. Verso, 2017.

Meagher, Sharon M., editor. *Philosophy and the City: Classic to Contemporary Writings*. State U of New York P, 2008.

Merrifield, Andy. *Magical Marxism: Subversive Politics and the Imagination*. Pluto Press, 2011.

———. *The Politics of the Encounter: Urban Theory and Protest under Planetary Urbanization*. U of Georgia P, 2013.

———. *The Amateur: The Pleasures of Doing What You Love*. Verso, 2017.

Meter, Kevin Van. *Guerrillas of Desire: Notes on Everyday Resistance and Organizing to Make a Revolution Possible*. AK Press, 2017.

Mieville, China. "Rejected Pitch." *Rejectamentalist Manifesto*, April 7, 2011. https://chinamieville.net/post/4406165249/rejected-pitch.

Millar, Kathleen M. *Reclaiming the Discarded: Life and Labor on Rio's Garbage Dump*. Duke UP, 2018.

Miller, Jim. *Rousseau: Dreamer of Democracy*. Yale UP, 1996.

Mitchell, W. J. T., Bernard E. Harcourt, and Michael Taussig. *Occupy: Three Inquiries in Disobedience*. U of Chicago P, 2013.

Negri, Antonio, and Rocco Gangle. *Spinoza for Our Time: Politics and Postmodernity*, translated by William McCuaig. Columbia UP, 2013.

NewsClickin. 2018. *Shack Dwellers' Movement in South Africa Continue Their Fight for Better Life Despite Threats*. https://www.youtube.com/watch?v=8YhHIAhJBZs.

Nussbaum, Martha C. *Political Emotions: Why Love Matters for Justice* reprint. Belknap Press, 2015.

Parkinson, John. *Democracy and Public Space: The Physical Sites of Democratic Performance*. Oxford UP, 2012.

Pauli, Benjamin J. *Flint Fights Back: Environmental Justice and Democracy in the Flint Water Crisis*. The MIT P, 2019.

Perkins, Tom. "On Urban Farming and 'colonialism' in Detroit's North End Neighborhood." *Detroit Metro Times*, December 20, 2017. https://www.metrotimes.com/detroit/on-urban-farming-and-colonialism-in-detroits-north-end-neighborhood/Content?oid=7950059.

Place Culture Politics. *Rebel Cities: David Harvey in Conversation with David Graeber*. https://www.youtube.com/watch?v=2SNj1ttIQBY. Accessed June 13, 2019.

Protevi, John. *Political affect: Connecting the Social and the Somatic*. U of Minnesota P, 2009.

———. "Rhythm and Cadence, Frenzy and March: Music and the Geo-Bio-Techno-Affective Assemblages of Ancient Warfare." *Theory & Event*, vol. 13, January 2010.

Ranciere, Jacques, and Donald Reid. *Proletarian Nights: The Workers' Dream in Nineteenth-Century France*. Verso, 2012.

Rediker, Marcus. *Villains of All Nations: Atlantic Pirates in the Golden Age*. Beacon Press, 2005.

———, and Cornell Womack. *Villains of All Nations: Atlantic Pirates in the Golden Age*. Beacon Press, 2005.

Reid, Herbert, and Betsy Taylor. *Recovering the Commons: Democracy, Place, and Global Justice*. U of Illinois P, 2010.

Reno, Joshua O. *Waste Away: Working and Living with a North American Landfill*. U of California P, 2016.

Ross, Kristin. *May '68 and Its Afterlives*. U of Chicago P, 2002.

———. *The Emergence of Social Space: Rimbaud and the Paris Commune*. Verso, 2008.

———. *Communal Luxury: The Political Imaginary of the Paris Commune*. reprint. Verso, 2016.

Routledge, Paul. "Convergence Space: Process Geographies of Grassroots Globalization Networks." *Transactions of the Institute of British Geographers*, vol. 28, no. 3, 2003, pp. 333–49.

Rudofsky, Bernard. *Architecture without Architects: A Short Introduction to Non-Pedigreed Architecture*, reprint. U of New Mexico P, 1987.

Salvage Editors. "Salvage Perspectives #1: Amid This Stony Rubbish." *Salvage*, July 2015. http://salvage.zone/in-print/salvage-perspectives-1-amid-this-stony-rubbish/.

Scott, James C. *Weapons of the Weak: Everyday Forms of Peasant Resistance*, reprint. Yale UP, 1987.

———. *Seeing like a State: How Certain Schemes to Improve the Human Condition Have Failed*. Yale UP, 1999.

Sedgwick, Eve Kosofsky. *Touching Feeling: Affect, Pedagogy, Performativity*. Duke UP, 1999.

Semetsky, Inna. "Deleuze's New Image of Thought, or Dewey Revisited." *Educational Philosophy and Theory*, vol. 35, no. 1, 2003a, pp. 17–29.

———. "The Problematics of Human Subjectivity: Gilles Deleuze and the Deweyan Legacy." *Studies in Philosophy and Education*, vol. 22, no. 3, 2003b, pp. 211–25.

———. *Deleuze, Education, and Becoming*. Sense Publishers, 2006.

———, editor. *Nomadic Education*. Sense Publishers, 2008.

———, and Diana Masny, editors. *Deleuze and Education*. Edinburgh UP, 2013.

Sennett, Richard. *The Conscience of the Eye: The Design and Social Life of Cities*, revised. W. W. Norton, 1992.

———. *Flesh and Stone: The Body and the City in Western Civilization*, revised. W. W. Norton, 1996.

———. *The Craftsman*. Yale UP, 2008.

———. *Together: The Rituals, Pleasures, and Politics of Cooperation*. Yale UP, 2012.

"Shack Dwellers' Movement in South Africa Continue Their Fight for Better Life Despite Threats. *The Dawn News*. n.d. http://www.thedawn-news.

org/2018/05/29/shack-dwellers-movement-in-south-africa-continue-their-fight-for-better-life-despite-threats/. Accessed April 10, 2019.

Shanin, Teodor. *Late Marx and the Russian Road: Marx and the Peripheries of Capitalism*. Monthly Review Press, 1983.

Sheller, Mimi. *Mobility Justice: The Politics of Movement in an Age of Extremes*. Verso, 2018.

Shiffman, Ronald, Rick Bell, Lance Jay Brown, and Lynne Elizabeth, editors. *Beyond Zuccotti Park: Freedom of Assembly and the Occupation of Public Space*. New Village Press, 2012.

Sitrin, Marina A. *Everyday Revolutions: Horizontalism and Autonomy in Argentina*. Zed Books, 2012.

———, Dario Azzellini, and David Harvey. *They Can't Represent Us!: Reinventing Democracy From Greece To Occupy*. Verso, 2014.

Skewes, Carlos. "De Invasor a Deudor: El Éxodo Desde Los Campamentos a Lasviviendas Sociales En Chile." In *Los Con Techo. Un Desafío Para La Política de Vivienda Social*, edited by Alfredo Rodriguez and Ana Sugranyes, translated by Dennis Pollard. Ediciones SUR, 2005.

Smith, Thomas S. J. "Material Geographies of the Maker Movement : Community Workshops and the Making of Sustainability in Edinburgh, Scotland." Thesis, U of St. Andrews, 2018. https://research-repository.st-andrews.ac.uk/handle/10023/12815.

Solomon, Susan. *Louis I. Kahn's Trenton Jewish Community Center: Building Studies 6*. Princeton Architectural Press, 2000.

Stanek, Łukasz. *Henri Lefebvre on Space: Architecture, Urban Research, and the Production of Theory*. U of Minnesota P, 2011.

Stavrides, Stavros. *Common Space: The City as Commons*. Zed Books, 2016.

———. *Towards the City of Thresholds*. Common Notions, 2019.

Stengers, Isabelle. *In Catastrophic Times: Resisting the Coming Barbarism*, translated by Andrew Goffey. Open Humanities Press, 2015.

———, and Jane Bennett. *Political Matter: Technoscience, Democracy, and Public Life*, edited by Bruce Braun and Sarah J. Whatmore. U of Minnesota P, 2010.

Stevens, Quentin. *The Ludic City*. Routledge, 2007.

Stewart, Kathleen. *Ordinary Affects*. Duke UP, 2007.

Svirsky, Marcelo, editor. *Deleuze and Political Activism: Deleuze Studies Volume 4: 2010*, supplement. Edinburgh UP, 2007.

Thompson, E. P. *The Making of the English Working Class*. Vintage, 1966.

———. *William Morris : Romantic to Revolutionary*. Pantheon Books, 1977.

Thompson, Michael. *Rubbish Theory: The Creation and Destruction of Value*, second edition. Pluto Press, 2017.

Thrift, Nigel, and Ash Amin. *Arts of the Political: New Openings for the Left*. Duke UP, 2013.

Traverso, Enzo. *Left-Wing Melancholia: Marxism, History, and Memory*, 2nd revised edition. Columbia UP, 2017.

Tsing, Anna Lowenhaupt. *The Mushroom at the End of the World: On the Possibility of Life in Capitalist Ruins*. Princeton UP, 2015.

———, Nils Bubandt, Elaine Gan, and Heather Anne Swanson, editors. *Arts of Living on a Damaged Planet: Ghosts and Monsters of the Anthropocene*, 3rd edition. U of Minnesota P, 2017.

Tuan, Yi-Fu. *Space and Place: The Perspective of Experience*, reprint edition. U of Minnesota P, 2001.

Turkewitz, Julie. "Who Gets to Own the West?" *The New York Times*, June 22, 2019, U.S.

Turner, John F. C., and Colin Ward. *Housing By People: Towards Autonomy in Building Environments*. Marion Boyars, 2000.

Vasudevan, Alexander. *The Autonomous City: A History of Urban Squatting*. Verso, 2017.

Wall, Derek. *Elinor Ostrom's Rules for Radicals: Cooperative Alternatives Beyond Markets and States*. Pluto Press, 2017.

Wark, McKenzie. *Molecular Red: Theory for the Anthropocene*, reprint edition. Verso, 2016.

"We Are the 99 Percent." https://wearethe99percent.tumblr.com/?og=1.

Wells, Kate. "Detroit High School for Pregnant Teens Is Closing—This Time, for Real." June 5, 2014. https://www.michiganradio.org/post/detroit-high-school-pregnant-teens-closing-time-real.

Williams, Evan Calder. *Combined and Uneven Apocalypse: Luciferian Marxism*, reprint edition. Zero Books, 2011.

Winstanley, Gerrard, and Tony Benn. *A Common Treasury*, reprint edition. Verso, 2011.

Wolin, Sheldon S., and Wendy Brown. *Politics and Vision: Continuity and Innovation in Western Political Thought*, expanded edition. Princeton UP, 2016.

Writers for the 99%, A. J. Bauer, Christine Baumgarthuber, Jed Bickman, and Jeremy Breecher. *Occupying Wall Street: The Inside Story of an Action That Changed America*. Haymarket Books, 2012.

Young, Iris Marion, and Danielle S. Allen. *Justice and the Politics of Difference*, revised edition. Princeton UP, 2011.

Zerzan, John. *Future Primitive: And Other Essays*. Autonomedia, 1994.

———, and Lang Gore. *Why Hope?: The Stand Against Civilization*. Feral House, 2015.

Zibechi, Raúl. *Territories in Resistance: A Cartography of Latin American Social Movements*, translated by Ramor Ryan. AK Press, 2012.

Index

abstraction, 142, 150, 197; capitalist, 149

accumulation, 143, 145, 262; capital, 142, 150, 153, 157, 158, 160, 161, 164, 186, 215, 231; commodity, 186; salvage, 4, 11, 21, 41, 55

action, 47, 61, 243, 290n17; collective, 179; contestatory, 87; creative, 90; mass, 242, 245. *See also* political action

activism, 26, 38, 176, 206, 243, 276n18; anticapitalist, 11; contemporary, 11, 242; forms of, 5, 9; political, 9, 11, 22, 252, 292n22; radical, 47, 263; salvage, 67, 79, 263

activists, 1, 2, 262, 263, 269n16, 280n11; citizens and, 173, 175; networks of, 243; political goals of, 169

activity, 58, 160, 189, 191; political, 25, 26, 159, 164, 178, 184; spatial, 152, 153. *See also* salvage activity

aesthetics, 75, 83, 89, 180, 243, 291n2; anarchist/DIY, 88; art as, 28; deflationary, 86; social, 145

affects, 23, 60, 62, 63, 112, 141, 167, 176, 187, 222–23, 249; anticapitalist, 79–87; capitalist, 68–79, 86, 94, 188; craftwork

and, 111; disempowering, 132; ecosystem of, 34; employment of, 222; experience of, 91; geographies of, 161; loving, 79, 80; Marxist, 76; movement and, 194; multitude of, 129, 222; politics and, 43, 87–96, 188, 218; potentialities of, 67; producing/protecting, 44; relationships, 103; rhythmic, 139, 193, 194; shimmering, 78

affinity, 179, 180, 181; groups, 242, 243, 247

agency, 59, 194; democratic, 61; diminishment of, 274n14; feeling of, 274n13; indeterminate, 168; political, 60, 83, 261; sense of, 51

Agora, 191, 194, 195, 195 (fig.), 198, 203, 207; plurality/activity and, 192; Pnyx and, 191–92, 192–93

Alexander Technique, Dewey and, 271n2

alienation, 49, 50, 98, 120; affective, 78, 94; capitalist, 4, 76, 93; consumerist, 90; desire and, 75; reification and, 6, 12, 76, 82, 93, 98, 120, 185, 274

"Amid this Stony Rubbish" (Salvage), 17

anarchism, 213, 265n3, 277n4; politics and, 88–89

www.ingramcontent.com/pod-product-compliance
Lightning Source LLC
Chambersburg PA
CBHW030639270326
41929CB00007B/131